TRADE WARS
AGAINST AMERICA

TRADE WARS AGAINST AMERICA

A HISTORY OF UNITED STATES TRADE AND MONETARY POLICY

William J. Gill

PRAEGER

New York
Westport, Connecticut
London

Copyright Acknowledgment

The author and publisher gratefully acknowledge permission to reprint material from *The Intimate Papers of Colonel House*, Volumes 3 and 4, edited by Charles Seymour. Copyright 1928, 1956 by Charles Seymour. Reprinted by permission of Houghton Mifflin Company.

Library of Congress Cataloging-in-Publication Data

Gill, William J.
  Trade wars against America : a history of United States trade and monetary policy / William J. Gill.
      p.   cm.
  Includes bibliographical references.
  ISBN 0-275-93316-4 (alk. paper)
  1. Protectionism—United States.   2. United States—Commercial policy.   3. Monetary policy—United States.   4. International trade. I. Title.
  HF1756.G53   1990
  382'.3'0973—dc20   89–29765

Copyright © 1990 by William J. Gill

Library of Congress Catalog Card Number: 89–29765
ISBN: 0–275–93316–4

First published in 1990

Praeger Publishers, One Madison Avenue, New York, NY 10010
A imprint of Greenwood Publishing Group, Inc.

Printed in the United States of America

∞™

The paper used in this book complies with the Permanent Paper Standard issued by the National Information Standards Organization (Z39.48–1984).

10 9 8 7 6 5 4 3 2 1

Contents

Free Trade is the negation of organisation, of settled and consistent policy. It is the triumph of chance, the disordered and selfish competition of immediate individual interests without regard to the permanent welfare of the whole.

Joseph Chamberlain, in his Preface to
The Case Against Free Trade, John Murray, London, 1911

Introduction

Presidents and prime ministers constantly warn of the dangers of a future trade war. But it is abundantly evident that we have already been engaged in an all-out trade war for at least twenty years, and on some industrial fronts for a good deal longer. Trade war is being waged worldwide and the primary target is the United States—the biggest, most lucrative, most open market extant.

Virtually every other country on earth is waging trade war against America, while our government surrenders one industry after another to imports from abroad, imports that are frequently illegal under the international GATT code as well as U.S. trade law.

American industries are the sacrificial lambs offered up every day on the high altar of "free trade." Yet free trade—as envisioned by Adam Smith in his *Wealth of Nations* in 1776, refined by Ricardo with his theory of comparative advantage early in the Nineteenth Century, and preached interminably in university economics courses for a century and more—does not exist on this planet. Nonetheless this myth, which has now assumed the status of theology, is so firmly fixed in the modern mind that no one in authority dares speak out against this hungry Moloch as it insatiably eats up our plants, our jobs, our research, our towns, our cities, our present and our future.

Strong language? If you think so, I suggest you visit Youngstown or Cleveland, the industrial suburbs of Chicago, or the ghost towns up and down the Monongahela River that feeds into the Ohio at Pittsburgh, formerly the industrial heart of America, and once the world's redoubtable "Arsenal of Democracy." Today, virtually all the steel mills of these and many other cities are empty and silent and the subsidiary industries that supplied or serviced them no longer exist.

Nor is the industrial blight spawned by our government's trade policy limited to the "rust belt" of the Northeast and the Midwest. Imports have taken the bloom off the computer rose in California's Silicon Valley; dried up space satellite firms on Route 128, the high-tech road around Boston; shut down textile mills throughout the South; put shoe factories out of business in no less than forty states; closed fishing tackle plants in Florida, television assembly facilities in Tennessee, pipe and tube companies in Texas. Indeed, no region of the country can escape the fatal economic fallout of unrestrained imports.

Economists and misinformed journalists blame the blight on the loss of America's "competitive edge." The hard fact is that no U.S. industry, no matter how technologically advanced and cost-productive, can long withstand the onslaught of subsidized imports from abroad. American corporations, even with the wisest, most prudent management, simply cannot compete with the governments of foreign countries. Yet this is precisely what the U.S. government, by blindly pursuing free trade, forces our corporations to do.

For more than a dozen years I have worn two hats: one as an author and writer, the other as a consultant to American industries on their international trade problems. During that period the industries I have worked with have fought more than twenty trade cases—all but one successfully. Yet every one of these industries has continued to decline. Why? Because our government has either refused to grant effective import restraints as provided by law, has winked at the restraints it has ostensibly allowed so foreign exporters could easily avoid them, or has actively collaborated with foreign governments in selling my client industries down the rivers of the world.

My interest in international trade predated my professional involvement by more than a decade. Through much of the 1960s, while writing on a broad range of subjects, I was the chief executive officer of the Allegheny Foundation, T. Mellon & Sons, Pittsburgh. At least as early as 1965 I could see the giant U.S. trade deficits looming over the horizon, although it was to be a half-dozen years before they actually developed.

Toward the end of the sixties I worked with my friend, Max Bishop, on a project to head off the trade deficits we could see were coming. Ambassador Bishop was then serving as the director of the World Affairs Council of Pittsburgh after a distinguished career in the State Department as an expert on the Far East. Together, we drew up a blueprint for a World Trade Center designed to develop practical plans and formulas aimed at helping the United States expand its exports and achieve a more realistic trade policy.

Originally, I recommended the Trade Center be established at Carnegie-Mellon University in Pittsburgh. However, the trustees were against this so the initial grant of $1,500,000 was made by the Allegheny Foundation to a university that is better left unnamed. I signed the first check with misgivings and they were confirmed. The money was obviously wasted. Certainly it had no discernible effect upon the nation's trade balance, which finally popped over the horizon toward the end of Richard M. Nixon's first term as President.

Fighting in the trenches along the Potomac since 1975 in defense of a number of beleaguered American industries I have learned from firsthand and often painful experience what our workers and corporations are up against. It is not merely the predatory trade practices of Japan and the other countries invading our markets. It is far more the unrealistic policies and attitudes of our own government officials, from Presidents on down, that have brought us to the dangerous pass in which we are now caught.

However, I know it would be unrealistic to suggest a precipitous wholesale overthrow of current policy. It would be impossible for the United States to withdraw from its addiction to free trade overnight. This is why I propose a careful step-by-step return to sound trade and fiscal policies, a program that can be carried out over a reasonable period of time with minimal pain, though there are sure to be some hangover effects after the prolonged free trade binge America has been on for so long.

I have written this book from an American viewpoint. But it is my conviction that every nation in the world would ultimately benefit from a rejection of, and gradual withdrawal from, the subsidization of exports under the false banner of free trade. For one thing the present frenetic state of world trade is a conscience-less waste of the earth's resources. Thousands of ships plough and pollute the oceans as they carry our oil, coal, ores, and scrap metals to the Far East so the Japanese, Koreans, and Chinese can convert them into automobiles, machine tools, steel, TV sets, VCRs, and other products shipped back to the American market for sale here.

Subsidized trade is contributing substantially to the mounting threat to the planet's environment. Certainly, the hyped-up government-owned-or-supported smokestack industries of Japan, Korea, or even Hungary are helping to widen the already gaping hole in the ozone layer that protects us from potentially harmful effects of the sun's unfiltered ultraviolet rays. Environmental controls in these and scores of other industrial countries are either nonexistent or in a very primitive stage.

Beyond the growing threat to the environment, beyond the waste of resources, there is the toll taken by free trade upon the lives of millions of innocent people, upon their communities and, indeed, upon the very infrastructure of civilized society.

It is not only the hopeless plight of the five hundred thousand American steelworkers whose jobs have disappeared since the 1950s,[1] nor even in the nearly ten million others thrown out of work by plant closings and layoffs between 1983 and 1988,[2] that we see the ravages of wide open trade. French farmers are ruthlessly uprooted from the land their families have tilled for centuries to satisfy the demands of the European Community as it moves toward a homogenized market. Italian tailors, perhaps the world's best, are threatened with extinction as clothes made in Korea or Hong Kong flood the world's stores, often with counterfeit labels. Even Japanese rice planters see their livelihood jeopardized by the silly insistence of U.S. trade negotiators that Japan import rice from the Carolinas or Louisiana.

The toll exacted by free trade is also political. It causes endless quarreling and disputation among nations, heightening international tensions, rather than lowering them as our State Department professes to believe. In addition, free trade provides the "cover" for the world drug market, most painfully the smuggling of billions of dollars worth of cocaine and heroin past the harried and overworked officers of the U.S. Customs Service. Moreover, the world is belatedly awakening to the risks inherent in the proliferation of nuclear and chemical weapons, again under the effective camouflage of "free" trade, while at the same time the defense industrial base of the United States—indeed, of the entire West—is dangerously eroded by this same false philosophy.

Alexander Hamilton and our other founding fathers understood that any nation that desires to remain politically independent must also protect its economic independence and strive toward as much self-sufficiency as possible. The whole concept of nationhood rests upon this premise. Only those nations which intend to eventually surrender their sovereignty completely will abandon protectionism in trade to the extent that the United States has in recent decades.

Obviously, the world has changed so dramatically that a retraction to the trade practices of the old nation-states of the past may no longer be feasible. On the one hand you have the emergence of multiple ministates that were colonies not so long ago; on the other you see the gradual consolidation of older independent states into multinational amalgamations. Thus, the economic convergence of the European Community is now so far advanced that its member nations cannot retreat and will probably have to keep marching in lock step toward a United Europe, perhaps incorporating along the way some or all of the countries that just yesterday comprised the Soviet Bloc in Eastern Europe.

It is for the Europeans to decide whether they wish to give up their ancient nationhoods and merge into a supranational state. But they should do so with their eyes open, conscious that they will be forced to give up not only economic independence but political sovereignty as well.

Moreover, there are the more emotional matters of language and customs and tradition that must be resolved. Will Europe speak English or French? German or Spanish? Italian or Polish? Of course, there is always the possibility that the Soviet Union may decide these momentous questions for Europe, particularly in the wake of the arms control agreements that are dismantling the military deterrence that kept the Red Army at bay for more than forty years. The shimmering goal of a United Europe could conceivably collapse into the abyss of an expanded Union of Soviet Socialist Republics that would embrace all of Europe, and eventually the world.

But what I have written in this book is predicated upon the world as it exists at this time—the world every nation and individual must deal with on a day-by-day basis short of the cataclysmic changes capable of transforming the global political structure into something quite different from what we have at present. Transformations are taking place all the time within nations, as witness the Islamic revolution in Iran, the upheavals that created sixteen additional Communist "Peoples Republics" in the single decade ending in 1985, and the ostensible overthrow of Communist regimes in Poland, Hungary, East Germany and Czechoslovakia in 1989.

However, it is the global ball I have tried to keep my eye on while attempting to devise a way to restore the manufacturing and technology base of my own country, the United States of America. For as the stock market dives of 1987 and 1989 again revealed, the economy of the whole world rests upon the shoulders of America. When Wall Street shudders the economic earth shakes for months.

If we collapse, the world will collapse with us. Therefore, it is in the interest of all countries, including the Soviet Union, which the United States has helped feed and finance since 1917, that America be rescued from the free trade trap that now paralyzes so much of our economy. Who can forget, so quickly at least, that it was the announcement of yet another large monthly U.S. trade deficit that triggered the 1987 market crash? And, less visibly, Nicholas F. Brady, soon to be Secretary of the Treasury, was reported to have told a group of businessmen that his presidential commission's[3] investigation of the 1987 crash traced its origin to the "enormous" selling of U.S. Treasury bonds by the Japanese.[4]

Internally, we have been slowly garroting ourselves and our capital base with the ever-growing socialist-inspired welfare schemes fed by more than five decades of almost unbroken federal budget deficits.

Externally, the United States has been financing and building socialism, and even communism, throughout the world. The government-owned or subsidized industries in dozens of countries from Europe to the Far East have been sustained by American capital via such multinational lending machines as the World Bank, the International Monetary Fund, and, most importantly for the past two decades, the big commercial banks like Citibank and Chase Manhattan.

The foreign industries that these giveaway lenders financed increasingly turned out products—steel, automobiles, TV sets, etc.—that were exported to the American market to zap our own homegrown industries and eliminate the jobs of our best-paid and most productive workers.

A decade ago, the *Harvard Business Review* published the accompanying chart based upon a report in *The Economist* which graphically illustrates how our private sector industries are forced to compete with a largely socialized world. The "black holes" in this chart represent government-owned industries, or the degree of government ownership, in eighteen noncommunist industrialized countries. The white circles are reserved for predominantly privately-owned industries, with the black segments of these indicating the approximate percentage of government ownership.

Keep in mind as you view this chart that many of the white circles should be black—or partially black—because government ownership or subsidization of ostensibly private companies is often hidden in foreign countries. In Japan, for instance, under-the-table government subsidization to pump up exports is a way of life. But Japan is far from alone in concealing its socialistic practices.

Looking at the chart, you will note that by an alphabetical accident, the United

Scope of State Ownership

Exhibit I
Scope of state ownership

	Posts	Tele-communi-cations	Electricity	Gas	Oil production	Coal	Railways	Airlines	Motor industry	Steel	Ship-building
Australia	●	●	●	●	○	○	●	◑	○	○	NA
Austria	●	●	●	●	●	●	●	●	●	●	NA
Belgium	●	●	◔	◔	NA	○	●	●	○	◑	○
Brazil	●	●	●	●	●	●	●	◔	○	◕	○
Britain	●	●	●	●	◔	●	●	◕	◑	◕	●
Canada	●	◔	●	○	○	○	◕	◕	○	○	○
France	●	●	●	●	NA	●	●	◕	◑	◕	○
West Germany	●	●	◕	◑	◔	◑	●	●	◔	○	◔
Holland	●	●	◕	◕	NA	NA	●	◕	◑	◔	○
India	●	●	●	●	●	●	●	●	○	◕	●
Italy	●	●	◕	●	NA	NA	●	●	◔	◕	◕
Japan	●	●	○	○	NA	○	◕	◔	○	○	○
Mexico	●	●	●	●	●	●	●	◑	◕	◕	●
South Korea	●	●	◕	○	NA	◔	●	○	○	◕	○
Spain	●	◑	○	◔	NA	◑	●	●	○	◑	◕
Sweden	●	●	◑	●	NA	NA	●	◑	○	◕	◕
Switzerland	●	●	●	●	NA	NA	●	◔	○	○	NA
United States	●	○	◔	○	○	○	◔	○	○	○	○

Legend:
- ○ Privately owned: all or nearly all
- ● Publicly owned: all or nearly all
- ◕ 75%
- ◑ 50%
- ◔ 25%

NA – not applicable or negligible production
*Including Conrail

Adapted from a chart in *The Economist* (London).
December 30, 1978 and reprinted with special permission.

Source: Reprinted by permission of *Harvard Business Review*. An exhibit from "State-Owned Business Abroad: New Competitive Threat" by Kenneth D. Walters and R. Joseph Monsen (March–April 1979). Copyright © 1979 by the President and Fellows of Harvard College; all rights reserved.

States is positioned at the very bottom of the heap. Only our postal service and segments of our electric power industry and our railroads are owned by the government. All other American industries are privately owned.

However, in the rest of the industrial world, government-owned black holes predominate. In Austria, Brazil, Britain, France, West Germany, Holland, India, Italy, Mexico, South Korea, Spain, Sweden, and even Switzerland virtually all or most of the large essential industries are socialized totally or in part. In the remaining nations—Australia, Belgium, Canada, and Japan—there is also a high degree of government ownership.

There has been some privatization of these industries in very recent years, most notably in Great Britain. But the 1978 chart reproduced here reflects the socialized world that put so many U.S. companies and manufacturing plants out of business in the twenty-five-year period 1960–1985, when so much of the damage was done to American industry. Moreover, privatization, though promising, has not substantially changed the dismal picture reflected in this chart.

Only the United States has thus far escaped the socialist plague. We are the lone major nation left on earth with an essentially privately owned industrial base. We are the only nation still generating substantial real capital, in spite of the dangerous erosion of our industries and the siphoning off of our capital for internal social welfare schemes, wasteful foreign aid, and reckless unsecured lending to all and sundry abroad.

If you were to add the communist countries to this chart, and the relatively undeveloped nations of Latin America, Africa, and Asia where government ownership is rampant, you will get an even more vivid picture of the magnitude of the "comsocialist" competition targeting American industries and markets.

What you can also see in this chart is that the United States is down at the very foundation—indeed, it *is* the foundation—shoring up the whole world economy, as noted earlier. As also noted, the stock market's free fall in '87 dramatically demonstrated this. When prices fell on Wall Street, stocks immediately began to crumble in every other market from London, Paris, and Bonn to Tokyo, Hong Kong, and Sydney. The sell-off was global, but it was the New York stock exchange dive that took all the others with it. Conversely, as Wall Street slowly pulled out of its dizzying dip, and stock prices recovered, most other markets around the world also revived.

For nearly a century America has been playing the hard role of Atlas holding up the world economy. We managed to accomplish this truly amazing feat because until recently our industrial production had given us a spine of steel, and the preservation of our largely free enterprise system had provided the capital required to buy a good deal of what the rest of the world produced.

Although our spine is not yet broken, the tragic fate of our steel industry would indicate that it is at least fractured. Indeed, free trade has done severe damage to our whole economic nervous system. But we are not industrially

xvi   Introduction

paralyzed as yet. It will take a tremendous effort to restore America's mighty industrial machine. But it can, and must, be done. At the end of this book specific suggestions are set forth for dealing with the trade crisis, the absolute first step that must be taken before the rebuilding of America can commence.

In the time remaining in this twentieth century, America can yet point the way to the brighter tomorrow promised by the technological advances still being made all around us. Certainly, environmental problems must be given much higher priority lest they cancel out the progress made via science. That they have already done so in some vital spheres is painfully apparent. Still, Britain cleaned up the Thames after centuries of pollution, and the air of America is far more breathable today than it was before auto emission controls a decade ago.

The first order of business is, plainly, to put our own American house in order, to rebuild the industries destroyed by our past trade policy, to revitalize the cities and towns that depended upon those industries, to reduce the federal budget deficits that have soared toward outer space during nearly two decades of horrendous trade imbalances. Once we have reestablished the American model on a more firm foundation of sane trade and sound money we will be in a better position to ask other nations to follow.

America still has the capacity to lead the world to higher ground, the current crop of doomsayers to the contrary. Trade is the right place to start forging the future. But before we can begin, it will be useful to dig beneath the surface of the myths manufactured by generations of theorists and examine the true terrain hidden by the mythology, both in the present and in the past.

TRADE WARS
AGAINST AMERICA

Chapter 1.

Reagan Roulette

It occurs to me that as I approach the end of my presidency that the unparalleled resistance that greeted our policies and that we still face, despite our unparalleled success, was born of more than an ordinary political clash. . . . Our arrival in Washington represented not another skirmish among partisans, but a collision of constellations.

> —Ronald Reagan in his Farewell Address
> to the U.S. Chamber of Commerce,
> May 1, 1988

Ronald Wilson Reagan, the fortieth President of the United States of America, was engulfed by problems as he departed from Washington for Moscow and his fourth summit meeting with Mikhail Gorbachev, secretary-general of the Communist Party of the Union of Soviet Socialist Republics. Just the day before, the House of Representatives had voted overwhelmingly to override Reagan's veto of the trade bill Congress had been laboring over for several years. Although the President knew the Senate probably would uphold him, the man he hoped would be his successor in the White House, George Bush, was in trouble because of the unpopular reason given for the veto. Reagan had sent the whole trade bill back to Capitol Hill because he did not like the provision to give workers sixty days notice when a plant was forced to close.

To most Americans the plant closing provision of the trade legislation seemed only fair and reasonable. They had seen millions of their fellow citizens summarily thrown out of work as literally thousands of industrial plants shut down in the face of an unrelenting invasion of imports now in its third decade.

Yet the familiar airy wave of Reagan's hand and the sunny smile seemed to dismiss all cares as the President boarded *Air Force One* on that rainy Wednesday before the long Memorial Day weekend of 1988. The President appeared to carry the nation's myriad problems lightly, so lightly that many questioned whether he really understood them. Yet whether he was conscious of it or not, Ronald Reagan was taking with him to Moscow as heavy a load as any man had carried in all human history. Prometheus, chained to the rock of the world for giving fire to mankind in defiance of Zeus, could not have shouldered a heavier burden than this President.

Reagan's burden was not only heavy, it was nuclear—and capable of exploding on a hundred fronts all at once. Indeed, the international trade and monetary problem had been detonating all along that crucial line almost daily for several years and had set off a shocking stock market crash the previous October. But the President had shrugged off the crash and the import invasion that shut down plants and crippled whole communities. After all, he could point proudly to the longest run of prosperity and expansion in the country's history as evidence that his open-door trade policy was working. Unemployment was at its lowest point in years. The other economic indicators were almost all up, and America had seemingly shaken off the effects of the market's devastating dive the year before.

In spite of the euphoria, hundreds of thousands of men and women who had once worked in well-paid jobs in steel, electronics, textiles, shoes, or automobile production were idle or laboring in low-pay dead ends. The industrial landscape of the United States was littered with factories and steel mills silenced and padlocked, most of them permanently.

Unlike the Great Depression of the 1930s, when the machinery had been maintained in most factories, the import invasion of our era has gutted the nation's plants, emptying them of equipment. Ironically, the machinery and assembly lines, considered antiquated by most economists, had been sold off to eager buyers from Japan and other countries said to have surpassed America in technology and efficient production.

While the United States exported its machinery and technology to the world, foreign interests more than doubled their cumulative assets in America to almost $1.5 trillion, and by 1988 we had become by far the biggest debtor nation on earth. Our total foreign debt shot up nearly 37 percent to $400 billion in one year, 1987, and was approaching $1 trillion in 1990. The British and Japanese particularly, but others, too, were on a massive buying binge in the United States, grabbing up industries and real estate from Maine to California and across the Pacific to Hawaii. Britons purchased four hundred American companies for some $32 billion in 1988, and the Japanese snatched plants and properties worth $12 billion more. British, Japanese, Korean, Taiwanese, and European factories so dotted the industrial landscape that the map of America looked as though the country had caught smallpox.

John M. Berry, an astute financial correspondent for the *Washington Post*, reported in 1988 that "the nation's need for foreign capital to finance its overall international deficit reached a record annual rate of $165.9 Billion in the fourth quarter'' of the previous year.[1] This news came on the heels of a temporary wholesale retreat of foreign money from U.S. investment markets, which some observers, among them Nicholas Brady, the future Secretary of the Treasury, believed touched off the Wall Street crash that saw the Dow-Jones average plummet 508 points on October 19, 1987. Actually, that numbing day brought the market's fall since its historic high of 2,722 on August 17 to nearly 1,000 points, a sell-off that wiped out more than a third of all stock values.

America's dependency on foreign investment had reached the point where foreign interests could control the movements of our markets, whether in real estate, in corporate stocks, or in U.S. Treasury bonds. This means they can also influence interest rates, including mortgages, which now routinely move up or down at the whim of traders in Tokyo, Bonn, or London. New issues of Treasury bonds can be manipulated at will by the Japanese alone and three big financial institutions in Tokyo, including the mammoth Fuji Bank, were designated as ''primary dealers'' of U.S. government securities by the Federal Reserve System, giving Japan additional leverage over the American economy.

Tokyo has replaced New York as the banking center of the world, and in 1988 Japanese banks lengthened their lead over American banks in assets. According to the Bank for International Settlements, Japanese banks had $1.4 trillion in international assets—more than double the $630 Billion held by U.S. Banks.[2] Indeed, Japanese banks dominated all lists of the world's largest financial institutions and no American bank was any longer near the top ten.

Japan's meteoric rise to leadership in the world of finance had been fueled by trade. America's retreat, conversely, was also largely caused by trade—''free'' trade that permitted unrestricted imports that had undermined the nation's industrial base and curtailed its productive capacity.

While Japan's banks were basking in the favor of the gods said to reside on Mount Fuji, many American banks were going broke. There have been hundreds of bank failures in the past decade and in 1987 alone there were 184, the largest number since the Great Depression. Moreover, some one thousand, four hundred banks were on the ''problem list'' of the Federal Deposit Insurance Corporation and the savings and loan industry was one vast disaster area.

Even the biggest American banks were in deep trouble, and L. William Seidman, chairman of the Federal Deposit Insurance Corporation, warned in December 1989 that commercial bank bailout costs may rise sharply in the 1990s. Chase Manhattan was forced to add $1.6 billion to its growing reserve fund as early as May 1987 to offset bad loans to the Third World. The Bank of America posted a huge $955 million loss for 1987, largely because of a $1.1 billion addition to its reserves for future loan losses in developing countries. And Citicorp, parent of Citibank, absorbed a whopping $2.5 billion loss in the second quarter of 1987 for the same reason.

Things were so bad for BankAmerica that its chairman, A. W. Clausen, former president of the World Bank, had to go begging in Tokyo for a bailout. A consortium of nine Japanese banks agreed to help pull BankAmerica out of the red,[3] thereby enlisting, or solidifying, another powerful ally for Japanese exports to the United States.

The Federal Reserve reported that as of June 30, 1986, the nine largest U.S. banks had lent over 99 percent of their total capital to Latin American borrowers alone.[4] As bad as that may seem, it was an improvement over 1982 when the same banks had 146 percent of their capital committed to the Latinos, who were then just beginning their long de facto default.

Still, the *Wall Street Journal* noted that ''the Federal Reserve and the International Monetary Fund have persuaded . . . the big banks to lend the Latins a good deal more in the hope that something good may come of it.''[5] But what came of it was that the U.S. Treasury was now floating bonds to bail out the Latins so they can pay off some of the debt, or at least the interest, owed to the U.S. private banks. Inevitably, it is the long-suffering American taxpayer who gets stuck with the bill.

Ostensibly at least, the critical condition of American banks and industries did not deeply trouble Ronald Reagan winging his way toward the summit. Trade was near the top of the agenda the President and his aides would discuss with Gorbachev in Moscow. Publicly, much more had been made of disarmament, and the Senate was still debating the Intermediate Nuclear Force (INF) treaty as Reagan left Washington. Just that afternoon, Sen. Jesse Helms of North Carolina, leader of the conservative opposition to the INF, admitted he was ''licked'' after an amendment to improve verification was defeated; and on Friday, May 27, the Senate ratified the treaty by a 93 to 5 vote so Reagan could deliver it to Gorbachev at the summit.

Despite the focus on disarmament, informed citizens knew that trade was inextricably tied to arms control. In exchange for the INF treaty, progress on (START), and a relaxation of emigration for dissidents, the Soviets wanted huge credits, more U.S. technology and heavy machinery, and the most favored nation status that would open wide America's doors to imports from the USSR.

Implicit in many of the stories about glasnost was the threat that Gorbachev might go if the United States and the other developed nations failed to rescue the Soviet economy. Thus, the additional burden of shoring up Gorbachev was insinuated into Ronald Reagan's baggage.

Elsewhere in the heavy portfolio President Reagan carried with him to Moscow was an assortment of political problems, all piling up in an election year in which he hoped to see his Vice President, George Bush, follow him into the White House. The bare enumeration of these problems was enough to convey the impression of an administration under siege: Panama, Nicaragua and the Contras, Irangate, the Persian Gulf war, rumblings in the Mideast—all these and more appeared to be circling Reagan's wagon.

Crucial as some of these crises were, the trade issue struck much closer to home. Almost a non-issue in the presidential campaigns of 1980 and 1984, trade had emerged as one of the transcendent concerns of the decade, along with Narcotics, nuclear arms and ''Star Wars.''

The cumulative trade deficit for the Reagan years was approaching $1 trillion, not coincidentally the same astronomical figure forecast for the U.S. foreign debt by 1992. Moreover, a very large part of the $1 trillion (billions had become passé) federal budget the President submitted to Congress for fiscal 1989 could be tracked to our long-running imbalance of payments in trade.

Of the $486 billion earmarked for social programs in the trillion-dollar 1989 Reagan budget, a substantial portion was for welfare, adjustment assistance, and other costs stemming in no small part from the decline in industrial jobs. Moreover, a considerable share of the huge federal deficits rolled up in the 1980s was traceable to the decline of corporate and individual income taxes caused by the plant closings or by companies driven out of business by imports. On top of these was the most obvious fact that America was borrowing heavily from abroad to buy imports, and the interest on these loans also added to the budget deficit.

The national debt soared to $2.2 trillion officially by 1988, though J. Peter Grace, who had headed the presidential commission on government waste, claimed the "real debt is between $4-and-$5 trillion" when "all the other hidden debts Congress refuses to tell its citizens about" are included.[6]

Interest paid by the Treasury on only the official debt was close to $160 billion in 1988 and probably would reach $200 billion by 1990.

Inflation, which had remained deceptively low during most of Ronald Reagan's first five years as President, suddenly quadrupled in 1987 as the consumer price index soared from 1.1 percent in 1986 to 4.4 percent. Actually, the real inflation rate was much higher, and in the Washington metropolitan area the price of a home—the single largest consumer cost of every family who can afford to buy one—was up nearly 25 percent in one year through March 1988.[7]

A good bit of the new inflation had been generated by a precipitous drop in the value of the dollar in international exchange, a decline deliberately induced by the then Secretary of the Treasury, James A. Baker III, beginning September 1985. This move was taken to slow the ballooning trade deficits. Instead, it made them larger. The $130 billion trade shortfall of 1984 climbed to nearly $150 billion in 1985, $170 billion in 1986, and an announced $171.2 billion in 1987; but it was probably closer to $200 billion, and it appeared headed for another disastrous performance in 1988.

In spite of the dismal record of Baker's 1985 devaluation, the Treasury was forever chirping about the "improvement" in trade brought about by increased exports. Actually, the trade imbalance was being narrowed by new mumbo-jumbo methods of calculating the deficit. The Commerce Department, charged with concocting the monthly trade figures, actually announced in January 1988 that before the end of that year it would report the "real" trade deficit, which previously had been reported only quarterly.[8] One wonders what Commerce had reported in between quarters all through the years.

Apparently no one had told Treasury Secretary Baker in 1985 that devaluations never work and have always and everywhere made things worse. A Texas lawyer who had been chief of staff in the Reagan White House until 1985, Baker may not have known that four devaluations had been attempted in the preceding seventeen years, all in efforts to reduce the chronic balance-of-payments deficit caused by our government's stubborn adherence to the myths of free trade. (One attempt was made under Lyndon Johnson, two under Richard Nixon, and the fourth, a de facto devaluation, was tried with disastrous results in the Carter administration.)

There was, however, a man sitting at Baker's elbow who had been involved in every one of these prior devaluations and who gave the nod for yet another suicidal leap off the monetary cliff. Paul Volcker was chairman of the Federal Reserve Board when Baker worked out the Plaza Pact in New York with the finance ministers and central bankers of our principal trading "partners."

Volcker, a Chase Manhattan graduate, had been president of the New York Federal Reserve Bank and later chairman of the Fed's board during the Carter devaluation. Previously, he had been Under-Secretary of the Treasury for Monetary Affairs and chief chef of the two Nixon devaluations. And he was in a Treasury policy post when Lyndon Johnson tried *his* devaluation. If Baker was acting from lack of experience in 1985, Volcker certainly could not cop that same plea of innocence.

Devaluation was only one of a number of myths Reagan and Baker bought in the misleading hubris surrounding the trade issue. Another was the equally insidious fiction that imports fight inflation. This was disproved in the late 1970s by a Labor Department study which found that prices prevailing in the four principal industries then under import restraints—specialty steel, color television sets, footwear, and textiles—had all been *anti-inflationary* during a period of the greatest peacetime inflation in U.S. history. The study, entitled "Price Behavior of Products Under Import Relief," was conducted by the Labor Department's Bureau of International Labor Affairs in 1979 and updated in 1981, when substantially the same anti-inflationary results were found to be still prevailing for the protected industries. In fact, the prices of certain high-alloy specialty steel products made by American companies had declined while protected by import quotas and voluntary restraint agreements.

Moreover, the whole historic experience of the United States gives the lie to the imports-versus-inflation myth, for it was the economies of scale enjoyed by American industries under our traditional protectionism that held prices down, not imports.

The chief cause of inflation is government spending. But for most of the first 125 years of the republic, Customs duties on imported goods paid the greatest part of all costs for operating the federal government—more than 90 percent in the early decades, and still in the 40 to 50 percent range before the Wilson administration overturned the protective tariff in 1913. Customs duties were then replaced by the income tax as the chief source of the Treasury's revenue. It is obvious, from even a cursory glance at history, that import restraints fight inflation. Yet the myth persists that the contrary circumstance prevails.

The endemic inflation that has afflicted our country for three decades, with the exception of the earlier Reagan years, has occurred during the devastating explosion of imports into the U.S. market. Our standard of living, built by sound money and protectionist policies, is declining as the government borrows increasingly from abroad to pay for the import binge.

Yet another free trade myth is that trade promotes peace. It obviously did not in the case of the United States and Japan, both of which could boast that the other was its number one trading partner prior to World War II. United States–Japan trade was the second largest bilateral trade in the world then. The largest was between Germany and England. So much for trade promoting peace.

For decades it has been an article of faith at the Treasury and the Federal Reserve that a paper money economy, hyped up by never-ending increases in government and consumer spending, could be kept going indefinitely. After all, paper money—like any currency—reflects the confidence people have in the economy, in the government, in themselves.

However, with America it had always been implicit that the value of the dollar rested securely on the nation's productive capacity. Now that productive capacity is fast breaking down. Indeed, in many vital areas of industrial production it has disappeared almost entirely or eroded to a point where its revival is impossible, at least under the trade policies so fanatically followed by Ronald Reagan and a long line of his presidential predecessors. The experience of the steel industry is a classic case in point.

There is no better gauge of the relative decline of American productive power than this: in the 1950s the United States had nearly 60 percent of the world's total steel capacity; in 1988 it was under 12 percent—with the Soviet Union, the European Community, and Japan all ahead of us.

Since 1974 more than seven hundred steel production and related facilities have closed, twenty-five steel companies have terminated operations entirely,[9] and employment in this crucial industry plummeted from over 650,000 persons in 1953 to less than 150,000 by 1987. During the decade 1974–84, import penetration of the American steel market doubled from 13 percent to 26 percent.[10] According to the American Iron Steel Institute, the total penetration was actually 34 percent when imports of finished products using steel are factored in.

The trickle-down effect of steel plant closings is incalculable. We do know that from 1974 to 1986 steel companies, in addition to closing seven hundred plants, shut down forty more facilities involved in mining and processing iron ore and coal, plus fifty-eight additional factories which manufactured fabricated steel products. But the impact on trucking companies and railroads, on electric power and natural gas companies, on construction and home building, on retail and wholesale business—on the countless suppliers who depended upon the seven hundred steel plants and the ninety-eight other facilities permanently shut down—this will never be accurately measured.

The Labor Department assures us that the multiplying factor is "only" one and a half support jobs lost for every one steel industry employee thrown out of work. Even assuming that this modest multiplier is correct, the more than

500,000 jobs that have disappeared in steel since the 1950s caused at least 750,000 others to vanish for a total of over 1,250,000 jobs wiped out by this one vital industry's painful decline.

But the University of Illinois, in a study done for the Illinois Chamber of Commerce, found that no less than 3.2 support jobs are generated by every one production job in steel. This would place the fallout from steel's 500,000 lost jobs at well over two million.

These employment losses were not made up by the increase in "service industry" jobs, as the economists kept telling us. Most of the jobs lost in steel's long slide were high-paying positions that enabled the workers to buy decent homes, own several family cars, and often send their children to college.

Many of the 1,250,000-to-2,000,000 men and women thrown out of jobs dependent on steel never worked again. Those who did too often found the "service" jobs they were forced to take paid but a fraction of the wages they had earned in steel and its satellite industries. The less fortunate wound up as "street people," their lives and their families shattered forever.

The financial side of the steel picture has been just as dismal as employment. In 1986 the steel industry in the United States lost more than $4.2 billion, bringing the total for five consecutive years of losses to an aggregate of almost $12 billion.[11] Although 1987 and 1988 saw an improvement, the upswing came only on a greatly reduced production base.

Contrary to the propaganda that the domestic steel industry fell behind because of its alleged failure to update its technology, American steel companies had spent more than $8 billion for new plant and equipment from 1981 to 1986, in spite of the staggering losses during those same years. However, this was accomplished through borrowing and the debt-to-equity ratio in the steel industry soared to 197.7 percent in 1986, the highest on record. Still, the steel industry was only following the sad example set by the U.S. government.

None of this weighed heavily, if at all, on Ronald Reagan as he landed at Helsinki for a little rest and relaxation en route to the Moscow summit. There were, however, a few things that should have concerned him in the context of his impending meetings with Gorbachev. One was a report in Wilson C. Lucom's Washington *Inquirer* about a recent press conference at the American Enterprise Institute on the implications of the INF treaty. Participating were a group of experts on arms control, all of whom had held high posts in the Reagan administration.

The group included Frank Gaffney Jr. who had been the Pentagon's top arms control official until the autumn of 1987; Richard Perle, who had served as Assistant Secretary of Defense for International Security Policy and had been given credit for paving the way for the INF; Sven Kramer, ex-director of arms control at the National Security Council; and Michael Mobbs, a former assistant director of the Arms Control and Disarmament Agency.

Presumably, this was a group that knew something about arms control. But what they said at the press conference, according to Peter Samuel of the *Inquirer*, was that "Reagan Administration tinkering with the Intermediate Nuclear Force (INF) treaty" had "actually made the document more damaging" to American security after Reagan and Gorbachev signed it in Washington the previous December.[12] Among other things, the post-signing adjustments had, Gaffney emphasized, "retroactively fashioned" INF in such a way that it now inhibits U.S development of high-technology non-nuclear systems.[13]

The concerns of the Gaffney group added to the dismal forecast made by the outgoing commander of the North Atlantic Treaty Alliance, Gen. Bernard Rogers, in October 1987—*before* Reagan and Gorbachev affixed their signatures to the INF treaty. At a briefing of the Marshall Group in the Reserve Officers Association (ROA) building on Capitol Hill, General Rogers stated candidly that INF would eliminate NATO's ability to deter war in Europe. For nearly forty years NATO had kept the peace. But the man who had commanded the alliance's forces for eight of those years was telling us that NATO's mission was about to be crippled.

There was a sobering silence in the ROA board room when General Rogers finished his briefing. A number of the men around the table had held important commands with the U.S. Armed Forces in Europe and around the world. Two others had been American ambassadors to the Soviet Union. Although Rogers later went public with his evaluation of INF, members of the group were then hearing it for the first time. Finally, the silence was broken by the obvious question.

"Did you give the president the same appraisal of the INF treaty that you just gave us?"

"No," replied General Rogers, "I never was given the opportunity." He then told how he had requested a meeting with President Reagan and flew from NATO headquarters to Washington in the belief he would see him. But when Rogers got to the White House he was told Reagan was busy with a young people's group and the General was shunted off to the then director of the National Security Council, Frank Carlucci.

Thus, the President of the United States, in preparing to sign the "most significant" arms control treaty in history, did not avail himself of the advice and council of the man who had commanded NATO for eight critical years, the one man who undoubtedly knew more about the full implications of that treaty than anyone in the West.

General Rogers did tell the Marshall Group, in response to a later question from the president, Stuart L. Hannon, that if the INF was signed and ratified the emphasis in NATO would obviously have to be on conventional forces.

But in June 1987, when INF was still a gleam in Gorbachev's eye, George C. Wilson, the veteran Pentagon correspondent of the *Washington Post*, reported an interview with the outgoing U.S. Army Chief of Staff, Gen. John A. Wickham, Jr. Although Wickham said today's Army was strong and mobile, there was something that worried him. As Wilson put it in his lead, the Chief of Staff was concerned that the U.S. Army *"would run out of supplies after only a few months of intense fighting because there is no national production base to support it."*[14]

It did not take the INF treaty to reduce America to this dangerous state, so dangerous that it might be interpreted by a potential enemy as an open invitation to war, conventional or otherwise. Trade—free and open trade—had done that job. But the gamble President Reagan was taking in playing arms control roulette with Mikhail Gorbachev would shift the West's principal deterrence from nuclear to conventional forces—at the very moment there was "no national production base to support it."

The Reagan game had become an ominous one indeed and it threatened to become far more ominous for Ronald Reagan's successor in the White House.

But to know how this dangerous game of international roulette in trade and arms had brought us to this perilous point, it is necessary to look back, to resurrect from the grave of history things that America has long forgotten.

Chapter 2.

Genesis

A free people should promote such manufactories, as tend to render them independent on others for essential, particularly military supplies.

—George Washington,
message to the First Congress
of the United States, 1789

The impression created by modern economists is that the United States bubbled up to its present, or just past, position of economic preeminence thanks to our government's policy of opening the American market ever wider to foreign imports in its dedicated pursuit of free trade. The reality is that the diametric opposite is true: America was built on firm and steadfast protectionism and it was the protectionist principle that gave our people the highest standard of living the world had ever known.

In the beginning there was a vast undeveloped continent inhabited by scattered tribes of Indians. There were no foreign aid funds available to the early settlers; no World Bank to finance the building of roads, dams, or power plants; no big lenders to shower unsecured loans on the Colonies. There were a few British investors willing to help pay the passage for some of the adventurous souls who came here. The investors hoped that a profit might one day be realized from trading with the natives, or mining gold, or some other amorphous scheme.

The settlers were driven here in quest of religious or political freedom or simply a chance to eat and live a little better than they had at home, although Goethe and some other romanticists later attributed their courageous flight into the unknown as another historic act in the great Faustian drama that has driven

Western man to the ends of the earth and now, in our era, to the moon and toward exploration of the stars.

For the most part the first Americans were forced to carve their farms and homes and infant industries out of the wilderness entirely on their own. Theirs was a constant battle for sheer survival—against the elements, the Indians, the thousand and one tribulations of a people set down in a strange and hostile land. All they had was their physical strength, common sense, and an abiding faith in God. But with these they generated the superhuman effort that slowly created a nation the like of which had never been seen in all recorded history.

Agriculture took priority. Merely to grow enough to feed one's family was counted an achievement. But some few industries soon sprang up. Shipbuilding was encouraged by England, whose great forests had all but disappeared by the mid-seventeenth century. Fisheries quickly followed and were among the first of our export industries. Tobacco was a cash crop many colonists counted on to earn that greatest rarity, hard money.

In the earlier part of the Colonial period, as the industrial revolution was dawning in England, iron making was begun in Massachusetts, Rhode Island, Connecticut, and Virginia.[1] Hemp was grown to make cordage for the ships but linen sails came from the mother country, as did most other manufactured products. From the very beginning the Crown and the City, London's close-knit imperial-financial partnership, adopted a mercantilist policy toward the Colonies, which were required to provide England with raw materials in exchange for manufactured goods and minimal amounts of specie.

Ernest Ludlow Bogart, in his incisive book, *Economic History of the American People*, makes the point that inter-Colonial trade developed along the coast from Gloucester to Savannah and soon equaled the trans-Atlantic trade with England and Europe.[2] A lively trade also developed with the West Indies, where sugar plantations provided the molasses New England made into rum to swap with African chieftains for slaves. It was on this trade that the early fortunes of Salem, Newport, and Boston were built.[3]

From 1700 until the outbreak of the Revolution the American trade imbalance with England was horrendous: we bought eight times as much from Great Britain as they imported from us.[4] The circuitous trade with the West Indies, Africa, Spain, Portugal, Italy, and occasionally a few other countries where the Crown permitted our ships to sail, partially paid for the huge trade deficit. But it was Britain that profited most handsomely.

Lord Sheffield estimated that in the first seventy-five years of the eighteenth century England extracted upwards of £30 million from the American colonies in this tangential trade, on top of the direct exports sent in payment for the goods imported from Britain.[5] This was a huge sum for those times; and when one reflects that it was extracted from the sweat and toil of a people numbering only one million in total population near the end of that period, we begin to get a dim idea of how oppressively the Crown and the City's mercantile policy must have weighed upon our forebearers.

Even bibles could not be printed in the American Colonies because they had to be imported from England. The exceptions were German bibles, which were published in Pennsylvania because they did not compete with the English product, a New and Old Testament translated into a phonetic Indian tongue, and several Colonial editions in English that apparently escaped the notice of the British officials charged with policing industrial production in America. Indeed, enforcement of the laws passed by Parliament at Westminster to keep the Colonies in economic subjugation were not always as rigidly enforced as the King and his ministers would have liked. If they had been, the iron foundries that supplied the materials for the musket makers and gunsmith forges would have been completely suppressed and the American Revolution may not have erupted, or certainly not as early as it did.

After the French and Indian War, which George III, with some justification, thought his Colonial subjects should help pay for, the mercantilist Acts of Trade were more rigorously applied. Moreover, these statutes were expanded to include more products that could only be shipped to England, among them bar and pig iron, lumber, and hides. On top of this, the sailing routes of American vessels were further restricted to keep our ships from carrying manufactured cargoes from European ports, a temptation many of our intrepid sea captains had succumbed to during the seven years of war with France.

Other measures to limit our trade were also implemented, most notably by the despised Townshend Acts, probably influenced by Adam Smith, who helped Lord Townshend, the Chancellor of the Exchequer, draw up the postwar budget designed to squeeze more revenue out of the Colonies. Smith, the inventor of free trade, apparently had his hand in the statutes that stiffened Customs enforcement in America, placing heavy import duties on a wide range of items, including wine, oil, lead, paint, and tea. Thus, from its inception in the agile but erratic mind of Adam Smith, free trade was a one-way street intended to benefit one country at the expense of another, or even all others.

The response of the Colonies was to adopt nonimportation agreements which, in 1769, cut deeply into imports from England and forced repeal of the Townshend Acts, though the tax on tea was kept to sustain a vestige of royal authority—and to goad the Bostonians into staging their historic tea party. This event, led by "the prince of smugglers," John Hancock, brought on the "intolerable acts" which closed the port of Boston, annulled the charter of Massachusetts, and quartered upon the people the red-coated soldiers sent to enforce British law and royal decree. The stage was thus set for Lexington and Concord in April 1775 and the Declaration of Independence fifteen months later on July 4, 1776.

Modern historians and writers have passed over the decisive role played by British trade policy in igniting the American Revolution. But a century ago the memories of Americans were not yet so dimmed as they are today. John A. Logan, in his 1886 book, *The Great Conspiracy*, a probing search into the causes of the Civil War, remarked on the motivation of the First Congress in enacting a protectionist Tariff Act as its very first substantive legislation in 1789:

None knew better than its [the First Congress] members that the war of the American Revolution grew chiefly out of the efforts of Great Britain to cripple and destroy our Colonial industries to the benefit of the British trader, and that the Independence conquered was an industrial as well as a Political Independence; and none knew better than they, that the failure of the subsequent political Confederation of States was due mainly to its failure to encourage and protect the budding domestic manufactures of those states.[6]

   Taxation without representation was the battle cry of the Revolutionary War. The mercantilist trade policy of Great Britain was its underlying cause. Yet today Americans have meekly surrendered their economic independence to a slogan— ''free trade''—and slavishly accept the mercantilism of Japan and a host of other foreign countries that are brazenly killing off our industries and robbing our citizens of their jobs.
   As John Logan noted, the First Congress of the United States gave top priority to passage of protectionist legislation, again in stark contrast to the charades staged by the Congress on the trade issue in recent times. President George Washington, having urged adoption of such a measure for ''the safety and interest of the People,'' signed the trade bill into law on July 4, 1789, the first Independence Day under the new Union created by the Constitution. From this significant date until 1913, the first year of the tragic presidency of Woodrow Wilson, America pursued an essentially protectionist trade policy, more so at some times than at others, but always protectionist.
   Washington was not the only prominent protectionist of his day. Both Alexander Hamilton, the first Secretary of the Treasury, and Thomas Jefferson, Secretary of State, were proud to count themselves protectionists. (Although the term ''protectionist'' had not yet been coined, their beliefs were explicit in their words and actions.) Hamilton and Jefferson disagreed on many things, but on this issue they marched in unison. James Madison, who with Hamilton and John Jay had authored the Federalist Papers that brought about the Constitutional Convention, was also an open and avowed protectionist.
   The fact that the Tariff Act of 1790, which strengthened and broadened the original trade legislation, was carried by an overwhelming three-to-one margin in the House of Representatives is indicative of the staunch protectionist position of most of the founding fathers. But of them all, it was Hamilton who most clearly saw the absolute necessity of a firm policy to protect our infant industries in order to maintain our hard-won independence.
   As Secretary of the Treasury, Hamilton was entrusted with the herculean task of placing the United States on a sound financial footing. The paper currencies issued by the Continental Congress and by the separate states during the period of the Articles of Confederation had depreciated drastically in value. Inflation was out of control and threatened to snuff out the life of the new republic.
   Hamilton understood that a sound currency had to be based upon two essential ingredients: confidence in the government, and the production of the people. The only way to achieve both, then as now, was—and is—protection of agri-

culture, industry, and commerce. Wisely, Hamilton insisted on the United States paying off its crushing war debt in order to establish confidence. But he was equally insistent that protectionist measures be adopted because Hamilton knew, far better than most modern economists, that a viable economic system must be built upon the energy, inventiveness, and productive capacity of the people. He also saw through the transparent fallacy concocted by Adam Smith and his disciples—that imports combat inflation. This is what Hamilton wrote on what is still today the principal fallacious argument for free trade:

"When a domestic manufacture has engaged . . . a competent number of persons, [his product] invariably becomes cheaper . . . than was the foreign Article for which it is a substitute. The internal competition, which takes place, soon does away with every thing like Monopoly, and by degrees reduces the price of the [domestic] Article to the minimum of a reasonable profit on the Capital employed."[7]

It was not only a matter of sound economics but, in the prophetic view of Hamilton, Washington, and other founders, protectionism was the soundest philosophy for guaranteeing the greatest good for the greatest number of people. They believed with the Anglo-Irish statesman-philosopher, Edmund Burke, that government was "a contrivance of wisdom to provide for human wants" and men and women have "a right that those wants should be provided for by this wisdom."[8] Burke's belief was rooted in the Aristotelian conviction that morality and politics are—or should be—one and the same. To separate them is to cast off responsibility for maintaining the welfare of the governed, which is precisely what most of our "pragmatist" Presidents have done in the name of free trade since the reign of Woodrow Wilson.

Hamilton wrote in his message to the first speaker of the House that "not only the wealth, but the independence and security of a Country, appear to be materially connected with the prosperity of manufacturers. Every nation . . . ought to endeavor to possess within itself all essentials of national supply. These comprise the means of Subsistence, habitation, clothing and defense."[9]

George Washington, the commander who had welded a rag-tag militia into a fighting force that defeated the best-trained troops of England and Germany, was particularly emphatic on Hamilton's last named point, defense. In his initial message to the First Congress, Washington stressed that freedom and independence depended upon the people's ability to manufacture their own products, "particularly military supplies."

Indeed, how can any nation aspire to true independence unless it strives for self-sufficiency? Dependence upon imports, on the scale now assumed by the United States, cuts the ground from under our independence—economically *and* politically. The Japanese lobbyists and their American hirelings swarm all over Washington, D.C., and repeatedly kill or soften protectionist legislation. Moreover, the U.S. Treasury now finds itself so beholden to Japanese purchases of government bonds that the executive branch behaves as though it is securely in

Tokyo's pocket. It apparently never occurred to the White House or to the Congress, as the Japanese and others racked up the tremendous trade imbalances that contributed so heavily to the record budget deficits of the 1980s, that it is much healthier to generate domestic revenues by encouraging American industrial growth than to rely on foreign financiers to bail out our Treasury.

Fortunately for the early development of the nation Alexander Hamilton had a firmer grasp of the hard realities of promoting and preserving America's economic well-being than his modern successors at Treasury. He not only saw that the fledgling United States had to restore its credit by paying old bills incurred by the Continental Congress and the individual states, he also knew that protection for domestic industries could produce an enormous bonus above and beyond the direct benefits derived from building an indigenous manufacturing base. Hamilton, and those Secretaries of the Treasury who followed him for the next five generations, relied on import duties to pay the lion's share of government expenditures.

For decades, the duties collected by the Customs Service on imports provided almost all the Treasury's funds. Additionally, with some exceptions, the import duties were responsible for annual surpluses in the Treasury, and as late as 1914 they were still the primary source of our government's revenue.

Hamilton and those who came after him were able to pay off a good deal of the debt left over from the Revolutionary War and the runaway inflation that followed with the monies from Customs. If the recurring threats of war with France and Britain during the 1790s had not forced the United States to build and maintain a strong navy, the Customs duties may have been able to retire the debt entirely in that one decade.[10]

In spite of Hamilton's brilliant stewardship of the Treasury, which laid a solid foundation for the economic miracles America was to perform throughout the ensuing century, he was savagely attacked by his many enemies.[11] The economic illiterates of the day, including the small but vociferous claque of messianic freetraders, opposed his protectionist policies. States-rights proponents fought his efforts to establish the government on a strong Federalist basis. Political rivals were jealous of his influence with Washington, who regarded Hamilton almost as a son. And all manner of men, among them some who, like Jefferson, should have known better, resented Hamilton's undoubted aristocratic tendencies.

One action Hamilton took is still open to question, though he may not have had a viable alternative at the time. This was the creation of the First Bank of the United States, with four-fifths of the stock subscribed by private investors who were to profit substantially over the twenty-year life of the Bank. Nonetheless, the notes of the bank were firmly based upon specie, with the dollar backed by gold and silver. The Mint Act of 1792 set the value of gold at fifteen times silver, the ratio equal then to bullion values. The First Bank of the United States and the currency system established by Congress on Hamilton's recommendation was a far, far cry from the present Federal Reserve system with the dollar based on little more than the imprint of a high-speed printing press upon paper.

Yet the first central bank did set a bad precedent. It encouraged the government to borrow, and the temptation to do so was not easily resisted. With the threats of war and the expenditures made to strengthen our defenses, the national debt swelled to over $6 million by 1796. This forced the government to sell its stock in the Bank of the United States. Although it made a profit of $671,860 on the sale, and realized dividends of $1,101,720 during the years it had held the stock, the government was cut out of the much greater dividends paid by the bank in the fifteen years it had remaining before expiration of its charter.[12]

In spite of the debt accumulation, the Customs duties handed the Treasury a substantial surplus almost every year. When the Jefferson administration negotiated the Louisiana Purchase in 1803 with Napoleonic France for a total of $15 million, there was a $5 million surplus in the Treasury thanks to the $12,438,000 in import duties collected the year before.

The surplus enabled the government to float the bond issue for the biggest real estate bargain in history without recourse to either a temporary loan or to new taxes.[13] Thus, the protectionist policy of the United States, from which our sizeable Customs revenues steadily flowed, played the major role in doubling the territory of the country in the most painless possible way—without taxes, without costly short-term borrowing, and without war.

In addition, the high costs of the successful military operations against the Barbary pirates were offset totally by the increased revenues produced by the expanded Tariff Act of 1804.[14] The pirates had taken a heavy toll of American shipping in the Mediterranean and hostilities dragged out for four years before the Marines landed on the shores of Tripoli and, in June 1805, defeated the Arabs who had declared war on us in 1801.

The battles with the pirates of the Barbary Coast for a time diverted attention from a far more serious situation that was developing on the high seas as America struggled to establish trade with the rest of the world. British men-of-war were hailing down our merchant ships, boarding them, and taking off all sailors they deemed to be subjects of the Crown. The United States government protested, but the British seemed to know our presidents would always turn the other cheek to their aggression on the seas. Appeasement was paving the way for war and in 1812 it finally came.

Chapter 3.

War, Peace, and Protectionism

It is time we should become a little more Americanized and, instead of feeding the paupers of Europe, feed our own, or else in a short time we shall all be paupers ourselves.[1]
—Andrew Jackson in 1824

The first real war the United States engaged in after creation of the Union was over trade. Americans thought they had the right, under the doctrine of freedom of the seas, to trade with all sides even while the nations of Europe were fighting for their lives in the prolonged and bloody Napoleonic wars. The British, quite understandably, thought otherwise.

The pacifist policies of the reigning Republican Party, lineal ancestors of today's Democrats, had so weakened the armed forces of the United States that the British, although their navy and army were widely deployed, believed in 1812 that they could safely teach the upstart Americans a lesson. By 1814 it appeared that their conjecture was correct: British redcoats marched into Washington, set fire to the Capitol and the White House, and chased President Madison and his wife Dolly out of town.

Andrew Jackson, however, was an American cast from a different mold and he was bent upon avenging the invasion of his country. In a remarkable series of victories below New Orleans in late 1814 and early 1815 he repeatedly defeated a far superior force of England's best troops with a motley collection of frontiersmen, militia and even a pirate "navy" under Jean Lafitte. This battle, fought in three separate stages over nearly a month, cost the British two thousand casualties, against only seventy-one for the Americans. Ironically, neither side knew that a peace treaty had been signed at Ghent in Belgium two weeks before the final victory.

The Madison administration's posture of weakness in the face of an obvious threat of war before the invasion is in explicable except in the context of the peculiar American mindset, which prevails in many quarters even to our own day, that the United States is somehow impervious to attack. There certainly was no fiscal reason for the economies Madison imposed upon our army and navy. After years of enjoying a brisk trade with most of the belligerents in the Napoleonic wars, the economy of the country was thriving.

In 1811, Customs duties accounted for more than $13 million, or nearly 99 percent of the Treasury's total revenues. As a result, the Treasury enjoyed a huge (for that day) $5 million surplus and it would have been no hardship for the people if this money had gone into strengthening the armed forces as a deterrent to war. Yet the President and his cabinet, under the apparent delusion that the country was immune to war, further cut back defense expenditures in the wistful hope this peaceful gesture would somehow waft the war clouds away.

During the hostilities import duties were doubled in an effort to offset the sudden increases in funds needed for the Army and Navy. However, Customs revenues declined precipitously because Britain had been our chief trading partner and had traditionally absorbed the biggest share of U.S. exports until war broke out.

In spite of the drop in Customs duties during the War of 1812, the tariff still managed to produce most of the government's revenues. Indeed, in 1813 tariffs accounted for 93 percent of the Treasury's income, though thereafter they shrank to under 60 percent in 1814 and to less than 50 percent in the following year. By this time peace had been restored, and a whole new set of problems confronted the nation. Chief among them was the mountain of debt piled up by the war. On January 1, 1816, the indebtedness of the United States reached $127,334,000, and astronomical figure no one could have conceived of a few years earlier.

The debt problem was exacerbated by a postwar invasion of imports, primarily from Britain, that shut down scores of American factories, many of which had been built to help the nation defend itself against British aggression. Rabbeno in his *American Commercial Policy* wrote that "The English manufacturers . . . rushed as if to the attack of a fortress." And like the walls of Jericho, and all the great ports of the United States in recent times, the walls came tumbling down. Imports, valued at less than $13 million in 1814, soared to $147 million two years later.

The British were not secretive about their intentions. They openly dumped their goods on the American market at a loss in order to capture our commerce, much as the Japanese, Koreans, and even the Europeans and English are doing today. A member of Parliament named Brougham boldly argued in the House of Commons: "Is it [not] worth while to incur a loss upon the first importation, in order by the glut to stifle in the cradle those rising manufactures in the United States which the War had forced into existence contrary to the natural course of things."[2]

Fortunately, the Congress and the executive branch both hastened to protect the devastated domestic industries. President Madison and his Secretary of the Treasury, Alexander J. Dallas of Pennsylvania, recommended swift action and Congress passed the strongly protectionist Tariff Act of 1816 by a healthy margin. The vote in the House of Representatives was 88 to 54 with the North and West voting overwhelmingly in favor of the legislation. Even the South and the Southwest, which in later years violently opposed the tariff, provided 23 votes for the 1816 trade bill in the House.

The battle for this historic trade law, which added tremendous impetus to the policy of self-sufficiency initiated by Washington, Hamilton, and Jefferson, was led by a rising generation of political leaders—Henry Clay of Kentucky and John C. Calhoun of South Carolina most prominent among them. Logan noted that "no man labored harder and did more effective service in securing passage" of the act than Calhoun, who ironically—indeed, tragically—was to become the most forceful opponent of protection, carrying his fight against it to the point of espousing the dangerous doctrine of "nullification" and encouraging South Carolina and other states to refuse to collect tariffs at their ports of entry.

In 1816, however, John Calhoun championed the Tariff Act in the interest of the security of the nation, observing in the House debate that "liberty and the union" of the United States depended upon the principle of protectionism. "Neither agriculture, manufactures, nor commerce, taken separately, is the cause of wealth," stated Calhoun. "It flows from the three combined and cannot exist without each."[3]

The Tariff Act of 1816 was designed to rebuild and substantially strengthen the protective wall which had crumbled so quickly before the onslaught of British dumping in the wake of the War of 1812.[4] In the nineteenth century higher tariffs were usually enough to deter uneconomic import invasions because industry in England and Europe, our only competition then, was virtually all in private hands. A privately owned company can only absorb losses from dumping its products abroad for a limited period. If the firm fails to knock out the domestic competition in the market targeted within a reasonable time, it may find itself in deep financial trouble.

Today, government-owned or subsidized industries wage trade wars against American manufacturers for years, knowing that in the end they can bring even the mightiest U.S. corporations to their knees. Thus, higher tariffs are no longer necessarily a strong deterrent, but often merely an irritant the treasuries of the socialized world can scratch away at indefinitely until they have captured our markets and replenished their losses from the higher prices they eventually impose. Moreover, foreign governments and industries know it is *they* who can count on protection from the government of the United States, which perversely denies protection to its own industries and workers while granting it, in effect, to all others.

In 1816, however, the higher tariffs soon put a stop to most British dumping. An immediate surge of prosperity swept America as factories reopened and new ones were built to meet the increased demand. All sectors of the economy—

manufacturing, agriculture, and commerce—benefited from the new protection. Unhappily, in this same year the act chartering the Second Bank of the United States narrowly squeaked through the House of Representatives, passed the Senate, and was approved by the president. The first bank had died in 1811 when Congress refused to renew its charter. But it was now felt, at least by a slim majority, that a central bank was required to help service the burdensome debt incurred during the war.

In fact, $21 million of the new bank's $35 million total capitalization was in the funded debt of the U.S. Treasury. The $14 million capital balance was equally divided between subscriptions by the government and by private investors. But once again, as with the first central bank, the private group had effective control: the President of the United States was permitted to appoint only five directors; the outside investors could name the remaining twenty, which meant the monetary policy of the bank—and eventually of the country—was decided by a small group of individuals.

Although foreign investors were ostensibly forbidden a vote, everyone knew they could actually exercise great influence under the monetary table. Overall, the structure of the Second Bank of the United States was quite similar in substance to the present structure of the Federal Reserve. Today, the President gets to name five members of the Fed's board of governors, but he has nothing whatever to say about naming the real controlling group, the Open Market Committee, which is hand-picked by the private stockholders who actually own the Federal Reserve Bank and, therefore, decide policy.

Still, the Second Bank of the United States, unlike the present Federal Reserve, was pledged under its charter to redeem its paper notes for gold and silver on demand. But in spite of this precaution, the reckless monetary and lending policies of the Second Bank soon plunged the country into a panic, the first of its kind in our history.[5] The advantage given American manufacturers and workers by the Tariff Act of 1816 and broader protection in the 1818 bill melted away temporarily as credit tightened and prices fell too far, too fast.

Although a tougher trade bill failed in 1820 by one vote in the Senate, the Tariff Act of 1824 put the nation back on its increasingly protectionist track, though it was nearly derailed for the first time by sectionalism. Curiously, in the vote on this legislation, New England joined the South in opposition. The commercial and shipping interests in Boston and other ports were inclined toward an open-door free trade, but the votes of the expanding industrial mid-Atlantic states like Pennsylvania and New York, plus the Midwest and Kentucky and Tennessee, carried the day by a slim five-vote margin, 107–102.

Henry Clay, the speaker of the House, played the decisive role in this legislative battle, and from there on was identified as the leader of the American system. However, it was Andrew Jackson, then senator from Tennessee, who emerged as the truest and toughest protector of the nation's interests.

In 1824, all three of the leading candidates for the presidency in the election of that year were protectionists—Andrew Jackson, Henry Clay, and John Quincy

Adams. If Senator Jackson had compromised and voted against the Tariff Act, he could have picked up enough support in the West and North to become president. But he voted for the bill and stated afterward that he would not have changed his vote to place himself ''in the Presidential chair.''[6]

John Quincy Adams was elected over Jackson with support from Clay, who was rewarded with the position of Secretary of State. This infuriated Jackson. He felt betrayed by his fellow Westerner, and he never forgave Clay.

In 1828 Jackson was not in the Senate and therefore did not take an active role in the confused tariff fight of that year. Calhoun believed he could defeat the tariff by increasing the duties on raw materials to make the legislation unpalatable to Northern manufacturers. But as he was to do so many times in his career, John Calhoun outsmarted himself. The ''unpalatable'' bill was swallowed whole by the Congress, though again the majority of the New England delegation in the House joined the South in opposition.[7]

The Tariff Act of 1828, passed with the complicity of Calhoun, angered the plantation owners of the South and in the volatile years leading up to the Civil War the tariff and slavery issues became inextricably intertwined. But it was the tariff that first touched off talk of secession below the Mason-Dixon line. Dr. Dewey has lucidly set forth the reasons why the South opted for free trade:

The South with its natural advantages for the growing of cotton, rice and tobacco, and with abundant rude slave labor, was devoted solely to the production of a few staple agricultural commodities, and witnessed with indifference if not with impatience the building up of diversified industries and manufacturing cities. Indifference and impatience were converted into open hostility as soon as it was felt that this development was at the expense of its own profit. By her natural resources the South was equipped for magnificent development of manufacturers . . . but the institution of slavery necessarily restricted the productive genius of the South and forced her industries into grooves from which there was no escape. The interest of the South obviously lay in free trade with England, which was its principal customer for cotton, hemp and tobacco; and it was ingeniously reasoned that a tax on imports was in incidence a tax on exports.[8]

There is evidence that England encouraged the South in this mistaken reasoning. The Crown and the City longed for a restoration of the mercantile system of Colonial days, and the slaveholding South was willing to accommodate this ambition. In the end, the South's twin stands for free trade and slavery both conspired to bring it down. If the South had surrendered slavery and adopted protectionism, it could have joined the North and West in the great industrial buildup of the late nineteenth century and shared in the general prosperity that transformed America into the promised land the Pilgrim fathers had envisioned when they set sail on the *Mayflower* for the New World.

During World War II and the period immediately following it, ''the productive genius of the South'' was permitted to develop, though the development would have been carried much further if it had not been for the federal government's free-trade policy. The textile industry, which came to be centered in the Carolinas, Georgia, and Virginia, is among those domestic industries hardest hit by imports. Many textile mills have closed, leaving whole communities devastated and thousands of workers out of jobs. Steel mills have been shut down in Birmingham, Alabama, and other Southern industries have also been curtailed.

Through these painful experiences, the South has gradually become a stronghold of modern protectionism, though there is great hesitancy to call this valid principle by its proper name. Old beliefs die hard, as we are witnessing in our own time with the survival of most of the myths of free trade—after they have been proven fallacious for decades.

Chapter 4.

Jackson's Greatest Battle

The Bank cares not whether [the President] is benefitted or injured. It takes its own time and its own way.
—Nicholas Biddle, president of the
Second Bank of the United States[1]

In the nineteenth century the overwhelming majority of people in America saw the trade issue in a much more clear and realistic light than today. Few saw through the tinsel facade of the free trade theory better than Andrew Jackson. When he was elected President in 1828 with John C. Calhoun as Vice President, the antiprotectionist faction expected Jackson to scrap the tariff and raise the banner of free trade. Instead, he permitted the strongly protectionist Act of 1828 to remain in force except for some small changes in 1830.

Two years later, Jackson's predecessor in the White House, John Quincy Adams, authored a trade bill as chairman of the House Committee on Manufacturers that did reduce some duties but preserved the protectionist spirit of the existing law. This Tariff Act of 1832 carried in the House by 132 to 65, with Virginia and North Carolina supplying enough votes for it to split the South right down the middle, 27 to 27. New England was also evenly divided, 17 to 17. But the mid-Atlantic states, the West (now the Midwest), and the border states of Tennessee and Kentucky were overwhelmingly in favor of this protectionist measure and supplied the bulk of the support.

In spite of the heavy majority vote for the 1832 Act, South Carolina called a convention on November 24 and passed a nullification ordinance declaring the law "null and void" in that state and decreeing that import duties would not be collected at its ports after February 1, 1833.

Jackson had tried to send the nullifiers a warning several months before when he told a South Carolina congressman who was setting out for home: "Tell . . . [the Nullifiers] from me that they can talk and write resolutions and print threats to their hearts' content. But if one drop of blood be shed in defiance of the laws of the United States I will hang the first man of them I can get my hands on to the first tree I can find." [2]

Senator Thomas Hart Benton of Missouri overheard Senator Robert Hayne of South Carolina expressing doubt the President would go that far. "I tell you, Hayne," Benton replied, "when Jackson begins to talk about hanging, they can begin to look for the rope." [3]

Tom Benton knew a thing or two about Andrew Jackson's character. In Nashville some years earlier Old Hickory had come after Benton with a horsewhip. Benton's brother, Jesse, shot Jackson twice and very nearly killed him. Yet within weeks General Jackson was leading troops into battle against the marauding Creek Indians.

Calhoun, Hayne, and the other free trade firebrands in South Carolina turned a deaf ear to Jackson's warnings against nullification. Quietly, without fanfare, the president dispatched a ship of war and a small squadron of revenue cutters to Charleston and sent Gen. Winfield Scott to command the land defenses against any rebellion. Jackson repeated his promise to arrest the nullification leaders and try them for treason. And on December 10, 1832, he issued his famous Proclamation on Nullification.

Jackson restated the government's duty to collect the tariff, branded nullification unconstitutional, and denied the claimed right of secession. "To say that any state may secede from the Union," he declared, "is to say that the United States is not a nation." He appealed to his "fellow-citizens of my native State"* to cease their acts of disunion or bear the "dreadful consequences" of treason.

John Quincy Adams pledged his support of Jackson, as did Sen. Daniel Webster of Massachusetts. Even in the South the majority appeared to support the President. In South Carolina itself pro-Unionist militia were drilled by Joel Poinsett. But Robert Hayne, who had left the Senate to become governor of South Carolina, vowed to perish "beneath its ruins" rather than submit.[4] And John C. Calhoun rode north to resign as Vice President and take Hayne's former seat in the Senate. Apparently the sentiments of the citizens he talked with along the way softened Calhoun's resolve. Although he did resign as Vice President, on January 4, 1833 he strode into the Senate chamber and swore to uphold and defend the Constitution of the United States.

Martin Van Buren replaced Calhoun as Vice President. This sprightly little Dutchman from Kinderhook on the Hudson, along with other Jackson advisors,

*Jackson was actually born c. 1765 in the Waxhaws, a southern bulge in the North Carolina border, that should have been in South Carolina but was not. He missed being born in Ireland, where his two brothers were born, by only two years, his parents having emigrated from Country Antrim, in 1763.

had been whispering caution in Andy Jackson's ear. When Henry Clay pulled his Compromise Tariff Act out of the Congress and sent it to the White House in tandem with the president's requested "Force Bill" authorizing use of the military to collect the revenue, including import duties, Jackson reluctantly adopted the weaker tariff in order to have the full power of the companion legislation to put down rebellion. As his biographer, Marquis James, put it: "Old Hickory winced as he signed the tariff bill."[5]

However, the Compromise Tariff was still to a very large extent protectionist. It provided for a gradual reduction of tariffs over the following nine years to an eventual average level of 20 percent on duty-covered items. As it turned out, the lowest tariff was only in effect for a few months in 1842 and was superseded by more protectionist legislation. Meanwhile, Andrew Jackson was nursing his disappointment at having compromised, perhaps the only time in his life he had taken an easier way out on a matter of principle. Of the nullifiers he wrote, with obvious regret: "I thought I would have to hang some of them and I would have done it."[6]

Having missed that opportunity, which some historians believe would have averted the terrible Civil War that blew the country apart twenty-eight years later, Jackson won a great victory in another battle in the year 1832—his courageous fight for the dissolution of the Second Bank of the United States, which he correctly perceived had placed too much power in the hands of a few.

Under the brilliant but arrogant direction of its president, Nicholas Biddle, the Bank dominated the financial affairs of the nation and had become a political force unto itself. Much like the Federal Reserve today, the Second Bank of the United States could promote prosperity by loosening up on credit or plunge the country into recession by contracting the supply of money and forcing banks to recall or tighten up on loans.

Biddle put politicians in his pocket by simply granting them loans that were never called—except when he wanted their vote. He won over the agricultural regions of the South and West, which traditionally had been opposed to the Bank, by showering credit upon the planters and farmers. He gained the support of a majority of President Jackson's cabinet, including the Secretary of the Treasury, Louis McLane. Biddle boasted, not without justification, that he had more power than any President of the United States.[7]

Secretary McLane, and the Bank's other allies in the executive branch, advised Biddle to wait until after the presidential election of 1832 before asking the Congress to vote on renewal of the charter. But Biddle audaciously threw the gauntlet down at Jackson's boots: "The bank cares not whether . . . [the President] is benefitted or injured," he proclaimed. "It takes its own time and its own way."[8] Biddle then made the additional mistake of allying himself with Henry Clay, who hoped to replace Andrew Jackson as President.

No man, or combination of men, living or dead, could challenge Old Hickory in such a blatant manner. A true aristocrat with a sense of honor honed by his Celtic ancestors over centuries, Jackson wore a deep scar in his skull from a sabre cut administered by a British officer whose boots he had refused to clean as a youthful captive in the Revolutionary War. Jackson had left several men dead on dueling fields, littered the South and West with the bodies of Indians in his recurring campaigns, defeated the best troops England could throw into the line at New Orleans, and successfully challenged the Spanish in Florida to bring that state into the American Union. Moreover, he would soon face down France in a bitter dispute over a debt owed the Treasury, and he was to go after a would-be assassin with a cane, charging into two pistols blazing away at him, both of which jammed in what a firearms expert believed a one-in-one-hundred-thousand chance. Although he was one of America's most devoted owners of race horses, Andrew Jackson simply was not fazed by odds.

Biddle tried every trick in the lobbyist's book to get the Congress to override the President's threatened veto of the bill to recharter the Bank of the United States. He bought congressmen and senators left and right with loans and outright bribes; he curried favor with the cabinet and kept the Secretary of the Treasury and others planting seeds of dissension at the White House; he went to the grass roots, where he had planted millions of dollars in loans, and whipped up scores of petitions and appeals for rechartering the Bank.

Biddle did win the first round when Congress approved the renewal of the charter. But Jackson promptly picked up that gauntlet too, throwing it back at the legislative branch with a veto message that should be required reading for every American, or, for that matter, for anyone interested in preserving freedom:

> Distinctions in society will always exist under every just government. Equality of talents, of education, or of wealth, can not be produced by human institutions . . . every man is equally entitled to protection by law. But when the laws undertake to add . . . artificial distinctions . . . to make the rich richer and the potent more powerful, the humble members of society, the farmers, mechanics, and laborers, who have neither the time nor the means of securing like favors to themselves, have a right to complain of the injustice of their government. Its evils exist only in its abuses. If it would confine itself to equal protection, and, as heaven does its rains, shower its favors alike on the high and the low, the rich and the poor, it would be an unqualified blessing. In the act before me, there seems to be a wide and unnecessary departure from these just principles.[9]

Nicholas Biddle called the Jackson message "a manifesto of anarchy" and pulled out all the stops to override the presidential veto. Daniel Webster, already in the Bank's debt for $22,000, got $10,000 more to lead the pro-Bank phalanx in the Senate. Biddle used the Bank's funds to distribute thousands of copies of a Webster address advocating renewal of the Bank's charter, and he tried to weaken Jackson in the public eye by drumming up support for Henry Clay in the Kentuckian's campaign to succeed to the presidency. But on July 13, 1832, the President's veto was sustained. The Second Bank of the United States was dead. Andrew Jackson considered it the greatest victory of his career.

Biddle did not give up. He kept coming back with rechartering schemes. But the President defeated him every time. The coinage of gold and silver was resumed after a long interruption and the country entered a period of unprecedented prosperity, fueled by sensible protectionism on the trade front and sound currency in monetary matters. However, a rapid increase in state banks, all issuing their own notes without sufficient backing, and the practice of the Treasury in accepting these notes in sales of federal lands, soon produced an abusive boom. To head it off, President Jackson directed the Secretary of the Treasury to take only specie for land sales, and a depression followed in 1837 after Jackson had left Washington to return to his beloved Hermitage plantation in Tennessee.

This depression lasted some years and gave the Free Trade League an opportunity to drive home the same arguments here that had been used in England for the repeal of the corn laws, a series of actions by Parliament that marked the end of that country's protectionist policy by 1846. In that same year tariffs were cut substantially by the U.S. Congress and when a spurt of prosperity followed the advocates of free trade naturally claimed credit.

However, it was obvious that other factors were responsible for the vigorous upturn. America's war with Mexico, which broke out in 1846 and lasted until 1848, was the initial impetus. A bigger boost, opened up by this war, soon followed. It was the discovery of gold in California that lifted the American economy onto a higher plateau than it had ever experienced before.

William D. Kelley, a leading member of Congress from Pennsylvania, wrote in the introduction to an 1872 book of his speeches on the trade issue, that the lure of gold and the ensuing surge of expansion westward created "great markets for our productions [sic] of every kind, thus increasing our trade and quickening every department of industry."[10]

An avid free trader who had seen the error of his ways when lower tariffs shut down factories and mines all over the country, Congressman Kelley remarked that whereas "1847 had been a good year for farmers, mechanics, miners and merchants, 1857 was a good year for sheriffs, constables and marshals" foreclosing on bankrupt farms, factories, mines and stores.[11]

Unlike so many of today's devotees of free trade who refuse to acknowledge that their theories are responsible for any of the nation's economic ills, Congressman Kelley's eyes were opened by the hard times that plagued the land in the late 1850s. He became a member of the American school of economics which had come to prominence under the aegis of the protectionist philosopher, Henry C. Carey of Philadelphia, author of the *Principles of Political Economy*. Carey, in turn, had inherited many of his ideas from his father, Mathew Carey, the famed Dublin-born newspaper editor and book publisher who was one of the key founders of the protectionist movement in the early years of the Republic.

The philosophy of the Careys, based as it was upon common sense and hard experience, had won wide acceptance in the young nation; and the few deviations from it, as in 1846, were corrected when they were proven wrong. Protectionism had enabled Americans to conquer the continent and to provide the people with a steadily rising standard of living. But in one corner of the country, the people had listened to a different drum. Now the South was preparing to march to it.

The spark ignited by free trade in the nullification battle, and fed by the pro-slavery issue for three decades, was about to explode into the great tragedy of the War Between The States, the bloody Civil War that was to claim nearly five hundred thousand American lives and leave the old agrarian society of the South shattered in the ruins. The North, despite the terrible toll that cost it almost three times as many fatal casualties as the Confederacy, was to miraculously emerge stronger than ever, with a mighty industrial complex ready to take on the world in the trade wars that were to come after Appomattox.

Chapter 5.

The Agony and the Glory

I have long thought it would be to our advantage to produce any necessary article at home which can be made of as good quality and with as little labor at home as abroad . . .

—Abraham Lincoln in an address
on his way to Washington,
February 15, 1861

The Civil War plunged America into its greatest agony. But out of the crucible of four years of terrible struggle the nation came forth into a period of peace, prosperity, and expansion the like of which the world had never seen. The remarkable recovery and growth of the United States between 1865 and 1900 was accomplished under a firm policy of protectionism, which indeed was the primary engine driving industry and agriculture forward.

During the hostilities the tariff played a major role in financing the army and navy and it played the most important part in paying off the war debt and placing the nation on a sound financial footing in the postwar era. Without the higher Customs duties collected on a greatly extended list of dutiable imports during and after the Civil War it is doubtful that the United States could have dug itself out of debt for many decades.

The tremendous expansion of industry, the spread of agriculture across the Great Plains and beyond, the building of our mighty cities—none of these would have been possible without the customs revenues that kept our Treasury on a sound money course and the protectionism which created the healthy climate for growth.

The Civil War may be said to have begun on December 20, 1860, when South

Carolina seceded from the United States a little more than one month after the election of Abraham Lincoln as President but a full three months before he was inaugurated. This first secession was followed by the rapid seizure of forts, arsenals, and other military installations throughout the South.

On February 8, 1861, six more states seceded and Jefferson Davis was proclaimed president of the new Confederate States of America. The incumbent President of the United States, James Buchanan, took no effective action from Washington to quell the spreading rebellion, leaving Lincoln to deal with the crisis when he took office.

In his inaugural address, Abraham Lincoln held out the hope for national reconciliation, assuring the people of the southern states that "their property and their peace and personal security" were not endangered. "There has never been," he said, "any reasonable cause for . . . apprehension." He then repeated what he had said so many times before: "I have no purpose, directly or indirectly, to interfere with the institution of slavery in the states where it exists. I believe I have no lawful right to do so; and I have no inclination to do so . . . ."

However, Lincoln denied the right of individual states to secede from the Union, just as Andrew Jackson had done during Calhoun's ill-advised effort to "nullify" the tariff a generation earlier. But he urged patience and proclaimed: "Intelligence, patriotism, Christianity, and a firm reliance on Him who has never yet forsaken this favored Land, are still competent to adjust, in the best way, all our present difficulty."

The response of the fanatics, devoted as much to the inane concept of free trade as to the inhuman system of slavery, was to fire on Fort Sumter. The following day President Lincoln issued his first call for volunteers and ordered the navy to blockade Southern ports to cut off imports to the Confederacy and halt the exports it needed to trade for weapons abroad.

Unfortunately, Lincoln's Secretary of the Treasury, Salmon P. Chase, failed to act with equal dispatch on the Union's financial front. Chase, after whom the Chase Manhattan Bank is named, refused to recommend a tax system adequate to carrying the heavy burden of war,[1] much as Ronald Reagan refused in recent times to raise taxes to pay for the strengthening of our national defense, an inexplicable stratagem which predictibly helped produce the crushing budget deficits of the 1980s.

In 1861, Customs duties provided nearly 95 percent of the government's total revenues but the funds received fell far short of the heavy requirement laid upon the Treasury by the war. At year's end there was a deficit of $417 million and it belatedly dawned on Chase that something drastic had to be done. He finally agreed to float sufficient loans to carry the alarming expenditures needed for the defense of the Union.

In January 1862, the Congress, as Davis Rich Dewey points out, "adopted a more determined policy" and set about enacting a series of measures, including an income tax, to properly finance the war. David A. Wells, later special commissioner of revenue, said that the revenue and tariff acts of 1862 were based on the principle of the Irishman at Donnybrook Fair: "Whenever you see a head, hit it; whenever you see a commodity, tax it."[2]

F. W. Taussig tells us, "Every thing was taxed, and taxed heavily."[3] In fact, some items were taxed as many as a dozen times as they moved through the manufacturing process. To compensate industry for these added costs, however, and to make certain that Customs duties continued to produce a fair share of the required revenues, the Congress passed a succession of "war tariffs," the most far-reaching protectionist measures in our history. One of these, the Tariff Act of 1864, increased the average duty on imports covered by Customs to over 47 percent.

It was this act, signed into law by Abraham Lincoln, that remained essentially in force for the next two decades, and laid the solid foundation for fueling the great expansion of American industry, agriculture, and commerce that amazed the world.

As Dr. Taussig testifies, the statesmen responsible for the war tariffs "were protectionists and did not attempt to conceal their protectionist leanings."[4] Indeed, there was no reason for Lincoln and his fellow protectionists to "conceal" what clearly was in the best interests of the United States. They knew what our politicians today have forgotten: that no nation can long survive—as a real nation—without protection of the national means of production, its defense production base, the jobs of its people, and a sound currency based upon output and not undermined by eternal inflation.

During the war years, 1861–65, the tariff produced nearly half the total revenues collected by the Treasury.[5] But, as already noted, the tariff and the multiple war taxes could not possibly meet all the demands of the lengthy struggle with more than a million men under arms in a nation of then less than thirty million people. Still, the loans that were belatedly floated were quickly bought up by citizens in all walks of life.[6] The people knew the Union was in a life and death struggle for survival and they rushed to help in any way they could.

It is interesting to note that during the Civil War there was no market in London or Paris for U.S. government bonds, but only for Confederate bonds which, of course, wound up being worthless.[7] This meant that through the war years very little foreign capital came into the country and the tremendous industrial expansion was financed almost totally by Americans, proving once again what a free, independent, and determined people can do on their own under a realistic economic system.

The South, equally determined and independent, was defeated more by its past adherence to free trade than by the disparity in population or by any lack of military ability. Indeed, historians are still awed by the courage and skill of the Southern soldier and his unwavering devotion to the cause of the Confederacy. Moreover, in Robert E. Lee, Stonewall Jackson, and others, the South undoubtedly had the superior generals, as their far smaller casualty lists testify.

However, when the war began, the North had more than 90 percent of the nation's manufacturing capacity. The Northern states obviously had taken full advantage of the national policy of protection; the South just as obviously had not. Although the benefits of that policy had been equally available to the Southern states, they had settled for an agrarian economy that acquiesced in playing the role of provider of raw materials to the factories of the North and to the mercantilism of England. A similarly unrealistic approach has captured our present day policymakers in Washington, with long-range results that could one day prove as disastrous for the whole nation as it did for the Confederacy, unless a realistic trade policy is again adopted.

Salmon P. Chase, despite his rash delay in devising adequate financing early in the Civil War, can be credited with establishment of the national banking system which he started as an antidote to the inflationary issuance of paper money by the state banks that had proliferated in antebellum days.[8] By 1862 there were nearly fifteen hundred banks with notes in circulation. The notes, in turn,were based upon "a great variety of securities,"[9] and a dwindling number of them could be redeemed in gold. During the war there were an estimated seven thousand different types of notes in circulation and as many as five thousand more kinds of counterfeit notes.[10]

The National Banking Act of 1863, buttressed by additional legislation in 1865, proved an important pillar of the nation's expanding financial structure for many years to come. These laws made it easy for numerous state banks to adopt national bank charters. But the principal accomplishment was to provide a currency that was uniform throughout the country.[11] There was no longer any doubt as to what a dollar was worth.

It was the tariff, however, that continued to be the foundation and mainstay of both the national finance and the fast-growing agricultural-industrial base of the United States, providing more than a third of the Treasury's total revenues in the immediate postwar period, and some 60 percent from 1872 onward. Customs duties generated the funds that made it possible for the federal government to dismantle the pervasive system of internal taxes, including the income tax, within a few years after the war, and to pay all the interest on the war debt which the import levies eventually enabled the Treasury to pay off entirely. Moreover, the Customs revenue permitted the Treasury to resume specie payments for government obligations and ultimately to restore full gold backing for the dollar.

In March 1869 President Ulysses S. Grant, in his first inaugural address, assured the world that the United States would pay every dollar of its indebtedness in gold to protect the national honor. The premium on gold at the time was hovering around 30 percent, and, as Dr. Dewey informs us, "The government would have failed to secure credit on a paper basis."[12]

Fortunately, the Customs Service collected import duties in gold and the revenues from these plus the prudent policies of Secretary of the Treasury John Sherman of Ohio eventually erased the premium on gold entirely. From a low in 1865, when the dollar was worth only fifty cents, and often less, in gold, it had come all the way back by January 1879 to parity.

Full parity would have been achieved much sooner if it had not been for two financial panics that temporarily slowed both industrial progress and the effort to resume gold backing for the dollar. The first of these was the Black Friday stock market crash in the early autumn of 1869 which was triggered by the abortive attempts of two notorious Wall Street speculators, Jim Fisk and Jay Gould, to corner the gold market via a wild spending spree.[13]

Within two days Fisk and Gould ran up the premium on gold nearly 25 percent before their manipulation boomeranged and sent all markets into a precipitous dive. A lot of innocent bystanders were hurt on Black Friday but the broad-shouldered young country quickly shrugged off its losses and again surged ahead.

The second postwar panic, in 1873, proved more serious and resulted in a prolonged depression, particularly in the large agricultural segment of the economy. There is substantial evidence that this depression was brought on by a combination of an effort to curtail protectionism and by a growing campaign to hike the supply of paper money instead of staying the Treasury's course toward resumption of parity for gold and the dollar. Free trade and loose money policies that promote inflation behave like Siamese twins: one can't move without the other.

The farm community, which in the nineteenth century was the most populous part of America, was irritated by the tight money policy of the post–Civil War. Although most farmers were sharing in the general prosperity, many were not. Irritation led to agitation and the farm state representatives in Congress pushed for a reduction in tariffs. In the Act of 1872 they got their way and duties were reduced 10 percent on most items and up to 50 percent on salt and coal.[14] Imports threatened to rise sharply and industrialists decided to cut back on capital expenditures for plant and equipment, as must always happen when protective barriers are let down.

At about the same time European investors, having lost heavily in buying Confederate bonds during the Civil War, compounded their previous error. Europeans had come bounding back into America after the war to recoup their losses by investing heavily in railroads, industry, and U.S. government bonds. Now, in 1872–73, they thought the American agrarians would succeed in stripping the gold backing from the dollar, and thus from their loans and investments. The Europeans stampeded to cash in their U.S. holdings while the dollar was still convertible into gold. This drained our banks and the Treasury and on September 18, 1873, "came the shock of the decade" when the great banking house of Jay Cooke failed.[15] The New York Stock Exchange temporarily gave up the ghost and shut down.

The Treasury acted swiftly to stem the panic and on September 20 it began to buy bonds at par on gold and to pay interest in advance on the debt, neither of which it could have done if healthy surpluses had not piled up in the preceding years thanks to the gold collected on import duties. In spite of the Treasury's brave effort, too much damage had already been done and the United States plunged into its first lengthy depression in forty years.

The situation worsened when Customs collections dropped because of the reduction of duties that accompanied the decline in imports in the wake of the panic. The Treasury surplus vanished entirely for a while in 1874 and Congress made matters worse by voting to expand the circulation of greenbacks.

However, Congress, in an attempt to stimulate investment, restored tariffs in 1875 to rates prevailing before the cuts of three years earlier. Nonetheless it took time for industry to get its capital investment back on track and the depression dragged on until the latter years of the decade, though it was not felt as severely in some parts of the country as in others.

Just as the twin moves toward free trade and looser money helped bring on the depression, reverse actions toward protectionism and sound money eventually brought prosperity back. Restoration of full gold backing for the dollar began in January 1875 when the outgoing Republican Congress passed the Resumption Act directing the Treasury to redeem in coin all greenbacks presented for redemption.[16] The veteran chairman of the Senate Finance Committee, John Sherman, played an important role in framing this legislation, and, as Secretary of the Treasury, he was responsible for implementing it.

John Sherman came to the Treasury early in 1877 after the inauguration of President Rutherford B. Hayes, who wisely ended the painful period of Reconstruction by withdrawing federal occupation troops from the South. With Sherman's steady hand steering the Treasury's course the dollar sailed into the safe port of parity in the face of ominous inflationary winds blowing in from the West.

The Greenback Party, raising its loud and ill considered cry for more paper currency even if it meant less gold backing, was gathering strength and in 1878 it garnered a million votes in the Congressional election. But Sherman refused to be deterred by this vociferous minority. In January 1879, he had the dollar squarely back on a solid gold foundation.

Sherman was aided considerably in the redemption endeavor by the protectionist policy he had helped hammer out in the Senate with the tariff of 1875. The higher Customs duties brought more gold into the Treasury and encouraged manufacturers to resume the industrial expansion interrupted by the Panic of 1873. Agriculture also played its part and grain exports helped bring about favorable trade balances beginning in 1876. Both farm and manufacturing exports grew by leaps and bounds as the dollar strengthened in value.

Today, the opposite perception prevails at Treasury. With the support of the Federal Reserve, the Treasury Department believes *devaluation* of the dollar can bring about a balance of trade. Fortunately for America, in its greatest era of growth and capital formation, the Treasury was guided by men like John Sherman who knew better.

With protectionism and sound money policies jointly fueling the nation's progress, the United States soared into the position of economic preeminence that it was to hold for the next one hundred years. It was like a giant booster rocket blasting into outer space where the universal laws of physics took over and kept America in orbit as it rode out all the storms of the twentieth century— until the free trade missile finally caught up with it in the 1970s and slowed down the mighty engine of the world.

Chapter 6.

America Becomes No. 1

We cannot afford to have cheap labor in the United States.
                                        —William McKinley

By 1880 the United States of America had overtaken and surpassed England as the industrial leader of the world. Indeed, England, which had stubbornly persisted in its free trade policy, instituted in the 1830s, was now in third place. Germany, imitating our protectionism, was second behind America.[1]

The rise of America dazzled the world. Cities seemed to spring up out of the prairies. Railroads criss-crossed the country, binding all sections of the nation together with bonds of steel. Already by 1870 America had built nearly 53,000 miles of railroads, far more than then existed in all of Europe and enough to twice encircle the entire globe with many miles to spare.[2]

Another gauge of our country's astonishing progress in this period is the exponential increase in freight traffic. It is estimated that between 1860 and 1900 total domestic freight multiplied fifteen times from 50 million to 750 million tons annually.[3] In the early part of the era, the railroads and inland waterways more or less evenly divided most of the haulage between them but by 1900 pipelines had been built and were already transporting huge quantities of petroleum. All this was accomplished before motor vehicles came into their own.

Factories proliferated under protectionism. Between the outbreak of the Civil War and the end of the nineteenth century the number of manufacturing plants multiplied from about 140,000 establishments employing some 1.3 million people who were paid $378 million annually, to 512,000 with 5.3 million employees earning $2.3 billion a year. The value of manufactured products had risen in the same period from under $1.9 billion to more than $13 billion.[4] But, as Bogart observes, "the remarkable diversity of industries and increase in the volume of products is not revealed by the statistics of value."[5]

Nonetheless, the increase in productive capacity of the individual worker implicit in the statistics reflects the ability of protectionism to hold down prices, thereby increasing the standard of living. For it was the domestic competition, as Alexander Hamilton had long ago foreseen, that brings prices down, not imports from abroad as we have been led to believe in our uncertain era.

Protectionism had unleashed the inventive genius of the American people and the new products and innovations poured forth in a seemingly never-ending stream to create the great cornucopia of the industrial age. Though it has been downgraded in our era, much was made of the inventiveness of our people in those earlier, more confident times. No doubt this accounted for a good deal of our progress but as Bogart reminds us it was "most of all . . . the enormous domestic market" that made possible the profitable introduction of our citizens' inventions.[6] Without that market, which so many of our industries have now been deprived of through free trade, it was inevitable that the innovative spirit of our people would fade and flag. The number of patents has declined dramatically in proportion to the total population and will continue to decline until protectionist policies are restored.

In the post–Civil War years all sections of the country and all segments of the economy shared in the growing prosperity once the trade deficits of the earlier part of the period had been erased and full parity with gold restored to the dollar. The South, ravaged by war and oppressed by the occupation for a dozen years afterward, came back with the fair wind of protectionism. Railroad building resumed, new factories appeared, and by 1879 even cotton production surpassed pre–Civil War levels in our Southland, with the bulk of the crop coming from small farms and sharecropping rather than the big plantations of the past.[7]

The West became more heavily settled, with hundreds of thousands of new immigrants joining the quest for economic independence in America's wide open spaces. The magnet was no longer gold, as in the rush westward that followed the great discoveries of the metal in California in 1849. It was simply land and the chance to call the land your own. The Homestead Act of 1862 granted title to 160 acres of free land to settlers willing to till it for a minimum of five years and by 1870 eight million pioneers had thronged into the Midwest and the prairies beyond. One measure of the phenomenal growth of agriculture in this period is the fact that by 1900 there were twice as many horses and mules—twenty-four million in all—than in England, France, and Germany combined.[8]

Although farm animals were still most widely used, by 1880 no less than ten thousand patents had been granted for farm machinery. Huge steam tractors were doing more and more of the heavy planting and harvest work, and McCormick's famed reapers no longer had to be pulled by horses and mules as the country's industrial ingenuity blazed the way toward freeing the whole world from its ages-old slavery to the soil.

For the first time in history on a large scale the farmer could truly enjoy the fruits of his labor, at least in the United States. Europe still had its peasants but to call a farmer that in America would have earned you a black eye. Our farmers, many of whom had so recently come from Europe, were free men and the term *peasant* implied a bond bordering on ownership by another, something no American would then countenance. Yet, tragically, only a few generations later their descendants are docilely willing to work in industrial plants located in their own country but owned and supervised by Japanese and other foreign bosses.

Between 1850 and 1910 the population of the United States quadrupled from twenty-three million to more than ninety-two million in one of the greatest population explosions in all history to this century.[9] However, under our government's firm protectionist trade policy this soaring growth was not accompanied by all the increasing miseries we have witnessed in today's world of multiplying populations. There were, of course, pockets of poverty, which we seem destined to always have with us. But the prosperity generated by protectionism embraced a far higher percentage of people in America than it had in any time, in any place, and under any other system in the whole long history of mankind. Moreover, protectionism built the capital and provided the economic momentum that this country—and much of the world upon which we have showered our wealth— has been riding on ever since.

Along the way there were slowdowns and even setbacks, particularly when Washington was tempted, or shoved, into deviating from our traditional protectionism. In 1883, with the Democrats back in control of the House of Representatives, another attempt was made by the free trade lobby to roll back the tariff. Although it succeeded only to a limited degree (the duties on goods covered were reduced an average of 5 percent), this was apparently enough to throw a scare into the industrial community and another financial panic followed in 1884. Other factors were at work, of course. No doubt the rapid pace of the country's progress was due for a correction. But the pattern that had begun with earlier moves toward free trade and away from protection persisted. Every time the tariff was cut the bulls pulled in their horns on Wall Street—and Main Street— and a panic ensued. (The lone exception to this time, in 1846, was explored in a prior chapter. As Congressman William D. Kelley found, factors other than the tariff reduction brought on prosperity.)

The panic of 1884 brought on another widespread depression and, because of the earlier meteoric buildup of industry, much of which was now curtailed or shut down, for the first time a very large pool of unemployed appeared on the American scene. The labor movement began to gather strength and the Knights of Labor, founded as a secret organization in 1869, called a series of strikes in 1886. They proved disastrous for the membership, which the organization claimed had reached 730,000 that year.[10] Thereafter, the Knights of Labor faded into history. But the American Federation of Labor, formed in 1881 by skilled workers organized under the banners of their own trades and crafts, proved to have great staying power and persists to this day in the great amalgamation of the AFL-CIO.

Dr. Ernest Ludlow Bogart, late of the University of Illinois, gives this brief and accurate sketch of the early history of the American Federation of Labor: "Under the leadership of Samuel Gompers, who remained its president with the exception of one year from 1882 until his death in 1924, it grew steadily in influence, which was generally conservative, avoided political entanglements, and saw its membership increase from 220,000 in 1890 to 550,000 in 1900." Dr. Bogart goes on to write that "probably ten to fifteen per cent of the working population was enrolled in labor organizations by the end of the century . . . and by 1911 the membership of the affiliated [AFL] unions was 1,762,000 . . . "[11]

The American labor movement, unlike those in England, Europe, and South America, was not socialist in its origins nor, indeed, through most of its history to the present era. Although a few unions did come under communist control in the 1930s, almost all of these threw off the communists, who frequently masqueraded as tame socialists. Under the long presidency of George Meany the AFL-CIO became one of the nation's strongest bulwarks against Soviet influence.

In its formative stages the American labor movement was staunchly protectionist, as it is again today. In between, from about 1945 to 1970, many union leaders were caught up in the free trade fad that swept America from its moorings, and many more embraced the free-spending welfarism that has proved so inimicable to the interests of labor as well as to the rest of the population.

During its youth, the labor movement also made a serious strategic mistake, the one that effectively finished off the old Knights of Labor. The country was showing signs of bouncing back from the effects of the panic of 1884 when the outbreak of strikes in 1886 brought on a series of related lockouts, boycotts and other labor disturbances that slowed the recovery.[12] These troubles occurred during the initial presidency of Grover Cleveland, the first Democrat to occupy the White House since the incumbency of James Buchanan.

Cleveland proved a more forceful personality than Buchanan. A fiscal conservative, he nonetheless favored a less stringent form of protectionism than the country had been thriving under for so many years. Brought into office by the public dissatisfaction that resulted from the panic of 1884, he lost out four years later to Benjamin Harrison, a Republican and firm protectionist.

The swing back to stronger protectionism had already begun in the congressional elections of 1886 when the Republicans regained control of the House and kept their majority in the Senate by campaigning vigorously for higher tariffs. In this election, as in others in which the trade issue was a prominent feature, the Republican Party had the support of organized labor.

In stark contrast to the records of both major parties on trade in our era, the Republicans made good on their campaign promises and in 1890 the McKinley Tariff Act, named for the congressman who would one day be President, restored the reductions of the 1883 legislation and increased the average tariff on dutiable goods to nearly 50 percent.[13]

In leading the fight in the House for his act to "equalize duties on imports," William McKinley recognized, as very few in government do today, that the

American worker should not be forced to compete with the lower pay scales that then prevailed in Europe, much less the subsistence wages of the Orient or of the Soviet bloc. For if you do force this irrational competition upon our citizens, as both Republicans and Democrats have since the 1960s, there will be a reduction in the standard of living and the quality of life, as we have already witnessed in the United States over the past several decades.

In McKinley's day a notion had seeped into the minds of many Americans that protectionism was the policy of the great trusts and was therefore against the "common man." It is certainly true that industrialists piled up more profits under the protectionist policy. Pittsburgh steel barons like Andrew Carnegie and Henry Clay Frick never invested in new mills unless they were sure their investments were safeguarded by what they saw as common sense protection against imports.

Although these men, and their counterparts in other industries, piled up seemingly unconscionable profits, they also slashed prices. It is estimated that Carnegie's companies cut the price of steel nearly 500 percent in the post–Civil War period. But the benefits of the lower prices were slow to trickle down to the consumer, who saw only the opulence of the industrialists and vowed to take them down a peg or two.

At the same time the inflationists were telling the people that the annual federal surplus from Customs duties should be doled out to the needier classes of society and to the less prosperous sections of the country. One of many schemes for accomplishing this abiding dream was the free coinage of silver.

"Free silver" became the battle cry of the West, but it found many sympathizers in the South and East. Six new Northwestern states had recently been created, adding a dozen senators from that region to the upper chamber. This bloc, and their allies, were able to hold the McKinley Tariff Act of 1890 hostage to their drive for greater coinage of silver.[14] They thus succeeded in getting a new law, the Sherman Act, authorizing an increase in silver purchases by the Treasury which was obliged to pay for the silver in Treasury notes of full legal tender backed by gold.[15]

As so often happens, then as now, in congressional "coups" such as this, the legislation proved counter-productive. Customs duties, which had been preponderantly in gold before the Sherman Act, fell to less than 4 percent gold in September 1892. The Treasury's gold reserve plunged from nearly $230 million in 1890 to $177 million in 1892 and less than $132 million by 1894.[16] This brought a contraction of the paper money in circulation and hard times fell like a shroud over the entire country.

A second financial panic in 1893 came hard on the heels of another tariff cut. Even Bogart, more inclined toward free trade than protectionism, conceded that "the business uncertainty caused by the frequent tariff changes undoubtedly contributed to the prevailing economic disorder."[17]

Grover Cleveland had been elected President again in 1892 after four years out of office and he was widely blamed for the depression. After passage of the tariff reduction of 1893, which he supported, and the panic that quickly followed, Cleveland became increasingly unpopular. He acted courageously by obtaining repeal of the Sherman Act, an action needed to stem the stampede of gold out of the Treasury. But this only deepened public dissatisfaction with the President by turning the free silver Democrats against him forever.

The Cleveland administration was also plagued by the explosion of the violent Pullman strike in 1894 and the march of Jacob Coxey's "army" of unemployed on Washington. In 1896 the Democrats jettisoned Grover Cleveland to place William Jennings Bryan at the helm of their vacillating fortunes. Bryan was to be defeated three times in his strident bids for the presidency, losing twice to McKinley, who ran on the tandem issues of sound money and protectionism, and the third time to William Howard Taft in 1908.

Bryan's vivid promise, first made at the Democratic convention of 1896, to keep the country from being "crucified on a cross of gold," got the headlines. But the perception that he was antiprotectionist probably lost him more votes. The United States was firmly committed to protection as it drew near the end of the eventful century that had seen the country surge from an agrarian society still chopping farms out of a wild frontier to the mightiest manufacturing nation in the world, a nation that pointed the way for all mankind as long as it heeded the message of the American success story: *protectionism produces capital and it does so in such a way that the greatest number of people can share in the resulting prosperity.*

As the twentieth century stumbled from one tragedy to the next, Americans forgot their own lesson—indeed, their own history. Amid the turmoil that increasingly compelled our citizens to focus on the crisis of the hour, we lost our bearings until now, as another century beckons from over the horizon, we are increasingly adrift in an uncertain sea.

Chapter 7.

The Attack Begins

To reduce privilege by bringing down the tariff was a first priority
among many reformers.... [1]

—Otis L. Graham, Jr.
in *The Great Campaigns*

The twentieth century dawned bright and promising for America. Never before
had any country shared its wealth so broadly with so many of its people. The
American system, built on the solid foundation of protectionism and sound
money, was breaking through the ancient barriers of ignorance with new tech-
nologies, new inventions, new methods of production, new ways of doing many
things, from growing and harvesting crops to traveling between home and office
or factory. The future appeared to have no boundaries and, within a few years
the Wright brothers were to prove that even the sky would no longer be the
limit.

The nation had just recently come through a victorious war with Spain. President McKinley had been reluctant to intervene in Cuba but after the sinking of
the battleship *Maine* in Havana harbor he could no longer resist the popular
outcry for action stirred up by the yellow journalism of the time. Teddy Roosevelt
went charging up San Juan Hill and on to the Republican nomination for Vice
President in 1900.

Although the war lasted only four months, it proved expensive. Congress had
acted quickly to raise funds for the military operations, having apparently learned
a lesson from Salmon Chase's dilatory attitude of 1861. In 1898 a big loan was
authorized, excise taxes were widely imposed, and, for the first time, a tax was
levied on inheritances.[2] (The maximum inheritance tax was 15 percent.)

The tariff, so recently revised in 1897, was permitted to stand. It had produced 50 percent of the government's total revenues in that same year and both the Congress and the president probably felt Customs duties were doing their fair share. The war did cut the ratio of tariffs to total revenues to 37 percent in 1898 but it bounced back up to 50 percent the following year, and was to remain in the the 40 to 50 percent range until 1914.[3]

The ability of the tariff to carry such a substantial portion of the government's financial burdens in the period after the Spanish-American War was no small accomplishment. The war had given the United States heavy added responsibilities, including the administration of Puerto Rico and the Philippines. Our greater involvement in world affairs required a larger navy and army. In 1904 we took over the Panama Canal project from a French company and in the next dozen years it was to cost the Treasury more than $400 million, a staggering sum. Without the tariff revenues, none of this would have been possible.

Customs duties enabled the government to dismantle the war taxes by 1902 and to pay off a considerable part of the war debt. Indeed, the Treasury's surplus in that year was the highest since 1888 and credit for this must also go to the tariff.

The protectionist policy continued to create a healthy climate for expansion and as the United States grew more prosperous we could afford to import more goods from abroad, generally buying raw materials and other things we needed, or handmade and luxury goods not produced in our country. In short, protectionism was proving a boon to trade as well as to domestic industry, American workers, and the U.S. Treasury.

Nonetheless, as Bogart states, "a conviction was steadily gaining ground among tariff reformers that the tariff was largely responsible for the growth of large combinations"—the big business "trusts" feared and despised by more and more people. The trusts were also being tied, at least in the public view, to the sound money policies of the Republican Party, which was increasingly seen as too pro-business. But for the moment the Republican administration held fast to its principles.

In 1900 the Congress, with President McKinley's approval, passed a Currency Act officially placing the United States on the gold standard and committing the Treasury to maintain parity between gold and the dollar. The government's sound money policy and protectionism were now legally linked, giving the full and majestic sanction of the law to the explicit policy that had prevailed since the very beginning of the republic.

The presidential campaign of 1900 between McKinley and the "silver-voiced" standard bearer of the Democratic cause, William Jennings Bryan, was again fought out on these twin issues, with an added arrow aimed by Bryan at the "imperialism" he saw in the recent war with Spain. McKinley defeated Bryan by an even larger margin in both the popular and electoral vote than in 1896 and the country appeared irrevocably committed to protection and a sound currency. But less than a year later, while greeting citizens at the Pan-American

Exposition in Buffalo, New York, the president was fatally shot by Leon Czolgosz, the son of Russian immigrants and disciple of the anarchist Emma Goldman. William McKinley was the third Republican president to be assassinated within thirty-six years. Abraham Lincoln was the first in 1865; James A. Garfield in 1881; and now McKinley in 1901. Strangely, all three victims were ardent protectionists.

Theodore Roosevelt took over the White House after the assassination of President McKinley and transformed it into a command post directing a great expansion of government and the sweeping reforms of the Progressive Era. The Sherman Anti-Trust Act, enacted in 1890, was given a sharper edge for cutting the big corporations down to size. The Pure Food and Drug Act of 1906 increased the government's regulatory powers and the Interstate Commerce Commission, founded in 1887, acquired new policing authority. A Department of Commerce and Labor was given cabinet status in 1903 with jurisdiction over immigration, the census, and a host of other functions. The Navy was greatly expanded. Army engineers started building the Panama Canal. Public works proliferated and pensions multiplied. The federal bureaucracy, until now relatively small and manageable, suddenly blossomed like dandelions in the lawns of Washington.

As the cost of government grew, new sources of revenue and federal finance were sought. The tariff, which had borne the major share of the Treasury's load since 1789, was about to take a back seat to more "progressive" forms of fiscal transfusion. But before these changes could be enacted several more battles to dismantle the traditional system had to be fought.

The Progressives, basing their arguments on the deepening public suspicion of trusts and monopolies, prepared to wage war on four fronts. The first had as its objective the demise of the tariff. However, the substantial revenues that would be lost by killing off the tariff had to be replaced and that was to be the function of the graduated income tax, the second front of the attack.

The other two fronts, opened almost simultaneously, were, third, the restoration of the central bank which Andrew Jackson had finished off eight decades earlier in the face of Nicholas Biddle's bold attempt to buy Congress and, fourth, an amendment to the Constitution to elect U.S. senators by popular vote instead of by the state legislatures as the founding fathers had stipulated.

Combined, these four measures were to foist off a second American Revolution on a largely unsuspecting and complacent populace. This coup was accomplished within a very few years without the firing of a single shot. Indeed, it was fought out entirely on what appeared to be the open stage of public opinion and the legislative process. Yet in the wings the manipulators were pulling the strings that kept the politicians dancing to their tune while their propagandists softened up the voters with an unrelenting propaganda barrage on all four fronts.

The opening battle was the debate over a new tariff act in 1909. It had been a dozen years since Congress had tackled the trade question and during that time the media muckrakers had so thoroughly identified protectionism with the monopolists that even the Republican Party felt compelled to call for a change.

The focus of the battle in Congress became not so much the tariff per se as the income tax which was to replace it. The Progressive Republicans, led by Senator Robert La Follette of Wisconsin, teamed up with the Democrats under Representative Cordell Hull of Tennessee, in pushing for the graduated tax. Arrayed against them was a powerful triumvirate in the Senate—Cabot Lodge of Massachusetts, Elihu Root of New York, and Nelson Aldrich of Rhode Island.

President William Howard Taft stood aside from the dispute until June of 1909 when he sent Congress a suggestion that since the Supreme Court had declared the income tax unconstitutional some years earlier the Congress ought to propose an amendment to the Constitution to clear the way. But Taft, in a sophistic contradiction, himself proposed an income tax on corporations that was to serve as a revenue source while the constitutional amendment was wending its way through the state legislatures. The corporate levy was euphemistically termed an excise tax to get around the Constitution.[4]

The Payne-Aldrich Tariff Act, which encompassed the "excise" tax on corporations and produced, as a side effect, the constitutional amendment to authorize the graduated income tax, finally emerged after a long and bitter battle on Capitol Hill. Much to the surprise and chagrin of the muckrakers, it was enacted as an essentially protectionist law. American industry and workers were granted a temporary reprieve from the antiprotectionist onslaught. But Payne-Aldrich introduced a dangerous heresy into the administration of the tariff which in the end was to utterly destroy the protectionist principle upon which the nation was built.

The seed of the free trade takeover was cleverly planted in a provision granting the president the authority to control the rates of duties on imports. Until this act Congress had jealously guarded its responsibility, as clearly spelled out in the Constitution, "to regulate commerce with foreign nations." Moreover, this clause in Article I, Section 8, dealing with the "Powers of Congress," had been reinforced in Section 10, prohibiting the states from levying duties on imports or exports without consent of the Congress, reserving all such duties for the federal Treasury, and plainly setting forth that all laws dealing with imports and exports "*shall be subject to the revision and control of the Congress.*" (Author's emphasis.)

Now, in 1909, it handed the president the option to increase tariffs up to 25 percent of the value of goods imported from countries which discriminated against the United States in international trade.[5] The dangerous precedent was established: the executive branch had been given control over the Congress's constitutional prerogative to regulate trade. The first crack had been opened in the protectionist wall that for 120 years had guarded the interests of the workers and industry, agriculture and commerce of the United States.

Quite obviously, without a constitutional amendment the Congress did not have the authority to deliver these important functions of government over to the executive branch, nor did the President have the legal right to accept such authority from the Congress. Yet like so many other things in the long, slow surrender of the Constitution by the legislative branch, and the repeated usurpations of authority by the executive and the judiciary, the transfer of power over the nation's foreign trade was acquiesced by a public made malleable by misinformation.

The Payne-Aldrich tariff, masquerading as a protectionist law, proved to be a major wrecking ball in the long, slow but sure smashing of our Constitution's intrinsic structure. By implicitly paving the way for the income tax which had been declared unconstitutional by the Supreme Court in the previous decade, Payne-Aldrich blazed the way down the primrose path, not only for eventual extinction of the tariff and the system of protection, but for unsound money and the gradual loss of many liberties Americans of older generations took for granted. For the income tax, and the greatly expanded Internal Revenue Service it spawned, enabled the government to force open the doors into our homes and offices and privacy on a scale Washington, Hamilton, Jefferson, and the other founders could never have conceived. The guarantees they had so carefully embedded in the Constitution were now about to be filched from the American people in the name of progress.

Chapter 8.

The Overthrow

Mr. House is my second personality. He is my independent self. His thoughts and mine are one. If I were in his place I would do just as he suggested. . . . If any one thinks he is reflecting my opinions by whatever action he takes, they are welcome to the conclusion.[1]

—Woodrow Wilson

The American protective system was initially overthrown through the efforts of two men who openly proclaimed that their ultimate goal was the creation of a new world order, not only in international trade and finance, but in the sociopolitical realm as well. This pair, so similar in their thinking that they came to be regarded as almost one, were Woodrow Wilson and his alter ego, Edward Mandell House.

Sir Horace Plunkett called the Wilson-House relationship "the strangest and most fruitful personal alliance in human history."[2] Nothing sinister was suggested by this remark. Indeed, Sir Horace was a friend of both men. But contrary to his appraisal, the fruits of their collaboration were ultimately to prove tragic, not only for America, but for Europe and, in fact, for all mankind.

Woodrow Wilson was a professor and historian who became president of Princeton and, after less than two years as governor of New Jersey, was catapulted into the White House. Edward House, the man who, more than any other, put him there, was a quiet, unassuming Texan with a sharp mind that seemed to cut through human subterfuge to the very heart of large, momentous matters.

Both Wilson and House were quintessential products of progressivism. Wilson was an anti-Jeffersonian Democrat and although he claimed he was not a socialist he supported many of the "reforms" the socialists struggled to bring about. Albert C. Ganley, in his fine little book, *The Progressive Movement*, says that Wilson "moved far beyond" Theodore Roosevelt and other progressives "in recommending a limited amount of socialism. . . . "[3]

House, however, was seen by a close contemporary as "a pronounced radical . . . more advanced in his ideas than the persons he was working with."[4] Indeed, House, by his own admission, was an admirer of Karl Marx and of the European revolutionaries of 1848. This was reflected in his 1912 novel, *Philip Dru, Administrator*, in which the hero, obviously modeled on House himself, became the reformist dictator of the United States.[5]

Woodrow Wilson, as president of Princeton from 1902 to 1910, was also regarded by some as a "radical," although on a somewhat different plane, for trying to break up the old student eating clubs and other actions aimed against the traditions of the college. Elected governor of New Jersey in 1910 he "pushed through a broad program of progressive legislation"[6] and won national attention for his attacks on what were then regarded as the twin devils of the Left, the trusts and the tariff.

Edward House did not meet Wilson until November 1911 when the governor came to visit him at the Hotel Gotham on New York's Fifth Avenue. This fateful rendezvous resulted in what came to be seen by both as a mystical merger of their minds and personalities.

"A few weeks after we met," House said later, "and after we had exchanged confidences which men usually do not exchange except after years of friendship, I asked him if he realized that we had only known one another for so short a time. He replied, 'My dear friend, we have known one another always.' And I think this is true."[7] Professor Charles Seymour, later president of Yale, noted in the amazingly revealing four-volume *Intimate Papers of Colonel House*, which he edited, that House and Wilson communicated with each other in "a special code known only to themselves."[8]

Dr. Seymour also wrote that House believed he had a tacit understanding with Wilson to act in the president's behalf unless expressly told otherwise. "When Colonel House put a project before President Wilson, he did not expect affirmative commendation. He evidently took the President's silence for consent, for, as he once said, 'If the President did not object, I knew that it was safe to go ahead. . . . ' "[9]

House secured the crucial support of William Jennings Bryan for Wilson's presidential candidacy and laid the intricate plans which defeated his rivals, Sen. Champ Clark of Missouri and Congressman Oscar F. Underwood of Alabama, at the 1912 Democratic national convention in Baltimore. House was on an Atlantic liner en route to Europe when he received a wireless that Wilson had won, with Bryan's backing, on the forty-sixth ballot.

The Republican convention in Chicago a month later was the scene of the rupture that was to divide the GOP for most of the rest of the century into the two eternally warring camps, conservatives versus liberals. The original split came when President Taft was nominated and Theodore Roosevelt stormed out to form his "Bull Moose" Progressive Party. Dr. Seymour was correct in his appraisal that Roosevelt's defection "put Wilson in the White House," though Seymour would certainly agree it was House who pushed all the right campaign buttons, including the one which painted Roosevelt as a "wild radical."

Wilson won the election with a minority of 6,286,000 votes against the combined popular tally for Taft and Roosevelt of almost 7,700,000. Edward House virtually hand-picked Wilson's cabinet, selecting Bryan as Scretary of State, William McAdoo for the Treasury, and a free trade economist, D. F. Houston, to head the then very important Agriculture Department. House also deployed like-minded men to the key ambassadorial posts: Walter Hines Page to London, James W. Gerard to Berlin, Frederick C. Penfield to Vienna, Thomas Nelson Page to Rome, Brand Whitlock to Brussels, Henry Morgenthau to Turkey.

The tariff, symbol of the country's traditional protectionism, was the priority target after Wilson's inauguration in March of 1913. Colonel House had previously geared up for this attack by "educating" Wilson on its alleged evils,[10] persuading him that the tariff sustained the big business trusts so despised by the progressive movement.

One of the strongest arguments against protectionism, then as now, was that it allegedly spurred inflation. The tariff was blamed for a steady increase in prices that had been rising for some years, and, of course, big corporations were identified as the chief beneficiaries and the "common man" as its principal victim.

The theory that protection promotes inflation is today an article of faith, an *idée fixe* so deeply imbedded in the minds of bankers, economists, journalists, politicians and other "thought leaders" that any discussion of the subject is summarily dismissed. But in 1913 it was still possible to debate this issue and one of those who did was Dr. Taussig of Harvard. Although an advocate of free trade, Taussig nonetheless saw through the fallacious equation, protection = inflation.

"The rise in prices during the opening decade of the century was world wide," Taussig wrote. "Its main cause, in the judgment of almost all the economists, was the immense increase in the output of and supply of gold. . . . It was not proved, or susceptible of proof, that the tariff was the cause of the continuing rise in all prices throughout these years."[11]

The year 1913 was not one in which voices of reason were widely heard, however. The progressive revolution was in full flame and it was determined to burn down the great protectionist tradition that had undergirded the bridge across which America had traveled from undeveloped wilderness to industrial colossus.

Soon after taking office, President Wilson summoned a special session of the Congress to apply the torch to the tariff. The Democrats had gained complete control of both the House and Senate and they were ready to do the President's bidding. Representative Oscar Underwood of Alabama, chairman of the House Ways and Means Committee and a Wilson rival for the 1912 presidential nomination, already had a trade bill in hand, one that had been vetoed by William Howard Taft in the previous session.

The Underwood Tariff Act of 1913 sailed through the House in record time. The Senate, which used to be a more deliberative body, took a good deal longer to consider the measure. But with prodding from the President, who denounced the industrial lobbyists as "insidious" villains for trying to preserve some protection for their companies, the Senate finally approved the bill in September. On October 3, 1913 it became law.

This revolutionary act set the nation on the road to the free trade system which now prevails. There were detours along the way, particularly between the two world wars, but since 1913 the United States has been committed to free trade.

It is interesting to note that the principle articulated by President Wilson and the Democratic congressional leaders who successfully stormed the ramparts of protectionism in 1913 was precisely the same as the one foisted off on President Ronald Wilson Reagan to maintain free trade in the 1980s—"competitiveness." As Woodrow Wilson put it, "the object of the tariff duties henceforth laid must be effective competition, the whetting of American wits by contest with the wits of the rest of the world."[12]

Until then no one had been aware that America was lagging in "competitiveness"—or intelligence. On the contrary, it was perfectly obvious that we had outstripped the rest of the world in industrial and economic development. But Wilson knew revolutions could not be built on success stories. So our success was, rhetorically at least, turned into a failure that had to be corrected with a new slogan—"competitiveness," dredged up and dusted off seventy years later by Reagan in a vain attempt to camouflage the real reasons for the astronomical trade deficits of the 1980s.

The Underwood-Simmons Act slashed the old tariff right, left and sideways. Import duties on wool and woolen manufactures were cut from 56 percent to a little over 18 percent. Tariffs on iron and steel products were in many cases completely eliminated as steel rails, barbed and galvanized wire, iron in slabs and blooms, and Bessemer steel ingots went on the free list. Duties on sugar imports were wiped out,and with them, in time, much of the once thriving beet sugar industry which had brought prosperity to thousands of farmers and dozens of small towns in the West.

"A sweeping clause put all agricultural implements on the free list," Taussig noted, almost bowled over by the revolution he had helped wrought.[13] The tariffs on leather and shoes were tossed overboard, along with those on wheat and flour, cattle and meats, dairy products, coal, lumber, and a host of other items.

Ironically, the farmers and manufacturing workers of the West and Midwest, who had spawned the progressive movement in alliance with the South and the more radical elements of the East, were to be offered up as the first sacrificial lambs on the high altar of free trade. But the South and East were to have their turn too. The whole country was to be put up for grabs by foreign "competitors."

And most of the victims cheered, as they have in every revolution since Madame Guillotine began the decapitation of Western civilization two centuries ago.

The American lambs had their slaughter postponed, however, when World War I exploded in Europe less than a year later. And it was delayed again, for an even longer period, by World War II, which left Europe and Japan in rubble and America with the only industrial base still intact and the only agricultural production capable of feeding the war-torn world. Indeed, it was to be a half-century after the 1913 Tariff Act before free trade began to really devour our industry and a decade after that before most people even began to notice the devastation all around them. But during those fateful intervening years, free trade gnawed away at America's industrial innards, weakening our will to resist as it gradually increased our reliance on foreign production.

After the tariff barriers were breached, the "progressive" revolution galloped ahead on all its other fronts. The two critical constitutional amendments went into effect, one stripping state legislatures of their traditional power to elect U.S. senators, the other authorizing the income tax. The latter had been approved by two-thirds of the states, "barely in time," Dr. Dewey wrote, "to enable the Democrats to utilize this revenue . . . to make good the losses expected under the 1913 Tariff Act."[14]

As with so many other taxes levied in this century, the income tax began modestly: only 1 percent on incomes in excess of $3,000, or $4,000 for married couples, with small surtaxes ranging up to 6 percent on incomes from $20,000 to over $500,000. But the sluice gates had been opened, and from that point on the government was able to siphon off an ever-increasing portion of the earnings of individual citizens as well as the profits of corporations tapped since the 1909 Tariff Act bypassed the Constitution.

The year 1914 marked the end of Customs duties playing the dominant role in producing revenues to run the government, a role they had heroically played for 125 years. Beginning in 1915 the tariff started a long slide downhill in its relative importance as generator of revenue. The income tax, slowly at first, but with steadily mounting acquisitiveness, picked up the part, adding to it over the years until it reached an almost confiscatory role in some income brackets and took an unhealthy bite out of the wages and other earnings of the vast majority of our citizens.

Although it is acknowledged that taxes add to inflation, to my knowledge nothing has been done to compare the relative roles of the income tax vs. protectionism in generating the long and often accelerating rise in prices since 1913. Such a comparison would undoubtedly prove embarrassing to the free traders, for it would certainly show that the income tax has added exponentially to prices, whereas the protective tariff helped hold back inflation between George Washington's first administration in 1789 and Woodrow Wilson's "progressive" revolution of 1913.

The tariff not only paid most of the costs of government up until 1915, it also took that heavy fiscal load off the backs of our people and shifted it to foreign governments and exporters attempting to exploit the great American market.

Contrary to the belief of free trade advocates, tariffs on imports are not necessarily paid by American consumers. They are frequently paid by foreign governments subsidizing exports to the United States, as the files on numerous countervailing duty and dumping cases testify in the murky archives of our Treasury and Commerce departments. Moreover, the American taxpayer is an unwitting accomplice to these illegal subsidies, for a slice of his income tax dollar goes to the World Bank and other multilateral "lending" conduits that enable foreign governments to finance export subsidies.

One should qualify this by adding *our increasingly watered-down dollar*. For the other factor most modern economists fail to take into account in concocting their trade equations is the diminution of the dollar's value, not merely in foreign exchange, but in what it will buy in our own country, a diminution due in no small part to the rising costs of welfare, unemployment compensation, loss of tax revenues, and other ingredients that boil up out of the free trade stew our economy has simmered in for decades. There are other fires igniting inflation, of course. But this exceedingly hot and destructive one is summarily ignored, and the patently fallacious proposition that unrestricted imports dampen inflation is substituted in its place.

The income tax has proved a gargantuan destroyer of the dollar's value, as already noted. But there is another furnace, the biggest one of all, that has virtually incinerated real capital and capital formation in the United States. It too is a legacy of the 1913 overthrow of our traditional economics. For that critical year also saw the creation of the infernal debt machine known as the Federal Reserve System.

Chapter 9.

The Federal Reserve Coup

the Fed is not "just a central bank" as our European friends
think of their central banks. Nor is it just a regulatory agency.
It is both of these and more, and its effect on the nation's economic health is sometimes direct, more often subtle, difficult to
measure, and always pervasive. . . . none can question the extent
of its influence in our economy.[1]

—Charles E. Lord,
former Acting Comptroller
of the Currency

The Federal Reserve Bank is the greatest generator of debt in the whole long
history of man on Planet Earth. By comparison, all the combined central banks
of Europe in *La Belle Epoch*, before the Old World came tumbling down in
1914, were insignificant dwarfs.

In ancient times, King Midas was said to have the touch that turned everything
to gold. King Fed has devised a better formula: all the gold it touches turns to
paper in the form of everlasting debt. "We owe it to ourselves," was the battle
cry in and out of Congress from the reign of Franklin Roosevelt to the recent
past. But now we owe it all—our colossal two-going-on-three-trillion-dollar
debt—to the international bankers and a consortium of foreign countries from
ubiquitous Japan to pygmy dots on the map of a globe glutted with U.S. Treasury
bonds and other IOUs from Uncle Sam. All this, with the implicit promise of
heaven-on-earth for all men everywhere.

The Federal Reserve Act of 1913 sealed the fate of the American economy
for at least the twentieth century and, in all likelihood, far beyond. Moreover,

it affected the finances of all nations because the Federal Reserve Bank made it possible for the United States to borrow endlessly so it could lend and give away our funds to the rest of the world.

Creation of the Federal Reserve System was the final coup of the 1913 Revolution. Twice before the United States had given the central bank concept fair and extended trials. Twice the nation had decided to terminate the prolonged and painful experiments on the valid ground that a central banking system in private hands tended to create an oligarchy of finance that corrupted both the citizenry and the government.

Now, however, these two prior hard-fought battles for individual freedom were conveniently forgotten. There was no one left to remember the strong determined voice of Andrew Jackson defending "the farmers, mechanics, and laborers" against subjugation by the central bank financiers who bought congressmen like cigars—and discarded them just as casually when they were burned out.

The news media, skillfully managed by Edward House and the great barons of finance, perversely laid down barrage after barrage of enticing arguments and clever slogans, mowing down the careers of the courageous congressmen and senators who opposed the monetarist takeover. One exception was Robert La Follette of Wisconsin, who led the battle in the Senate against creation of the Fed and somehow survived to hold his seat and go on to become the presidential candidate of the Progressive Party in 1924. But more met the fate of Congressman Charles Augustus Lindbergh of Minnesota, father of the famed aviator, who was soon consigned to political oblivion.

The man who picked the first lock on the Treasury for the Federal Reserve was Nelson Aldrich of Rhode Island, chairman of the Senate Banking and Currency Committee. Ironically, Aldrich had been deposed by the Democrats' election sweep in 1912 and was no longer at center stage when the Federal Reserve Act was passed. But he had the dubious satisfaction of knowing that the law that was enacted was based on what was known as the "Aldrich Plan."

Before 1913 Aldrich was one of the most powerful men in the Senate. Journalist Lincoln Steffens called Senator Aldrich the "boss of the United States" in a 1905 article for McClure's magazine[2]—and that at a time when Teddy Roosevelt was President.

A friend of J. P. Morgan, Aldrich had married off his daughter Abby to John D. Rockefeller Jr. in 1901. Thus, in due course he became grandfather to the Rockefeller brothers, John D. III, Nelson, Laurence, Winthrop, and David, and to their sister, Abby. The senator's own son, Winthrop Aldrich, became chairman of the Chase National Bank and, in 1953, was named by President Eisenhower as ambassador to England. Winthrop's nephew, David Rockefeller, eventually took over the chairmanship of the bank (by then Chase Manhattan) and reigned as chairman for more than two decades.

When he first came to the Senate in 1881, and for many years after, Nelson Aldrich was a protectionist and sound money advocate. As late as 1909 in the battle over the Payne-Aldrich Act, he stood firm for protection and led the fight against the income tax designed to replace the tariff. There is evidence, however, that he had already begun to shift into a more ambitious camp before this, following faithfully, but on tip-toe, in the well-heeled footsteps of his friend, J. P. Morgan.

A disastrous panic in 1907 had produced demands for exhumation of the central bank interred by Andrew Johnson seven decades earlier. The press, echoing the line of the financial community, called for action to "stabilize" the financial system and President Roosevelt signed a bill in 1908 to create a National Monetary Commission to investigate the alternatives and possibilities. No one was surprised when Senator Nelson Aldrich was named chairman.

Aldrich took the new Commission off on a two-year tour of Europe that cost the taxpayers $300,000.[3] On this truly grand tour, the Commission studied the workings of European central banks which were busy financing the biggest arms buildup in history in preparation for World War I.

Nelson Aldrich and his entourage obviously learned their European lessons well. When they returned to the United States the Senator slipped off to Jekyll Island, Georgia, with a little group of bankers to frame the legislation that was to become the Federal Reserve Act. Bertie Charles Forbes, founder of Forbes Magazine, wrote of this historic meeting a half-dozen years later:

Picture a party of the nation's greatest bankers stealing out of New York on a private railroad car under cover of darkness, stealthily hieing hundreds of miles South, embarking on a mysterious launch, sneaking onto an island deserted by all but a few servants, living there for a full week under such rigid secrecy that the names of not one of them was mentioned lest the servants learn the identity and disclose to the world this strangest, most secret expedition in the history of American finance.[4]

Forbes, the father of Malcolm Forbes, said that Senator Aldrich laid down the law: "The utmost secrecy was enjoined upon all. The public must not glean a hint of what was to be done."[5] The bankers present at Jekyll Island are identified as Frank Vanderlip, president of the National City Bank of New York (now Citibank); Henry P. Davidson, senior partner of J. P. Morgan Company; Charles D. Norton, president of the Morgan-dominated First National Bank of New York (which later merged with National City cum Citibank); Benjamin Strong, another Morgan man, and Paul Warburg, a then recent immigrant from Germany who had joined the New York banking house of Kuhn, Loeb and Company a few years earlier.[6] Since J. Pierpont Morgan, so well represented on this drafting committee, was known to be the American affiliate of the Rothschilds of Europe, it is certainly not too much to say that the Federal Reserve Bank of the United States was tailored to the Old World's specifications. In fact, it is believed, on much evidence, that the "Aldrich Plan" was really written by Paul Warburg, a Rothschild protege.

Although B. C. Forbes's story about the birth of the Federal Reserve was pooh-poohed as a preposterous invention when it appeared in 1916, one of the participants in the conference, Frank Vanderlip, later confessed in his autobiography: "Our secret expedition to Jekyll Island was the occasion of the actual conception of what eventually became the Federal Reserve System. The essential points of the Aldrich Plan were all contained in the Federal Reserve Act as it was passed."[7]

Aldrich, for all his power, was unable to get his plan adopted immediately. Some Progressives were opposed to a central bank and the fight against the Fed was waged skillfully in the Senate by La Follette and in the House by the elder Lindbergh. Their efforts were supported, at least initially, by Sen. Elihu Root who presciently pointed out that turning over exclusive note circulation to the Federal Reserve was bound to expand inflation indefinitely. Although, the Fed has on occasion *contracted* the currency supply (with disastrous results in 1921 and 1929, to name but two), the predominant effect of its machinations over the last seventy-five years has been precisely what Elihu Root predicted—ever-rising inflation.

The combined efforts of La Follette, Lindbergh, Root, and others prevented the Aldrich Plan from coming to a vote in Congress during the Taft administration. It was to take the violent national campaign of 1912, and the election of Woodrow Wilson, to rescue the Federal Reserve Act from its legislative limbo. Originally, Wilson, like many other progressives, was against the scheme concocted on Jekyll Island. But as Professor Seymour gently puts it, "Wilson ultimately accepted House's arguments for centralized control of banking which materialized in the Federal Reserve Act."[8]

Once he got—or gave—the presidential signal to go ahead, the little colonel moved like a wraith behind the scenes, quietly shepherding the fateful bill through the Congress. Wisely, he permitted the law to bear the names of Congressman Carter Glass of Virginia and Sen. Robert Owen of Oklahoma, two popular and influential legislators. But as "the unseen guardian angel of the bill," it was House who summoned the great figures of finance and "progressive" reform to his presence to help him pressure the Congress. J. P. Morgan, Paul Warburg, and Otto Kahn, Walter Page and Bernard Baruch, Louis Brandeis and Henry Morgenthau—all of them trooped in and out of the little Texan's throne room in New York.[9]

With some brave exceptions, the press dutifully supported the legislation to create the new central bank. Still, the opposition was sufficiently strong to cause the Wilson administration to resort to subterfuge in guiding it through the Senate. Colonel House's men in the upper chamber held off bringing the bill to a vote until a number of senators had gone home for the Christmas holidays. Then, on December 20, 1913, they quietly smuggled it out onto the floor for a perfunctory debate. By December 23 the Federal Reserve Law was enacted. The United States of America had been sold down the international monetary river and the overwhelming majority of the people had not the faintest idea of what had been done. Indeed, to this day their descendants still don't know what happened.

The citizenry believes the Federal Reserve Bank is a government agency, subject to control by the three great branches of the government—legislative, executive, and judiciary. Actually, the Fed is owned by private shareholders, most of them representing the great commercial banks of Wall Street, which in turn owe extensive obligations to banks in Tokyo, London, Paris, Frankfurt, and other world finance centers.

The president does appoint the members of the Federal Reserve Board, but these must always be at least acceptable to the big commercial bankers or, preferably, products of the financial establishment like Paul Volcker, the Fed chairman who matriculated at Chase Manhattan.

Moreover, the Federal Reserve Board does not actually govern the Federal Reserve System. It serves more in the nature of an advisory body or a liaison group between the international banking confederation and the federal government. Policy is ostensibly set by the "Open Market Committee," which the *Wall Street Journal* calls "the Fed's key policy-making body."[10] It was the Open Market Committee that triggered the Crash of 1929 and the Great Depression that followed by summarily tightening credit in 1929 to a point where it garroted the national economy. This was the action that sent the world into its 1930s tailspin,—not the Smoot-Hawley Tariff Act of 1930, as the latter day mythmakers would have us believe.

It is not the purpose of this book to examine the labyrinthian ways of the Federal Reserve System. This has been done in authentic detail by others in recent times, including Thibault de Saint Phalle, a former director of the Export-Import Bank; author-scholar Eustace Mullins; Donald F. Kettl of the University of Virginia; and William Greider in his monumental 1987 book, *Secrets of the Temple: How the Federal Reserve Runs the Country.*

However, the Federal Reserve has played the key role in this era of one-sided free trade that is stripping the United States of its mighty capital-industrial base. Indeed, the Fed's policies have made this era possible and, through its support of the World Bank and other multinational lenders, it has indirectly, but no less certainly, stimulated the building of rival foreign industries in Europe, Japan, the Pacific Rim, Brazil, and even in Communist China, the Soviet Union, and in the rest of the Soviet bloc.

U.S. commercial banks have also played a major role in this suicidal drive to create and expand foreign competition for American industries and for the jobs of our workers. But the Chase Manhattan, Citibank, Bank of America, and others would never have been able to embark on their wild lending sprees of the recent past if they had not gotten the green light from the Federal Reserve.

The secret coup which the money changers in the Wall Street temples slipped over on the American people in 1913, with the support of Wilson and House and a compliant Congress, created the machinery which has governed the country's economy ever since. By destroying the protective tariff, replacing it with the income tax, and creating a privately owned central bank empowered to issue currency based upon debt, they turned over control of our government to a small band of bankers who preside over the Federal Reserve System.

Generations of Americans as yet unborn will still be digging themselves out from under the mountainous debt dumped upon the United States of America by the Federal Reserve and its multifarious subsidiaries and affiliates—the World Bank, IMF, Ex-Im Bank, et al. Free trade is taking America down the primrose path to economic slavery and the Fed has financed that march every step of the way.

Chapter 10.

Financing War

Without means of payments in dollars . . . the Allies would have been beaten before the end of 1917. America's entry into the war saved them. Before the American soldier, the American dollar turned the tide. . . . For Europe, what a stream of gold![1]
            —Andre Tardieu, French member of the
                    Allied Economic Commission

The Federal Reserve Bank came into being just in time to finance and help prolong World War I. Paradoxically, the war delayed the disastrous effects upon American industry and agriculture that would have resulted, if peace had prevailed, from the free trade Tariff Act of 1913.

Instead, the devastation of Europe wrought by World War I, and even more extensively by its bastard son, World War II, increased the demand for our products tremendously and, by so doing, held at bay the rape of America's markets for a half-century. This long reprieve from reality gave the one world–free trade syndrome ample time to capture the minds of the "thought leaders" who ostensibly control the nation's agenda.

At the outbreak of the war the United States had nearly 36 percent of the world's total industrial plant, far more than any other two countries combined. Germany was second with almost 16 percent; England, the innovative birthplace of the industrial revolution, had been so ground down in its dedicated pursuit of free trade that it was in 1914 a distant third with barely 15 percent of the total; France, for all its resources, plus the raw materials of a great colonial empire, had a scant 6.4 percent; and Russia, a latecomer to industrial development, could claim only 5.5 percent of the global aggregate, despite its relatively rapid growth over the previous decade.

Although the Triple Entente—Britain, France, and Russia—could boast an appreciably larger combined industrial base than Germany and Austria, the contending belligerents were roughly equal in war production capacity. But it must have been obvious to both sides that should the United States, the great industrial giant, jump into the war the balance of power would be preponderantly tilted in favor of whichever side we joined.

In 1914, however, America was in the grip of another of those painful depressions that had followed virtually every attempt to tamper with the tariff for nearly a century. Only this time the Underwood Tariff, combined with the creation of the Federal Reserve, had sent the nation's industrial leaders into such a panic that it threatened more lasting damage to the economy than any prior decline. *Bradstreet's Journal* reported "the largest number of business failures in our country's history," and Andrew Carnegie wrote President Wilson that he had "never known such conditions, such pressing calls upon debtors to pay."[2] By July the New York Stock Exchange, which had kept its doors open during the panic of 1907, was forced to close.

The great irony in this was that the Federal Reserve System had been sold to the people, or at least to the Congress, as the great preventative for future financial panics. Yet here we were, in the very first year of the Fed's existence, and the economy was already on the ropes. Moreover, this panic threatened to become the worst America had ever experienced, so great was the loss of confidence that followed upon the Revolution of 1913, with the lashes it had taken to the tariff, the bites the new income taxes would take out of the public's pocketbooks, and the fear inspired by creation of the Federal Reserve.

At this point, Dr. Otis L. Graham Jr. reports, "the bankers showed Wilson a golden opportunity to put idle funds to work by simply *allowing* Europeans to borrow in New York and spend the money in this country. The pressures were enormous, and there were no real counterpressures . . . Here was an apparently painless cure for America's economic troubles, and the enthusiasm for Allied loans and trade would certainly have broken Wilson politically had he blocked it. . . . "[3]

The *New York Times* strongly supported this fateful plan, hypocritically holding out the promise of a "peaceful penetration of the world's markets to an extent we have never dreamed of" by simply "bestowing our benevolence"[4] upon the Allies.

The great trap was thus baited and set. Woodrow Wilson bit and the loans sent U.S. products flowing to the Entente. The mightiest nation on earth was ensnared in the maw of Mars by the lure of loans to other nations on the promise that they would solve our own economic problems.

President Wilson's "second personality," Edward House, was soon bending all his efforts to persuade Wilson to plunge America into the war. Even before World War I began, the little "colonel" (his was an honorary Texas title) journeyed to Europe as the president's ex officio emissary and met with the Kaiser, as well as the leaders of England and France. He was in London when news came of the assassinations of the Austrian Archduke Ferdinand and his wife by Serbian gunmen at Sarajevo on June 28. House remained in England until July 21 and wrote the Kaiser in an attempt to reinforce the hope of his British friends for a peaceful settlement.[5] But events had gone too far. Europe stepped off the cliff into the abyss.

Of all the many factors that shoved Europe over the brink, the recklessness of the Russians probably provided the primary push. The Czar's order to mobilize his imperial armies on July 30, 1914 is regarded by many thoughtful historians as the flash point that touched off the explosion.

When the German army moved two days after the Russian mobilization, the Czar's ambassador in Paris, Alexander Izvolsky, exulted: "This is my war! My war!"[6] Others could share in his benighted boast, particularly the Czar's imbecilic minister of war, Sukhomlinov, and the minister of foreign affairs, Sazanov. It was Sazanov who went to Tsarskoe Selo on the afternoon of July 30 and persuaded Nicholas to give the order for Russia's mobilization, both of them knowing this would mean a general European war. That night the elderly German ambassador, Count Pourtales, came to Sazanov and pleaded with him to cancel the mobilization. Three times, the old Count begged Sazanov to have the mobilization cancelled. Three times, Sazanov refused. Pourtales handed him the note announcing Germany's declaration of war and walked to the window and wept.[7]

The Czar had not planned to go to war until 1917, but by that year the calamitous events he had triggered in 1914 had already swept him from his throne and sent millions of young men to their graves. Nicholas and Alexandra, their four young daughters, and the invalid Tsarevich were murdered on July 16, 1918 by the socialist revolutionaries (that is what they called themselves). The family doctor, the footman, cook, and maid—even the little girls' dog— were also killed.

As the twentieth century grinds down, the end of the terror touched off in 1914 is not yet in sight. The sins of the fathers of that fateful year are still descending upon the heads of their children, their grandchildren and great-grandchildren. It is only fair to inquire then what role the New America forged by the Revolution of 1913 played in the war that was to end all wars but instead ignited many more.

Although the United States was innocent of any conscious role in starting World War I, there is no doubt that it kept the war going for at least two years, and possibly longer, partly with "humanitarian" efforts like Herbert Hoover's food relief for Belgium. The hungry Belgians did get some of the food we sent, but more of it went through their country into Germany or to the Kaiser's troops in the north of France. Thus, the relief program helped the Germans hang in on the Western front.

More than offsetting the food received by Germany, however, were the massive shipments of arms, munitions, and other supplies that flowed from U.S. ports to England and France, courtesy of the American banks. J. P. Morgan became the Allies' primary loan arranger and purchasing agent in the United States.[8] Before long the "Morgan Loan" to England had swelled to more than $400 million, and by the time the United States entered the war in March 1917 the total loan to the Allies stood at $2,262,827,544.[9] That was more than twice the total "ordinary" revenues of the U.S. Treasury in 1917.[10]

Quite obviously, loans of this magnitude would not have been possible without the Federal Reserve System, the great borrowing machine that had begun to function just as the war started in Europe. Under the traditional American system of protection and sound money, the United States could not have floated the huge loans that kept Britain and France in the war. (Perhaps to demonstrate their "impartiality," the U.S. banks had also loaned $27 million to the Germans).[11]

By August 1915 Britain was in the throes of a financial crisis, France was broke, and Russia was collapsing economically. Two months earlier William Jennings Bryan had resigned as Secretary of State in protest of the Wilson administration's drift toward war. His successor, Robert Lansing, persuaded the president to permit larger loans to the Allies on the grounds that failure to do so would cause "industrial depression . . . financial demoralization, and general unrest" at home.[12]

Lansing was not alone in lobbying Wilson for an enlargement of the war loans. As the British ambassador to Washington, Sir Cecil Spring-Rice, wrote his foreign minister, Sir Edward Grey, "when it became apparent that a loan was necessary, many secret forces began to act in its favor."[13] Certainly one of these was the president's "dear friend," Edward House.

From the very beginning of the war, Colonel House had been acting as the British government's chief agent in the United States. Working closely with the ambassador, Spring-Rice, and with Sir William Wiseman, the British Intelligence chief in America, House pulled the strings that ultimately led to Wilson's decision to ask Congress for a declaration of war.

Increasingly embittered by the U.S. policy of sending arms, on credit, to the Allies, Germany stepped up its submarine warfare. Even before enlargement of the loan, a U-boat had sunk the British liner *Lusitania* off the coast of Ireland. The loss of nearly 1,200 lives, including those of 128 Americans on board, inflamed American public opinion against Germany, although most citizens remained opposed to our entry into the war.

Meanwhile, the British navy continued to stop and search U.S. vessels on the high seas with obvious impunity.[14] Formal protests were lodged in London, but the American ambassador, Walter Hines Page, whispered *sotto voce* to the British Foreign Office that the protests could safely be ignored.

In the summer of 1916, however, President Wilson appeared to foster a more even-handed policy. Nominated by the Democratic Party for reelection, he may have been trying to live up to his campaign slogan, "He kept us out of war!" Whatever his motives, he got Congress to empower him to deny the use of U.S. ports to any nation that discriminated against American commerce.[15] It was an obvious gesture against the British, who, in addition to searching U.S. ships and seizing our mails, were blacklisting American firms suspected of doing business with the Germans. Wilson also asked the Federal Reserve Board to rein in the bankers who were financing the arms trade.[16]

The president never used the powers Congress gave him to block foreign ships from our ports. Nor is there any evidence that the Federal Reserve paid any attention to his request to slow down the war loans. But he did win the election of 1916 by a more comfortable margin than his feeble plurality of 1912.

The last steps that waltzed America into the war were orchestrated by Edward House as conductor for the bankers, with the help of a dissonant finale sounded by the Germans and the ominous crash of the Czar's government in Russia. House played the press like a virtuoso. When the British deciphered the Zimmerman telegram from Berlin instructing the German ambassador in Mexico City, von Eckhardt, to seek an alliance with Mexico against the United States, it was House who urged that the telegram be released.[17]

When Wilson hung back and hesitated, House nudged him toward war and planted other stories in the media to whip up the war fever. When Sen. W. J. Stone of Missouri, chairman of the Foreign Relations Committee, balked at approving the arming of U.S. merchant ships, House urged Wilson to brand Stone and the other senators opposing him as "a little group of willful men" and fed the statement to the newspapers.[18] (Wilson went ahead and armed the merchantmen without Senate approval.)

When the President at last decided to ask the Congress for a declaration of war, it was to House he turned for help in preparing his speech. On many momentous occasions, it was House who literally dictated a speech, or at least its central ideas, and it was the President who himself typed out his friend's thoughts on a White House typewriter. This time Wilson jotted down their joint ideas and met again with House next day so the little Texan could make corrections and offer additional suggestions.

House was not shy about taking full credit for persuading Woodrow Wilson to declare war. "I made him feel, as Mrs. Wilson told me later, that he was not up against so difficult a proposition as he had imagined," House wrote. "In my argument I said that everything that he had to meet in this emergency had been thought out time and time again in other countries, and all we had to do was to take experience as our guide and not worry over the manner of doing it. I thought it not so difficult as taking a more or less ignorant, disorganized party in Congress and forcing it to pass the Federal Reserve Act, the Tariff Act, the Panama Tolls Act, and such other legislation as he had gotten through."[19] Wilson listened with "sympathetic attention." Then he acted. Thus was the die cast for America. And for the world.

Chapter 11.

Into the Caldron

The day has come when America is privileged to spend her blood and her might for the principles that gave her birth and happiness and the peace which she has treasured.[1]
　　　　　　　　　　　—Woodrow Wilson in his war message
　　　　　　　　　　　　　　　　　　　　　to Congress

On April 2, 1917, President Wilson went before the Congress and issued the call to war, forever ending this nation's historic policy of neutrality and non-involvement in the conflicts of foreign nations as set forth by George Washington in his farewell address.

With this speech, Dr. Seymour states, Wilson "launched the United States on what he regarded as a crusade for a new world order."[2] Indeed, the new order was already taking shape. On February 27, 1917 the socialist leader of the Russian Duma, Alexander Kerensky, screamed for the Czar to be "removed, by terrorist methods if there is no other way."[3] Riots broke out in St. Petersburg, and the army garrisons soon joined the mob under the blood red banner of socialist revolution. On March 15, Nicholas II resigned, believing by this act he could keep Russia in the war and save his country. The old order was thus already coming down when the Congress of the United States, on April 6, 1917, voted overwhelmingly for war.

The first order of business upon our entry into the war was the financial bailout of our bankrupt Allies. Lord Balfour, the new British foreign secretary, came to the United States to persuade the President to write off the enormous Allied war debt and advance new credits. En route to Washington, Balfour stopped off in New York to visit Colonel House. At a subsequent meeting in Washington on April 28 House and Balfour carved up Europe so that its future map would conform with the Allies' secret treaties. To a very large extent, the postwar world that later emerged from the Treaty of Versailles took shape at this private meeting.[4]

The Balfour mission to the United States proved an enormous success for the Allies. The bailout of Britain was easily arranged. Colonel House had cautioned the Secretary of the Treasury, McAdoo, to give "with a glad heart."[5] Lord Northcliffe, Britain's propaganda chief, took obvious satisfaction from McAdoo's "spending the nation's money like a drunken sailor" as some newspapers had charged.[6] Still, it was Edward House who called the tune on finance, as on almost everything else in the Wilson administration. And Northcliffe, Balfour, Wiseman, and other Allied officials never lost an opportunity to butter him up. Nor did Woodrow Wilson.

"I am grateful to you all the time, and everything you do makes me more so," the President wrote House in 1917. "Will you not write me again. . . . I devour and profit by all your letters."[7]

The little revolutionary in a top hat was only too happy to oblige. He was intimately involved in every major decision the President made during the war and at the Paris peace conference afterward. House picked many of the key people for the powerful war boards and commissions that invested the government, in many cases superseding the cabinet. In August 1917 when J. P. Morgan, Jr. stepped aside as purchasing agent for Britain and France, he was succeeded by a presidential commission comprised of three of House's friends—Bernard M. Baruch, who also ran the War Industries Board, Robert S. Brookings, and Robert S. Lovett. But these were just a few among many.

One of the great ironies of the Wilson Administration was that the President, who presented himself as a progressive crusader fighting for the "common man," was always surrounded by the moguls of Wall Street. J. P. Morgan's men occupied key seats of power and supplied a veritable regiment of top officials to Wilson's war councils, both from the firm itself or from its subsidiaries. William G. McAdoo, the secretary of the Treasury and the President's son-in-law, was joined by two undersecretaries from Cravath & Henderson, the Kuhn, Loeb law firm, and by Jerome Hanauer, who became Assistant Treasury Secretary in charge of Liberty Loans.

Herbert Hoover was persuaded by House to shift from European relief to the U.S. Food Administration. Eugene Meyer, whose family banking house was Lazard Freres in Paris, headed up the War Finance Corporation. Jacob Schiff, the senior partner of Kuhn, Loeb, did not have an official position but served importantly in an advisory capacity, perhaps because he was sensitive to the fact that two of his brothers were still in Germany advising the Kaiser's government on financing its war effort.

Paul Warburg was not quite so sensitive, however. He continued to serve on the Federal Reserve Board while two of his brothers, Max and Fritz, labored for the German war cause in Hamburg and Berlin. In fact, Max Warburg was the chief of the German Secret Service and Paul had himself been decorated by the Kaiser in 1912 while preparing the way for passage of the Federal Reserve Act.

Woodrow Wilson was aware of the Warburgs' German connections but he didn't think that should preclude Paul Warburg from keeping his post as vice chairman of the Federal Reserve Board after the United States entered the war against Germany.[8] The British appear to have been somewhat more concerned than the Americans, however. As early as November 13, 1914, England's ambassador at Washington, Spring-Rice, wrote Sir Valentine Chirol:

I was told today that *The New York Times* has been practically acquired by Kuhn, Loeb and Schiff, special protege of the (German) Emperor. Warburg, nearly related to Kuhn, Loeb and Schiff is a brother of the well-known Warburg of Hamburg [and] . . . is a member of the Federal Reserve Board, or rather THE member. He practically controls the financial policy of the Administration. . . . Of course, it was exactly like negotiating with Germany. Everything that was said was German property.[9]

The British had not done badly themselves at playing what Kipling aptly called "the great game." They had Sir William Wiseman in an apartment in the same building with Colonel House in New York where they continued their close collaboration after America's entry into the war. One of the things that deeply concerned them in the summer of 1917 was the Pope's call for a peace conference. This was the last thing any of the Allies wanted with victory so tantalizingly near. But House and Wilson were able to thwart the papal mediation effort, with the full cooperation of Britain, France, and Italy.[10]

When the president prepared his famed "Fourteen Points" speech, it was naturally House who advised him on which points to select and emphasize. Indeed, House and a hand-picked team of *outré* progressives had been working, with Wilson's approval, on this project for months. The ad hoc research group House had gathered was called "The Inquiry" and its secretary and guiding "genius" was Walter Lippmann, who was to influence a long succession of presidents from Woodrow Wilson to John F. Kennedy.

Lippmann was regarded by Britain's Fabian Socialists as their leading apostle in America. (Lenin, who had once been their man in Zurich, moved back to Russia in October 1917 in a sealed train provided by the German Secret Service headed by Max Warburg.) It was under the guidance of Lippmann and House that the Fabian vision of the brave new world first began to take shape in Woodrow Wilson's "Fourteen Points."

Wilson had sent House to Europe in October 1917 to represent him on the Allied War Council. While he was in London the Austrians routed the Italian army at Caporetto. This was a severe setback for the Allies, but a far more portentous one soon followed. On November 7, Lenin seized power in St. Petersburg with a promise to take Russia out of the war. With the Allied Eastern front collapsing, the possibility of a German victory suddenly loomed.

When House got back to Washington in mid-December he briefed the President on his mission and returned the following week to spend Christmas at the White House. On this visit he brought maps and other data assembled by Walter Lippmann's "Inquiry" group. The Fourteen Points were hammered out by Wilson and House at this and a subsequent meeting in early January. The speech that resulted had four main objectives. Seymour says the first was designed to persuade the Bolsheviks and Russia to "stand by the Allies."[11] Second, it was to "appeal to the German Socialists" to sharpen their suspicion that "their Government was not really waging a war of defense. . . . " Third, the Entente was to be put on notice that there "must be a revision . . . of the war aims which had been crystallized in the secret treaties."[12] The fourth objective was to mount what House called "a powerful liberal offensive" to marshal Americans behind the war effort.

House thought "the most eloquent part" of Wilson's Fourteen Points was the section devoted to Russia. In this, the president promised to give Bolshevik Russia "a sincere welcome into the society of free nations under institutions of her own choosing; and more than a welcome, assistance of every kind that she may need and may herself desire." It also contained a thinly veiled threat aimed at the other Allies, particularly Britain, to restrain them from interfering too forcefully in Russia.

"The treatment accorded Russia by her sister nations in the months to come will be the acid test of their good will, of their comprehension of her needs as distinguished from their own interests, and of their intelligent and unselfish sympathy,"[13] Point VI stated.

Wilson's generous appeal to the Bolsheviks, including the offer of a blank check on the U.S. Treasury, fell on deaf ears. They were already negotiating with the Germans when Wilson delivered his speech to a joint session of the Congress on January 8, 1918. Eight weeks later, on March 3, the Treaty of Brest-Litovsk was signed ending the war in the east and freeing the Central Powers to move their troops to the Western front.

One of the Fourteen Points was designed to hasten creation of the new world order Wilson and House so ardently sought. This was Point III of the president's speech which demanded "the removal, so far as possible, of economic barriers"[14] to world trade.[14] It was a clarion call for universal free trade and a declaration of war against protectionism.

In the spring of 1918 the German armies, reinforced from the east after the treaty with the Bolsheviks, very nearly broke the Allied lines in France. Fresh American troops helped the French and British drive the Germans back across the Marne. Fighting valiantly, the Yanks took Saint Mihiel, Chateau-Thierry and began the long, hard battle on the Meuse-Argonne line.

It was at this point, in September 1918, that House drew up the plan for the Covenant of the League of Nations and persuaded Wilson to unveil it at the Metropolitan Opera House in New York on the twenty-seventh of that month. The invitation for the President to speak at this kickoff for a Liberty Loan drive was issued by Benjamin Strong, president of the Federal Reserve Bank of New York. Actually Strong presided at this gala launching of the new order. Even Dr. Seymour, sympathetic as he was to House and Wilson, admits the plan for the League of Nations appeared to "threaten the creation of a super-state" with "the assembly of delegates as a sort of permanent world-parliament."[15]

There was, of course, nothing in the Constitution of the United States that gave a president authority to surrender our sovereignty to an international body. But Woodrow Wilson sought to appropriate that authority to himself and he very nearly succeeded.

Wilson's League of Nations speech had an immediate effect: it lured the Germans into an armistice. The very next day, Hindenburg and Ludendorff, facing the American divisions moving on the Meuse-Argonne and, looking over their shoulders at Allied breakthroughs in Austria and Bulgaria, urged Berlin to take President Wilson up on the promises held out in the Covenant he had proclaimed and in the Fourteen Points.

The Kaiser prepared to retire to Holland while the moderate Prince Max of Baden replaced Wilhelm's man as chancellor of Germany. The Prince sent a note to the President on October 5 urging negotiations on the basis of the Fourteen Points. The British military historian, B. H. Liddell Hart, has pointed out that the German armies were far from defeat in the autumn of 1918. Rather, as Liddell Hart states, the German Supreme Command "lost its nerve"—it "cracked, and the sound went echoing backwards until it had resounded throughout the whole of Germany . . . the moral impression, as ever in war, was decisive."[16]

The first thing Wilson did when he received the German peace offer was to contact House, who urged the President to "delay without seeming so" on the proposal until he (House) could get to Paris and confer with the Allies.[17] Wilson sent House off with "a virtual power of attorney" to decide the fate of the world.

"Colonel House thus came to Europe," wrote Seymour, "with all the authority of the President of the United States. . . . Characteristically the President gave him no instructions of any kind, apparently certain that House understood exactly what was in his [Wilson's] mind."[18]

In this Wilson may have been fatally mistaken, for this man who had never been elected to a major office in the United States, sat as an equal on the Supreme War Council in Paris with the prime ministers of Great Britain, France, and Italy—and meekly acquiesced in almost all the intricate designs of Lloyd George, Clemenceau, and Orlando. The Fourteen Points were postponed and the promises explicit in the President's League of Nations speech were also shelved. The terms concocted by the Entente, and approved by House, went forth to the German high command and laid the foundation for future war. But when Germany, already feeling betrayed by Wilson and the United States, agreed to the Armistice on November 11, 1918, Colonel House sent an exultant cable to Woodrow Wilson:

Autocracy is dead. Long live democracy and its immortal leader. In this great hour my heart goes out to you in pride, admiration and love.[19]

At eleven o'clock that morning the guns fell silent on the Western front to wait impatiently for another generation to rise and fill the places of the 8,538,315 men and women who had died in "the war to end all wars."

Chapter 12.

The Peace That Brought War

It staggers the imagination to think what the future may have
in store for the development of American banking.[1]
                    —Paul Warburg in a speech to the
                    Bankers Club, St. Paul, Minnesota

The United States emerged from World War I with a crushing debt, so burdensome that we still are paying it off after seven decades. The total indebtedness
surpassed $50 billion in 1921 but when subsequent military pensions, the vet-
erans' bonus, and hospital care for the seriously wounded were added, the
aggregate debt may have been three or four times that amount.

The national debt, which had been $1.2 billion in 1916, multiplied by more
than twenty times to almost $25.5 billion at war's end. On a per capita basis it
rose from $12 per person to $242. Although these figures appear modest in the
present age of hyperinflation, they could not even have been conceived in the
wildest dreams before the war. Except, of course, by the little group of men
who created the Federal Reserve.

Income taxes soared and myriad other levies were devised to help bear the
fiscal costs of war. Customs duties sank in significance, although in the early
stages, before America's entry into the conflict, the tariff was still the major
producer of revenue for the Treasury, generating 40 percent of the total in 1914,
30 percent the following year, and 28 percent in 1916.[2] But it was borrowing
that carried the heaviest load. Some $51 billion in short-term loans were floated
between April 6, 1917, and October 31, 1921, and billions more in long-term
bonds were issued by the Treasury.

Dewey informs us that ''a very considerable part of this huge debt was due to credits in behalf of European governments engaged in the war against Germany."[3] Yet at the Paris peace conference the European leaders behaved as though the Americans were indebted to them.

The 320,000 casualties the United States suffered in eighteen months of hard fighting in France were waved aside by Clemenceau and Lloyd George, whose countries had admittedly suffered much more. But there was little sense of the obvious fact that it had been Europe's war, despite America's decisive role in bringing it to a conclusion.

The peace table was stacked with the secret treaties the Allies had entered into before and during the conflagration, and the attitude was that these did not concern America. The other nations were out to grab whatever they could, and Britain alone took more than a million square miles of former German colonies and other territories. Only the United States wanted nothing except a guarantee that peace would be lasting.

However, America was represented in Paris by a curious collection of reformers, bankers, lawyers, and visionary idealists—all but a few seemingly far removed from the hard realities of European politics. Colonel House held forth at the luxury Hotel de Crillon he and his huge staff had occupied during the Armistice negotiations. More and more House acted as if he were the President of the United States, and it sometimes seemed as though he treated Woodrow Wilson as the office boy, which indeed may have been the role House conceived for Wilson as early as 1912. In public, however, he was careful to behave deferentially toward his friend.

President Wilson landed in France on Friday, the thirteenth of December, 1918. The following day he was welcomed in Paris by a "monster parade" House had arranged with the French socialists.[4] Indeed, House had arranged everything. Although the President did not stay at the Hotel de Crillon with him, House had a private telephone line from his bedside to Wilson's in the palatial mansion of Prince Murat on the Parc Monceau.

Wilson brought with him to Paris, on this and his subsequent trip, many of the same men who had sustained him in his battles to destroy the protective tariff, foster the Federal Reserve, and guide the United States into the war. Among them were Thomas W. Lamont of J. P. Morgan; the Morgan lawyers, John W. Davis and Frank Polk; Supreme Court Justice Louis Brandeis and his eventual successor on the high court, Felix Frankfurter; plus Walter Lippmann and the ever-present Paul Warburg, who found his brother, Max Warburg, on the German peace team.

The Secretary of State, Robert Lansing, came along for the ride, as did the lone Republican on the U.S. Peace Commission, Henry White. The President appears not to have noticed that the Republicans had won the congressional elections the week before the Armistice, although this indicated the war, and Wilson's policies, were not as popular with the American people as most historians have led us to believe.

Edward House hand-picked the American members of the Supreme Economic

Council, including Herbert Hoover for food, Bernard Baruch for raw materials, and Norman H. Davis for finance. Thomas Lamont and Vance McCormick were on the reparations committee, but House had effectively dispensed with that knotty problem during the armistice talks. He simply caved in to French demands for revenge, permitting France's finance minister, Klotz, to write the clause that Clemenceau & Co. were to interpret as a blank check on Germany.[5]

The French wanted reparations of $200 Billion and their attempts to extract payments contributed mightily to Hitler's rise to power and the outbreak of World War II. On the eve of *Der Fuerher*'s putsch, economist Wilhelm Roepke presciently warned that the reparations question was "upsetting the economic and political peace of the world."[6]

House did come up with terms for the takeover of the German navy, conditions even Lloyd George thought "excessive," and Marshal Foch deemed unreasonable.[7] The Germans obviously agreed for they scuttled their fleet at Scapa Flow rather than turn it over. Later, House made an agreement with his British friends to keep the U.S. Navy in second place to Britain's.[8]

Free trade got another big boost from the dour little Texan during the armistice talks that paved the way for the peace treaty. Insisting that the third of Wilson's Fourteen Points be hammered into the protocols to call for the removal of economic barriers to trade, House set forth a principle that has haunted American industries and workers ever since.

The Belgians raised an objection to the trade clause, pointing out that they needed protection from the anticipated dumping of German steel and other products in their markets. But the colonel would have none of that protectionist nonsense. "If we prevent her [Germany] from making a living," House said, "she will not be able to pay [the reparations]."[9]

This high-sounding notion has been extended in more recent years to apply to debtor countries in Latin America and elsewhere, giving them carte blanche to dump their goods in the American market so they may earn enough to pay interest on the loans from U.S. banks and the multinational lenders. The debtor nations are now almost all in de facto default, and millions of American jobs, to say nothing of taxes and corporate revenues, have been sacrificed to the fantasy originated in Paris.

Colonel House also played a major role in the territorial division of Europe and Africa and the Mideast that, with the reparations problem, were to set the fuse for the explosion of World War II and the interminable strife that has followed. In so doing, he was putting America's seal on the private agreements he had made with Lord Balfour in New York soon after the United States declared war.

Woodrow Wilson had been briefed on these arrangements by House and Balfour, though perhaps not as fully as he should have been. However, Wilson was not so much interested in the details as he was in fulfilling his vision of the Brave New World. Too often, substantive issues were simply swept aside.

Wilson became totally dedicated to the making of a "world constitution" in the meetings of the League of Nations Commission held in House's spacious chambers at the Crillon.[10] Indeed, the President wore himself out in these interminable debates, which often went on until midnight and after. Finally, on February 13, 1919, the Covenant of the League of Nations was completed. The following day it was presented to the plenary of the peace conference at the Quai d'Orsay.

The next day Wilson left for Washington in an attempt to win congressional support for his dream. He stayed in the Capitol only a very short time before returning again. In fact, from early December 1918 until the end of June 1919 the President spent only seven days in the White House. The rest of the time he was either in Europe or traveling across the Atlantic. He became more and more depressed and irritable, referring to Lloyd George and Clemenceau as "madmen." Once he burst out: "Logic! Logic! I don't give a damn for logic!"[11] He fell ill in Paris during the spring of 1919, and there is evidence he may have suffered a stroke in April. He showed symptoms of paranoia and even became gradually estranged from his friend, House.

The Germans refused to acknowledge their war guilt and for a time the Allies considered a naval blockade to starve Germany into signing the peace treaty.[12]. But after scuttling their fleet, the Germans finally agreed to sign. The ceremony took place at Versailles on June 28 with cannon booming and the flags of the victors flying. Even House was touched by the sight of the humiliated Germans. As he confided to his diary, "It was not unlike what was done in olden times, when the conqueror dragged the conquered at his chariot wheels."[13]

Wilson left for the United States the same day. House saw him off at the railroad station with a sense of foreboding. They were never to see each other again, and henceforth the colonel's letters to the White House went unanswered.

"My separation from Woodrow Wilson was and is to me a tragic mystery," House wrote later.[14] The real tragedy, however, lay in their friendship, a mysterious collaboration that spelled disaster for America and for the world, beginning with their overthrow of the American protective system and ending with sowing the seeds for future wars. They were not alone in sharing the guilt for the peace that brought more wars. But they put their seals to it, and House's fingerprints were all over the fateful Treaty of Versailles.

Chapter 13.

Brave New World

America doubtless welcomed the Russian revolution more keenly than many of the Allies.[1]

—John Pollock, English relief
worker in Russia, from
1915 to 1919

The remaining twenty months of Woodrow Wilson's presidency after his return from Versailles unfolds like a dark Euripidean drama. Finding the Senate unwilling to accept United States participation in the League of Nations without provisions to protect our sovereignty, Wilson went off on a grueling whistlestop campaign through the West in a vain attempt to sell the League to the people. On September 25, he broke into tears during a speech before several thousand in Pueblo, Colorado.

"I believe that men will see the truth," he said in closing. "[W]e are going to be led by it, and it is going to lead us, and through us the world, out into pastures of quietness and peace such as the world never dreamed of before."[2]

In the middle of the night, as the presidential train neared Wichita, Wilson suffered a "thrombosis of the brain," which his doctor told the press was "a complete nervous breakdown."[3] Rushed back to the White House, he had another apparent stroke a week later. Gene Smith, in his book *When The Cheering Stopped*, documents how the President's second wife, a woman with only two years of formal schooling, ran the administration of the United States government for nearly a year and a half.

Secretary of State Lansing said Wilson was in "such a condition that he was utterly unable to attend to public business."[4] Mrs. Wilson appointed men to two cabinet posts; one, D. F. Houston, whom she shifted from Agriculture to Secretary of the Treasury, was the academician Edward House had recruited to convert Wilson to free trade years earlier.[5]

The Senate, led by Henry Cabot Lodge of Massachusetts, twice refused to consent to the treaty Wilson had signed in Paris to bring America into the League of Nations. But Wilson said, in a note written for him, "I do not accept the action of the United States Senate as the decision of the Nation."[6] Still, the Constitution provided for such acceptance. The decision of the Senate stood.

Wilson wanted to run for a third term as President, but the Democratic Party leaders, realizing he was mentally, as well as physically, incapacitated, nominated Ohio newspaper publisher James Cox instead. Cox campaigned on the pledge to bring the country into the League of Nations—and lost in the biggest electoral vote landslide in a century. Wilson's Wall Street friends bought him a house in Washington's expensive Kalorama Triangle and there he died on February 3, 1924, a broken man.

Before his departure from the White House Woodrow Wilson fought one more successful rear-guard action for his free trade theology, which his messianic mind saw, quite correctly in this case, as the great stepping stone to the One World government he and Edward House had labored so ardently to create.

When the Republicans captured control of Congress in November 1918, they made known their intention to overthrow the Tariff Act of 1913 and restore the higher import duties that had previously protected American industries and the national economy. But preparations for a new trade law went forward slowly. The public and the Congress were preoccupied with the peace conference, the return of our soldiers from France, and Wilson's emotional battle for the League of Nations. But near the end of 1919 a protectionist trade act appeared imminent.

In December the Wilson administration intervened to block the trade bill with a strongly worded message to Congress which purported to be from the President. The fiction was still being maintained that Mr. Wilson was in control though everyone in Washington knew he was incapable of governing. The presidential message, probably written by or for Carter Glass, then Secretary of the Treasury, emphasized that foreign countries could not pay their debts to the United States unless we permitted them to sell their products in our country.[7] This, of course, was the principle promulgated by Colonel House in Paris when the Allies were dealing with the question of how the Germans might pay their reparations. It is doubtful the Congress bought this obviously destructive line of reasoning but the threat of a veto was implicit in the message and legislative action on trade was postponed for the remainder of Wilson's term.

The government of the United States, spurred on by war, grew exponentially under Wilson. Many of the wartime bureaucracies his administration created are still with us. It is doubtful we will ever be rid of them all.

Segments of the body politic went far to the Left. As Dr. Otis Graham states in his study of the period, "At least parts of the American public seemed to have been radicalized by the war, and this included some intellectuals. Woodrow

Wilson himself . . . mused to a friend in 1918 that the world would probably be moving to the Left and that he would be going with it.''[8]

Nonetheless, as Dr. Graham also points out, ''the Right was much stronger,'' and the triumph over Wilson and the League of Nations ''was not engineered by some manipulative business elite, but was a national phenomenon expressing the ultimate decision of the great bulk of the American people. . . . ''[9]

In Europe, and much of the rest of the world, however, the Left was on the rise. The seeds of socialism sown by Marx came into full flower with World War I, and much of the Old World was succumbing to its blandishments—and its bullets. Germany tilted to the Left during the Weimar Republic and plunged off the deep end into National Socialism under Adolf Hitler. In Italy, a socialist newspaper editor named Benito Mussolini ascended the throne of his wedding cake palace in Rome and instituted widespread statist reforms. France became more and more politically gauche and eventually elected socialist Leon Blum premier to pave the way for disarmament and defeat. Britain toyed with the Fabian Society's fantasies but postponed its slide into the socialist chasm when Ramsay MacDonald rejected the Left.

In Russia, meanwhile, the Union of Soviet Socialist Republics was being forged by a tight little band of ruthless fanatics who knew how to divide and conquer a confused and polyglot population. It is doubtful the Bolsheviks could have kept control, however, if it had not been for the substantial assistance they received from the United States. The Americans were fooled by the Communists at every turn.

John Pollock, an Englishman who served in Russia as a relief worker for four years ending in 1919, wrote that the U.S. mission under Sen. Elihu Root that arrived soon after the Bolshevik putsch hired interpreters and other staff people from among the Communist officialdom. ''The mission,'' Pollock said, ''in fact, was in the hands of its enemies, who, at critical moments, were thus able to render its best intentions nugatory.''[10]

Actually, some Wilsonians secretly, and often openly, saw themselves as the real advance guard of world revolution. Edward House pointedly stated on the heels of the Czar's abdication in March 1917, ''my friend [Wilson] has always held these convictions'' [regarding the ''liberation'' of the world's peoples, as the president had put it] ''but until Russia joined the democratic nations he did not think it wise to utter them.''[11] One reason Wilson delayed entering the war was because he feared taking America in on the side of the Russian autocracy would offend his most avid followers.

A week after Czar Nicholas abdicated, the revolutionary Kerensky regime was recognized by the United States and, with the collaboration of the Federal Reserve, nearly $200 million was ''loaned'' to the new Russian government. An American Red Cross mission arrived in St. Petersburg on August 7, 1917 and one of its members, Col. Raymond Robins, was to become a leading propagandist for the Bolsheviks.[12] More American help flowed to Russia after Lenin and his gunmen disbanded the Constituent Assembly in November 1917. George

Bakmetiev, Kerensky's ambassador to Washington, claimed the Bolsheviks, "after victory, transferred 600 million rubles in gold between the years 1918–22 to Kuhn, Loeb Company."[13] Whether this transaction ever took place may be open to question. But there is no doubt that the Federal Reserve Bank of New York became a heavy buyer of Bolshevik gold beginning in 1920, thereby helping finance the USSR at a crucial juncture.

Although Woodrow Wilson appears to have had recurrent misgivings about the Bolsheviks, he played the game that Lenin, Trotsky, and their numerous American apologists designed for him. Thus, William Boyce Thompson, another Red Cross officer who became an ally of the Soviets, could boast after hearing Wilson's Fourteen Points speech, that the President had "accomplished nine-tenths of what he [Thompson] had in mind."[14]

Far more damaging than his speeches was Wilson's prevention of effective Allied intervention in Russia when there was still time to have nipped the Communist world revolution in the bud. In this historic failure the President was aided and abetted by the slippery Welshman who had become prime minister of England, David Lloyd George. France's Clemenceau was for full-scale intervention in Russia after the Armistice and so was Marshal Foch.[15] But Woodrow Wilson and Lloyd George held out for half-measures they must have known would fail.

When Wilson finally did decide to intervene in concert with Britain and France, it was in a manner that seemed calculated to help, rather than hinder, the Soviets. A token American force landed at Vladivostok thousands of miles from Moscow and Petrograd where the fate of the revolution was being decided. An even smaller British military mission arrived at Archangel and the French sent a few units into the Crimea. Believing these minuscule military formations were just the beginning of a real invasion, the Bolsheviks in Moscow began packing their files as they prepared to flee.[16] But when it became apparent this was to be the extent of the Allied intervention, Lenin was jubilant. A new wave of terror began against opponents of the Bolsheviks and intensified when Lenin was shot and wounded by a rival Leftist.

Bruce Lockhart, the ex officio British agent in Moscow, later wrote: "The weakness of our landing force in the North resulted in the loss of the Volga line and in the temporary collapse of the anti-Bolshevik movement in European Russia."[17] In the Far East, the American landing, although augmented by a much larger Japanese force, had approximately the same effect on the White Russian resistance across Siberia. The U.S. commander, Maj. Gen. William S. Graves, made it clear in his book, *America's Siberian Adventure 1918–1920*, that he was under orders not to interfere with the Bolshevik revolutionaries, but merely to help the Czech Legion, comprised of former prisoners of war, in their attempt to escape from Russia.[18]

The heart was cut out of the native Russian resistance struggling against the Red Army when the feeble Allied forces withdrew early in 1920. It became obvious to everyone in Russia that there was no hope of succor from the outside world, particularly from America, the country so many had counted on for help against the Bolshevik terror. Instead, the United States tightened the Bolshevik grip on the throat of the Russian people by what many perceived as a great humanitarian act.

The Red Army, which may have driven all the way through war-weary Europe to the coast of France, was stopped on August 16, 1920, at the battle of Warsaw by a courageous Polish force under Marshal Josef Pilsudski. The Bolshevik attempt to break through to the West had cost Russia dearly. Much of the fighting had been in temporarily independent Ukraine, the breadbasket of Eastern Europe. The breakdown in transport and administration, originally brought on by war and revolution, was compounded by a draught and the struggle with Poland. There followed the worst famine in Russian history to that time. Before it was over an estimated five million people died.[19]

The Bolsheviks, reeling from the defeat in Poland, still fighting resistance forces in the Ukraine, beset by a thousand and one other problems, knew that if they could not feed the Russian population they would soon be out of power. At this critical juncture they turned once again to America.

Herbert Hoover, by now Secretary of Commerce in the Harding administration, cranked up his food relief organization for yet another rescue operation. Most of the nearly $100 million spent in Russia in 1921–23 came from private sources in the U.S., including the churches the Soviets were so intent on closing down. But Hoover did persuade Harding and the Congress to give him $18 million from a government wartime grain account, and the War Department and the Red Cross came up with millions more in medical supplies and equipment.[20]

No doubt the three hundred Americans who worked on the extensive food relief program in Russia were impelled by the best humanitarian motives. But as John Pollock had observed, in commenting on earlier American food relief efforts, the Bolsheviks were the real beneficiaries of such programs.[21]

Chapter 14.

The Rip-Roaring Twenties

So you see that old libel that we were cynics and skeptics was nonsense from the beginning. On the contrary we were the great believers.

— F. Scott Fitzgerald in "My Generation"

The election of 1920 set the stage for a reversal of the Wilson-House free trade policy and cleared the political decks for a return of the battered ship of state to the American home port of protectionism and, some hoped, to the principle of sound money secretly scuttled with the creation of the Federal Reserve System seven traumatic years earlier.

Before Congress could tackle the tariff, however, the country had to grapple with a short but fierce and destructive postwar recession that began in the summer of 1920. The Federal Reserve Bank of New York raised its rediscount rate from a little over 4 percent to 7 percent within eight months[1] and threw the banking system throughout the country into a panic. Loans were called all over the economic landscape and the stock market plunged from a high of 138 in 1919 to under 64 in 1921, cutting share values by more than half and driving many companies to the wall. Farmers were hard hit by the drastic retraction of credit and more than a million of them were driven off the land.

The Federal Reserve, which had been sold to the public in 1913 as the great palliative for panic, had precipitated one of the worst panics in our history. No doubt some tightening of credit was called for after the near runaway inflation engendered by World War I, though the steep decline in world commodity prices already underway probably would have cut prices in a less damaging way. But the draconian measures employed by the Federal Reserve to slow down the overheated economy was the equivalent of a thoracic surgeon curing the patient by sawing him in half. The country reeled under the impact of the Fed's axe and for a time the acrid stench of revolution was in the air.

The Left, encouraged by the Bolshevik victory over Russia, acted as though it was on the point of duplicating the feat in the United States. A wave of strikes erupted in the fall of 1918 and continued through the following year. As Graham observed, the labor unrest led the Left to believe it "might be within months of a seizure of power."[2] The Socialist Party, not yet completely divorced from its more bloodthirsty Bolshevik elements, polled an amazing 27 percent of the vote in a New York mayoralty election and no less than 34 percent in a similar contest in Chicago.[3] Race riots flared in several dozen cities and a wave of bombings was attributed to Bolsheviks and their sympathizers.

Even the Wilson administration was frightened by the Red scare and Attorney General A. Mitchell Palmer took vigorous action against revolutionaries from Russia and elsewhere who had infiltrated the United States. If the postwar panic had deepened into prolonged depression, the Left may have come closer to its goal. In the end, all it accomplished was to increase the margins of victory for conservative Republicans in the 1920 election.

Shortly after Warren Harding's inauguration the Congress went to work on an "emergency tariff" and enacted it in May 1921. This measure was primarily designed to prevent more farm failures by protecting American agriculture from a massive invasion of commodities dumped wholesale into the United States market by foreign countries anxious to earn Yankee dollars. The manufacturing sector, which now accounted for nearly 40 percent of the nation's employment, was only peripherally affected by the emergency trade legislation though it too had felt the painful bite of unfair competition from abroad.

At this point there began the longest congressional debate on trade in U.S. history, a debate in which the "progressives" proved, as they have many times since, that they could thwart the will of the people if only by delaying the legitimate demands of the overwhelming majority of citizens for a protracted period. Hearings on what was to emerge as the Fordney-McCumber Tariff Act began in January 1921 and the final bill was not enacted until September 1922.

In spite of the unconscionable delay, which occurred at a time when the Europeans were dumping their manufactured products in our market on an unprecedented scale, the law that finally won through was a spectacular victory for protectionism. The vote in the House of Representatives was 292 to 131 and was cast along almost straight party lines. In the Senate, the Republicans beat down the Democrats by an equally decisive margin, 48 to 25.

The Tariff Act of 1922 undid the revolutionary Underwood Tariff of 1913 and rolled back the free trade insurgents to square one. Indeed, Taussig claimed it "went beyond the acts of 1890, 1897 and 1909."[4] The duties on iron and steel products that had been eliminated in 1913 were restored, and the tariffs on sugar, wool, and textiles were sensibly increased. Just as sensibly, iron ore and other raw materials were continued on the duty free list. The average import levies on dutiable goods was raised from the then all-time low of 16 percent, the ineffective depth they had sunk to under Wilson, to a truly protectionist level of 40 percent.

However, as with several of the predecessor tariff acts, the 1922 law increased the powers of the executive branch over trade, thereby surrendering yet more ground clearly reserved for the Congress under the Constitution. The act also strengthened the Tariff Commission, giving that growing bureaucracy more jurisdiction over American industries and jobs. The results were soon apparent. Over the next six years there were some three hundred applications for tariff increases to help domestic industries squeezed by imports. About a hundred of these were investigated by the Tariff Commission, and the president granted tariff increases in only twenty-four cases. Twenty-four out of three hundred was hardly a promising record and probably discouraged many more industries from wasting legal fees by applying for relief from unfair imports.

Despite the drawbacks, the Tariff Act of 1922 represented a tremendous improvement over the 1913 law engineered by the previous administration. Nor did Calvin Coolidge follow the example of Woodrow Wilson, who had opposed a tariff increase in 1919 on the dubious ground that foreign countries had to be able to freely sell their exports in the United States in order to pay for our exports and loans to their countries.

Just as protectionist legislation, or the prospect of it, had always brought prosperity in the past, enactment of the 1922 trade act was immediately followed by an economic resurgence. Other factors contributed to the great boom of the twenties, of course. The Secretary of the Treasury, Andrew W. Mellon, persuaded Congress to approve a series of healthy tax cuts and, with added revenues from Customs duties, he achieved budget surpluses year after year. The national debt was reduced and nearly a third of the heavy war debt was retired by the end of the decade. The Federal Reserve eased credit and sent the discount rate down from 7 percent to 4½ percent and finally to 3 percent in the mid-1920s. All these measures spurred prosperity. But return to the healthy protectionist climate which gave American investors and industrialists the proven incentives to move forward was the proximate force behind the boom.

Industry managed to regain its momentum after the painful shakeout of the postwar recession and went on to set new production records. This was nowhere more apparent than in the automobile industry which multiplied its production to over 5.6 million vehicles by 1929. Moreover, newer industries were beginning to grow and thrive. Many different types of airplanes were being built and infant airlines started. Radio came into its own after the pioneering broadcast of the Harding-Cox election returns over KDKA, the Westinghouse station in Pittsburgh, and national radio networks soon came into being. Other developments in electronics, chemicals, metals, and other industries provided jobs at brand-new plants in towns and cities all across the land.

Local and regional manufacturing economies were created in scores of communities during the twenties and most of them were able to survive the Great

88 Trade Wars Against America

Depression, help see America through to victory in World War II, and sustain the national production base for two or three more decades before the devastating Japanese and other foreign trade invasions of the 1970s and 1980s knocked so many of them into the scrap heap of history.

The Roaring Twenties were not, of course, an unmitigated success for every segment of the population. Production line speed-ups often reduced workers to virtual automatons and many of them did not share at all in the zooming prosperity. Dr. Martin A. Larson makes the important point that the increased production in the automobile industry actually brought fewer jobs and reduced wages for workers in Detroit and other automotive manufacturing communities. In 1923, 241, 256 workers earned $407 million by producing 2.6 million vehicles with a wholesale value close to $1.8 billion. But in 1929 15,000 fewer workers earned $366 million by turning out more than twice as many vehicles valued at $3.7 billion.[5]

Dr. Larson emphasizes that "it would be a mistake to consider the employers simply cruel and rapacious in their drive for doubled or tripled production at lower cost; what they did was their only means of survival."[6] He points out that "at least a thousand manufacturers of automobiles and parts went bankrupt in the fierce competition prevailing during this period. Since the industrial workers had no unions at that time, they had no protection or any means of enforcing a demand for a better share of the profits, which, if obtained, would have increased their buying power in the market place. Any employer who voluntarily raised the pay of his workers or reduced his production requirements was simply forced into bankruptcy."[7]

It is Martin Larson's belief, and this writer's too, that this patently unhealthy, if not inhuman, situation was caused by the suicidal easy credit policy of the Federal Reserve System, a policy that made paper profits transcendent and guaranteed the great boom would eventually end in a disastrous crash.

The Federal Reserve touched off and continued to feed the fire under the speculative scramble by promulgating bargain-basement rediscount rates. In 1925 the Fed lowered the interest rates at the behest of Great Britain and France. Gold was flowing out of Europe to the United States because of our higher rates and the robust economic recovery following enactment of the 1922 Trade Act which made investment on this side of the Atlantic more attractive.

Britain had attempted to return to the gold standard but the pound was too weak to support such a move. The results were painful and all gold coins rapidly disappeared from circulation in the United Kingdom. France was having great difficulty making its debt payments. Germany had just been pulled out of the inflationary inferno by a large American gold loan to stabilize its currency. Austria, shorn of its old empire, was waltzing around the rim of economic disaster, as were most of the other countries of Europe.

Against this background, the Federal Reserve agreed that low interest rates in America would stem the gold drain on Europe. The first drop in U.S. rates in 1925 had only limited results and two years later the Europeans came back again. The old maestro of economic history, John Kenneth Galbraith, tells the tale thusly:

In the spring of 1927, three august pilgrims—Montagu Norman, the Governor of the Bank of England, the durable Hjalmar Schacht, then Governor of the Reischbank, and Charles Rist, the Deputy Governor of the Bank of France—came to the United States to urge an easy money policy. . . . The Federal Reserve obliged. The rediscount rate of the New York Federal Reserve Bank was cut from 4 to 3.5 per cent. Government securities were purchased in considerable volume . . . leaving the banks and individuals who had sold them with money to spare. . . . The funds that the Federal Reserve made available were either invested in common stocks or (and more important) they became available to help finance the purchase of common stocks by others.[8]

The Fed's easy money policy made buying stocks on margin all the rage, not only in New York, but in a number of other American cities that now boasted stock exchanges. There were a host of subsidiary elements contributing to the great boom that went bust in 1929. But the Federal Reserve's actions top the long list. A few of the others are worth a quick look before we examine the Great Crash and the depression decade that followed.

Encouraged by the Federal Reserve, U.S. commercial banks went on their second big international lending binge in the rip-roaring twenties. The first, during World War I, proved disastrous, but too many bankers seem eternally willing to forgive foreign borrowers their defaults even while calling in loans made to their fellow Americans.

Beyond lending generously abroad, our banks also promoted foreign securities in the New York money market. From 1921 to 1927 these often risky sales more than doubled: from $623 million to $1.3 billion. They tapered off somewhat after that, but remained abnormally high and still totalled $905 million in 1930.[9]

The sales of foreign securities in Wall Street further fueled the explosive boom of the twenties since a large part of the funds raised were spent on products made in America. It was the same principle upon which the Morgan loans of World War I were based. And, as Paul Studenski and Herman Krooss noted, it made the U.S. "dependent to a great extent upon loans to Europeans and on purchases of American products generated thereby."[10] The same writers correctly concluded that "this was not a stable foundation for prosperity."

The foreign loans also boomeranged on the borrowers. By increasing the already heavy demand for dollars, the loans further depressed foreign currencies and forced foreign governments to adopt ersatz exchange rates. "Thus," Studenski and Krooss inform us, "conditions were being prepared for a great world crash which would engulf the United States even more than any other country, since no other nation enjoyed greater prosperity or was more involved internationally."[11]

Another aspect of our international involvement that helped set the stage for the big blowout of 1929 was the cavalier attitude of foreign countries toward the debts they already owed the United States. The Bolsheviks in Russia led the way by simply "annihilating" (to use their word) the $200 million loan to the Kerensky government in 1917.[12] Since Russia got away with this, and even received additional aid from America *after* the debt was annulled, other countries naturally thought they should be forgiven too. Ultimately, all nations that owed us, with the exception of Finland, just stopped paying.

The problems with the foreign debt placed unbearable strains on America's banking system and contributed to the record number of bank failures in this dotty decade. From 1921 through 1929 no less than 5,712 banks gave up the ghost, further proving that the Federal Reserve shield supposedly protecting our banks was made of papier-mâché.

There was yet another factor that contributed to the instability of the era, one which most economists have ignored. The late Reverend Edmund A. Walsh, after whom Georgetown University's School of Foreign Service is named, explored this hidden factor at fascinating length in his 1931 book, *The Last Stand*.[13] An expert on the Soviet Union, where he had served during Herbert Hoover's rescue operation in the 1921–22 famine, Father Walsh presented substantial evidence that the Soviets began dumping products heavily on world markets in the late 1920s and continued their assault into the depressed thirties. The cut-rate exports were the external part of the Soviet Five-Year Plan and had two objectives: (1) to earn foreign exchange to finance Communist global activities, and (2) to depress prices worldwide in order to help create unemployment and unrest in the targeted countries.

A broad range of Soviet products were dumped in Europe and the United States—oil, timber, coal, manganese, matches, and cheap textiles.[14] Even wheat and other grains were exported at a time when people were starving in Russia and, in the latter stages of the operation, a cruel famine was devastating the Ukraine and claiming millions of lives.

Soviet trade agents in New York, London and other citadels of capitalism were, Walsh wrote, "authorized to underbid any market." Since costs in the Soviet Union, then as now, could not be pinned down, it was difficult to bring dumping charges against them. Eventually, a storm of protest swept the parliaments of Europe and there were loud echoes in the halls of Congress. But by the time the West awoke, in 1930 and 1931, the damage had been done.

Even President Hoover, ardent promoter of trade with the Soviets during the eight years he was Secretary of Commerce, was finally forced to take half-hearted action. Revelations of Soviet slave labor loading ships bound for our ports coincided with a Soviet sortie against American farmers. The Soviets were caught selling wheat short on the Chicago futures market. The price of wheat was driven down to less than eighty-seven cents a bushel, and the already hard-pressed farmers in the Midwest were painfully squeezed.[15] The U.S. tariff of fourty-two cents a bushel of wheat did not deter the Soviets for the good reason that tariffs, no matter how high, cannot deflect a socialist government bent on dumping.

It is difficult to assess at this late date just how much Soviet dumping actions contributed to the crash and the depression. But world commodity markets were vulnerable throughout the twenties and became dangerously depressed in the 1930s, seriously hampering efforts to rescue the economies of all nations affected by the collapse.

By early 1929 all the ducks were lined up in the Wall Street shooting gallery just waiting to be shot down: soft commodity prices, a weak banking system, the uncertainty of huge foreign loans, a lopsided distribution of income, and the stock market speculation building for several years towards its cataclysmic climax. At this juncture, the Federal Reserve began a series of puzzling moves that at first tossed more gasoline on the speculative fire and then, with the boom completely out of control, tried to douse the blaze by choking off credit, the same kind of action that had brought on the economic deluge in the early part of the decade. Tragically, this time the crash kept right on crashing for most of the next ten years.

Chapter 15.

Crash!

In 1929, at the time of the stock market crash, the Federal Reserve unfortunately did not move fast enough to increase bank reserves.... There was at that point an immediate need to restore liquidity through Federal Reserve action. It was not forthcoming.[1]

—Thibaut de Saint Phalle in
The Federal Reserve:
An Intentional Mystery

The Dow industrial average of selected blue chip industrial shares trading on the New York Stock Exchange went from 63.9 in 1921 to a high of 386.1 on September 3, 1929 and all the way down to 40.6 in 1932. It was one of the great roller coaster rides in financial history. Although the worst part of the Crash came during a half-dozen numbing days in late October of 1929, the market kept falling, with a few interruptions, over the next three years. When it reached bottom in the summer of 1932 some twelve million people were unemployed in the United States, millions more in Europe, and international trade and finance were crawling along with all the alacrity of a snail who had just taken an overdose of phenobarbital.

In the postmortem immediately following the collapse there was no audible mention that America's protective tariffs had played any role whatever in the debacle. That came later. The first widely advertised allusion to the tariff's alleged part in bringing down Wall Street's house of cards and prolonging the Depression surfaced in the platform the Democratic Party unveiled at the 1932 national convention in Chicago.

The Smoot-Hawley Tariff Act had, the Democrats charged, "created international economic hostilities, destroyed international trade, driven our factories into foreign countries, robbed the American farmer of his foreign markets, and increased the cost of production."[2]

There have been mountains of nonsense written into the platforms of both major political parties over the years, but this must top them all. Yet appendages have been added that heighten the indictment of Smoot-Hawley, including one that is a favorite of the Japanese—i.e., that this tariff act led directly to World War II. The Japanese long ago forgot Pearl Harbor. But then, so has almost everyone in Washington.

The salient fact the Japanese, and too many American economists, choose to overlook is that Smoot-Hawley was not enacted until more than eight months *after* the stock market crashed. Moreover, the act covered barely a third of all imports into the United States. Dutiable imports—the one-third affected—fell by $462 million in 1930. Since the law did not go into effect until June, the onus of the free traders' myth focuses on roughly half that figure, or some $231 million in a wide range of products shipped by scores of countries.[3] This statistic represented but an infinitesimal percentage of the world's total trade and certainly could not have begun to cause the mischief attributed to it.

Donald W. Bedell searched the record exhaustively in 1983 and concluded that tariffs had been "miscast as the villain in bearing blame for the Great Depression."[4] In entering Bedell's findings in the *Congressional Record*, Sen. John Heinz of Pennsylvania expressed the hope that Bedell's detailed analysis might help the Congress "reflect a more sophisticated—and accurate—view of economic history."[5] It was probably a forlorn hope, but Senator Heinz should be given credit for trying. Indeed, he is one of the most knowledgeable members of Congress on trade and as chairman of the Senate Steel Caucus in the 1980s, John Heinz took the lead in obtaining at least one exception to the Reagan administration's free trade policy. Senator Heinz and his colleagues in both the Senate and House Steel Caucuses should be credited with saving what is left of our vital steel industry and the nearly four hundred thousand jobs that still depend on it.

Herbert Hoover, the consummate liberal who has come down to later generations in the distorted guise of a rock-ribbed conservative, has traditionally been identified with the 1929 Crash and the Depression that followed. No doubt he must take some of the responsibility, but he had been President only a little more than seven months when the market collapsed. If his Democratic opponent in the 1928 election, Governor Alfred E. Smith of New York, had been in the White House in October 1929 would Wall Street have borne up any better? We will never know.

Hoover did misread all the signposts pointing the way to the Crash. As Secretary of Commerce he was chairman of a committee that surveyed the national economic scene for more than a year from early 1928 to 1929. When it was done, the Hoover committee issued a call for "acceleration rather than structural change" in the economy.[6] This may explain why, as President, Herbert Hoover appeared so reluctant to put a damper on the speculative binge. After all, if one urges "acceleration," and then sees the economy speed up, there must be a certain hesitancy to slow it down.

As Secretary of the Treasury, Andrew Mellon was the man on the spot when the explosion came, though it is difficult to fathom how much he had to do with detonating it. He was in his ninth year at the helm of the Treasury and had been in that position during the 1921 debacle so he could hardly plead inexperience. In addition, he was an ex officio member of the Federal Reserve Board, though there is some question as to how much influence he exerted on the behind-the-scenes owners and directors of the Fed. Still, Mellon had been a successful banker in Pittsburgh for many years before going to Washington so he at least spoke the language of the Federal Reserve's satraps, even if he did not always necessarily understand what they were up to. If he must share some of the blame for the crash, Andrew Mellon should also be given a good deal of credit for the seven years of prosperity that preceded it.

Benjamin Strong, the governor of the New York Federal Reserve Bank, is the figure several economic historians have zeroed in on as the man primarily responsible for the big boom that led to the bigger bust. Strong died in 1928 so there is no way of knowing whether he would have permitted the speculative spiral to keep soaring in the fatal year 1929. But there can be no doubt that he acceded to the demands of the Bank of England, and the central banks of France and Germany, to lower the rediscount rate of the New York Federal Reserve Bank in 1925 and again in 1927. It was these two actions that allegedly ignited the insanity on Wall Street, though the inaction of the Fed in the first eight months of 1929 was the final torch that ultimately burned America's financial house almost to the ground.

Thibaut de Saint Phalle, in his 1985 book *The Federal Reserve: An Intentional Mystery*, tells how Benjamin Strong usurped power over the nation's money supply. "It was Strong and his colleagues," de Saint Phalle informs us, "who turned [the Federal Reserve] . . . into an active force as an instrument of monetary, and later regulatory, policy."[7] But it was not the whole Federal Reserve System, nor even the Board appointed by the President of the United States, that dominated this policy. As the same writer notes: "In effect the power of the Federal Reserve Board over the U.S. monetary system was not in the hands of the Federal Reserve Board in Washington but under the control of Governor Strong in New York."[8]

Benjamin Strong persuaded Andrew Mellon to form the Fed's Open Market Committee, which has effectively controlled the money supply ever since through its purchases, or sales, of government securities. The waspish Celt, John Kenneth Galbraith, pays tribute to Ben Strong as "the first American since Nicholas Biddle to make an important reputation as a central banker."[9] It was a mantle that could be assumed only by a manipulative man strongly opposed to everything America once stood for, most especially individual freedom.

And what of the man who was President during most of the 1920s? Calvin

Coolidge may have had sterling qualities besides his taciturnity, but what was needed in those years was another President cut out of the same fighting mold as Andrew Jackson to put Ben Strong, the 1920s Nicholas Biddle, in his proper place.

The search for villains after the Crash turned up some who had previously been regarded as heroes. Charles E. Mitchell, chairman of the National City Bank and the man who halted a sharp drop in the market early in 1929, was arrested on March 21, 1933, and charged with income tax evasion by an ambitious young U.S. district attorney in New York named Thomas E. Dewey. Mitchell was acquitted but the government later won a judgment against him for more than a million dollars in back taxes and penalties.[10]

Albert H. Wiggin, chairman of the Chase National Bank, was unmasked as one of the premier villains when it was discovered he had sold short some 42,500 shares of Chase stock beginning a full month before Black Thursday, thus making a personal contribution to the Crash. Using a "front" company, he had financed the deal with a $6.5 million loan from his own bank. Wiggin picked up more than $4 million in profits on this one transaction at a time when investors not plugged into Chase's inside information were losing their shirts. Yet Wiggin was kept on as Chase chairman for an additional three years and the bank's board, in gratitude for the splendid example he had set, voted him a lifetime salary of $100,000 per year upon his retirement.[11]

Richard Whitney, president of the New York Stock Exchange, was arrested in 1938, also at the behest of Tom Dewey. Actually, it appears he had done nothing more, nor less, than myriad other stockbrokers of his time. He had borrowed heavily to support stocks he had bought on a falling market. If the stocks had gone up, he would undoubtedly have paid the loans. But his investments turned sour, including a bad bet he made on applejack, alias "Jersey Lightning," being in demand after repeal of the 18th amendment. Whitney would have been much better off if he had bet on Scotch whiskey, as Joseph P. Kennedy had done. With the help of James Roosevelt, the President's son, Kennedy got the jump on repeal in 1933 by importing Haig and Haig and John Dewar's Scotch under "medicinal" import licenses "months before Prohibition officially ended."[12] While "Jersey Lightning" languished in sales, Scotch became the whiskey of choice in America.

Whitney made a full disclosure and escaped going to jail. But as Professor Galbraith noted, Richard Whitney was identified with the Stock Exchange, "the symbolic center of sin."[13] This, of course, was *after* 1929, the year in which the stock market descended into hell. Before that the New York Stock Exchange had been widely regarded as every man's stairway to heaven.

The hunt for the culprits who had caused the crash continued through much of the 1930s. J. P. Morgan, Jr., suffered the indignity of having a midget placed on his knee for photographic purposes at a congressional hearing. What *that* was supposed to symbolize was doubtful, but perhaps the joker who dreamed it up had in mind depicting Morgan as one of the big bankers who bounced little citizens around on his knee, making puppets of a whole population. If this is what was intended, it wasn't too far off the mark.

But it was Andrew W. Mellon who became the top target. Franklin Roosevelt personally singled out the former secretary of the treasury as Villain No. 1.[14] An attempt to persuade a grand jury to indict Mellon on criminal tax fraud charges failed, but FDR would not give up. As far back as 1926, Roosevelt had called Mellon "the master mind among the malefactors of great wealth" and as president he seemed determined to prove his earlier accusation no matter how little evidence there was to support it.

The Board of Tax Appeals, stacked with New Deal appointees, conducted hearings over a four-month period in Pittsburgh and Washington. This civil case was supposed to focus on Mellon's 1931 tax return, but it went into every facet of the former Treasury Secretary's affairs. The government's evidence at times centered on gifts Mellon had made to the A. W. Mellon Educational and Charitable Trust, gifts of some of the world's greatest paintings. Ironically, these same paintings were to form the nucleus for the most munificent gift any private citizen has ever given to the people of the United States—the National Gallery of Art in Washington. But the Board of Tax Appeals was not going to disappoint Roosevelt. It scraped up enough technicalities to force Mellon—or rather his estate, for by this time Andrew Mellon was dead—to pay $485,809 plus interest in the settlement that finally was arrived at,[15] a considerable cut from the tax deficiency of $3,000,000 originally claimed.

The IRS investigation of Andrew W. Mellon was more than a personal vendetta ordered by President Roosevelt. It was an attempt to place capitalism itself on trial—or at least that shrinking segment of capitalism that then felt some responsibility for maintaining the nation's historic policies of protection and sound money.

Andrew Mellon may have acquiesced in the easy money policy advocated by Benjamin Strong of the New York Federal Reserve Bank. But he stuck to his guns on trade and helped shepherd through the Congress the protectionist Trade Act of 1922 as well as the Smoot-Hawley law of 1930. Moreover, he ran the Treasury Department on a solid sound money basis, bringing in budget surpluses almost every year and managing to pay off a full third of the terrible debt from World War I. His was to be the very last stewardship of the Treasury that adhered to the principles upon which Alexander Hamilton had built the solid foundation that made America a success. After Andrew Mellon came the deluge that drowned the dollar in the ever-rising sea of deficits and debt that we are still floating on to this day.

Chapter 16.

Assassinating Gold

England's departure from gold was the beginning of the end of stability. The world of trade and trust was thenceforth to be as compartmented until it looked like an egg crate.

—Broadus Mitchell
in *Depression Decade*[1]

When Franklin Delano Roosevelt was nominated by the Democratic party for the presidency in the summer of 1932 he went straight to Magnolia, Massachusetts, to get his marching orders from the capitalist-cum-Marxist, Edward Mandell House, the man who had used Woodrow Wilson to execute the secret Revolution of 1913 and manipulate America into World War I. It is not known what those orders, probably couched as "polite suggestions," were but James McGregor Burns informs us that House had been "quietly pulling strings" for some time to get Roosevelt the nomination.[2]

The little "colonel" had also helped turn on the financial faucets for FDR's campaign. "Large donations came from (Herbert) Lehman, Henry Morgenthau, William H. Woodin, Joseph P. Kennedy, Robert W. Bingham, and a score of other financiers, merchants and industrialists," Burns reports.[3]

Although the generosity of these plutocrats surely helped grease Roosevelt's road to the White House, if they had run Mickey Mouse against Herbert Hoover in that Depression year Mickey would have been elected in a landslide. As it was Roosevelt won with 472 electoral votes from 42 of the then 48 states and he received nearly 23 million votes to less than 16 million for Hoover.

Burns tells us that "Roosevelt had no program to offer."[4] But he did have a slogan—the New Deal—and that sufficed, as slogans have in most presidential elections of this century.

During the campaign Roosevelt denounced the budget deficits Hoover had been running up for the last few years. "Let us have the courage to stop borrowing to meet continuing deficits," he declared. "Stop the deficits."[5]

Actually, Herbert Hoover did set the example for Roosevelt and all the other big spenders who have occupied the White House down to the present day. Contrary to later popular belief, Mr. Hoover did not sit still on the federal budget while the country went to hell in a hand basket after the 1929 crash. He began almost immediately to adopt what later became known as "Keynesian economics" by spending far more than the Treasury was taking in. Public works expenditures rose from $3.3 billion, or 3 percent of the GNP in 1929, to $4.6 billion—9 percent of the GNP—in 1932.[6] Construction was started on new federal buildings, hydroelectric dams, improvements to rivers and harbors, and a host of other projects. Federal grants to states for highways more than doubled and the Emergency Relief and Construction Act of July 1932 authorized the new Reconstruction Finance Corporation to make huge loans to states and municipalities.[7] (The loans were transformed into outright gifts by the Congress in 1934.)

Hoover also increased taxes in an effort to pay at least part of this vast cornucopia he had opened. But this didn't help much with the deficit. The economy was in such a depressed condition that few people had much income to pay taxes on. Industrial production declined some 40 percent between mid-1929 and the end of 1931 and it fell even further after that. Somewhere between ten and fifteen million Americans were unemployed—nearly one-third of the total work force. Nor was it only the workers and farmers who had been hard hit. Literally thousands of millionaires had been wiped out by the stock market's continuing fall. Capital had evaporated, and what little money there was left had gone into hiding. The Federal Reserve had lowered the rediscount rate to 1½ percent to lure it out, but no one wanted to take another chance on borrowing after the great bath of 1929.

The situation worsened in mid-1931 when a banking crisis swept Europe. It started in May of that year when the Kreditanstalt, Austria's largest bank, showed signs of going belly up. Kreditanstalt had borrowed heavily from England and the United States and when it was on the verge of collapse the Bank of England, other central banks, even the Rothschilds, and the Bank for International Settlements, came rushing to the rescue.[8] But the strain on the resources of the rescuers was too much. Germany, which had suffered through six years of heavy trade deficits under the free trade policy of its pseudo-socialist Weimar Republic, became the next European economy to go down in flames. Central Europe was collapsing and the reverberations were felt in the farthest corners of the earth.

The United States, generous as always, tried to shore up the crumbling edifice. On June 20, 1931, President Hoover proposed a year's moratorium on all war debts. But "France delayed for dangerous weeks" and the failure of the Durmstadter und Nationalbank in North Germany brought on a government-imposed bank holiday. This brought down banks in Rumania and Hungary, sent a shock through Holland to England and across the Atlantic where it hit the shores of the United States like a tidal wave.

On September 31, 1931, came the final blow. Prime Minister Ramsay MacDonald, undoubtedly dancing to the tune dictated by the central bankers at the "little old lady of Threadneedle Street," took England off the gold standard. A clotche of other countries followed. The result was a wholesale liquidation of European holdings in the United States and a run on American gold, which was soon drained to dangerous levels in the vaults of the Federal Reserve. All the herculean efforts to rouse the U.S. economy over the preceding two years now counted for nothing as the stock market slide picked up more speed downhill. The siphoning off of our monetary gold by Britain and the Europeans was the reason for the deepening of the Depression and the trade wars that followed—not the Smoot-Hawley Tariff Act of 1930.

The European banking crisis, and England's resultant withdrawal from gold, touched off another wave of bank failures in America. The situation went from bad to worse through 1932 and at the end of the year, when France, Belgium, and four other countries defaulted on their debt to the United States,[9] it was as if an earthquake had shattered the lofty temples of Wall Street.

Jesse Jones, the tall Texan President Hoover had hailed up to Washington to run the new Reconstruction Finance Corporation, claimed that the five thousand U.S. banks that folded in 1932 would have numbered seven thousand more if it had not been for the government loans made through the RFC.[10] But the RFC could not stem the run on gold and within ten days in late February and the first days of March 1933 $400 million in gold was withdrawn from the banks. By the time Franklin Roosevelt was inaugurated on March 4, 1933, seventeen states had declared bank holidays and on that same day New York and Illinois joined this despairing club. "That was the knockout blow," said Jesse Jones. All the other states slammed the doors of their banks shut. Jones reached into the sky for a metaphor to describe the new crisis: "The economic sun was in total eclipse all over the United States."[11]

In his inaugural address Franklin Roosevelt told the country that the "only thing we have to fear is fear itself." That was on Saturday. On Monday he declared a national bank holiday, which merely threw a federal cloak over a fait accompli. However, Roosevelt must have taken lessons from Houdini, the great escape artist. When he began the removal of the bank holiday cloak a week later, as if by magic the "economic sun" began to shine again. The big banks stood firm, though not on their own feet. The RFC came to the rescue of such exalted eyries of finance as Chase, National City, Guaranty Trust, and Continental Illinois. The RFC, Jesse Jones' "fifty billion dollar baby," bailed them out—not with loans, but with capital investment in their preferred stock which the Congress had approved when it became apparent loans would not suffice.

The frenetic weeks that followed Franklin Roosevelt's ascension to power transformed the financial face of America. On March 10, after only six days in office, he took the United States off the gold standard with an executive order prohibiting the export of gold coin, bullion, or certificates except under license issued by the Secretary of the Treasury.[12] The banks' foreign exchange transactions were severely restricted. Circulation of Federal Reserve bank notes were greatly increased and the Fed augmented the capital investments of the RFC by making direct loans to nonmember banks.

Three more executive orders issued in April tightened the embargo on gold shipments abroad and forbade ownership of gold by any individual or institution—except coin collectors and the Federal Reserve banks. Although the United States had not always in its history technically adhered to the world gold standard, these actions marked a radical departure from the past. Henceforth, America would be on a paper money standard, which is increasingly seen as no standard at all.

Roosevelt's executive orders were buttressed by the Emergency Banking Act, which gave the President authority to declare war on gold just one day before he acted. In June 1933 the Glass-Steagall Banking Reform Act thoroughly overhauled the nation's banking system, providing for limited insurance of bank deposits, divorcing commercial from investment banking, and stipulating closer regulation of national banks.[13]

In the terrible crisis that confronted the nation in March 1933 when Roosevelt took over, his revolutionary actions were probably justified. All commercial banks were already closed before he had finished his first day in office. The country was paralyzed and it needed the healthy injection of hope which FDR promptly administered. In his first fireside chat on national radio he laid it on the line:

"There is an element in the readjustment of our financial system more important than currency, more important than gold, and that is the confidence of the people. Confidence and courage are the essentials of success in carrying out our plan. You people must have faith; you must not be stampeded by rumors or guesses."[14]

With these words Roosevelt put his finger on the pulse of the nation and though he found it beating ever so faintly, it soon appeared to revive. Confidence and courage. Those are the essential elements that must undergird any economy, any society, any country. Confidence and courage and faith. Franklin Roosevelt gave all of these to his fellow citizens at a critical moment in their nation's history. But, alas, man cannot live by words alone. The deeds which followed spoke much louder, much more forcefully in the annals of America.

Chapter 17.

New Deal

Lenin was certainly right. There is no subtler, no surer means
of overturning the existing basis of society than to debauch the
currency. The process engages all the hidden forces of economic
law on the side of destruction and does it in a manner which
not one man in a million is able to diagnose.

—Lord Keynes[1]

By taking the United States off gold, Franklin Roosevelt had set a high-risk
course. It was followed by a deliberate devaluation of the dollar, the first in our
history. What the president hoped both these radical moves would do was pump
up inflation. Prices of almost everything, from commodities to the most highly
sophisticated manufactured products, were debilitatingly depressed. The price
levels kept the bankers and investors at bay, hoarding their cash or keeping it
in government bonds.

Prior to Roosevelt's 1933 executive orders, much of the country's money had
been frozen in gold. FDR thought that by thawing this golden iceberg, and
forcing it into paper money or securities, he could float the economy to higher
levels of productivity and employment. Unfortunately, it didn't work.

In June 1933 an international monetary conference opened in London to which
Roosevelt sent his Secretary of State, Cordell Hull. Like so many who have
occupied that important office, from Thomas Jefferson and Edmund Randolph
to Henry Kissinger and George Shultz, Mr. Hull had his own agenda, one that
was quite different from the President's, at least for the moment. Cordell Hull
was a Southerner cut out of the same free-trade cloth as Calhoun and he was a
thoroughgoing Wilsonian internationalist in the bargain. Thus, Hull went to

London to promote free trade and started immediately to lobby for tariff reduction.[2] Roosevelt, however, had no thought of reducing tariffs at this time and he sent Raymond Moley, an advisor then more in tune with White House thinking, to rein in Hull.

The European countries, some of which were still on gold, tried to persuade Moley to have the President join in a pledge to eventually restore the international gold standard. Even Britain was in favor of this, since it would cost nothing right away. But a caveat to the promise was that in the interim period each nation would do all in its power to limit currency speculation in foreign exchange.

Apparently seeing this as a threat to his attempt to inflate the dollar, FDR demurred. Characteristically, he gave the opposite reason for his refusal. "Let me be frank in saying that the United States seeks the kind of dollar which a generation hence will have the same purchasing and debt paying power as the dollar value we hope to attain in the near future," Roosevelt cabled. "That objective means more to the good of other nations than a fixed ratio for a month or two in terms of the pound or franc."[3]

These words of Roosevelt may have a hollow ring today, but it sounded good at the time, at least in the United States. In London it infuriated Ramsay MacDonald and it stunned the Europeans. As Studenski and Krooss observed, "The Roosevelt message gave the coup de grace to the International Monetary Conference and eliminated the last small hope of bringing order out of the international monetary disruption."[4]

Franklin Roosevelt was a mercurial man, and what he said one day didn't necessarily apply the next. James McGregor Burns believed he had "three or four different personalities."[5] This apparent multiple schizophrenia led him to conduct conflicting experiments in government. Thus, within a year of issuing the nationalistic manifesto that scuttled the monetary conference in London, the president warmly embraced internationalism in trade and monetary matters.

The Trade Agreements Act of 1934 put the United States back on the Wilson-House free trade track of 1913 by a more devious route enticingly labeled "reciprocal" trade, though the slogan was studiously avoided in the law itself. In June 1934 the bill sailed through the Congress, as almost everything Roosevelt asked for did at the time, and it set the United States irrevocably on the free trade course it has followed ever since, though once again a war intervened to delay the full impact, as it had two decades earlier.

With dubious constitutionality, this trade act gave the executive branch authority to enter into treaties—euphemistically called "agreements"—with other nations without the required "advise and consent" of the Senate. The legislation also permitted the president to raise or lower import duties by up to 50 percent, a power exclusively reserved for the Congress in Article I, Section 8 of the Constitution. Although the Congress had surrendered this prerogative to the executive in previous tariff laws, these precedents hardly made either the old or the new legislation constitutional.

Between 1934 and 1940, Studenski and Krooss count twenty-three "reciprocal'' trade agreements which the United States entered into with other countries. These twenty-three de facto treaties affected over a thousand reductions in the import duties stipulated by Smoot-Hawley.[6]

Senator George Malone of Nevada examined the results of the 1934 Trade Agreements Act nearly a quarter-century after its passage in a book titled *Mainline*. He identified a number of points where this law had failed in the promises explicitly made for it in the legislation itself,[7] in the congressional debates, and in the 1932 Democratic platform that set the stage for the new trade act. These failures are worth enumerating in light of the fact that their evils still live with us today:

1 Instead of producing more revenues for the Treasury, as promised, the tariff had produced less and less each year.
2 Instead of opening up foreign markets to our exports, the agreements permitted other countries to close them while the U.S. ''continued to open its markets to the goods which these others produced.''
3 ''The 'retaliatory action' for which the Smoot-Hawley tariff was blamed, became itself vastly multiplied'' by the reciprocal trade treaties.
4 ''The economic hostilities which the Act was claimed to palliate, became a sustained and all but invisible cold war.''
5 ''The international trade which had been [allegedly] 'destroyed' by the former tariff not only was not restored . . . it dwindled year by year, as the figures show.''
6 ''The Act was to remove the causes which had 'driven our factories into foreign countries';'' instead, it created ''conditions which encouraged American factories to move abroad. . . . ''
7 ''The [Smoot-Hawley] tariff, it was claimed, had 'robbed the American farmer of his foreign markets.' Where—after more than twenty years—are those markets now?''
8 The tariff had been accused of ''increasing the cost of production,'' but ''the very *theory* of the Trade Agreements Act . . . is inflationary per se.''
9 ''Conferences designed to 'restore' international trade became conferences at which such trade was 'restored' by giveaway programs financed by the taxpayers of the United States, and by moves which further opened the *American* market to others wares.''
10 ''Exchange was 'facilitated' by imposition, by other nations, of the greatest and most diversified restrictions upon *our* goods that the world of commerce had ever seen.''

To Senator Malone's post-mortem of the 1934 Trade Agreements Act could now be added a long list of other failures to live up to the promises made for this law and the subsequent acts that have descended from it. The 1934 legislation was one of the early manifestations of the shift of the Roosevelt administration's overall foreign policy into the murky realm of internationalism. Other actions damaging to America's sovereignty and well-being followed. It was preceded some months earlier by another action which was to prove equally fateful for this nation and for the world—United States recognition of the Union of Soviet Socialist Republics.

Tragically, President Roosevelt agreed to formally recognize the USSR at the very time when that country was deliberately starving millions of people to death in the Ukraine and other parts of the Communist realm. The state-sponsored famine was a well-kept secret, though Walter Duranty, Moscow correspondent of the New York *Times*, and other foreign newsmen in Russia, knew about it and simply withheld the information from the outside world. It was not the first case of Western journalists censoring their own dispatches to curry favor with the Soviets, nor would it be the last.

With the black veil of public ignorance draped over the terrible events taking place in the Soviet Union, Maxim Litvinov, the USSR's foreign minister, arrived in Washington on November 7, 1933—the sixteenth anniversary of the Bolshevik coup. His trip had been promoted by businessmen hoping to increase trade with Russia, among them James Mooney of General Motors and Thomas Morgan of Curtiss-Wright and Sperry Gyroscope. After Litvinov and Roosevelt signed the protocols at the White House in mid-November, the foreign minister went to New York. William Leuchtenberg tells us what transpired:

"At a farewell dinner for Litvinov at the Waldorf-Astoria, executives of the House of Morgan, the Pennsylvania Railroad, the Chase National Bank and other firms feted the Soviet emissary. Thomas Watson, president of International Business Machines, asked every American, in the interest of good relations, to 'refrain from making any criticism of the present form of Government adopted by Russia.' "[8]

And what of all the sugarplums—those visions of tremendous profits—which had these illustrious leaders of American finance and industry dancing so enthusiastically to the Bolshevik ballet? "The benefits did not materialize—there was no substantial increase in trade . . . ," Leuchtenberg writes.[9]

As for the political benefits, the Soviets had agreed to tone down their revolutionary propaganda in the United States. Instead, it was greatly increased. Nor did recognition by America restrain the Soviet in international relations. Three years later it was involved in the bloody civil war in Spain where Soviet officers directed the mass murders of thousands of civilians, including hundreds of nuns and priests. And in 1939, Stalin teamed up with Hitler to carve up Poland and start World War II.

In 1934 John Maynard Keynes journeyed to Washington to offer advice to President Roosevelt. In the past, Keynes had been all over the economic map, sounding like a protectionist one month, a free trader the next; a monetarist at any given moment; admitting the failure of monetarism in almost the next breath. At times Keynes appeared to embrace socialism. But he had gone to Russia and seen that socialism doesn't work, and he came home to England in a somewhat penitent mood.

Keynes was just concocting his magnum opus, *The General Theory of Money*, an elaborate economic model built upon the ideas of one of his young students at King's College, R. F. Kahn. The core of the theory was Kahn's "multiplier," which a biographer of Keynes succinctly describes as "the relationship between a change in investment and the alteration in the size of national income which that change caused.''[10] Keynes gave the example of a government spending £500 to employ one man for one year in public works and this small sum multiplying up, or down, through the economy as the £500 were spent, creating additional employment as it circulated. Keynes seized Kahn's multiplier to bolster his argument for greater budget deficits as a means of spending Britain out of its economic doldrums.

On his 1934 trip to the States, Keynes got a mixed reception. Roosevelt didn't know what the don was talking about and balked at what he called Keynes's "whole rigmarole of figures." Keynes, for his part, remarked after the meeting that he had "supposed the President was more literate, economically speaking."[11]

Keynes had more success in winning over some key people around Roosevelt— Harry Hopkins, Leon Henderson, and Lauchlin Currie at the White House, Harry Dexter White at Treasury, and Marriner Eccles, the chairman of the Federal Reserve Board.[12] By 1935 he had converted them all to his deficit spending theories, though Eccles, and perhaps some of the others, were already inclined in this dangerous direction.

However, it was two more years before Roosevelt fully embraced Keynes's recommendations, though his administration had been chalking up record peace-time budget deficits in its frantic efforts to spend the country out of the economic hole. Another stock market plunge on October 19, 1937, persuaded the President he had not been doing enough on the spending front, as Keynes had warned. For the next fiscal year he submitted a more imaginative budget, which included a big increase for public works, though ostensibly he continued to deplore the deficits he was fostering.[13]

The recession of 1937–38 should have convinced Roosevelt that something more than liberal spending was required to restore the nation's economy. But having dug the deficit hole deeper, he appeared unable to climb out of it. Moreover, his administration went flailing—and failing—off in other exotic directions as it kept reaching for the brass ring on the New Deal merry-go-round.

When they can't get things to work at home leaders of great nations have historically tended to seek solutions abroad. By 1936 Roosevelt had already staked out a more internationalist approach. In December of that year the United States signed the Tripartite Accord with Great Britain and France, which Studenski and Krooss found to be "shrouded in mystery."[14]

The Treasury issued one of its tranquilizer pills to deepen the mystery still further, saying the Accord pledged the three countries "to foster those conditions which safeguard peace and will best contribute to the restoration of order in international economic relations . . . [and] to avoid as far as possible any disturbance of the basis of international exchange." A free trade prayer was also offered, pledging the United States, Britain, and France "to relax progressively the present system of [import] quotas and exchange controls with a view to their abolition."[15]

A codicil to the Tripartite Accord arranged for each of the three nations to sell gold to the others at a price fixed on a twenty-four-hour basis. The American Stabilization Fund, which came out of all this, bought up pounds or francs or gold whenever the dollar rose in foreign exchange. But it did not hold onto foreign currencies for more than the twenty-four hours stipulated in the Accord, converting pounds and francs into gold every day.[16]

It remained for subsequent international agreements to find better ways to deal the United States out of dollars, but for the time being this proved an efficient way for foreigners to raid the Treasury. Every day the French and the British were free to juggle their currencies in a manner best suited to the trade and monetary conditions of that particular twenty-four hour period. In a later time the Japanese were to improve on the currency juggling act, but they must have learned a few turns from the profitable example set in Paris and London in the late 1930s.

Nonetheless, as has happened so many times, our nation's naiveté ultimately appeared to protect it. Someone has said that "Americans are like the drunk falling down stairs whom everyone thinks has just killed himself but is miraculously unhurt." This was certainly true in the instance of the Tripartite Accord.

The eventual effect of the currency juggling in Paris and London was that the United States got all the gold, albeit at prices that were temporarily advantageous to France and Britain. By the end of 1939, when the Accord came to an end, America had a virtual corner on the world's gold supply,[17] a situation that was to make the dollar truly almighty in international finance for the next quarter-century.

The Federal Reserve and the Treasury got more deeply into the gold game at the same time the Tripartite Accord was announced, if not unveiled. Gold acquisitions were "sterilized" by the Treasury by isolating them in an inactive account, and no new gold certificates could be issued against them. Further, new government bonds were sold to banks in amounts equal to net gold acquisitions.[18] This had the effect of increasing the national debt, and also the interest paid out by the Treasury, while giving the impression to the untutored eye that the dollar was getting stronger backing with gold. In the Treasury Department, since at least 1933, everything has been done with mirrors.

In spite of these moves, or perhaps because of them, the recession of 1937 ensued and forced the Treasury to cut back on its "sterilization" of gold. At this stage of the aging New Deal nothing seemed to work. Failure of the devaluation of the dollar was followed by the failure of the Federal Reserve to pump up inflation with low interest rates. Failure of deficit spending to restore the economy was followed by the failure of the international monetary moves. Those were followed by yet another failure of still larger deficits. And so it went. The Roosevelt administration went from one failure to the next.

Broadus Mitchell pronounced the judgement: "The New Deal failed . . . ," he wrote, "for at the end of six years of effort (in 1939) the nation still had some 10,000,000 unemployed."[19]

But the voters didn't seem to notice the failure. They kept electing Democratic

Congresses right through the thirties and in 1940 they reelected Franklin Roosevelt to an unprecedented third term. By then, however, the war in Europe was finally pulling America out of the Depression as we again delivered arms to the Allies on credit.

The New Deal proved costly. The national debt ballooned by billions and the dollar never again regained anything approaching its pre-Depression buying power. Federal expenditures in a single year (1935) were estimated to be some $1.5 billion more than the United States had spent in the first 124 years of its history up to the creation of the Federal Reserve and the beginning of the dismantling of the protective system.[20] The federal debt was $17.9 billion in 1930 and most of that sum represented the loans left over from World War I. By 1940 the debt was more than $53.1 billion, a $35.2 billion increase in a single decade and almost all of it derived from domestic welfare and public works as defense expenditures were cut to a minimum.[21]

Despite the many reciprocal trade agreements the United States had entered into after passage of the 1934 trade act, total trade still lagged far behind the levels of the 1920s. Exports in 1929 were over $5.2 billion; in 1939 they were under $3.2 billion. Imports followed much the same pattern: in 1929 they were just below $4.4 billion; in 1939 just over $2.3 billion.[22] Obviously, foreign trade had not recovered any more than the depressed domestic economy.

However, all this was about to change. The series of "little wars" that began with the Japanese invasion of Manchuria in 1931 and escalated with the Italian invasion of Ethiopia in 1935, the Spanish civil war in 1936, the Japanese attack on China in 1937, and the surrender of Czechoslovakia at Munich, culminated in September 1939 with the joint German-Soviet assault on Poland.

In July, at the President's behest, the Congress approved an extraordinary defense spending bill of $12 billion and by April of 1940 defense expenditures reached $35 billion, substantially more than the total the United States had spent on its defense forces in all of World War I. The New Deal was giving way to the new era of perpetual war in the name of peace.

Chapter 18.

Global War

Not since the dark days of the Revolution had the American people confronted so dire a military menace or so staggering a task as during the Second World War.[1]
        —Arthur S. Link in *American Epoch*

The outbreak of World War II in September 1939 rescued Franklin Roosevelt's failed New Deal from the condemnation of history and gave U.S. trade a sudden and vigorous lift. Leon Henderson, commissar of the all-powerful wartime Office of Price Administration, reported the war's initial side effects on the national economy:

"The impact upon American markets was immediate. Memories of the first World War—memories of insatiable demand, of shortages, of inflation—were rekindled and there was an immediate and sharp increase in buying. Prices rose precipitately, basic commodities and basic raw materials both jumping 25 percent in the single month of September. A speculative boom was on."[2]

The British and the French rushed in with orders for war matériel. Factories that had been in mothballs, or limping along at much reduced capacity, suddenly sprang to life. Employment went up at once, rising 10 percent within the first four months. Wages shot up even faster, with payrolls increasing 16 percent in the same period. The Federal Reserve index of industrial production stood at 106 percent of the 1935–39 average in August. At the end of December it hit 125.[3]

This initial spurt proved short-lived. As Europe settled into the euphoria of the "phony war" after Poland's collapse, the Allies believed they might get along without U.S. arms. They hung onto their pounds and francs and gold and

the boom in America sputtered out in the early spring of 1940. The Wehrmacht
and the Red Army appeared to be busy consolidating their division of Poland.
Soviet forces had met courageous resistance in Finland. On the Western front
all was quiet on both sides of the Maginot line. Then came Blitzkrieg.

On April 9 the Germans invaded Denmark and Norway. A month later, on
May 10, their armored divisions, attacking under cover of Stuka dive bombers,
slashed into Belgium, Holland, and Luxembourg. Within four days they had
pierced the French defenses near Sedan. By the end of May Italy administered
what Roosevelt called the "stab in the back" to France. On June 14, the German
armies marched into Paris as their Russian allies prepared to occupy the Baltic
states and move against Rumania.

The Neutrality Act, designed to prevent repetition of the Morgan Loan and
other conditions that led America into World War I, had been invoked soon after
the German-Soviet dissection of Poland. Other legislation forbade American
vessels from trading with belligerents and American citizens were prohibited
from traveling on ships of any nation at war.

With the fall of France, President Roosevelt waved aside the Neutrality Act
and stepped up arms shipments to beleaguered Britain. Politically, this was a
risky thing for FDR to do in the election year 1940. Antiwar sentiment was
running high in the country and although the majority of Americans favored aid
for England, particularly after the bombings of London and other cities began,
polls found that less than 10 percent wanted war with Germany.[4] Yet Roosevelt,
who was openly trying to help Britain against Germany, was elected over Wendell
Willkie for an unprecedented third term in November after pledging "again,
again and again: Your boys are not going to be sent into any foreign wars."[5]

In January 1941 the President asked Congress for legislation to ship supplies
"to those nations which are now in actual war with aggressor nations." Britain
was the only major power resisting aggression at this time and Britain was broke.
So Roosevelt proposed that instead of lending money to England so it could buy
American arms, the supplies be paid for at the end of the war in goods and
services.[6] Passage of the Lend-Lease Act two months later, according to historian
Arthur S. Link of Northwestern University, "converted the United States from
a friendly neutral . . . into a full-fledged nonbelligerent, committed to pour out
all its resources if need be to enable Britain to bring Germany to her knees."[7]

On November 17, 1941, a special Japanese envoy, Saburu Kurusu, came to
the White House carrying the torch of peace. While the warlords in Tokyo made
preparations to send the Japanese fleet against Hawaii, Mr. Kurusu and his
colleagues smiled and talked interminably in meetings with the president, the
secretary of state and other U.S. leaders. It was a performance that was to be
repeated time and again from the 1960s onward as the Japanese launched their
trade wars against the automobile, electronics, steel, and virtually all other
manufacturing industries in the United States. The crucial difference is that the
U.S. government defended the country in 1941; it surrendered in the trade wars
of our era.

On December 7, 1941, Japanese war planes descended out of a Sunday morning sky on the sleeping U.S. fleet at Pearl Harbor. When they completed the attack, 2,323 American sailors and soldiers were dead, hundreds more wounded, and our Pacific fleet destroyed. Eight battleships had been knocked out, along with three cruisers, as many destroyers, numerous aircraft, and military installations. It was a terrible defeat, but it galvanized the American people behind the president and the war effort.

Overnight the steel mills and auto factories, aircraft plants and shipyards— the whole mighty industrial base of the United States—swung into all-out action as our then vast merchant marine started carrying arms and munitions and supplies to distant battlefronts. For the next four years the nation was united in the tremendous task of defeating powerful enemies on two fronts half a world apart and of arming allies from the steppes of Soviet Russia to the African Sahara, from the gorges of China's Yangtze to England's Thames. No other nation could begin to tackle such a mammoth undertaking. No other nation had an industrial base that could begin to compare with America's.

THE ROAD TO BRETTON WOODS

Within a week after Pearl Harbor, the secretary of the treasury, Henry Morgenthau, Jr., instructed his assistant, Harry Dexter White, to plan for setting up an Inter-Allied Stabilization Fund in order ''to provide for a post-war international monetary stabilization arrangement; and to provide a post-war 'international currency.' ''[8]

Neither of these ideas was original with Morgenthau. Both had been kicking around monetary circles for some time and their foremost exponent was none other than John Maynard Keynes, who had influenced the deficit drift of the New Deal during the Depression years. Specifically, what Keynes wanted was a central world bank to finance the world economy he envisioned; a global clearing house to facilitate the fixing of the relative exchange values of national currencies in international trade, and the creation of a *quantum* of international currency called the ''bancor'' which would not behave in what Keynes regarded as the unpredictable and irrelevant manner of gold.[9]

Keynes and Harry Dexter White had become acquainted during the English economist's earlier sallies in Washington and soon after America's entry into the war they met again. Almost at once there was a divergence in their thinking. Probably White knew the Congress would never sit still for a global central bank, let alone a world currency that would put the dollar in the shade indefinitely. Moreover, White had some ideas of his own about trade and monetary matters, not to mention the cogent thoughts supplied him by his friends, whose connections reached into mysterious corners of the murky world of finance and intrigue.

While practically everyone else in the country bore down on winning the war, Harry Dexter White and his coterie focused on the shape of things to come— after the war. What became known as the ''White Plan'' for the Bretton Woods monetary conference began with a memorandum recommending a world bank modeled on the Reconstruction Finance Corporation, a quite different vision than Keynes' plan. Eventually, White's plan evolved into what was to become the present World Bank—alias the International Bank for Reconstruction and Development—and the International Monetary Fund.

The structuring of the IMF and the World Bank was a long and laborious process that occupied hundreds of people for most of the war years. By April 1943 the project had advanced sufficiently for drafts of both the Keynes and White plans for currency stabilization to be sent to thirty-seven countries that were invited to send technical experts to a conference in Washington.[10]

Ultimately, White won out. Keynes, and Great Britain, bowed to Harry Dexter White and the reality of America's predominant power. Keynes agreed to White's proposal for an International Monetary Fund, which incorporated some of his ideas for exchange stabilization, and he accepted White's World Bank, though it was a far cry from the world central bank he wanted.

The World Bank born at Bretton Woods had no authority to issue currency in the munificent manner of the Federal Reserve or the Bank of England. Its primary function was to make loans to countries for development, and for its first fifteen years the World Bank's chief concern was rebuilding Europe. Thereafter most of its attention, and its loans, focused on the Third World.

The International Monetary Fund, which became a suprabank dishing out loans to undeveloped countries, was primarily designed to stabilize foreign exchange. At Bretton Woods, most of the world's major currencies were pegged to the dollar, which in turn was pegged to gold at a fixed price of $35 per ounce. In short, the dollar was to provide paper cover for an ersatz gold standard, albeit a frozen one.

The United States, alone among all IMF member nations, was pledged to buy or sell gold within the narrow range of one-fourth of one percent of the $35 fix.[11] Thus, if a country gained a surplus of dollars in international trade, American aid, or ways more devious, all it had to do was turn them in to the U.S. Treasury and cart off our gold.

At the time the Bretton Woods Agreement was signed, in the summer of 1944, the United States owned at least 70 percent of the world's known monetary gold. The temptations the IMF arrangement offered foreign countries were obvious, but Congress was persuaded to place its trust in the integrity of our trading partners. Who could believe they would ever carry off America's gold? With such naiveté Americans have delivered their gold, their jobs, their industries—the very security of their nation—to the assumed goodwill of others who, quite naturally, put their own self-interest first.

After the war the big raids on Fort Knox by foreign central banks were temporarily postponed because the exigencies of rebuilding Europe depended upon America's largesse, not only our willingness to deliver—gratis—food, fuel and factories, but also to keep open our doors to foreign imports. There were, nonetheless, a series of almost invisible heists of our gold via the Bretton Woods fix. By the late 1950s a third of America's gold had vanished offshore. It was easy, even during the postwar period of large U.S. trade surpluses, for central banks to get our gold since a large part of the foreign aid we doled out was in dollars. It was no great trick to exchange aid dollars for gold at the bargain basement price of $35 an ounce. In short, we actually *paid* other countries to take our gold.

Chapter 19.

Bretton Woods

There can have been few international meetings in the history
of such convocations where public comprehension of what was
occurring or even what was being attempted was so slight.
—John Kenneth Galbraith
on the Bretton Woods Conference[1]

The world often perceives things in a quite different way than they actually are,
and this was the case with the Bretton Woods agreement. For the most part,
people in America, or at least those who knew or read about the monetary
arrangement, thought it a good thing for the country since it firmly established
the dollar as transcendent in world trade and exchange.

There were a few exceptions. Some in the Congress, most cogently Sen.
Robert A. Taft of Ohio, had grave doubts about the International Monetary Fund
and the World Bank. But the influential news media was for it, along with
economists and the academy. The same people were also in favor of the Dum-
barton Oaks arrangement that was preparing the way for the United Nations.
And, most important, the Roosevelt and Truman administrations went flat out
to win congressional approval for both the Bretton Woods treaty and the Dum-
barton Oaks concoction.

In Britain, however, there were deep suspicions that at Bretton Woods the
pound sterling would be sold down the Thames for a mess of porridge consisting
of an indigestible mixture of American dollars tied to all that gold the Yanks
had stored in Fort Knox. In May 1944, John Maynard Keynes addressed the
House of Lords to reassure his countrymen that the British pound would not be
sacrificed on the altar of American gold at the forthcoming conference in New
Hampshire.

"The external value of sterling shall conform to its internal value as set by our own domestic policies, and not the other way around," Keynes vowed.[2] Then, in an impassioned plea for the Lords approval of the agreement he had worked out with Harry Dexter White, Keynes ascended to rhetorical heights reached by few others even in that golden age of empty promises.

"Was it not I," Keynes asked the Lords, "when many of today's iconoclasts were still worshippers of the Calf, who wrote that 'Gold is a barbarous relic'? Am I so faithless, so forgetful, so senile that at the very moment of the triumph of these ideas when, with gathering momentum, governments, parliaments, banks, the press, the public, and even economists, have at last accepted the new doctrines, I go off to help forge new chains to hold us fast in the old dungeon? I trust, my Lords, that you will not believe it.[3]

Two months after selling his compromise with Harry Dexter White to the House of Lords, Keynes checked into the old resort hotel at Bretton Woods in the White Mountains of New Hampshire. He and the more than seven-hundred other delegates from forty-four countries had at last assembled for the United Nations Monetary and Financial Conference to sprinkle their blessing on the plan that was, in its most important essentials, the product of the fertile imagination of Harry Dexter White and his mysterious friends.

One of the primary stated objectives of the conference was to "reduce obstacles to international trade" and to bring about "the harmonization of national policies of member states."[4] More than harmonization, the actual goal was *homogenization* of all nations into the One World state conceived by Marx, promoted by men of influence like Edward Mandell House, and, of course, financed by the capitalist system, most especially by America.

The treaty that came out of the three weeks of meetings at Bretton Woods in July 1944 acknowledged the dominance of the United States in the postwar trade and monetary world while at the same time charting the course for America's ultimate decline. Everything possible was done to accommodate other nations at the expense of America. And the principal vehicle for the undoing of our financial structure, as well as the dismantling, over time, of our then unsurpassed industrial base, was to be Harry Dexter White's brain child, the International Monetary Fund.

All IMF member nations were to contribute to the Fund on the Marxist principle of "from each according to his means, to each according to his needs." Since the United States was the only major nation with any substantial means in 1944, the results of the IMF plan were predictable. For openers, the United States was tapped for the lion's share of the IMF capitalization. Britain, broke as it was, got assessed the next largest "quota."

Contributions to the IMF were supposed to total nearly $9 billion initially, with one third of each contribution in gold. But the United States had more than two-thirds of the world's monetary gold in 1944 so it was only natural that the other countries should feel no compunctions about chiseling on their gold quotas, as many of them did. But there was an additional, and even more effective, way for the other IMF members to wage war on the dollar while they skewered our industries and workers with their subsidized exports to America. Two-thirds of each contribution our trading partners made to the International Monetary Fund could be made in their own highly inflated currency—*at the official rate of exchange*.

Anyone with even the most cursory knowledge or experience with foreign exchange knows that, with few exceptions, there are always at least two rates of exchange: the official rate and the real rate available on the black market. The disparities between official rates and the real rates of exchange can be very wide. In China in 1945–49 the real, or black market, rate reached as much as 100 times the official exchange.

Thus, the IMF arrangement, from its very beginning, was designed to put the United States and its dollar at a terrible disadvantage. America got taken both coming and going. We imported goods at official rates of exchange, thereby enhancing the opportunities for dumping in our market; and we exported at the same official rate when our products were actually worth much more in the countries they were shipped to. Of course, this gave rise to myriad private arrangements between importers and exporters in which some allowances were made for the disparity in exchange rates. Nonetheless, when the time came for nations to square their current accounts through the IMF "stabilization" process the official rates prevailed and the dollar almost always took a beating.

Another dodge was an escape clause in Article XIV of the Bretton Woods treaty that permitted member nations to shelter themselves under restrictions until they deemed their economies strong enough to adhere fully to the IMF rules. As a result European countries avoided complete currency convertibility until 1961 and the Japanese remained protected by the Article XIV umbrella as late as 1964.[5] Almost all less developed countries are under it to this day.

Actually, few nations other than the United States have ever observed the IMF convertibility rules entirely. They continue to rig their currencies to give their subsidized industries every advantage over the dollar. Japanese juggling of the yen, kept artificially rigged against the dollar for decades, served the dual purpose of keeping imports out of Japan while making it easy for Japanese exporters to penetrate the American and European markets with goods sold at prices that bore little relationship to the "fair market value" prevailing in Japan. In fact, this was a prime reason for Japan's great success in world trade.

The final nail in the coffin of America's future status as a trading nation was a point Keynes had hammered home in his grandiloquent speech to the House of Lords. Under the Bretton Woods treaty, the IMF was given the power to proclaim a particular nation's currency "scarce" whenever it was much in demand because of persistent trade surpluses. At that juncture, the "lucky" nation's trading partners could, with impunity, impose exchange restrictions and import restraints against the "scarce currency" nation's products.[6]

It was readily foreseeable in 1944 that for many years to come the United

States would stand virtually alone among major trading countries as a "scarce currency" nation—and that was the way it worked out for the next quarter-century until America's own chronic trade deficits began to appear in the early 1970s. The IMF gave other nations the perfect cover to bar their doors to American exports while enjoying free access to the much larger, more lucrative U.S. market.

The price America initially paid for digging its own trade grave at Bretton Woods—the side deals made with Britain and the others to bring them into the IMF fold—was astronomical. As a start, there was a $3.75 billion loan for England engineered by Keynes with interest set at 2 percent. (The greater portion of the much larger lend-lease to Britain was simply wiped off the books.) In *The Age of Keynes*, Robert Lekachman observed that "many Englishmen judged [the loan] an ungenerous act."[7] In spite of this ingratitude (which I do not believe represented the majority view), the United States was to add exponentially to its gift-loans to Britain, virtually financing the socialist Labor government of Clement Attlee in its sweeping nationalization of British industries just after the war.

The Bretton Woods conference adjourned on July 21, 1944, the day after a group of anti-Nazi Germans tried to blow up Adolph Hitler. At the final dinner in the New Hampshire hotel where the world's monetary future was sealed for the next quarter-century and beyond, John Maynard Keynes made a late entrance. "Spontaneously everyone in the room stood up in complete silence while he made his way to his chair. It was an unspoken moving tribute to the master, the true prophet of this gathering."[8]

Keynes may have been the prophet of Bretton Woods. But the treaty itself was the work of another man. Howard M. Wachtel correctly identified the real architect of Bretton Woods in his 1986 book, *The Money Mandarins*: "The IMF," Wachtel said, "was Harry Dexter White's great achievement."[9]

Unfortunately, most economic historians lightly pass over the highly culpable background of Harry Dexter White. Yet this is central to an understanding of the treaty that came out of Bretton Woods and of the monetary system under which the United States surrendered most of its gold and a substantial part of its strategic industrial base.

White was named by two confessed couriers for the Soviets— Whitaker Chambers and Helen Bentley—as among the covert agents who delivered classified U.S. government documents to them.[10] There was substantial evidence that he was "handled" by Jacob Golos, the same spymaster who managed the Rosenbergs and the atomic espionage ring.[11] And the Federal Bureau of Investigation "identified White's involvement in the Communist apparatus from more than thirty sources."[12]

White played a key role in the conquest of China by the Communist forces of Mao Tse-tung by delaying shipment of U.S. gold to Nationalist China to stabilize its currency.[13] Runaway inflation undermined confidence in the Kuomintang government and contributed mightily to the Communist victory.

We need be reminded that the loss of China led directly to both the Korean and Vietnam Wars with their combined casualties of 112,267 Americans killed and 256,587 wounded.[14] Further, it is estimated that as many as sixty-two million Chinese lost their lives during Mao's long and bloody rule, and several millions more died—and are still dying—in Vietnam, Laos and Cambodia. In the context of the human suffering he helped cause, Harry Dexter White's "accomplishment" in this one operation alone proved highly profitable to the Communists.

Edgar Ansel Mowrer, in his memoir *Triumph and Turmoil*, tells what happened when the Soviets took Berlin: "What they had not stolen they had bought with U.S. occupation marks, the plates for printing which had generously been handed them by Harry White of the U.S. Treasury."[15] It is said to have cost the American taxpayers at least one million dollars a day for our occupation forces to buy up the Russian counterfeit marks made from the plates White gave them.

White did everything in his power to deliver all of Germany to the Communists and he was the real author of the "Morgenthau Plan." In his original memo to Secretary of the Treasury Morgenthau, White recommended postwar Germany should be divided up among Russia, Poland, France, and Denmark and what remained should be stripped of all industry and reduced to a "goat pasture."[16]

What was to be done with the Germans who couldn't make a living after the country's industry was dismantled? The late Carroll Quigley of Georgetown University in his magnum opus, *Tragedy and Hope: A History of the World in Our Time*, said "the millions of surplus population [would] be, if necessary, deported to Africa."[17]

Morgenthau actually sold White's plan for the dismemberment of Germany to President Roosevelt and important provisions from it found their way into the Yalta agreement that delivered Eastern Europe to the Soviets. Whole provinces of Germany were given to Communist Poland so Russia could more comfortably push its own western borders further into Poland. Even after Roosevelt died in April 1945 and Harry Truman became President, American and British forces occupying West Germany with the French were ordered to let the Russians dismantle German factories and ship them by rail to the USSR.

White also tried to engineer a $10 billion loan for the USSR and in March 1943 he attempted to help the Soviets in a different way. At a hearing of the House Banking and Currency Committee on a monetary stabilization bill the Treasury proposed, Hugh Scott, later Republican leader of the Senate, bluntly told White, "This bill would give the Russians a veto over any devaluation, in fact over any change in the value of any other nation's currency."[18] White tried to dissemble, but Scott refused to let him off the hook. "The Treasury plan was thereafter quietly abandoned," Hugh Scott recalled. "No record of this hearing remains in the files of the House Committee."[19]

After the Bretton Woods treaty was approved by the Senate, Harry Dexter White was named by President Truman in 1946 to be Executive Director of the U.S. Mission to the International Monetary Fund. He left abruptly in early 1947 when disclosures of Soviet infiltration of the U.S. government came to light. This was long before Senator Joseph McCarthy came to prominence.

On August 13, 1948 White was summoned before the House Un-American

Activities Committee. He denied almost everything, of course. But he left Washington within hours after the hearing and traveled to his farm at Fitzwilliam Depot in New Hampshire. There he reportedly died of a heart attack a few days later.

Harry Dexter White's "accomplishments" for the Soviet Union lived long after him. Indeed, they are still with us. Surveying the nation's industrial landscape today, much of it demolished by foreign competition financed by our taxpayers via the World Bank and the International Monetary Fund, the question might be posed as to whether Mr. White envisioned a "Morgenthau Plan" for America when he was sculpting the Bretton Woods Treaty.

Chapter 20.

The New Age

There seems to be no inherent obstacle to the gradual advance
of Socialism in the United States through a series of "New Deals."
—Arthur M. Schlesinger,
"The Future of Socialism."
Partisan Review, 1947[1]

With the end of World War II, the One World lobby—many of its members
secret socialists, not a few covert communists, but the majority simply innocent
lambs led to the fleecing—began to see the unfolding of their most fantastic
dreams, though not necessarily in ways originally envisioned.

The atomic bomb had created a climate of fear and an atmosphere of foreboding
which changed the psychology of the world. Yalta and the Red Army had sealed
the fate of Poland and Central Europe for at least a generation. Harry Dexter
White and his cohorts had put America's gold, as well as our trade markets, up
for grabs at Bretton Woods. A large slice of U.S. sovereignty had been turned
over to the United Nations at the founding meeting in San Francisco with Alger
Hiss appropriately presiding as secretary general. Now the task before the glob-
alist coalition was to shift large supplies of U.S. capital, including our then
incomparable industrial base, out from under the American people and into the
insatiable maw of a voracious world.

Hardly anyone paused to add up the costs of the war years. Of the more than
16,000,000 Americans who had served in the armed forces, 1,078,162 had been
reported on the casualty lists, no less than 407,316 of them dead. Millions more
had been uprooted from their family homes and scattered about the country to
labor in defense plants, with great disruption to their lives—so great indeed that

to many the disruption was permanent. The human costs of the war were incalculable and must appear remote, if not unreal, to today's generation.

The financial costs of the war were still being paid by U.S. taxpayers four decades after it ended, and the mountainous debt it piled up cut deeply into the real income of the people. Between July 1, 1940, and June 30, 1946, the federal government spent a total of $387 billion, some 95 percent of it for the war effort.[2] Although taxes soared into the economic stratosphere, the Treasury relied heavily on loans. Indeed, 40 percent of the money came from the banks—twice the percentage of World War I.[3] Interest rates were kept very low during the war, but interest is still being paid on the war loans and will be for many years to come. As Studenski and Krooss noted, "the already close alliance between the Treasury and the Federal Reserve System was cemented more firmly" by the war.[4]

Customs duties, which had paid so much of the costs of previous wars, sank to insignificance during World War II, accounting for less than half of one percent of the Treasury's revenues in most of the war years. Instead, as already noted, the burden was shifted to taxes and bank loans. The national debt, which stood at $43 billion in 1940, multiplied more than six times to $270 billion on June 30, 1946.[5] Indeed, the U.S. had spent almost as much on lend-lease alone in the half-dozen years of World War II as the total accumulated national debt acquired in the entire preceding century and a half of the Republic.

The debt was, moreover, a sharp two-edged sword. Not only did it cut a large and lasting hole in taxpayers pocketbooks, it put the United States on the dangerous road of high inflation where, with a few temporary pauses, it has remained ever since. Unfortunately, there was little attempt to pay off the debt, as the U.S. had hastened to do after all its prior wars. In fact, the post–World War II debt reduction program lasted only two fiscal years—1947 and 1948—and nipped only $17 billion from the $270 billion owed. After that America was increasingly committed to carrying the dual load of foreign aid and Cold War defense costs. Debt retirement became a forgotten issue and the taxpayer meekly acquiesced in shoveling out money for the eternal interest due the banks and other lenders as the value of the dollar declined, first at home and later abroad.

Actually, the total global costs of World War II were beyond counting. Even estimates of the dead vary widely, ranging from twenty million fatalities to the World Almanac's calculation that "some forty-five million people lost their lives in the war."[6] C. Hartley Grattan, writing in Harper's Magazine in 1949, placed the financial cost of the six years of hostilities, including all the vast destruction of whole cities, and even countries, at four trillion dollars.[7] But a year later the U.S. secretary of the army, Gordon Gray, said the ultimate cost of modern war was about four times the direct and immediate cost. Extrapolating from that multiple, William Henry Chamberlin estimated "the ultimate cost of the second World War as some sixteen trillion dollars."[8] This did not, of course, take into account the subsequent costs to the West for defending itself for decades against the threat posed by what Winston Churchill called "the bringing of Asia to the Elbe."[9]

Tragically, the United States, with the very best of intentions, helped fasten the iron grip of "Asia" on Central and Eastern Europe. Nearly $3 billion in American aid was distributed in Poland, Czechoslovakia, Hungary, and the other countries of this region through the United Nations Relief and Rehabilitation Agency (UNRRA). Unfortunately, the first administrator of UNRRA, Herbert H. Lehman, governor and later U.S. senator from New York, "allowed himself to be persuaded to distribute (the UNRRA) relief through the *de facto* Soviet-controlled governments in the conquered European countries," according to Eugene W. Castle in his book on foreign aid, *The Great Giveaway*[10].

The U.S. army became more broadly involved in postwar relief efforts through the Armed Services Civilian Supply Program which dispensed more than $6 billion in emergency aid funds in West Germany and Japan between 1945 and 1951.[11] Hundreds of millions more dollars flowed to France, Italy, and Austria under a similar but separate aid program designed to help former enemies as well as allies recover from the ravages of the war.[12]

All of these were designed as temporary measures and they proved to be only warmups for the really big aid efforts that followed, efforts that have become embedded in the U.S. annual budget process and which the recipients now look upon as "entitlements." The first program in this category resulted from the Truman Doctrine announced by the President on March 12, 1947 to defend Greece and Turkey from communism. Over the four decades since these two countries have received more than $20 billion in aid from the United States. Yet even this ambitious program paled by comparison with the Marshall Plan unveiled three months later at the Harvard commencement by Gen. George C. Marshall, the Secretary of State. A little background may help clarify how and, more importantly, why, the Marshall Plan came about.

In July of 1945 the British electorate, in perhaps the most perverse action ever taken by a people in a democratic government, voted out of office the man who had led them successfully through the blazing fire of war to victory. Winston Churchill was retired as prime minister and replaced by Clement Attlee, a Fabian socialist and leader of the Labour Party.

Although it owed billions of pounds to the United States, as well as substantial sums to Canada and its other dominions, England embarked on the excruciatingly expensive program of nationalizing its major industries and transforming the government into a cradle-to-grave welfare state. The British taxpayers, to this day laboring under the crushing burden placed upon them by the socialist Labour government of the postwar period, could not, of course, pay for this incalculably costly binge entirely. Thus, the American taxpayer had to pick up a substantial portion of the bar bill.

First came the huge U.S. loan of $3.75 billion engineered by Maynard Keynes in his final raid on the U.S. Treasury and the wiping out of some $20 billion in

lend-lease owed us. But by mid–1947, barely a year after Congress had approved
the loan, all but a fraction of it had been used up in the socialist spending spree.
An alibi was quickly concocted, blaming Britain's embarrassment on U.S. demands for convertibility of the pound, which was hard-pressed because the loan
had enabled England to import needed machinery and other goods from America
on too fast a track for the decimated British economy.[13] More funds were urgently
needed for Labour's costly experiments.

The Marshall Plan was then devised to bail out not only Britain but the socialist
economies of France, Italy and the rest of Europe as well. The Soviet Union
and its satellites were included in the original munificent offer, made by Secretary
of State George Marshall in his speech at Harvard in June of 1947. But Josef
Stalin, in perhaps the most stupid decision he ever made, turned it down.

Over the next five years the Congress committed $17 billion in Marshall Plan
aid[14] and there is no denying that it went a long way toward reviving the shattered
economies of the United Kingdom and Western Europe. However, it also contributed substantially to the strengthening of socialism in European countries,
thereby enabling them to subsidize their industries and penetrate the American
market on a large scale for the first time since the dumping campaigns that
followed in the wake of World War I.

Quite obviously, the English and the Europeans could not have afforded their
expensive experiments in nationalizing their industries without the help of American taxpayers, many of whom were soon to lose their jobs to subsidized exports
from Europe. Additionally, the Marshall Plan, and all the other foreign aid
programs constructed upon that model, greatly accelerated the movement of U.S.
industries to foreign countries. Indeed, the Marshall Plan spawned the age of
the multinational corporations in which we now live.

In terms of the cost to the American taxpayer, the tab has been astronomical.
The House Foreign Operations Subcommittee on Appropriations added up the
bill in 1971 after a quarter-century of foreign aid and found that the net dis-
bursements to other nations then totaled $138,446,200,000. Moreover, the net
interest paid on what the Treasury borrowed to disburse those billions was
$74,434,597,000, bringing the grand total to $212,880,797,000. In 1990 the
total is more than twice that amount and by the end of the century, if the present
pace of foreign aid is sustained, it will total at least $1 trillion. That is almost
exactly the figure of the Bush administration's entire budget request for FY 1990
and, separately, the estimated debt the U.S. will owe to foreign countries some
time in the early 1990s. The national debt, which is something else again, is
already approaching the $3 trillion mark.

Still, no one in Washington seriously asks whether America can *afford* to
continue its foreign aid and loan giveaways. It is obvious that question—and
the payments on the principal and interest borrowed to dole out the largesse—
will be left to future generations, who will undoubtedly decide that their ancestors
of the present day were addlepated spendthrifts.

Chapter 21.

Forging the GATT

The [GATT] Agreement and the Charter [of the International Trade Organization] are predominantly the products of United States initiative and leadership in the cause of general trade barrier reduction.[1]

—William Adams Brown, Jr., in
*The United States and the
Restoration of World Trade*

On March 24, 1948 fifty-three countries represented at the United Nations Conference on Trade and Employment held in Havana signed a charter which was to have brought into being a UN agency to be known as the International Trade Organization. Although the ITO never got into orbit, primarily because a skeptical U.S. Congress withheld its consent, the Havana Conference nonetheless spun off a satellite that was to eventually carry on most of the work originally assigned the ITO. This satellite, which has since became a powerful arbiter of international trade disputes, is known as the GATT, alias the General Agreement on Tariffs and Trade, headquartered in Geneva.

The way was cleared for creation of the GATT in the 1945 extension of the reciprocal Trade Act of 1934. The extension, which went well beyond the 1934 measure in delivering yet more congressional control over trade to the executive branch, was passed by a confused and befuddled House and Senate in the wake of the death of the bill's principle sponsor, Franklin Roosevelt. It was a time when the Congress was trying its level best to cooperate with the new President, Harry Truman, as he grappled with the terrible problems of the postwar world.

Senator Robert Taft of Ohio led a well-reasoned, rearguard battle against the new trade act and at one point he was joined by an eloquent Democrat, Sen. Joseph O'Mahoney of Wyoming, who saw through all the blarney to the heart of the matter. Allen Drury, in his revealing book, *A Senate Journal: 1943–1945*, wrote of the high drama on the Senate floor on June 12, 1945 when O'Mahoney clashed with his party's leadership, directing his remarks at Walter George of Georgia. How, wrote Drury, paraphrasing O'Mahoney's remarks, could the senator from Georgia "contemplate without concern in an age of creeping totalitarianism the abject surrender of Congressional control over tariffs? Everywhere . . . the governments of free men are at bay. A great step will be taken toward totalitarianism," O'Mahoney warned, "if Congressional review of tariff reduction is not restored."[2] Drury, then a correspondent for United Press, observed that "the Senate sat in rapt silence as two of its giants tangled head-on."[3] But in the end the leadership had its way. O'Mahoney and Taft were outnumbered: the vote in the Senate was 54 to 21 for the act. The Congress, once again ignoring the Constitution, had handed the president more of its clearly stipulated power to govern trade.

Even more important, and barely perceived at the time, except by Senators Taft, O'Mahoney, and a few others, the Congress was helping transfer yet another piece of the nation's sovereignty to an international organization, this time to the GATT. Slowly but inexorably, over the years since the Havana Conference, the GATT organization in Geneva has increased its jurisdiction over American trade.

It is obvious that most other countries ignore, or find ways around, the GATT's strictures concerning *their* trade. Certainly they have had little noticeable effect upon Japan and the Pacific Rim countries. But the United States religiously adheres to the dictates of the trade gnomes in Geneva as it surrenders more and more of our home market and export trade rights to a foreign bureaucracy that sits in judgment upon trade disputes in an area still plainly reserved for the Congress by the Constitution of the United States.

Erich Roll admiringly states in his book, *The World After Keynes*, that the GATT continues to "exercise a favourable effect in promoting the oneness of the international economy."[4] It does so, however, on the basis of actions that are clearly unconstitutional.

Senator Malone pointed out that after approval of the International Trade Organization had been blocked in the Congress its Siamese twin—the GATT—was brought into being by "executive proclamation."[5] Thus, the familiar maneuver of an end run around the Constitution was supplemented by yet another around the Congress. George Malone put the proper name on the GATT. It was, he said, "our economic Yalta."[6]

Although Congress did not formally approve the GATT, it has appropriated funds for U.S. participation in this multinational monstrosity for almost four decades. In the early stages, the Truman administration was hampered in its efforts to internationalize our trade policy entirely because the Congress prevented our entrance into the ITO. But even the Republican eightieth Congress empowered the president to negotiate tariff reductions under the GATT.

The first Republican House and Senate since the Hoover era passed the Trade Agreements Extension Act of 1948, thereby revealing that both major political parties were merging in support of free trade. The Republican Party had been the protector of American jobs and industries since its first presidential standard bearer, Abraham Lincoln, took office in 1861. Now, however, it was demonstrating an unseemly willingness to compromise.

The Grand Old Party did tie some strings to the Trade Act of 1948. It took the Tariff Commission out from under the heavy thumb of the executive branch with several actions built into the new law. It severed the commission from the GATT negotiating process, forbade the commissioners to participate directly in policy making within the executive, and barred commission staff members from voting on proposals under consideration by interagency groups. The Congress also transferred the influential Committee for Reciprocity Information from the Tariff Commission to the Department of Commerce.[7]

Most promising, the Republican Congress established the peril point process intended to give American industry and workers some measure of protection against the trade giveaways the executive's bureaucrats were designing under the GATT. The 1948 Act ordered the president to submit to the Tariff Commission a list of all articles the administration planned to negotiate on in future international trade talks. The commission, in turn, was directed to study each article and notify the president within 120 days what limit must be placed on any trade concession without causing or threatening serious injury to the domestic industry producing the same article. This was the peril point. It reversed the "escape clause" procedure built into previous acts which required that U.S. industries prove injury first before higher tariffs or import restrictions could be made.[8] In other words, the patient had to show he was on his deathbed before any medicine could be prescribed. The peril point attempted to at least permit a diagnosis before sending our industries and jobs to the morgue.

However, the election of 1948 brought the Democrats back into control of both houses of the Congress and another Trade Agreements Extension Act in 1949 repealed the peril point procedure. It also put the Tariff Commission's staff back into the executive's pocket, and granted the president two more years to try again on the ITO, beef up the GATT, and trade away what tattered remnants were left of the traditional American protective system.

Unfettered once again from the "archaic" constitutional restraints limiting the executive's authority over trade, the Truman administration went all out. It took part in the third round of the GATT negotiations at Torquay in England and, without peril points to inhibit it, the U.S. negotiating team very nearly gave away the store. Fortunately, the Europeans were so intent upon building the ITO temple in such a way that they would have maximum control over all the trade-money-changing that the march toward the New World Order was temporarily slowed. During this lull the Congress, in 1951, managed to restore the peril point and the U.S. negotiators were restrained from agreeing to tariff cuts below those established by the Tariff Commission as the points of no return for American industry.[9] However, the 1951 Trade Act left the escape clause intact for cases brought by domestic companies and workers seeking relief from imports and it remains in effect to this day.

Although the International Trade Organization never got off the drawing board as a result of the changes and delays Congress threw in its path during the Truman years, the GATT began to rise, phoenix-like, from the ashes of the ITO. What we have today is an International Trade Organization masquerading under the guise of the GATT, which has assumed virtually all the functions planned for the ITO.

Chapter 22.

Cold War/Hot War

If freedom is to survive, it is essential that neither the U.S.A. nor the Soviet Union win . . . we must realize that a victory for either side would be a defeat for socialism.

—R. H. S. Crossman,
Labour Member of Parliament, in
New Fabian Essays[1]

The Cold War that suddenly turned hot when the Communist armies invaded South Korea on June 25, 1950, greatly stimulated U.S. trade with the rest of the world and escalated the growth of the federal government's fiscal budgets, launching them on the trajectory that has seen them explode from under $50 billion per annum to over the trillion-dollar mark less then forty years later, a multiple on the magnitude of twenty times in one generation.

Indeed, by January 1953 when Harry S. Truman left office, six months before the end of the Korean War, he had spent approximately twice as much in eight years as had all the Presidents of the United States combined from 1789 down to 1940.[2] The miracle is that the value of the dollar has not evaporated entirely in the years since.

The Korean War had its origins at Teheran and Yalta during World War II. In those momentous Big Three conferences Franklin Roosevelt, with a reluctant Winston Churchill acquiescing, urged Josef Stalin to enter the war against Japan and take over Manchuria, although it was obvious at Yalta that the American forces, with British Commonwealth support, had already defeated the Japanese. The ultimate surrender of Japan was only a matter of time, and this was apparent long before the atomic bomb was ready for its devastating work.

The Soviets waited until Japan signaled surrender before taking over Manchuria and immediately they began to arm the Communist Chinese with supplies seized from the Japanese armies. The Nationalist Chinese were soon being whiplashed by Chou En-lai's well-armed Communist forces and by the runaway inflation induced, or at least exacerbated, by the machinations of Harry Dexter White in undermining their currency.

The U.S. Commander of the China theater of operations at war's end, Gen. Albert C. Wedemeyer, repeatedly warned of the dangers inherent in U.S. insistence upon Chiang Kai-shek's collaborating with Mao Tse-tung.[3] This policy was to be the prototype for U.S. dealings with many countries under siege by Communist insurgents. General Wedemeyer explained it cogently:

We had rendered confusion worse confounded by making our aid and support conditional on the establishment of a Chinese Government deemed to be democratic by both ourselves and the Communists,'' he wrote. ''Since the Communist view of what constitutes democracy is diametrically opposed to that of the free world, we had impaled the Chinese on the horns of an insoluble dilemma.[4]

Had General Wedemeyer's warnings been heeded, China could have been saved the terrible bloodbath its people underwent under Mao, a quarter-century of terror in which many millions of people died. Moreover, if the Communists had not captured China, America would have been spared the prolonged agonies of the Korean and Vietnam wars.

There are those who believe, with much evidence on their side, that although the seeds of the Korean War were obviously planted before the loss of China to the Communists, the invitation for the attack across the thirty-eighth Parallel was issued to the Soviets in Berlin. Beginning early in 1948 the Soviets began a series of escalating probes against the Western Allies' access routes to Berlin. Meeting no real resistance, the Soviets began the full-scale land-route blockade of Berlin on June 24, 1948. This was just days after the new German currency was issued to supersede the occupation marks the Russians had been using for three years thanks to Harry Dexter White, who had delivered the engraving plates to them from the U.S. Mint.

An Allied task force was hastily formed under Maj. Gen. Arthur G. Trudeau, commander of the First U.S. Constabulary Brigade, and dispatched to the Elbe to await the order to cross and exercise the legitimate agreed-upon rights of the Western Allies to maintain access to Berlin. Tragically, the order never came.[5] Clement Attlee, the British Labour prime minister, and his fellow socialists in charge of the French government, persuaded President Truman to adopt the alternative option of the Berlin airlift to avoid direct confrontation with Stalin's Red Army. The hard probability is that there would have been no confrontation. The United States and Britain still had a monopoly on atomic weapons and Stalin knew that war with the West would have been suicide for the Soviets at this juncture.

The press played the successful supply operation as a victory for the West, but Stalin interpreted it as additional evidence that the United States and its allies were bent upon appeasement. Robert Murphy, the State Department's chief representative in Germany at the time, later wrote that "the Berlin blockade . . . caused Soviet leaders to downgrade United States determination and capability, and led, I believe, to the subsequent Communist provocation in Korea."[6]

With Soviet tanks spearheading their advance the North Koreans struck and two days later President Truman decided to commit U.S. forces in support of the UN action condemning the Communist aggression. American troops rushed in from Japan and managed to hold the Pusan perimeter in the southeast corner of Korea through the summer until Gen. Douglas MacArthur had sprung his amphibious end run around the Communist lines with the surprise landing at Inchon. Truman then approved the drive north as our forces quickly mopped up in the south.

What happened after this is still the subject of debate. The critical conference of the Korean War was held on November 6, 1950. Three days earlier MacArthur had warned that the Chinese had fifty-six divisions—498,000 men—massed above the Yalu River. He informed Washington that he was ordering Air Force Gen. George E. Stratemeyer to unleash his B-29s against the Yalu bridges.

President Truman at once summoned his advisors to Blair House to ponder MacArthur's order. Left to his own devices, Harry S. Truman probably would have let the order stand. But in his memoirs, *Years of Trial and Hope*, Truman tells why he revoked it:

Assistant Secretary of State Dean Rusk pointed out that we had a commitment with the British not to take action which might involve attacks on the Manchurian side of the river without consultation with them.[7]

Truman told his Joint Chiefs of Staff to convey to MacArthur "what Dean Rusk had set forth." MacArthur was ordered, in a dispatch signed by Secretary of Defense Marshall, "to postpone all bombing of targets within five miles of the Manchurian border."[8]

MacArthur protested vigorously. He later wrote that he was on the verge of asking to be relieved of his command. He stayed only because he feared his army "might become demoralized and destroyed" if he departed.[9]

On November 26, 1950, more than two hundred thousand Chinese Communists swarmed down across the Yalu and descended on the American forces strung out along two lines in North Korea. A half-million more were to follow, dealing the United States its worst military defeat in history. Despite this, the Americans and South Koreans, with token help from a handful of other UN members, fought the Chinese hordes to a standstill. By March the Allies had regained the initiative. At this point, Truman decided to negotiate a truce. MacArthur opposed his president's decision, pointing out that the Communists were now on the run. Instead of begging for a truce, he urged that the United

States issue an ultimatum to the Communists to leave South Korea or risk destruction. On April 11, Truman removed MacArthur from all his Far East commands.

America suffered 157,530 casualties in Korea, including 54,246 dead. Three-fifths of these casualties were suffered *after* MacArthur's recall and the start of the two-year truce talks at Panmunjom.[10]

Both trade and domestic production increased sharply during the Korean War. Imports shot up from well under $10 billion in the year before the war to nearly $17 billion in 1953. Imports in 1939 were only about $3 billion, so the increase was almost six times the pre-World War II level.[11]

Exports also rose, though foreign aid purchases in the United States accounted for much of this since exports actually paid for by other countries, following an initial big run-up after 1949, remained fairly steady from 1951 through 1953. In one sense, America was already running a trade deficit during these war years because imports exceeded paid-for exports, as distinguished from the aid giveaways financed by our taxpayers, in three out of the four calendar years between 1950 and 1953.[12] In short, our trade surpluses were becoming an illusion created by the tax funds Americans were shoveling out for foreign aid programs.

Inflation soared during the early part of the Korean conflict. At President Truman's request, Congress passed the National Defense Production Act granting the administration broad powers to control the economy. The new law went into effect on September 9, 1950, and Truman clamped a lid on consumer installment credit ten days later. When this failed to slow inflation appreciably the president declared a state of emergency in mid-December and imposed price rollbacks on automobiles and at the same time froze wages in the auto industry and extended rent controls. The inflation rate dropped to 4 percent in the last eleven months of 1951, less than one-third the annual rate in the last half of 1950.[13]

The controls probably did not have as much effect upon the inflation rate as Truman's draconian tax policy. The President was determined to put war costs on a pay-as-you-go basis and in some cases taxes exceeded those of World War II. Three separate tax laws were enacted during the Korean War and income taxes rose as high as 92 percent for individuals and 52 percent for corporations with a hefty excess profits tax that hiked the effective rate on some corporations up to 80 percent,[14] plus excise taxes on many items which took an additional bite out of consumers' pocketbooks.

There were, however, some salutary results from Truman's tough tax policy. In addition to combating inflation, the rate of borrowing by the government was reduced to about half that of World War II. Moreover, the federal deficits were kept fairly low, totaling less than $18 billion for the three years of the Korean War. Government expenditures rose from $47.5 billion in FY 1951 to $64.7 billion in 1953, with all of that increase due to defense spending which more than doubled during those same years from $22 billion to over $50 billion.[15] By contrast with Lyndon Johnson's profligate "guns and butter" policy during the Vietnam War, Truman cut back non-defense spending severely.

John Snyder, the secretary of the Treasury, was a prudent man by comparison with most of his successors and, with Truman's backing, he tried to keep interest rates low so the government would not have to pay exorbitant costs for the necessary borrowing. This led to a bitter struggle between the Truman administration and the Federal Reserve, which wanted to increase interest rates, ostensibly to fight inflation. Since Truman and Snyder were already doing all they could do through fiscal policy to hold down prices, the Federal Reserve's monetary moves appeared self-serving for they could only increase the earnings of the shareholder banks that own the Fed.

Rates on Treasury bonds had been kept low during and after World War II, and when the Federal Reserve threatened to increase the interest on long-term government bonds to 2 1/2 percent in late 1950 the president and Secretary Snyder opposed it. Truman was "scathingly denounced"[16] in the press for having the temerity to oppose the invisible moneylenders in the Fed's sacrosanct temple, and a lengthy struggle ensued.

Ultimately, Truman compromised and the Treasury and the Federal Reserve entered into an "accord" on March 4, 1951, which the sages of Wall Street and the media hailed as a great victory for monetarism. The Fed did make some concessions to the President, although it came out the clear winner, as it almost always does in any dispute with the elected representatives of the people. After continuing large purchases of government bonds for a few months to save the president's face, the Federal Reserve sharply reduced its level of buying after June 1951 with the result, according to Studenski and Krooss, that "discounts and advances in 1951 reached the highest levels since 1928 and in 1952 they were higher than at any time since World War I."[17]

Thus, the Fed got its way. Interest rates rose after the compromise of March 1950, went through the 2 1/2 percent barrier set by the Treasury as the limit on long-term borrowings, and eventually ended the era of low rates that had enabled the United States to finance hot-and-cold-war spending but which also enabled millions of Americans to buy homes at reasonable mortgage rates, automobiles and appliances at low interest, and aided the post-war expansion of industry.

Chapter 23.

The Golden Age

Our British friends must wonder what change has softened up
the descendants of their original American colonists who fought
so fiercely against a tax of a penny a pound on tea and their
restrictions on our export and import shipping.[1]
—Willard F. Rockwell,
Founder of Rockwell International

When Gen. Dwight D. Eisenhower was elected president in his landslide 1952
victory over the Democratic Party's Adlai E. Stevenson III, the voters obviously
hoped for a substantive change in the political direction the country had been
launched upon since Franklin Roosevelt's ascent to power two decades earlier.
What they got was something less than they had wished. Nonetheless, the Eisenhower years are looked upon as the great Golden Age of America, the cul-
mination of nearly two centuries of strenuous effort by this nation to bring the
good life to the broadest possible range of the population.

President Eisenhower's first popular move was to end the Korean War, if not
with a victory, at least on terms viewed as acceptable by the American people.
He later admitted that the only way he got the Communists to agree to the truce
was to threaten them with nuclear destruction. That U.S. forces had successfully
tested a devastating hydrogen bomb at Eniwetok Atoll just days before his election
undoubtedly lent additional weight to the threat. This and the fact that Eisenhower
had been the victorious World War II Allied commander in Europe obviously
gave the Chinese and North Koreans—and their Soviet sponsors—serious second
thoughts about prolonging the peace negotiations at Panmunjom. They took what
they could conveniently get, or already had, and called it quits.

The trade, monetary, and fiscal policies forged by twenty years of Democratic Party rule were continued almost without alteration during the Republican administrations of Dwight Eisenhower. Initially, Ike and his Secretary of the Treasury, George Humphrey of Ohio, did trim the last federal budget Harry Truman had submitted to the Congress. But when the first of three relatively mild Eisenhower era recessions loomed in late 1953, they quickly reversed themselves. Frightened by the prospect that the first Republican President in two decades might become the reincarnation of Herbert Hoover, Secretary Humphrey reportedly told Arthur Burns, the chairman of the president's Council of Economic Advisors, "We must not let this happen; you must tell us what to do."[2]

Burns, a Columbia University professor and director of research for the National Bureau of Economic Research, soon became the dominant influence in shaping fiscal policy. As Edward S. Flash, Jr., was to write, "Burns enjoyed full rapport with the President."[3] Later to become chairman of the Federal Reserve Board in the Nixon-Ford administration, Arthur Burns drafted the Eisenhower 1954 *Economic Report* and greatly influenced the new federal budget.

Although he had been thought to be anti-Keynesian, Burns surrounded himself with New Dealers and he persuaded the President to increase federal spending. Expenditures for housing, highways, and other federal programs went up by the billions and defense spending was maintained at very high levels. All thought of reducing the federal debt was abandoned after only one year of a small debt retirement. Personal income taxes had been cut earlier in the Eisenhower administration. The corporate excess profits tax and some excise levies were eliminated. But Social Security taxes were increased, though not enough to offset the revenue losses from the tax cuts and deficit spending naturally followed. The ghost of Lord Keynes could sit back in quiet satisfaction that his theories would be as diligently pursued by the Republicans as they had been by the Democrats.

Trade flourished in the wake of the Korean armistice, the initial slump in defense-related shipments being more than offset by the new sense of confidence felt throughout what was then called the Free World. America's power was thought to be invincible, despite the nagging fact it had settled for something less than victory in Korea. The non-Communist nations may not have felt entirely safe and secure, but people believed they had a capable protector in the United States, which had more than made up for the failure of most of the other United Nations to fully join in halting Communist aggression in Korea. Although the public was largely unaware, the United States was soon involved in Indochina, where it quietly began financing the French forces against the Viet Minh.

The Korean War had hardly slowed America's surging nondefense industries, and in some cases had brought them to new heights. By keeping defense spending high, the government provided a base for continued high production and employment, as well as the critical research and development that kept the country on the cutting edge of new technology. Still, the growth was in a wide variety of industries and not all of it was related to spinoffs from defense. This growth initially increased U.S. exports as the foreign demand for American products rose worldwide.

Television manufacturing led the way in generating the capital for the boom in consumer electronics and by 1960 there were some twenty-five domestic companies producing TV sets. Other firms shared in the bonanza, including furniture makers who turned out television cabinets, and glass producers making the "envelopes" containing TV screens. By the beginning of the 1950s electronics, which included radios, record players and tape recorders, in addition to TV receivers, was already a two-and-a-half-billion-dollar business and by the end of the decade that figure promised to double.

Air transport came into its own, spawning a huge network of terminals serving virtually every city and town of any size in the country. By 1952 there were thirty-five scheduled airlines employing close to one hundred-thousand people and carrying nearly thirty-million passengers over domestic and overseas routes totalling more than 188,000 miles. Moreover, the airlines were hauling over a quarter-billion ton-miles of freight each year in the early 1950s and this impressive total increased almost every year.[4]

The chemical industry and its versatile offspring, plastics, added a dazzling array of new products to domestic and world markets. At the beginning of the Eisenhower years chemical and related businesses employed well over seven hundred thousand workers and contributed more than $8 billion in the value added to their products through manufacturing.[5]

Appliances that every woman wanted for her home became far more widely available and affordable. This was due to the lower prices at which American manufacturers were able to profitably sell these products because of the dramatic reduction in costs they enjoyed through the economies of scale provided by increased production. Most of these appliances ran on electric power supplied by the private power industry at rates that remained relatively stable throughout the decade of the fifties. More and more homes were heated with natural gas and there were already more than three hundred thousand miles of gas pipelines snaking beneath the soil of America and well over a billion dollars a year was being spent on new lines.[6]

Automobile and truck production soared during this decade, approaching ten million cars and other vehicles annually. When Eisenhower took office in 1953 there were nearly sixty million licensed vehicles on the roads. When he stepped out of the White House in 1961 the number had shot up to almost eighty million[7] and many families owned two or more cars. Once again, prices had stayed relatively even because of the lower manufacturing costs associated with heightened domestic production.

The oil industry, spurred by the increases in automotive vehicles, chemicals and electric power, expanded exponentially. Nationwide more than 120,000 service stations and garages employing over 5 hundred thousand people sold petroleum products valued at well over $8 billion at the dawn of the Eisenhower era.[8] Eight years later all of these impressive figures had grown remarkably. But increasingly the crude oil was coming from abroad—from the Mideast, Africa, and South America, where the huge American oil companies, which now considered themselves "multinational," were investing billions of dollars in pumping oil out of deserts, jungles, and the floors of oceans.

Undergirding all of America's booming industrial superstructure was our gigantic and innovative steel industry. Domestic steel production soared past 100 million tons per annum during the Korean War, supplying not only the nation's critical defense needs, but the burgeoning consumer demand as well.

Steel made possible the construction of thousands of new factories, of hundreds of thousands of miles of highways, of countless office buildings, schools, shopping malls, hotels, motels, airline terminals, research facilities, power plants, university dormitories, and a host of other structures. New specialty steels brought on the Jet Age with lighter heat-resistant engines, helped put man into space, developed new surgical instruments and amazing medical machines, paved the way for deeper and more efficient drilling of oil and gas, and ushered in computers with new superconductor metals.

More than 650,000 people were employed in the steel mills of Pittsburgh, Chicago, Birmingham, Detroit, and dozens of other communities in the 1950s. Indeed, it was steel that made these cities and forged them into industrial centers. For every one production job in basic steel, the Labor Department estimates that one and a half more jobs are created. That meant some 1,625,000 people employed, directly or indirectly, by the American steel industry during the 1950s.

In 1988 the average employment in this most basic of all industries was a little over 160,000, with only 120,000 production workers, a record low.[9] Thus, the number of jobs dependent upon steel has dwindled to barely 400,000. No less than 1,225,000 of America's most productive and best-paying industrial jobs had simply disappeared, most of them wiped out by illegal imports from mills owned or subsidized by foreign governments, mills often built with American investment or foreign aid, though not under the restraint of U.S. environmental requirements.

The prodigious expansion of steel and other industries in the 1950s gave Americans the highest standard of living that any generation of people has ever enjoyed on this planet. The material accomplishments, which contributed immensely to a psychological sense of well-being, were achieved through domestic production, not trade. In fact, trade contributed very little to the gross national product. Imports accounted for just a little more than 3 percent of the GNP in the earlier part of the decade and rose only fractionally toward its end. [10] Exports as a percentage of GNP were 3.6 percent in 1950 and 4.1 percent ten years later.

Meanwhile, the GNP, which had been $347 billion in 1952 when Eisenhower was elected, rose steadily to well over $500 billion by 1960.[11] Since the value of the dollar remained relatively constant, this probably represented more real per capita economic growth than the nation has achieved in any decade since, given the inflation that has afflicted the country for the past thirty years. (I include the Reagan era in this. Inflation rates were obviously doctored in the 1980s and even before, as were trade and other government statistics.)

Amidst the general euphoria that prevailed in America during the Eisenhower era, deep and lasting social and political changes were taking place and these were often more visible than the economic changes—particularly those attributable to international trade, which, so far as the public was then concerned, were practically nonexistent.

On the domestic scene, the civil rights movement was beginning to stir. The Supreme Court, in *Brown v. Board of Education* (1954), ruled that a black girl should not have to walk or be driven past her neighborhood school to attend a school with members of her own race in another part of town. The same court later turned around 180 degrees and in a series of other rulings it held that children, white or black, must be bused out of their neighborhoods to achieve racial integration. Meanwhile, President Eisenhower ordered U.S. Army troops in September 1957 to enforce a federal court order for integration of Central High School in Little Rock, Arkansas.

Labor unrest also marred the Eisenhower era, though strikes were less violent than in earlier times. In 1959, however, a 116-day steel strike, the longest in the nation's history, had a depressing effect upon the whole economy and it opened the door wide to the invasion of subsidized steel from abroad. In their 1982 book, *America's Competitive Edge*, Congressman Richard Bolling of Missouri and investment banker John Bowles tell what happened during the prolonged steel strike: "Imports increased to 4.4 million tons, exports dropped to 1.7 million, and steel trade went permanently into a deficit," they wrote.[12]

The McCarthy-Army controversy occupied interminable hours of television time and established the tremendous power of this new media. It ended with a clear defeat for the senator from Wisconsin who had taken the lead from previous congressional critics of subversion in the government. The convictions of twenty-seven leaders of the Communist Party in two separate trials in New York and Los Angeles on charges of plotting to overthrow the government by force, the executions of the Rosenbergs for atomic espionage, Alger Hiss's imprisonment, the indictment of Owen Lattimore in the Amerasia affair, the lifting of J. Robert Oppenheimer's security clearance, and numerous other cases related to the struggle between the United States and the Soviet Union—all of these were suddenly erased from the public consciousness by Joseph McCarthy's fall. Internal security became, overnight, a dead issue.

In the world arena, the United States retreat, begun in Korea, was marked by our failure to act in the Hungarian Revolution of 1956 after openly encouraging the captive nations to rise up against their Soviet oppressors. The battle for Hungary was doomed by the Suez crisis that broke just as the freedom fighters won control of Budapest. The Israeli invasion of the Sinai, and the joint British-French attack on Egypt, provided the media smokescreen behind which the Soviet tanks moved back into Hungary.

An even more dangerous defeat was in store for the United States three years later when Fidel Castro rode triumphantly into Havana after the U.S. Department of State cut off arms supplies to the Cuban government of Fulgengio Batista. The Soviets had now established a base on Cuba, not only for their submarines and missiles, but for export of the Communist revolution to Central and South America.

In the realm of modern weaponry, the United States fared better. The atomic submarine *Nautilus* was launched in 1954 and by 1960 Capt. Edward L. Beach skippered the USS *Triton* around the world entirely underwater, a feat that would have been impossible without its atomic engines. The Soviet's surprise orbiting of *Sputnik* in the fall of 1957 was quickly matched, and soon surpassed, by American accomplishments in space, beginning with the launching of the first U.S. satellite from Cape Canaveral in January 1958. What few people knew was that the United States could have beaten the USSR into space by two years had the army team at Redstone Arsenal been given the green light in time.

The death of Josef Stalin soon after Dwight Eisenhower's first inauguration in 1953 at first seemed to promise a new era in U.S.-Soviet relations, particularly when the Korean truce was signed in June of that year. But before Ike left office eight years later the obstreperous Nikita Khrushchev was banging his shoe on the podium of the United Nations in New York after shouting at Vice President Richard Nixon in the famous Moscow "Kitchen Debate" of 1959. The U-2 incident, in which the Soviets shot down a high-flying American spy plane, gave Khrushchev an excuse to cancel a summit meeting with Eisenhower in 1960. Many of the hopes of 1953 had died away eight years later.

If the Republican and Democratic parties were merging on foreign policy issues during the Eisenhower administrations, the homogenization was even deeper, if less apparent, in the related realm of international trade and monetary affairs. The mistake citizens most often make in trying to differentiate between the two major parties is to focus on the rhetoric rather than the reality. To grasp the latter they should focus on the people placed in nonelective offices of the executive branch, who often possess more power in the day-to-day operation of the government than the Congress does in forging our laws.

We have already noted the influence exerted by Arthur Burns on President Eisenhower. But there were others during this period who bear mention. The Dulles brothers, John Foster and Allen, controlled—or so they thought—the State Department and the Central Intelligence Agency. Actually, it would be more accurate to say that both brothers were controlled by the people under them. One in the State Department who quietly influenced trade policy as well as the more visible events connected with foreign affairs was Douglas Dillon, undersecretary of state.

Toward the end of Eisenhower's tenure, Dillon took an active part in U.S. trade actions. In fact, the GATT negotiations at Geneva in 1960–62 came to be known as the "Dillon Round." It was a round in which many more American industries and jobs got knocked out of the ring. During the Dillon Round the President "authorized tariff reductions below the peril point on several commodities in order to obtain desirable concessions, particularly from the Common Market,'' according to an official report of the U.S. International Trade Commission.[13]

Dillon, one of those nominal Republicans who believe in blending into the woodwork of both parties, was a Wall Street investment banker and the son of the founder of Dillon Reed, a firm that has impartially placed its partners in high government positions under both Democrats and Republicans. Indeed, Douglas Dillon himself slid over from the State Department at the end of the Eisenhower era and into the office of Secretary of the Treasury under John F. Kennedy. Martin Mayer in *The Fate of the Dollar* writes that Kennedy asked Douglas Dillon to be Secretary of the Treasury because, Dillon said, it would give public credence to his determination to stabilize the dollar. ''The shock of the gold market was the only reason I came in,'' Dillon added.[14]

It was a shock that was to have a lasting effect upon U.S. trade and monetary affairs. Indeed, the shock was more like an earthquake, or at least a tremor, that disclosed the gaping cracks in the wall of gold that supposedly had guarded the soundness of the dollar.

Chapter 24.

Out with the Gold

The year 1958 was a watershed. In that year, for the first time, dollars held by foreigners exceeded the value of the U.S. gold stock in Fort Knox.

—Howard M. Wachtel in
The Money Mandarins[1]

It is a measure of the perspicacity of the Keynesian economists who infested our government and other institutions that virtually none of them displayed any concern whatever about the gaping cracks in the nation's gold vaults that were apparent in the early 1950s. Although the United States appeared to register large trade surpluses throughout this decade, the balance of payments was titled heavily against us in all but one of those ten years. This was due to the ongoing foreign aid programs and to large and steady increases in American capital investment abroad coming on top of the steady upswing in imports. Indeed, between 1951 and the end of December 1961 the U.S. balance of payments had gone in the red to the tune of an aggregate $18 billion, a horrendous sum for those relatively innocent times.

On June 18, 1957 the Secretary of the Treasury, George Humphrey, testified before the Senate Finance Committee and rather reluctantly admitted that the nation's monetary gold supply was already down to $22.4 billion. What had happened to the approximately $8 billion more reportedly on hand at the end of World War II? It had simply melted away as the foreign countries quietly called it in with the sight drafts we had so charitably given them in the form of aid, investments, and our open-door policy for imports.

Up until this point the economists had assumed the gold in Fort Knox was completely safe. No one dreamed our friends would be so brash as to present their drafts at the Treasury's window, though if they had looked a bit closer in 1953 they would have discovered that $1 billion in gold had gone out in that one year alone. Five years later, however, our trading partners began to get really serious about calling in the gold at the bargain price of $35 an ounce.

In 1958 $3 billion in gold was hauled out of the United States, mostly to central banks in Europe, but some to private gold markets in London, Hong Kong, Beirut, Macao, and Tangier. "By 1959," Studenski and Krooss tell us, "something very much like panic had replaced the previous feeling of indifference in the nation's financial centers. How to stop the gold flow had become the most crucial problem in the minds of many economic, monetary and fiscal experts."[2]

As in the Reagan years the federal budget deficits were blamed for everything. These were said to have created uneasiness abroad about the reliability of the United States and its dollar. For FY 1958 the budget had been increased $5 billion to $72 billion, a budget that the chairman of the Senate Finance Committee, Harry F. Byrd of Virginia, called "a luxury budget on a global basis."[3]

No doubt the ballooning federal budget was a factor in the outflow of gold. Deficits are bound to force down the value of any currency over time, and the dollar is not exempt from this ancient law. But there was a more fundamental reason for the gold outflow. This was that the Europeans, and others, knew a good thing when they saw it and U.S. gold at $35 an ounce was a good thing indeed. Our foreign friends held reams of paper giving them claims on our gold under the Bretton Woods Treaty. Gold had risen as high as $46 on some of the private exchanges and on the black market in India it was over $100 an ounce.

France led the first great raid on America's gold. Charles de Gaulle had staged his dramatic comeback in mid-1958 and was installed as premier on June 1. France then forged a new constitution and de Gaulle became president of the Fifth Republic in December. He executed a draconian devaluation and introduced the "new franc." The French wanted their new currency to be backed by as much gold as possible. They held all those dollars they had picked up via exports to the U.S., the old Marshall Plan aid, and investments American corporations were showering upon France. All they had to do was turn them in to the U.S. Treasury and cart off the gold.

Only a decade earlier the Federal Reserve Board had boasted its "financial strength and authority" was so great it could offset, at will, "the credit and monetary effects of any likely movements of gold."[4] In the late 1950s, the Fed's boast sounded arrogant and empty as the French accelerated the exodus of gold from the United States.

Unfortunately, the belated embarrassment of the Fed could not save the American jobs and industries that had already been offered up on the One World altar constructed at Bretton Woods from the murky malarkey cooked up during the Wilsonian Revolution of 1913 and during Roosevelt's New Deal.

Senator George Malone took a partial inventory of the damage done during the 1950s to U.S. industries by imports encouraged by the free trade policies now advocated by both political parties and came up with some disturbing case histories. The U.S. Department of Labor listed, in May 1955, no less than 156 "distressed areas" with high unemployment, 119 more than in 1953.[5] As Senator Malone pointed out in his book, *Mainline*, much of this unemployment was due to the steadily rising tide of imports.

Textiles, still shifting from their historic home in New England to the lower-wage states of the South, now found competition coming from the Orient, particularly from Japan. Twenty communities where textile manufacturing was the predominant industry wound up on the distressed areas list and five others, where textile plants were the second most important employers, were also designated as distressed.

The manufacture of machinery was already one of the industries hardest hit by imports and Senator Malone noted that high jobless rates, "reflecting injury caused by competitive imports from abroad, has brought distress to 19 areas and contributed to distress in nine others."[6]

Mining was another of the chief victims of free trade. Gold, manganese, tungsten, and fluorspar were all affected. Senator Malone pointed out that "in 1955, ninety percent of the zinc and lead miners in the United States were walking the streets, unemployed."[7] What had happened to them is a classic case of the surrealism engendered by our aid-and-trade policies.

"The United States provided Britain with funds with which to purchase a stockpile of [lead and zinc] metals," Malone wrote. "Then, in 1953, Britain began to release the stockpile to the United States. At what price? At six cents a pound under the market. Thus Britain was given—by us—the money to buy a stockpile, which they used to undercut our market. The perfectly natural result occurred. Our mines shut down."[8]

The senator added that within two years U.S. production of lead and zinc was cut in half. The Tariff Commission belatedly recommended relief for these industries in the form of higher tariffs. But the Eisenhower administration turned it down because, as Senator Malone said, such action would "not accord with our foreign policy."[9]

Coal mining suffered "from the impact of tremendous imports of foreign waste oils, including shipments from the Middle East and Indonesia," Malone reported.[10] The result was that coal mining communities topped the Labor Department's list of distressed areas, with thirty-three of them so labeled. The Senator conceded that "the situation would be worse were it not for the export of American coal to countries which, like Britain, formerly were large producers for their own export trade."

There is an obvious anomaly in America shipping coal to Newcastle, once the greatest coal export center in the world. While we sent billions in foreign aid to England so the socialist government there could keep some of its workers employed, our coal exports put other British workers on the unemployment rolls. The fuels used to power the ships that hauled the coal across the Atlantic added to the real cost of delivering the product to English ports. But this waste was considered somehow beneficial.

Mercury production, a small but crucial industry, is a textbook model of what was to happen in a number of industries as U.S. foreign policy took precedence over American companies and jobs. After World War II, a cartel was formed in Europe with the open objective of capturing the world market in mercury. While Marshall Plan aid pumped billions of dollars into European countries to rebuild their economies, the cartel slashed the price of its mercury to $45 a flask delivered in New York. The prevailing U.S. price at the time was $191, and the result was inevitable.

American mercury producers were knocked for a loss and Canadian and Mexican production of mercury ceased entirely. With North American production down for the count, the European cartel then proceeded to gouge their customers on this side of the Atlantic. During the Korean War, with domestic mercury production crippled, the cartel blithely raised the price of mercury to $240 a flask and in 1954 the price was still going up, hitting $265 offloaded in New York.[11]

The free trade purist may ask from his ivory tower why U.S. producers did not climb back into the ring and take on the mercury cartel when the price had risen again to profitable levels.

But once a domestic industry is gutted, it takes time and capital to bring it back. Skilled workers have scattered in search of other jobs. Sales staffs cannot be reassembled overnight. Investors, already badly burned, know the power of the cartel, and know also their own government will not protect them. They are naturally reluctant to walk through the flames a second time.

Other industries were beginning to feel the bite of unfair, and often illegal, imports during the Eisenhower era. Farm and garden implements began coming in from Germany and Japan. Table cutlery and chinaware from these same countries flooded the U.S. market and virtually wiped out domestic producers. Even in the chemical industry there was high unemployment due to imports in four of the distressed areas designated by the Labor Department.

Shipbuilding was also becoming an endangered industrial species during the Eisenhower years, due to the strange policies fostered by free trade and foreign aid. This industry, which thrived even during Colonial times as an exception to Britain's mercantilism, had played a vital role in the development of America. Not only our foreign trade, but transport on the myriad inland waterways of the nation, depended upon our ability to build ships.

During World War II, however, a shift in policy took place. Senator Malone, an engineer by profession, observed that scores of Liberty ships launched in U.S. yards were equipped with old fashioned reciprocating engines. "Yet at the same time," he wrote, "we supplied turbines and diesels to other nations, and these . . . were installed in foreign-built ships. When the war was over these vessels were ready for the fast competitive carrying trade. Our Liberty ships . . . went into the mothball fleet."[12] Overnight, America's merchant marine was "obsolete." The merchant fleets of all other maritime nations grew, while America's shrank.

Labor costs were a primary factor in the transfer of registry of many American ships to foreign flags. Nearly a thousand vessels were soon flying the flags of Panama, Liberia, and Honduras, though most of these ships were owned by U.S. companies. The Associated Press reported on December 1, 1989 that "As of July 1986, more ships above 1,000 gross tons capacity flew Panama's flag than any other—3,620 [ships] with a capacity of 42.1 million gross tons. The Soviet Union was second and Liberia third." American crewmen could not compete with the cutthroat wages paid crews from Africa or Central America. No one, except the maritime unions, asked *why* American sailors and ship officers should have to compete with these low-wage countries. The crews joined the unemployment rolls and most U.S. shipyards stopped building ships.

Japan, East Germany, Sweden, and a host of other countries took over the shipbuilding industry, dominated for two centuries by the United States. Costs were the chief factor in this shift. U.S. yards were saddled with heavy taxes to help pay for foreign aid. They also had to pay big unemployment insurance bills to cover workers who kept losing their jobs to foreign competition, and they were hobbled with the red tape of numerous government regulations. Under these circumstances competition with the Japanese or Swedes or virtually any foreign maritime nation soon became a losing game, especially where U.S. aid and investments were helping build the overseas yards.

In 1946 there were nearly 5,000 vessels with total deadweight of almost 51 million tons flying the U.S. flag. Today there are only 721 ships totaling less than 25 million tons deadweight under the Stars and Stripes although international trade has increased exponentially during the four intervening decades.[13] America's once proud and mighty merchant marine has been all but scuttled by the policies of the United States government.

Farmers, then as now, were not exempt from the axe of the free trade executioners, although they have foolishly come to believe, in common with many manufacturers, that their salvation lies in exports. Dairy farmers were already feeling the import pinch in the 1950s and their once thriving export markets had virtually evaporated, dropping from sales averaging almost five million pounds a year prior to Roosevelt's Trade Agreements Act of 1934 to 387,000 pounds in 1952. Deprived of their traditional export markets, dairy farmers were whiplashed by a massive invasion of foreign cheeses, butter, and other products. Thousands of them had to sell their farms for whatever they could get, and not infrequently the buyers were foreigners.

Wheat exports before the 1934 legislation averaged close to 215 million bushels a year and in the next seven years plummeted to less than 56 million. With the advent of foreign aid they picked up sharply, of course. By 1953 wheat exports were over 219 million bushels, but the American taxpayer was footing the bill and the foreign aid giveaways kept the world price of wheat depressed, which hardly benefited the farmer.

Agriculture price supports by the U.S. government not only failed to offset the price depressants of the foreign aid export program but they added to the farmer's tax bill, along with those of all other citizens. The high-flying middlemen, exporters, and insider speculators continued to benefit from the subsidies-plus-aid. But the family farmer was being driven off the land by his government's policies. There were 5,382,162 farms in the United States in 1950. By 1959 that number was down to 3,703,894, a drop of 1,678,268.[14] Total farm employment in the same decade went from 9,926,000 to 7,057,000, which translated into a loss of 2,869,000 agriculture jobs in a single decade.[15].

Total farm production continued to rise despite this decline. The big factory farms owned by corporations, and increasingly by foreign interests, could afford the expensive equipment and other methods of boosting yield that the smaller farmer could not buy, let alone compete with. Cheap imports may only have hastened his departure from the farm that had been in the family for many generations. But many a farmer would have stayed to pass the land on to his children if he had not been faced with additional competition fostered by his own government.

The loss of manufacturing jobs did not quite equal the decline in agriculture employment during the 1950s but a serious erosion had started. An estimated 700,000 manufacturing jobs were lost to imports in the years 1956 to 1960 alone.[16] Moreover, there was a noticeable shift underway from manufacturing to so-called service industries. The emphasis in the new age of the "hired gun"— the salaried manager—was less on production and more and more on the bottom line of the balance sheet.

The imports flowing into the United States did more than kill off jobs and farms and industries. As previously noted, they handed over billions of paper dollars to the foreign central banks, who were turning in the dollars for gold at the U.S. Treasury. Although Americans were forbidden by law to buy gold with their dollars, foreigners were not.

As the U.S. balance of payments deficit continued to climb, the gold drain threatened to become a hemorrhage. In both 1959 and 1960 the imbalance owed by the Treasury came dangerously close to $4 billion—nearly $8 billion for just two years. Next to imports, which topped $15 billion in 1959, the greatest outflow of dollars was the U.S. investments pouring overseas. Between 1950 and 1960 our "direct" investment abroad almost tripled to nearly $32 billion and the overall total of private international investments made by Americans was closer to $50 billion, according to a Treasury Department report.[17]

The multinational corporations were stampeding to Europe and the Far East to escape the higher wages the American labor unions were demanding, and they were being encouraged in this exodus by the free trade policy then strongly supported by the AFL-CIO. But it was the United States government that was encouraging both the corporations and the labor movement in their joint flight from reality.

Instead of inhibiting imports, cutting back on foreign aid and reducing American investments in other countries, the Eisenhower administration encouraged increases in all three. Ritual noises were made that the Treasury and Federal Reserve were "concerned" and keeping an eye on the gold transfers. But the third and worst recession of the Eisenhower era, beginning in 1958 and still going in 1960, appeared to paralyze everyone.

At the helm of the Treasury during this period was Robert B. Anderson, who had succeeded George Humphrey. An accountant, Anderson had been named chairman of the National Youth Administration in Texas by Franklin Roosevelt. One of his protegees at NYA was Lyndon Johnson, who became leader of the Democrat-controlled Senate in the 1950s. Anderson had been the go-between for Harry Truman in the battle between the Treasury and the Federal Reserve which resulted in the 1951 "accord" that restored the Fed's ascendancy after a temporary erosion of its power. A condition of the compromise Anderson worked out was promotion of William McChesney Martin, then a young Assistant Secretary of the Treasury, to chairman of the Federal Reserve Board.[18]

In the waning days of the Eisenhower administration Bob Anderson accompanied Douglas Dillon to Bonn to plead with Chancellor Konrad Adenauer to help bail the United States out of its gold drain predicament. The old chancellor listened politely but made no commitments. Perhaps he was in no position to promise anything. *Die Bundesbank* made the real decisions when it came to Germany's monetary affairs, just as the Federal Reserve and the claque that controls it does in America. Ultimately it was the central bankers who would tell both countries what to do.

Chapter 25.

The Kennedy Round 1

This nation will maintain the dollar as good as gold, freely interchangeable with gold at $35 an ounce, the foundation stone of the free world's trade and payments system.

—John F. Kennedy in a
message to the Congress,
July 1963

John F. Kennedy injected the gold issue into his 1960 campaign for the presidency against Richard M. Nixon, implying that he had the answer to the outflow of gold and the related international trade and monetary problem. After his razor-thin victory, however, the young man from Massachusetts found that the answer was more elusive than he had led the public to believe. The campaign rhetoric simply did not wash in the seething caldron of world economics.

During the critical transition period before his inauguration, Kennedy named to cabinet and subcabinet posts what political historian Theodore White accurately called "as visionary a group of thinkers as have ever held the ear of any chief [executive] in modern times."[1]

The composition of the team Kennedy initially appointed to tackle the trade–balance-of-payments–gold-outflow problem was typical of the personnel he deployed into every agency and department of the government. George W. Ball, a Washington lawyer and a Leftist since his student days at Northwestern, was named chairman of the monetary task force. A close friend of Adlai Stevenson, Ball now was to become Undersecretary of State for Economic Affairs, later succeeding Chester Bowles as the No. 1 Undersecretary when Bowles was shipped off to New Delhi as ambassador. At State, Ball participated in the dismantling of the Department's internal security program ordered by the Secretary of State, Dean Rusk.[2]

On Ball's pre-inaugural monetary team were Otto Eckstein of Harvard, Paul Samuelson of the Massachusetts Institute of Technology, and Robert Triffin of Yale—a Belgian educated at Harvard who had worked for the Federal Reserve, the International Monetary Fund and as an advisor to the Europeans on their new Payments Union. Others on the Ball task force included Joseph Pechman of the Brookings Institution, Robert Roosa of the Federal Reserve Bank of New York, and Edward M. Bernstein, who had served as Harry Dexter White's deputy during the construction of Bretton Woods.[3]

Predictably, the Ball task force came up with recommendations guaranteed to exacerbate U.S. trade problems, make the balance of payments worse, and chart a course for siphoning off yet more of our gold. In addition to the economic controls they championed, such as a thinly veiled wage-price control mechanism, they also urged a full-scale return to the Keynesian principle of juggling the federal budget to better manage the economy.

However, the Ball group's most *outré* recommendations were reserved for trade. In *The Fate of the Dollar* Martin Mayer summed them up in a sentence: "To remedy the balance-of-payments deficit, Kennedy should seek much greater liberalization of foreign trade, elimination of [import] quotas and restrictions everywhere and tariff reductions of 50 percent on trade around the globe."[4]

In brief, what the Ball brigade prescribed was a much more lethal dose of the same poison that was already killing us. Although Kennedy was unwilling to swallow the hemlock whole, the Ball task force's trade nostrums were later almost all adopted when the Congress approved the Kennedy Round agreements negotiated in Geneva under the auspices of the GATT. In 1961, however, the incoming president and his Secretary of the Treasury, Douglas Dillon, tabled the trade agenda temporarily and focused on the monetary suggestions.

Ball's team wanted the European countries to jettison the limitations they almost all had on their citizens making capital investments in the United States. At the same time Ball's group advised Kennedy to establish "close surveillance over private capital outflows."[5] (Not *curb* the outflows, mind you. Just *watch* them as they went sailing off.)

Moreover, the Ballists suggested Kennedy persuade the IMF to entice borrowers to accept their loans in foreign currencies, rather than the favored dollar, in order to hold down the balance of payments. And finally, they thought the Treasury should "undertake a study of [the] desirability of continuing free gold markets."[6] In Washington, there is nothing quite like a study to solve all problems. Words speak much louder than actions on the Potomac.

Kennedy, perhaps realizing the Ball group had gone a bit too far for the times, formed another, smaller committee to deal with the international trade and monetary mess. As chairman he appointed Allan Sproul, former president of the Federal Reserve Bank of New York. Others included Treasury's Douglas Dillon, and Walter Heller, chairman of the President's Council of Economic Advisers.

Within a few weeks after his inauguration John Kennedy delivered a message to Congress, presumably formulated by the Sproul committee, strongly reaffirming the commitment of the United States to protect the sacred cow of Bretton Woods—the convertibility of the dollar into gold at $35 per ounce. The $35 gold idol had taken on the aura of the biblical golden calf in the years since Harry Dexter White had fashioned it and every president was required to kneel before it to demonstrate his subservience to free trade and the One World state that would ultimately evolve from it.

Aside from the commitment to $35 gold, Kennedy's message was the prototype for hundreds, maybe thousands, of pronouncements on trade and monetary matters that have flowed from the White House and the Treasury in an unending stream for, now, more than a quarter century. Like Ronald Reagan in the late 1980s, John Kennedy placed his hopes in 1961 on expanding exports, encouraging investment by foreigners in the United States, maintaining our foreign aid and military assistance programs at high levels, and strengthening the International Monetary Fund.

There was one point, picked up from the Ball task force, which Kennedy made in his message that marked a major change in America's approach to monetary matters. He said the United States would be willing to *borrow* from the IMF to acquire foreign currencies, thereby reducing the demand of foreign central banks for dollars which could then be converted into gold. This was probably the first time any President had ever openly admitted America's need to *borrow* for such a purpose though it certainly would not be the last, as the trillion-dollar foreign debt that the Reagan administration steered the country toward so forcefully demonstrates. As Howard M. Wachtel wrote in his 1986 book, *The Money Mandarins: The Making of a Supranational Economic Order*, in the 1960s, "Crisis management, instead of institutional reform, became a habit that the U.S. government has not broken."[7]

However, it was becoming apparent, even in the sixties, that the $35-an-ounce golden calf would eventually have to be sacrificed. The question was whether the United States would have any gold left after the formula dreamed up by the druids of Bretton Woods had taken us completely to the cleaners. From 1945 when it was reported at close to $30 billion, the U.S. monetary gold supply had plummeted to $18 billion, a drop of some 40 percent.

Instead of biting the bullet and repudiating the $35 idol, Jack Kennedy decided to stick with the globalists and give their dangerous plan for a new world economic order the old Harvard try. In October of 1961 he approved the creation of the "Gold Pool" to inhibit speculation and stabilize the price of gold. By this time the foreign central bankers had discovered, or been persuaded, that their predatory raids on Fort Knox might pull the plug from their own thriving economies. It didn't take much acumen to figure that one out. If the U.S. economy came tumbling down, theirs was sure to follow since the products all of them produced had become addicted to the American market. A temporary halt in their calls on U.S. gold was obviously in order.

The leading industrial countries, including the United States, all kicked in some gold to the Gold Pool fund but the United States, as usual, got hit for the lion's share—fully half of the $270 million total. This fund was used to drive down the gold price if it went over $35 an ounce. Thus, the pool was nothing more than an arsenal for storing ammunition for the long-drawn-out war on gold that had begun in 1933. At first the Gold Pool worked, but just how successful the central bankers' war has been over the long haul can be measured in the 1990 price of gold, which was bouncing over $400 an ounce. From the monetarist point of view that is a tremendous improvement over 1979 when it topped $875 during the Carter inflation. But $400 is a far cry from $35, and a fair gauge of what has happened to the dollar in the intervening years.

Arthur Schlesinger, the Kennedy administration's house historian, wrote in his book, *A Thousand Days*, that the president "used to tell his advisers that the two things which scared him most were nuclear war and the payments deficit."[8]

There was reason for John Kennedy's deep concern over both the balance of payments and the threat of nuclear war. In June of 1961 he went to Vienna for a summit meeting with the bumptious Bolshevik, Nikita Khrushchev, who threatened the United States with extinction if it opposed Soviet expansion. Kennedy had already blown the Bay of Pigs invasion of Cuba in April when he had refused to give the U.S.-trained Cuban exile brigade air cover, thereby delivering them to the tender mercies of Fidel Castro.

Emboldened by their Cuban victory and the young President's demeanor at Vienna, the Soviets defiantly erected the Berlin Wall in August to halt what had become an exodus of people out of East Germany. Then, in the autumn, the Soviets began a series of nuclear tests with bombs that far exceeded in destructive power any exploded before or since. One blast was over fifty megatons and some reports claimed it was twice that powerful. Either way, it was enough to wipe out the metropolitan area of New York City.

The Soviets had set off these bombs in the face of a unilateral test ban moratorium declared by President Eisenhower. Kennedy waited six months before responding to the Soviet's nuclear demonstration. It was not until April 1962 that he ordered resumption of U.S. nuclear tests, though of course they could not be conducted on the scale of the Soviet explosions.

Through all this, and afterward, Kennedy's advisors kept up a constant drumbeat urging him to seek "parity" with the Russians in nuclear weapons. Following deployment of the Minuteman missiles, the United States had strategic superiority in spite of the Soviets' possession of much larger warheads.

The most prominent exponents of unilateral disarmament in the Kennedy-Johnson years were Robert Strange McNamara, the Secretary of Defense; Dean Rusk, the Secretary of State; and Walt Whitman Rostow, who shuttled back and forth between the White House and the State Department, always in powerful positions despite the fact he had been twice rejected for security clearance by State and declared a security risk by Air Force intelligence during the Eisenhower years.[9] Rostow had been the leading intellectual light of the Massachusetts Institute of Technology's Center for International Studies (CENIS), a CIA-sponsored think tank that had tapped the big corporations to help Rostow & Company chart what he proclaimed as an "end of nationhood" for the United States and the "world community."[10]

In December 1960, during the critical transition period, Rostow flew to Moscow with Jerome B. Weisner, then director of MIT's electronics research laboratory and soon to become President Kennedy's chief scientific advisor. Among the Soviet leaders they met with was Vasily Kuznetsov, deputy foreign minister of the USSR, who complained that the United States was building a first-strike strategic force aimed at the Soviet Union. The Soviets, of course, were even then preparing for their multimegaton tests of the following fall which were to give them a far greater first-strike capability than the U.S. possessed, then or now.

Rostow and Weisner returned from Moscow with word that the Russians felt hemmed in by our nukes and all we had to do was be nice and go for "parity." This meant that the United States would stand still—indeed go *backward*—in the strategic arena, while we gave the Soviets time to catch up.

Implementation of this suicidal plot was placed in the hands of Robert McNamara, who promptly proceeded to eliminate or shelve a whole array of America's most effective or promising weapons. In June 1964 the American Security Council's *Washington Report* itemized a dozen systems which had cost American taxpayers many billions of dollars to develop but which had been consigned by McNamara to the scrap heap. These included the Skybolt and Pluto missiles; the X-20 Dynasoar; B-70 bomber; 195 Bomarc-A missiles; Nike-Zeus, a tested ABM defense against nuclear attack; the navy's Typhoon frigates and weapons systems, and 129 Atlas missiles which alone had cost $5.4 billion.[11]

Thus, as the United States plunged ever deeper into the Vietnam War, the Secretary of Defense was dismantling America's defenses, with the support of his allies in the White House and State Department.

Walt Rostow became, in 1964, director of the National Security Council. "He has," said President Lyndon Johnson, "the most important job in the White House, aside from the President."[12] Earlier, in his first stint on the NSC staff in 1961, Rostow played the key role in steering the United States into its first major troop commitment in Vietnam.

During the first year of the Kennedy Administration Rostow waged an intensive lobbying campaign from his White House base to win support for his idea to send ten thousand U.S. Army infantrymen into the Mekong Delta, where the Viet Cong was having some success. In the autumn, Rostow accompanied Gen. Maxwell Taylor, who was being brought back as Army Chief of Staff, on a tour of Vietnam. They returned to Washington with a strong recommendation for sending ten thousand American troops into Vietnam. Previously, the United States had a small number of military advisors in Indochina. But now the first organized troop commitment was to be made.

Before Taylor returned to the Pentagon in 1961, the Joint Chiefs of Staff had successfully resisted Rostow's plan on the grounds that the United States should not get trapped into another bloody land war in Asia as it had in Korea. But Rostow outflanked the Joint Chiefs, using Taylor to roll up their line. Kennedy, thoroughly mesmerized by his visionary advisors, gave the order Rostow had been urging for a year. In January 1962 the first of the ten thousand troops went in. America was on the hook in Vietnam, and it was to be eleven years before we got off.

During the revolutionary decade of the sixties, the nation's will was fractured and the United States transformed into a submissive tool of every country that wanted to exploit us, whether in the name of "mutual security" or on the trade and monetary front, or both.

The Cuban missile crisis in October 1962 revealed that the nation's neuro-logical system was already paralyzed. Although the crisis was hailed as a great victory for the United States and for its President, it was, as we now know, a dismal defeat. After a brave speech announcing that Russian missiles were in Cuba and would have to go, Kennedy surrendered his insistence on on-site inspection to verify that the weapons had actually been removed. Moreover, he ordered the withdrawal of U.S. Thor and Jupiter missiles deployed in Britain, Italy, and Turkey, something the Russians had not even requested.

Russian ships sailed out of Cuba with tarpaulins over the crates in which the missiles had been brought to the island. But the Senate Preparedness Subcom-mittee, after testimony from all the U.S. intelligence chiefs, concluded in May 1963 that not one of them could guarantee the missiles had actually been removed. Moreover, the Senate panel stated, the intelligence officials "readily admit that, in terms of absolutes, it is quite possible that offensive weapons remain on the island concealed in caves or otherwise."[13] Fidel Castro's sister, Juanita, defected in June 1964 and told a Brazilian newsman that "in Cuba there are long range ballistic missiles which are well camouflaged."

Reports of this kind continued to trickle into intelligence files all through the years since and occasionally they leaked out to the media, which for the most part ignored them, at least until they surfaced briefly in the 1988 presidential primary campaigns. By then no one was any longer interested. The Reagan administration, which as a rule enjoyed little credibility with the media, suddenly was accepted as the final authority. Officials denied missiles were in Cuba and that was that.

Ronald Reagan, taking his cue from a long procession of his presidential predecessors, had made it policy to ignore disquieting information, whether about missiles in Cuba, the consequences of budget deficits, or the closings of literally thousands of industrial facilities shut down by illegal imports in clear violation of U.S. trade laws.

Chapter 26.

The Kennedy Round 2

"It is a legitimate American national objective to see... an end
of nationhood as it has been historically defined."
—Walt W. Rostow in *The United States
in the World Arena*[1]

As the Kennedy administration stumbled from one foreign policy defeat to the
next, it was paradoxically able to achieve some measure, or at least appearance,
of stability on monetary matters though there was to be no truce in the trade
wars that were taking an ever-rising toll of America's industries and jobs.

The central bankers, meeting frequently in Basle, had, as we have seen,
decided to cooperate with Washington in defending the Bretton Woods arrangement by joining the United States in organizing the Gold Pool. This didn't happen
overnight, however. In fact, it took many long, acrimonious months of negotiations.

The Germans led the way in March 1961 by revaluating the mark upward, a
rather painful process for them since they had to give up some of the gold they
had so recently acquired from the United States. The Dutch soon fell in line
too, but the British, French, Italians, and Japanese at first refused to budge.
They had learned the great advantage of keeping their currencies undervalued
as they shipped their subsidized products into the U.S. market and they did not
want to let go. After all, if you can maintain low prices on your exports via
artificial monetarism, why raise the prices and make the products more expensive
just so American industries can be more competitive in their home market?

Nonetheless, the German revaluation had set in motion a chain of events that
eventually overcame the objections of our more recalcitrant trading "partners."

The higher-valued mark had touched off a run on the German currency around the world. A dangerous monetary expansion that would bring on worldwide hyperinflation was threatened as the central banks tried to cope with the rising demand for the Deutsche mark. Their alarm grew as foreign currencies continued to flow into Germany. Of course, the revaluation would not have sustained an inflow of foreign currencies seeking to buy marks if Germany had not had a strong balance of payments position brought about through a realistic trade policy.

The 1961 run on the German mark eventually forced the other European countries to revaluate their currencies. But for a brief spell the mark had appeared to take the place of the dollar as the currency of international choice and it served as a lightning rod so the dollar could sail through the storm, if not unscathed, at least not too deeply scarred. The demand for the Deutsche mark took the heat off U.S. gold. But this was only a temporary respite and a more lasting mechanism was furnished by creation of the Gold Pool, which brought the dollar back into the comforting but dangerous port of Bretton Woods.[2]

The Gold Pool held fast through all the remaining crises of the Kennedy administration—a stock market dive in May of 1962, the Cuban missile crisis that fall, mass civil rights demonstrations in Washington the following summer, and the growing problem of Vietnam. In spite of everything, Kennedy was able, in July 1963, to tell the Congress that the dollar was still "freely interchangeable with gold at $35 an ounce."

The biggest one-day drop in the history of the New York Stock Exchange on May 28, 1962 had sent shivers down the spines of the central bankers assembled at the Bank for International Settlements in Basle. It may also have nudged them toward considering Washington's plans for trade liberalization, which were thought to be much too radical even by Europe's socialists.

The central bankers, having eased up for a while on tapping the gold in Fort Knox, eventually saw they could make up for this concession by increasing their countries' product invasions of the American market. More open access to the great dumping grounds in the United States was the least painful way of keeping their own factories and farms going. But it took the U.S. negotiators years to convince the Europeans that America was actually *willing* to put more of its industries out of business if only they would join us in cutting tariffs further.

In the domestic debate over the Trade Expansion Act of 1962, the Kennedy administration centered its argument for more trade liberalization on the need to meet the new challenge of the recently created European Common Market. The Japanese were not yet seen as major players in the game since the U.S. and Europe then shared some 80 percent of the world's total exports.

The campaign to capture public opinion and build congressional support was carefully planned and adroitly executed. The State Department's invisible bureaucracy acted as quarterback and George Ball played fullback, bruising his way into the enemy line. The "enemy" was perceived to be American industry and, though no one on the Left would say so openly, labor was also looked upon as a stumbling block.

Ball warned the National Foreign Trade Convention in New York in November 1961 that "the process of tariff reduction involves the acceptance of some degree of structural adjustment by individual industries."[3] Ominously, Ball added that the old method of limiting our negotiators "to trading on an item-by-item basis" would have to be scrapped in favor of "across-the-board cuts."

After George Ball had softened up the line, *the* ball was handed off to President Kennedy who pranced around the right end of the National Association of Manufacturers with a speech in New York, and through labor's guard in another stemwinder at the AFL-CIO convention in Florida. Ernest Preeg, who chronicled the history of the Kennedy Round for the Brookings Institution, wrote that "the manufacturers were surprisingly receptive to the President's appeal . . . while George Meany [president of the AFL-CIO] gave unqualified support from the labor group."[4]

In January 1962, the president carried the fight to Congress, calling for "a wholly new approach—a bold new instrument of American trade policy." Kennedy cited "five fundamentally new and sweeping developments [which] have made obsolete our traditional trade policy." These included the European Common Market, pressure on the balance of payments, the need to accelerate growth, the Communist trade offensive and, believe it or not, the need to create new markets for Japan and the developing countries.[5]

The Democrat-controlled Congress dutifully passed the requested legislation, giving the executive branch authority to negotiate tariff cuts across the board up to 50 percent with a very few exceptions to protect the national security. With practically the whole U.S. industrial base being offered up at the GATT negotiations, the national security provision was almost a joke.

A sop was thrown to labor in the legislation providing for "adjustment assistance" to U.S. workers and companies injured by the increase in imports anticipated from the slashing of the tariff. In the 1970s and 1980s this writer attended a number of hearings before the U.S. International Trade Commission in which presidents of labor unions described adjustment assistance as nothing more than "burial insurance" for the jobs of their members. But in 1962 this provision was seen as a great coup for labor.

The propaganda barrage for passage of the Trade Expansion Act of 1962 was so deafening that it is doubtful organized labor, powerful as it then was, could have defeated the bill. Preeg notes that "Howard Petersen of the White House staff, with massive help from the Commerce and State Departments conducted a saturation campaign, using flashy trade promotion literature that included separate brochures for each state."[6]

Treasury's Dillon and Commerce's Luther Hodges promised that higher trade surpluses would result from the increased exports envisioned from the tariff cuts to be negotiated with the Europeans and Asians. But it was George Ball who came closest to enunciating the ultimate goal of the New Frontier trade policy. In a speech written by or for Ball, and delivered by George McGhee, Undersecretary of State for Political Affairs, the Rostowian vision of a nationless world community was evoked, a community "involving all the varied activities and aspirations of man."

"Trade is the warp and woof of such a community," Ball-McGhee proclaimed.[7] The final votes on the Trade Expansion Act in the Congress revealed how far down the free trade path the United States had descended. The bill was passed in the House 298 to 125 and sailed through the Senate on September 19, 1962 by an overwhelming 78 to 8. On October 11 John F. Kennedy signed it into law.

The average tariff on dutiable U.S. imports had plunged from 54 percent in 1933 to 12 percent thirty years later and now what remained was to be cut in half. But the precipitous reduction in tariffs from 1933 to 1962 tells only a part of the story. So many imported items had been placed on the free list in those intervening years that the ratio of Customs duties collected to the total value of imports had declined to barely 5 percent. And so many dodges were being developed to get around paying any Customs duties at all that the actual ratio was undoubtedly much lower. By comparison, the United Kingdom maintained a ratio of Customs to total imports of well over 25 percent and many countries were higher than that.[8]

A seemingly unrelated incident that spring gave Kennedy an opportunity to lash the steel industry, traditionally the strongest opponents of free trade. On April 10 the United States Steel Corporation announced price increases averaging $6 a ton on a number of its products. This was soon followed by seven other domestic steel companies hiking their prices.

Kennedy was infuriated and FBI agents were deployed to seek evidence of any collusion. The agents, carried away by the president's personal interest in the investigation, and spurred on by Attorney General Robert Kennedy, went banging on doors in the middle of the night. A newsman suspected of knowing more than he had reported about the story was routed out of bed in the wee hours and questioned.

Roger Blough, the chairman of U.S. Steel, quickly got the message. He rescinded the price increases for his corporation within a few days after Kennedy publicly denounced them and the other steel companies followed suit. Whether all this was in any way connected with the Kennedy campaign for a new trade act is open to question, but there is no doubt whatever of the fear the president's actions inspired in the business community. Nor was the fear unwarranted. The *Congressional Quarterly* later reported that antitrust actions skyrocketed under Kennedy, taking off from less than 300 in the last year of the Eisenhower administration to 2,079 in 1962.[9]

It is ironic, even tragic, that the Kennedy administration chose this particular period to go after American business. Industry had its hands full trying to cope with the increased competition from abroad, where our antitrust laws did not reach and where socialist trusts were leading the assault against the U.S. market. To put the costly and time-consuming burden of fighting antitrust cases on the back of our businessmen was to give aid and comfort to foreign producers and, indeed, to cut deeply into the competitiveness of the United States in international trade.

In the summer of 1963 attention was focused on the historic Senate battle over ratification of the Nuclear Test Ban Treaty. This first important arms control pact had been initialed at the Kremlin on July 25 by Nikita Khrushchev and by Averell Harriman, who was acting that day as the representative of President Kennedy. Another more formal signing took place on August 5 when the secretary of state, Dean Rusk, flew to Moscow with the UN ambassador, Adlai Stevenson, and Senator Hubert Humphrey. News photographs flashed around the world showing this distinguished group gaily toasting the treaty with Khrushchev and his commissars. The millennium was dawning once again.

On December 19, 1962, less than two months after the Cuban missile crisis, Nikita Khrushchev wrote in a secret letter to John Kennedy that the "time has come to put an end once and for all to nuclear tests."[10] Moreover, Khrushchev promised to meet the U.S. "halfway" on the issue of on-site inspection. Eagerly, Kennedy rose to the Pavlovian bait. Like Ronald Reagan in 1987, Jack Kennedy couldn't resist the promise of on-site inspection. In 1963, however, the Russian negotiators whittled the inspections from an opening number of ten all the way down to zero. But that didn't deter Kennedy. He swallowed the Soviet demands, approved the treaty and went all out for the Senate's consent.

When the final vote came, on September 24, 1963, only 19 senators voted against the Nuclear Test Ban Treaty; 80 voted for it. It was the supreme masterpiece of the Kennedy administration, ranking even above the Trade Expansion Act.

While the Test Ban Treaty was being negotiated in the spring of 1963, Kennedy's trade warriors were starting the struggle for multilateral across-the-board tariff cuts under the GATT's leaky umbrella in Geneva. The U.S. delegation was headed by Christian Herter, former Republican governor of Massachusetts and Secretary of State in the later Eisenhower years. A conscientious public servant, Ambassador Herter was painfully afflicted with a rheumatic ailment that had left him crippled for years. At Geneva, with his physical condition deteriorating, it must have been exceedingly difficult for him to conduct such intricately complicated negotiations. Tough is the proper word for trade talks. As *The Times* of London put it not long before the Geneva conference opened in May 1963, "Nothing shows the perversity of human affairs more clearly than tariff negotiations."[11]

Meeting at the Palais des Nations where Woodrow Wilson's old League had collapsed in the 1930s, the negotiators assembled on May 16. Christian Herter, acting as President Kennedy's special trade representative, urged "the maximum liberalization of trade" that would begin with "across-the-board, equal percentage linear cuts." For openers he suggested tariff reductions of 50 percent.[12]

The spokesman and chairman of the European Economic Community, Foreign Minister Eugene Schaus of Luxembourg, immediately objected to the "linear" cuts, sensibly insisting, "on some formula," as Preeg put it, "for reducing disparities where the tariff rate for a particular product was much higher in one country than in another."[13]

Herter held fast for the more sweeping across-the-board linear cuts, but the EEC flatly rejected the American proposal. The French minister of finance and president-to-be, Valéry Giscard d'Estaing, left the meeting before it ended, ignoring the pleas of the U.S. delegation. Nonetheless, a compromise was adopted, though few thought it contained much substance. The German economics minister, Ludwig Erhard, principal author of the compromise, admitted: "We have agreed on the shell of an egg. What will be in the egg we do not know."[14]

What Christian Herter and the other Americans had discovered at Geneva was that the United States no longer had the clout it had enjoyed in the long postwar era just past. The Europeans were feeling their oats, and on occasion they could behave with downright arrogance. Uncertainty still hovered over the dollar, and the European central bankers probably thought they had gone far enough in shoring up the U.S. currency without giving in to our more fanciful demands for more free trade.

Kennedy and his monetarists had tried, unsuccessfully, to get the Europeans to shoulder more of the financial burden for NATO. A quarter-century later Reagan was still trying, with little more to show for his efforts than his predecessor. For more than forty years the United States has patiently borne its disproportionate share of Europe's defense while the Europeans increased their exports to America and mined what was left of the gold in Fort Knox. In spite of the cosmetic covering the central bankers had helped Kennedy place over the dollar, the gold kept trickling out of the United States.

When John Kennedy took office in 1961 there was still a way out for the dollar. The short-term liabilities owed to foreigners were only slightly above the estimated $17.8 billion gold left in the vaults. By cutting the country loose from Bretton Woods then, and revaluing the remaining gold at a more realistic price, confidence could have been restored in the dollar. Some temporary inflation may have followed in the wake of such a move, but it would have been insignificant compared to what has happened since.

Unfortunately, Kennedy was so psychologically tied to the symbol of the golden calf sculpted by Harry Dexter White in 1944–45, he could not bring himself to renounce the ridiculous $35 per ounce formula. To have done so would have been tantamount to renouncing the Left's vision of world government and no president since Woodrow Wilson had been more completely under that spell than John Kennedy.

Indeed, it was Kennedy's incessant moves to hasten establishment of the global millennium that brought him to Dallas on November 22, 1963 to mend his sagging political fences. The American people still were able to perceive the dangers in such rash actions as the test ban treaty, unilateral disarmament, a Soviet base in Cuba, and dismemberment of the tariff in the name of free trade.

Kennedy was in deep political trouble throughout the country, but nowhere more than in the South.

Lyndon Johnson later recalled a "Texas poll, taken a few weeks before his trip, showed that only 38 percent of the people approved of what he was doing as President."[15] Johnson noted that by contrast the same poll showed the conservative Democratic governor of Texas, John Connally, with 81 percent approval. On the morning of Jack Kennedy's arrival in Dallas, Texas newspapers reported a new statewide poll showed him trailing Senator Barry Goldwater, his most likely Republican opponent in 1964.

"He had come to Texas for politics," Lyndon Johnson bluntly stated.[16] Waiting for him, on the sixth floor of the Dallas Book Depository Building on Elm Street, was a young ex-Marine Marxist named Lee Harvey Oswald, who had defected to the Soviet Union and returned to Texas with a Soviet wife. Others may have been waiting too. John Connally, wounded riding in the car with the president, heard shots coming from different directions.

John Kennedy never reached the Dallas Trade Mart where he was scheduled to speak. His body was flown back to Washington on *Air Force One* that afternoon. The jet took off from Dallas minutes after the new President, Lyndon Baines Johnson, was sworn in by a federal judge who had come aboard hurriedly at the airport. A brief era of our history had ended in tragedy. The legacy of that era is still with us.

Chapter 27.

All the Way with LBJ

As *Air Force One* carried us swiftly back to Washington after the tragedy in Dallas, I made a solemn private vow: I would devote every hour of every day... to achieving the goals he [John F. Kennedy] had set.

—Lyndon B. Johnson[1]

Lyndon Baines Johnson, the rough-hewn Texan who became thirty-sixth President of the United States when a Marxist assassin's bullet cut down John F. Kennedy, wasted no time promulgating the sweeping social revolution his predecessor had begun. The Congress had blocked many of Kennedy's more ambitious schemes for dragging the country further Left. But Johnson, the former Democratic leader of the Senate, was an accomplished arm-twister and within a few years he had wrestled a bewildered Congress into approving the tremendous transformation under which the American society has lived ever since.

President Johnson's first moves were directed at managing the crisis he had inherited as a result of the assassination in Dallas. He knew that many suspected him of complicity in the crime, as well as the Soviets and Castroites who had so captivated the gunman, Lee Harvey Oswald.

"The atmosphere was poisonous and had to be cleared," Johnson later wrote. "I was aware of some of the implications that grew out of that skepticism and doubt. Russia was not immune to them. Neither was Cuba. Neither was the State of Texas. Neither was the new President of the United States."[2]

Eugene Debs Rostow, who was helping his brother Walt and Dean Rusk steer the State Department further Left, suggested Johnson appoint and investigative commission headed by Chief Justice Earl Warren.[3] The new President saw that a "credible" commission under the man who presided over the Supreme Court of the United States could smother the dangerous rumors abroad in the land.

Lyndon Johnson understood perfectly the explosive implications of the FBI report that Lee Oswald had visited the Soviet embassy in Mexico City shortly before the assassination in Dallas. That embassy was known to be the KGB headquarters in North America. Knowing the embassy was under close surveillance the Soviets freely admitted Oswald had been there, though they claimed his visit had nothing to do with the subsequent murder of President Kennedy.

Johnson rewarded the Soviets for their "cooperation" by giving top priority to ramming through Congress a bill for huge shipments of American wheat to the perennially starving USSR. He considered the food-for-Russia legislation the major test of his new presidency and when the House, following the Senate's example, approved it on Christmas Eve 1963 Johnson felt "at that moment the power of the federal government began flowing back to the White House."[4]

Actually, it was apparent that Johnson had seized the reins of power as he stepped onto the presidential stage, reassuring his benumbed countrymen more by the appearance than the substance of his actions. It was obvious he had no intention of blaming the Soviets for the assassination, and appointment of the Warren Commission underscored his decision not to risk war. The nation, relieved that Armageddon had not yet arrived, responded with grateful alacrity.

When the New York Stock Exchange opened on Monday after the Friday murder of Kennedy it shot up a record 32 points. Wall Street, always more taken with illusion than reality, was obviously of the belief that the new President would be more "conservative" than the former one. The schizophrenic Street likes to think the market does better when there is more traditionalist leadership in power, although the more myopic, particularly among the bankers, cling eternally to the utopian vision of a One World millennium.

Lyndon Johnson hastened to bolster the hopes of both conservatives and liberals in a speech to a joint session of Congress on November 27, the day after the stock market's encouraging performance. While sketching a pinkish picture of the future calculated to delight the Americans for Democratic Action, the President reassured conservatives by promising, "We will keep our commitments from South Vietnam to West Berlin."[5] The problem was that the continuing outflow of our monetary gold, which inexorably whittled away the value of the dollar, was making it excruciatingly difficult for the United States to hold the far-flung lines it had established around the world to contain communism.

Our allies, most especially La Belle France, having become hopelessly hooked on the trade and monetary bonbons we had fed them for two decades, were more determined than ever to take full advantage of the U.S. open door for their exports. They had come to regard the American market as a modern El Dorado which provided them with an inexhaustible supply of dollars to cash in for gold at the Treasury's tormented window. Since Lyndon Johnson appeared to our trading partners as an even softer touch than John Kennedy and his predecessors, the outflow of gold, temporarily slowed earlier in 1963, soon began to pick up once again.

The renewed raids on Fort Knox were aided and abetted by a new floating crap game dubbed "Eurodollars." These were vast accumulations of U.S. dollars doled out via trade, aid, military assistance, and less licit means to virtually every country on earth. Between 1958 and 1963 the central banks, mostly in Europe, but increasingly in such exotic offshore enclaves as Panama and the Bahamas, had piled up uncountable billions of these free-floating dollars. Rather than turn them all in at the Treasury for gold, and thereby risk bringing the whole house of cards down on their own heads as well as ours, the central bankers prudently decided it was time to show some restraint. The Eurodollar began circulating as an international currency.

Loans were made between countries in Eurodollars and beginning in 1958 some European nations gave their private citizens the right to possess Eurodollars for their own accounts. Thus, they no longer had to turn their dollars over to the central banks, providing a greatly added incentive for salting away American cash in secret accounts in Switzerland and the other esoteric shelters blossoming in the Caribbean and around the Pacific Rim. In 1963, the London merchant banking house of S. G. Warburg underwrote the first Eurodollar bonds, a modest issue of $15 million for highway construction in Italy.[6] Much bigger Eurodollar deals were soon forthcoming.

Although circulation of Eurodollars abroad tended to take the pressure off the dollar and the dwindling U.S. gold supply, it created other problems. For one, the U.S. Treasury and Federal Reserve could not control Eurodollars as they did the circulation of domestic dollars: the Eurodollars were simply beyond the reach of U.S. regulation, a potentially explosive situation that kept the people at the Fed and the Treasury tip-toeing around the corridors of their respective temples in a state of perpetual trepidation. For another, Eurodollars presented foreigners with an almost irresistible temptation to cart off America's gold. Early in 1965 the French, having let up a bit after carrying away tons of our gold over the preceding decade, could no longer resist snatching more.

On February 14, President de Gaulle sent America an unwelcome valentine: Get the world back on the gold standard or face an immediate and accelerated conversion of France's Eurodollars into gold. As Howard M. Wachtel succinctly put it in *The Money Mandarins*, "De Gaulle had effectively declared war on the dollar. . . ."[7] Looked at another way, however, it is conceivable de Gaulle may have been making a brave last-ditch effort to bring the world back to monetary reality.

Lyndon Johnson, busy directing the war the United States had taken off France's hands in Vietnam, failed to react in any telling way. Instead, he once again turned the other cheek. De Gaulle and the Bank of France responded by stepping up their legalized heist of American gold. Rather than take thirty tons a month, as it had been doing, France now upped the ante substantially. All through 1965 and most of 1966 the Eurodollars poured into the U.S. Treasury from Paris and our gold poured out.

Fortunately, the Germans and Japanese, both running trade surpluses against the United States that could also have been turned into gold, refused to join de Gaulle's attack on the dollar. The Germans in particular cooperated in defending America's bedeviled currency and Great Britain agreed to shut down the London private gold market to give the dollar a little more breathing room.

Perversely, it was the Johnson administration that seemed determined, through ineptitude, to shoot the dollar down. The President, at the outset of his tenure, took a fast swipe at cutting the federal budget deficit from $102.2 billion to $97.9 billion for fiscal 1964. But he pushed through an election year tax cut in the same year just as the costs of the Vietnam War were rising and this doomed the federal government to large deficits for years to come. Moreover, Johnson insisted on plunging into the tremendously costly "War on Poverty" programs when Vietnam War expenditures were mounting rapidly in 1965. And he became obsessed with slashing U.S. tariff revenues by bulldozing yet another trade agreement into place at Geneva.

President de Gaulle pulled France out of the Gold Pool just as the United States was on the verge of getting the across-the-board tariff cuts it had been crusading for in the GATT negotiations. This was in June 1967 and the signing of the Kennedy Round trade agreements at Geneva at the end of that month gave the monetarists yet another straw to grasp just as the Gold Pool was sinking. Pushed, shoved, and bedazzled by Lyndon Johnson's trade team, several score nations sacrificed their farmers and workers for the promised pot of gold—or at least Eurodollars—at the end of the free trade rainbow.

President Johnson knew he was offering up proportionately more American jobs and farms than any other country. But he wrote off the protests of the soon-to-be-liquidated industries, workers and farmers as the squeals of just more "nervous special-interest groups."[8]

Only a month before his fateful journey to Dallas, Kennedy had submitted to the Tariff Commission a list of U.S. products to be put on the GATT's chopping block. As an official document of the commission's successor, the U.S. International Trade Commission, has it, the Kennedy list "included nearly every one of the articles enumerated in the TSUS" (Tariff Schedules of the United States).[9] Nothing was to be exempt from the free trade guillotine. The peril points that had previously given some protection to specific American-made products had already been decapitated by Kennedy's Trade Expansion Act of 1962. The Congress had again abdicated its Constitutional responsibility to govern trade. The President now had virtually unlimited power to decide the economic future of millions of Americans. No Oriental despot could have seized that power more avidly or used it with less regard for the consequences than Lyndon Baines Johnson. He assessed this power accurately in his memoirs, writing that in trade matters, "I had inherited authority that gave me more flexibility . . . than any other previous President."[10]

The negotiations resumed at Geneva in 1964 with Christian Herter still the chief American negotiator. Three years later the talks were still going on, but by then Herter was gone. William Roth was heading the U.S. team with Michael Blumenthal, later Secretary of the Treasury in the Carter cabinet, as his deputy. Among the other members of the coordinating group were Eugene Rostow, then Undersecretary of State for Political Affairs; and Anthony Solomon, Assistant Secretary of State for Economic Affairs, who later had a long run as president of the Federal Reserve Bank of New York.

The Europeans were generally opposed to the draconian 50 percent tariff cuts the United States insisted upon. Most of them were bewildered by what they correctly regarded as the naiveté of the Americans. It was inconceivable that a nation would want to auction off its industries and workers and farmers in pursuit of an obviously illusory ideal. However, they came to see certain advantages in the illusion for themselves, mainly keeping the U.S. market accessible to their products. If the Americans insisted upon committing suicide, why, Monsieur, the Europeans would be pleased to help them.

However, one disastrous thing that the Kennedy Round accomplished once it was in operation was to open Europe, as well as America, to a wholesale invasion of imports from Japan and the rest of the Orient. Europe, unlike America, eventually reacted and closed the door at least partly to imports from the Far East. But the United States, which takes its sovereignty much less seriously, has kept its door wide open while industry after industry has fallen before the subsidized imports from Japan and the Pacific Rim, thanks in no small part to the Kennedy Round tariff cuts.

At Geneva in 1967 Lyndon Johnson's boys would not be denied. They didn't get quite all they wanted. The Europeans still had enough spunk and wisdom to refuse to give away the whole store, or at least all at once. But Roth, Blumenthal, and the rest managed to get most of what they were after. Erwin Canham, editor of the *Christian Science Monitor*, estimated that "tariffs affecting four-fifths of the world's trade will be cut by over one-third" by the agreement reached at Geneva.[11]

Actually, the tariffs on numerous items were slashed 50 percent or more and were eliminated entirely on many others. Metals and metal products, chemicals, textiles, and apparel—all came in for drastic reductions. But machinery and transportation equipment, both American strongholds at the time, felt the heaviest and sharpest cuts. Indeed, they accounted for more than half the dollar value of all products affected by tariff reductions of 50 percent or more.[12]

The Geneva agreement was signed on June 30, 1967, just hours before President Johnson's authority ran out under the Trade Expansion Act. Michael Blumenthal, a naturalized citizen, affixed his signature on behalf of the United States. Lyndon Johnson later wrote that "The Geneva talks demonstrated that despite powerful isolationist pressures in all nations, the world community still had the vision to move together as partners, on the principle of fair shares for all."[13]

Two decades later the world can look back and see that it was the Japanese who got most of that "fair share"—indeed, the lion's share. Korea, Taiwan, Hong Kong, Singapore, and other Asian nations also got far more than their fair share. None of these were even considered factors at the time the GATT treaty was signed. All of the Pacific Rim countries enjoyed LDC—Less Developed Country—status, which permitted them to protect their own markets while they raided widely in the West.

Japan, though obviously not an LDC, behaved like one when it came to protecting the Japanese market. It is still, after more than twenty years of endless palaver over opening itself to American and European exports, one of the most deviously defended markets on earth. U.S. companies have spent hundreds of millions of dollars trying to penetrate it, with precious little success.

The Japanese long ago discovered that American trade negotiators were only too happy to live on polite Japanese smiles, nods of seeming agreement, and outright deception. Of late the Japanese have reverted to the arrogance of the warrior Samurai, encouraged by the spineless approach of the United States government and the certain knowledge that Japan now owns enough U.S. Treasury bonds to torpedo our national economy if they decided to unload them on us all at once.

Europe went through a period of permitting its industries to be decimated by the Japanese in the name of the false god of free trade. England still permits imports of Japanese automobiles, television sets, and other products that keep hundreds of thousands of chronically unemployed English workers idle. But most of the other European nations sobered up long ago when they found the *schnapps* distilled at Geneva in 1967 gave them more hangovers than old Bacchus ever could.

Only the United States still piously genuflects before the GATT god in the old temple of the League of Nations at Geneva, while blindly offering up what remains of our industries to appease the insatiable appetites of the Orient and Europe.

In his political autobiography, *The Vantage Point*, Lyndon Baines Johnson ruefully remarks, "A few months after the successful negotiations of the Kennedy Round agreements, another dangerous crisis broke."[14] The crisis was actually nothing new: it was the old balance of payments problem that had been siphoning off our gold for years. This time it had been exacerbated by the across-the-board tariff cuts at Geneva, which quite obviously were going to make the U.S. balance of payments much worse.

Revaluing gold then, or permitting it to be revalued by the free market, would have helped rescue the dollar though it would not have solved all our monetary problems. A true rescue calls for a return to a sound trade system so that the dollar can once again be solidly based upon production. Nonetheless, if President Johnson had tossed out the Bretton Woods formula in the late 1960s, the runaway balance of payments dilemma could have been slowed.

Instead, Johnson opted for another bandaid on all the others that had been applied to our trade and monetary wounds. This was the "Two-Tier Agreement" spawned by creation of something called the Special Drawing Right (SDR) in Rio de Janeiro in 1967 and officially brought into the world at Stockholm on March 17, 1968. Perhaps President Johnson and his European counterparts may have thought they would enjoy a little Irish luck by ushering in the "Two-Tier" on St. Patrick's Day. If so, they were right—for at least a little while.

The Two-Tier Agreement, which effectively replaced the international Gold Pool scuttled by France's withdrawal, established a dual gold market. One face of this Janus was branded with the indelible $35-per-ounce for monetary gold; the other permitted a controlled private market where the gold price could fluctuate, but within reason. To take the heat off monetary gold the SDR was to substitute for gold in IMF payments. Initially backed by the dollar, within a half-dozen years the SDR was to consist of a mixture of currencies and gold.[15]

The Rio-Stockholm two-step was choreographed by Guido Carli of the Bank of Italy, although the original concept is attributed to Eugene Birnbaus, who had matriculated at the IMF, the Commerce Department, and the White House before landing at that favorite pub of the monetarists, the Chase Manhattan Bank.[16] Prominent roles in concocting the SDR and the "Two-Tier" were also played by William McChesney Martin, chairman of the Federal Reserve Board, and Henry Fowler, Secretary of the depleted Treasury.

With Lyndon Johnson waving Harry Dexter White's $35-an-ounce golden banner from the battered ramparts of Bretton Woods, the central bankers solemnly promised not to buy or sell gold in private markets, thereby threatening speculators with the possibility that gold might actually fall *below* $35. As it turned out, the price of gold did drop for a time, though not for long.

Two political events contrived to bolster the dollar in 1968: the riots in France during the spring, and the massive Russian invasion of Czechoslovakia in August. The attempted revolution in France failed but it put tremendous pressure on the franc and forced de Gaulle to let up on his war to capture more of America's gold. In fact, the Bank of France had to sell off about half its monetary gold to support the franc and a humbled de Gaulle accepted a $1.3 billion bailout in the form of a standby credit from a consortium of nations. Not surprisingly, Lyndon Johnson's brand was on the bailout. Indeed, the American President had rounded up the other countries and persuaded them to save the French franc and de Gaulle's face, though the president of France had been raiding our gold for years.

The Soviet invasion that ended the brief "Prague Spring" in Czechoslovakia undermined the Deutsche mark and touched off a flight of the German currency to America. After another of its recurring periods of euphoria, Europe once again realized that in the final analysis it had to depend upon the United States to protect it against the Red Army. The heat was off the dollar and the U.S. gold supply, at least for a time.

On the surface, Lyndon appeared to have lucked out on the monetary front, though he had lost on virtually all others. In reality, however, he had presided over the demise of what remained of the sound money and trade system established by Washington, Hamilton, and the other founders.

Lyndon Baines Johnson and the compliant Congress that served him, rather than the nation, had eliminated the last gold foundation undergirding the dollar. From parity soon after the Civil War, to the 40 percent gold backing set during the Wilsonian Revolution and creation of the Federal Reserve, to 25 percent in the time of Truman, the dollar had descended all the way under LBJ to a zero gold support. And while he was at it, Johnson had the Congress kill off the dollar's redeemability in silver and the silver content of U.S. coins.

Lyndon Johnson had clung to the $35-an-ounce formula the alchemists had concocted at Bretton Woods. The price America paid for defense of this tin god was a high one indeed. But a far higher price was being paid by thousands of our men in Vietnam for the no-win policy the Johnson administration imposed upon the United States while the spiritual fabric that had bound our nation together was torn asunder and scattered by the tempest of rebellion.

Chapter 28.

The Wages of No-Win War

The fact is that the Defense Department, the budget bureau, and the President were lying to the Treasury, the Economic Advisors, and the Fed [about the costs of the Vietnam War].
—Martin Mayer in *The Fate of the Dollar*[1]

As president, Lyndon Johnson liked to have the people believe he could do anything. Anything at all. He waged war in far-off Vietnam and he declared war on poverty at home. The list of laws he tunneled through the Congress ranged from civil rights to food stamps, automobile tire safety to prevention of juvenile delinquency. There were some two hundred laws enacted during the little more than five years he was chief executive. A calligraphed listing of these acts presented to him by his cabinet fills two entire pages in his autobiography. The list is headed: "With these acts President Lyndon B. Johnson and the Congress wrote a record of hope and opportunity for America."[2]

What actually was written, however, was a record of war without the will to win, and despair, deceit, and debt—a debt so huge that even with a prudent trade and monetary policy it is doubtful the United States could pay it off for many decades to come.

The combined public and private debt of the nation had topped one trillion dollars in 1962 and another half-trillion was added to it by the end of 1968. The federal government's debt in that year approached $350 billion, or $1,727 for every man, woman, and child in the country. In 1910, before the Wilsonian era, the per capita federal debt had been $12.41 with a population less than half that of the 1960s. After four wars, all undertaken by Democratic administrations, our national debt had multiplied nearly one hundred and forty times. Moreover, state and local government indebtedness was growing at an even faster pace than the federal. As late as 1950 state and local debt had been only about 10 percent as large as the federal debt. By 1967 it was 40 percent and still rising.[3]

President Johnson's determination to ram his costly social programs through Congress while expanding the war in Vietnam was a fatal mistake, compounded by his stubborn insistence on maintaining foreign aid and trade as usual and upholding Harry Dexter White's $35 gold even if it meant emptying out Fort Knox.

Johnson did manage to keep the war at a relatively low level of action long enough to get himself elected president in his own right. In 1964 he waged a hypocritical campaign against Sen. Barry Goldwater of Arizona. While the president preached "peace," the press portrayed the Republican candidate as a war monger likely to blow up the world with nuclear bombs. The 1964 election, which Lyndon Johnson won by a landslide, was the most bitterly fought of this century and it left the nation permanently polarized.

It was in 1964 that Johnson unveiled his "Great Society" in a speech at Ann Arbor, Michigan. In it he called for "an end to poverty and racial injustice" and painted a glowing picture of the world to come "where the meaning of our lives matches the marvelous products of our labor."[4] The President gave no credit to the British Fabian Socialist, Graham Wallas, who had envisioned *The Great Society* a half-century earlier in his book of that title.[5] Perhaps Johnson had never heard of Wallas, though Walt Rostow and the other Leftists schooled in Britain who surrounded the President must certainly have been familiar with the socialist theorist's work. At any rate, Johnson's "Great Society" richly evoked the Fabian dream, particularly the Wallas book's last chapter, "Organization of Happiness" though there were echoes of other Wallas chapter headings in Johnson's speech, certainly "Organization of Thought" if not "Organization of Will."[6] There was very little will in the Johnson administration, as its prosecution of the Vietnam War demonstrated.

Once he was inaugurated in 1965 Johnson wasted no time escalating the war. He may have been justified in this—if he had had any intention of winning in Vietnam. Tragically, he did not. Still, he did not want to lose either. Lyndon Johnson simply let his advisors—Dean Rusk, Walt Rostow, Robert McNamara, and all the others—alternately play on his residual patriotism and feed his abiding desire to be seen as the President of Peace.

No military force in all history ever had to fight under conditions like those imposed upon the brave men of America's Army, Navy, Marines, and Air Force in Vietnam. They did not just fight with one arm tied behind their backs; they had *both* arms lashed to the gates of Robert McNamara's erratic Pentagon. All the ancient rules of war were tossed out the window and interminable instructions governing the most minute actions of forces a half-world away flowed in an unending stream from Washington.

Faced with a ruthless enemy, America's fighting men acquitted themselves with high courage and great restraint. Under McNamara's "Rules of Engagement'' they often found themselves surrounded by the stealthy Vietcong or the disciplined North Vietnamese Army and were not permitted to fire until their situation became desperate.

This kind of suicidal warfare was an everyday occurrence in Vietnam. Yet McNamara's Rules of Engagement were themselves covered up and it was not until 1985—ten years after the fall of Vietnam—that the Defense Department declassified them at the behest of Senator Goldwater. The Senator then inserted them in the *Congressional Record*. Over a three-day period—March 6, 14 and 18, 1985—these irrational rules took up twenty-six pages of the *Record's* small print.

Barry Goldwater remarked that ''These layers of restrictions, which were constantly changing and were almost impossible to memorize or understand, although it was required of our pilots . . . granted huge sanctuary areas to the enemy.''[7] Although we lost hundreds of our pilots over North Vietnam, they were never permitted to bomb really strategic targets. Airmen contended that one bomb could have knocked out a huge hydroelectric dam, cutting off most of the Communist country's power, flooding its food supply, and probably forcing an end to the war. But that single bomb was never dropped on that critical target.

An Air Force pilot told me of sighting whole divisions of the Communist Army fleeing across the DMZ to their sanctuary in the north in the fall of 1968. But President Johnson called another bombing halt and gave Ho Chi Minh's forces time to regroup for yet another invasion, thereby depriving the American and ARVN forces of still another victory. ''Every time we win, Washington takes it away from us,'' the pilot said. It was a theme one heard over and over again in Vietnam.

Belatedly, it is now widely recognized that there was not one, but two Vietnam Wars. The first was the real war our men and their allies kept winning in Vietnam. The other was the war we lost every night on the television evening news. Even the Tet offensive of 1968, presented by the press as a dismal defeat for the U.S. forces, is today seen for what it actually was—a major victory. Like all the other victories, however, it was stolen from us by the strategists in the Pentagon with the complicity of defeatists in the news media. There were, of course, many newsmen who reported the war with integrity and courage. Unfortunately, the ''straight'' story often didn't fit the preconceived picture of the conflict adhered to by the editors and columnists in New York and Washington, who always had the last word in the morning papers or the last cut for the TV evening news.

Ironically, McNamara and Rusk led Lyndon Johnson to believe, soon after he became president, that the war would be over by 1965.[8] But when 1965 came the war was just beginning to build toward its tragic climax. The Communists had broken their pledge to leave Laos neutral, a pledge extracted in a solemn agreement engineered by Rusk and certified by the Soviets. Laos, as President Eisenhower had warned John Kennedy, was the key to Indochina. Once it was negotiated away by Dean Rusk it was only a matter of time before Ho Chi Minh began using it to unlock the back door into South Vietnam and Cambodia.

The assassination of President Ngo Dinh Diem and members of his family—barely a month a before President Kennedy's assassination in Dallas—was a turning point. As Johnson understood, it had "created more problems for the Vietnamese than it had solved."[9] The Viet Cong stepped up their terrorism during the political turmoil that followed Diem's death and Hanoi increased its troop and weapons movements down the Ho Chi Minh Trail.

Strangely, McNamara covered up the Soviets' heavy involvement in supplying the Communist forces that were taking an ever rising toll of American casualties. The late Mendel Rivers, chairman of the House Armed Services Committee, told me in a 1966 interview that he repeatedly urged the Secretary of Defense to remove the "classified" label he had imposed for several years on the reports of Russian ships offloading weapons and matériel at Haiphong. But McNamara, with the cooperation of the media, continued to keep this important information from the American people.

Congressman Rivers said that one morning he received a report that five more Soviet ships had come into Haiphong the night before. He called McNamara and told him that if he didn't declassify the Soviet arms shipments to Vietnam, he would go out on the floor of the House that afternoon and declassify the information himself. McNamara waited several more hours, according to Rivers, apparently hoping some magic way could still be found to keep the lid on the Soviet role in the Vietnam War. Then, just before noon, Mendel Rivers was notified the wraps were at long last off.[10]

It must not be thought that this attempt, successful for so long, to hide vital information from the American public was an aberration. It was but one of a thousand and more coverups implemented during the Vietnam War. Indeed, coverup became policy. And the policy was clearly enunciated in a classified document entitled "Study Fair" which was disclosed in January 1965.[11]

"Study Fair" was prepared for the U.S. Arms Control and Disarmament Agency by the Institute for Defense Analysis. The underlying theme of the twenty-seven-page policy paper was that to end the arms race and prevent nuclear war, not only information for the public had to be restricted, but information provided by intelligence agencies to the President and other officials must also be rigidly controlled. For, as the study contended, there is "significant danger in information which is 'too informative'." To offset the danger that the President might be too well informed, "Study Fair" stressed "the need for restraint in providing and obtaining certain kinds of intelligence." This included turning off "the cameras" conducting surveillance of Soviet activities from our satellites.[12]

Lyndon Johnson extended the coverup policy articulated so bluntly in "Study Fair" not only to disarmament initiatives but also to the fiscal aspects of the Vietnam War. As Martin Mayer informs us, the war was costing up to $10 billion more each year than the administration admitted.

Senator Richard Russell of Georgia, the respected chairman of the Senate Armed Services Committee, quietly informed William McChesney Martin, the chairman of the Federal Reserve Board, that President Johnson and Secretary McNamara were permitting military expenditures to soar far beyond their budgeted limits.[13] Not only were they concealing this from the press and the public, they apparently were hiding it from the Secretary of the Treasury, Henry Fowler, and from other key administration officials responsible for government finance. At least Fowler denied the reports that began leaking in the press that the war was costing up to $10 billion more each year than Johnson and McNamara were letting on.[14]

Still, Lyndon Johnson's budgets should have made a Hottentot suspicious. Federal expenditures topped $100 billion in FY 1966 but by some legerdemain the Treasury came up with a surplus of $2.2 billion. The following year the magic marker didn't work so well and as spending zoomed to more than $153 billion a modest $3.6 billion deficit was confessed. It was not until 1968 that the magnitude of Johnson's wild spending spree became wholly apparent. Expenditures hit nearly $173 billion and the deficit was over $19 billion (some say $25 billion), a record except for the huge deficits of World War II. Between FY 1965 and FY 1968 the federal budget had increased an astounding 45 percent.

There was however no serious attempt to cut back on foreign aid or other international commitments and the balance of payments predictably worsened as our trading partners sent their exports flooding into the U.S. market on the first wave of the Kennedy Round tariff cuts generated at Geneva. The Europeans were initially the big beneficiaries, particularly the Germans and the French.

"What was most disturbing," Martin Mayer says, "was the way the Europeans kept down the prices of the manufactured goods they exported even as their other prices rose."[15] The Common Market took some of the credit—or blame—for this. But "rationalization," the new-found cover word for additional socialization of industries, played an even greater role. The Europeans were driving one another's workers into the ranks of the unemployed with their continental free trade arrangement and they decided to export more of their unemployment to the United States. Perversely, heavy American investment in Europe helped make this feasible. An estimated $6 billion in U.S. capital was exported overseas in 1967 alone. For all anyone knew, the *invisible* outflow, including Eurodollars held by U.S. firms in foreign banks and fed from there into overseas investment via subsidiaries, could have been twice the acknowledged estimate.

The European plants built with American dollars were enjoying economies of scale that permitted them to keep their export prices low while taking full advantage of the higher prices prevailing in Europe. Since they knew, even then, that the U.S. government would merely wink at this dumping and the related illegal subsidies, the trade war against America went up another nasty notch. The Japanese, seeing the Europeans get away with murder in the U.S. market, slyly joined the parade.

The only thing that seemed to trouble our trading "partners" was whether the United States would have sufficient reserves, especially in gold, to make up for its chronic payments imbalance. To help the Treasury keep paying through its gold window, the foreigners, particularly the Japanese, began buying U.S. government bonds, cutting themselves in for a large slice of interest paid by our taxpayers while they expanded their targeting of American industries.

Everyone seemed to benefit from the greatly increased spending abroad on the Vietnam War, as well as expenditures for NATO and the Pacific alliance. Everyone, that is, except the United States.

The French had the inside track on much of the private business in Vietnam so a healthy chunk of our war dollars bounced from Saigon to Paris. The Germans and the British quietly grabbed more of our export markets while our domestic industries focused on producing for the U.S. armed forces. The LDCs, most notably Brazil and Korea, took full advantage of the low-interest loans from the IMF and World Bank, in addition to the more direct aid from the U.S., to build new industries that would soon be knocking out our own. And the Japanese, now joined by Taiwan and other Pacific Rim countries, gobbled up everything in sight and much that was hidden, or at least unnoticed. Who, for instance, could complain about the millions of dollars American servicemen were spending in the Far East on their R&R leaves from Vietnam?

Flailing about for ways to hold back a bit on his rising deficits, President Johnson took another misstep in approving the budget for FY 1967, one that was to have long-range effects in inhibiting domestic investment in new plant and equipment while speeding up the capital outflow. Desperate to get his hands on ready cash to pay for his two wars—the one on poverty, the other in Vietnam—Johnson did away with the 7 percent investment tax credit designed to encourage investment in America. This produced more revenue initially. But it had a devastating effect on U.S. industry and played no small role in turning the industrial heartland of the nation into the "rust belt."

While foreign factories, many of them constructed by U.S. multinational corporations, enjoyed economies of scale, in part provided by exports to the wide-open American market, our domestic plants began to wither from lack of new investment. There were exceptions, of course. Some U.S. industries kept pouring in capital to build new plants and buy more up-to-date equipment. But even during the Vietnam buildup they often found they had to operate their modernized plants at lower capacity because of the import invasions and the increasing predilection of the Pentagon to buy abroad. This meant higher costs on the products domestic companies did produce, costs the producer either had to pass on to the consumer, abandon a product line entirely, or go offshore to take advantage of lower wage rates.

The effect of Johnson's ill-advised moves were devastating and inflation began its inexorable rise toward the outer limits of public confidence. At this dangerous juncture, in 1967, another event shook the world. It was more like a tremor on the Richter Scale at first. But the consequences are still felt more than two decades later.

Chapter 29.

The Dawn of Hyperinflation

Inflationism . . . is an instrument of destruction; if not stopped very soon, it destroys the market entirely . . . It is an expedient of people who do not care a whit for the future of their nation and its civilization. It is Madame de Pompadour's policy: *Apres nous le déluge.*[1]

—Ludwig von Mises

In the wee hours of June 5, 1967, President Lyndon Johnson was awakened by a call from Walt Rostow, his chief national security advisor. Rostow informed the president that war had broken out in the Mideast.[2] Though it is not clear from Johnson's account whether Rostow gave him many details, Israel had attacked Egypt and was fighting Jordanian troops for control of Arab Jerusalem.

The war was not entirely unexpected. The United Nations had withdrawn its peacekeeping force from the Sinai and the Gaza Strip on May 19 at the request of Egypt's Gamal Abdel Nasser, who had mobilized his armed forces a few days earlier. The Egyptian army had then occupied the Gaza Strip and closed off the Gulf of Aqaba to Israeli shipping. U.S. intelligence had learned the Israelis were preparing an attack, but Israel's prime minister, Levi Eshkol, had led President Johnson to believe his forces would delay action for a "limited period" while the U.S. tried to work out a negotiated solution through the UN.[3] Instead, Israel unleashed a blitzkrieg.

The American-supplied-and-equipped Israeli army quickly defeated the Egyptians, littering the Sinai with Soviet-made tanks and driving on to the Aqaba and Suez. The Arab Legion retreated from Jerusalem and the West Bank into Jordan and Israel invaded the Golan Heights and Syria.

What followed the lightning "Six-Day War" was an upheaval of the world trade and monetary system that eventually led to abandonment of part of the Bretton Woods agreement—the critical part that had siphoned off nearly two-thirds of America's monetary gold supply.

Meanwhile, President Johnson, beset by so many crises, was handed another during the Six-Day War which called up all of the administration's considerable cover-up talent. Indeed, it was a classic case of crisis management as laid down by Study Fair.

In his autobiography, Lyndon Johnson devotes only one paragraph to the surprise Israeli attack on the U.S. Navy's *Liberty*, an intelligence ship monitoring the war from international waters off the Sinai in the Mediterranean. Obviously intent on soft-pedaling the incident, Johnson goes so far as to lie about the *Liberty*'s casualties, stating that "ten men of the *Liberty* crew were killed and a hundred wounded."[4] The actual casualties, as he certainly knew, were 34 Americans dead and 171 others wounded.

The assault on the *Liberty* by Israeli war planes and surface craft lasted nearly two hours and only the most courageous action by the ship's captain and crew kept it from being sunk. No less than 821 rocket and machine gun holes perforated the *Liberty* and Israeli torpedo boats blasted a forty-foot hole in the ship's side.

James M. Ennes, Jr., one of the *Liberty*'s surviving officers, documents in his book, *Assault on the Liberty*, that "White House intervention prevented any timely rescue."[5] In fact, four jets dispatched from an aircraft carrier about thirty minutes flight time from the battle scene were called back on the personal command of the Secretary of Defense, Robert McNamara.[6] Moreover, a second rescue flight from the same carrier apparently was called off on President Johnson's own order.

The Secretary of Defense and the President of the United States were obviously more concerned with covering up the attack than in saving the crew of an American ship under fire, even when they knew it was in danger of being sunk with all hands because the rubber life boats had been deliberately destroyed by the attackers.[7] This disgraceful exercise in crisis management is thoroughly documented by Lieutenant Ennes, who was so severely wounded that he spent many months in navy hospitals, where he began years of research on his book.

The attack on the *Liberty* was followed some months later by North Korea's seizure of another U.S. intelligence ship, the *Pueblo*. James Ennes believes the one encouraged the other.

The cumulative effect of these and other similar incidents added to a gradual decline in confidence in the United States spurred by our failure to win the Vietnam War. This was not only reflected on the world political stage. It was mirrored in the decline of the dollar and the flight to gold and foreign currencies. If a country cannot uphold its own interests or defend its own fighting men, its currency and credit are guaranteed to erode.

The Mideast War touched off the age of hyperinflation. All the elements were there long before: wild spending for both welfare and war, the balance of payments problem due to our trade and aid policies, and the resulting reduction of America's gold supply. Other countries, including France and Britain, had suffered through periods of violent inflation in the wake of World War II but somehow America had appeared immune. Now, however, the cost of living began to climb sharply in the nation which had rightly prided itself on its long history of improving the lot of the greatest number of its citizens.

Lyndon Johnson's economic advisors all knew the situation was getting out of hand. In concert with the Federal Reserve, they did their best, by their limited lights, to dampen the fires blazing all around them. With the Fed calling the tune on rediscount rates to the banks, interest rates were increased to their highest level since 1921.[8]

On January 1, 1968, the President unveiled a sweeping program aimed at defusing the balance of payments bomb. All new U.S. private investment in continental Europe was to be put on hold. Investments in Australia, Canada, Britain, and Japan were to be reduced to 65 percent of the levels obtained in 1965–66. An all-out campaign to promote exports was launched. American tourists were subjected to more rigid foreign exchange controls. U.S. banks were severely restricted in their overseas lending.[9]

None of these programs worked as planned. American companies with big Eurodollar deposits in foreign banks found it easy to get around the offshore investment restrictions. The banks, and the tourists, discovered it was a simple matter to evade the foreign exchange and travel controls. Indeed, American travel abroad in 1968 set a new record and hiked the tourism deficit to $4 billion.[10] Moreover, the export promotion program was an almost total dud, though the Department of Commerce manufactured impressive figures based upon the bureaucrats' everlasting fantasies.

The trade surplus the United States was still running on its books by juggling foreign aid and other figures went down an unhealthy 40 percent in 1968 from the previous year. The biggest "peacetime" federal budget deficit in history churned up mountains of loose cash and American consumers were spending more and more on imports from abroad. On top of all this, two prolonged strikes, one in our Western copper mines, the other in the steel industry, gave foreign producers greatly expanded beachheads in the U.S. market for steel and copper.

Although the bitterest harvest of his international trade and monetary programs was still in the future, Lyndon Johnson had taken enough of a beating on Vietnam and other fronts, and he decided to call it quits. On March 31, he announced toward the end of a televised speech on Vietnam that he would not seek reelection. Despite his later disclaimers, LBJ obviously had bowed to the political winds blowing so fiercely against him. Sen. Eugene McCarthy of Minnesota, an opponent of his Vietnam policy, had come close to defeating the President in the New Hampshire primary on March 12. Four days later Sen. Robert F. Kennedy of New York declared his candidacy, breaking a previous public pledge to support the incumbent Chief Executive.

Lyndon Johnson's announcement that he was leaving failed to calm the country. On the contrary, it only fanned the spreading flames of protest against the president and the government. The year 1968 went down as the most tumultuous and divisive since the Civil War.

On January 30 the Communists launched the Tet offensive in Vietnam. They killed thousands of civilians and their terror added 350,000 more refugees to the ever growing population uprooted from their homes. U.S. forces suffered nearly 3,200 casualties, 416 of them fatal, in the first week of the Tet and the South Korean casualties were over 3,100 with 784 dead. However, the Communists lost more than 15,000 of their men and Gen. William C. Westmoreland, the American commander, was perfectly correct in reporting that the enemy had "suffered a military defeat."[11] However, the news media robbed Westmoreland and his forces of their victory and in June a vacillating President called the general home to kick him upstairs to the Joint Chiefs of Staff.

The Mideast flared again in February 1968 with clashes on the River Jordan and strikes by Israeli war planes deep into Jordan. In April came the assassination of Martin Luther King and the riots that followed. Student rebellion broke out on many campuses that same month. A march on Washington, organized by the Southern Christian Leadership Conference, left thousands of people camped during May and June in "Resurrection City," a jerry-built enclave occupying sixteen acres of public parkland. The objective of these marchers was to push for more antipoverty programs, and in this they largely succeeded.

Robert Kennedy was fatally shot in Los Angeles by a Marxist Arab, Sirhan Beshara Sirhan, as he emerged from a celebration of his California primary victory on the night of June 5. In that same month the Communists renewed their attacks in Vietnam, although the "peace" talks had begun in Paris only a few weeks before and the United States had tried to mollify the enemy by sending its senior champion of appeasement, Averell Harriman, as our chief negotiator.

The national nominating conventions commanded public attention during the summer months. Early in August at Miami Richard Nixon was named as the Republican standard bearer and Governor Spiro Agnew of Maryland as the GOP vice-presidential candidate. On August 28 Sen. Hubert H. Humphrey of Minnesota became the Democratic nominee and he chose Sen. Edmund Muskie of Maine as his running mate.

Riots disrupted the Democratic convention in Chicago. Mayor Richard J. Daley, the old-line Democratic boss of the city, called in the National Guard and some backup army troops to support the Chicago Police Department, and was criticized for the harshness with which he put down the riots. However, the critics never seemed to consider Daley's alternative, which was to permit the rioters to take over the convention entirely.

The week before the Chicago convention the world had been treated to a spectacular demonstration of the way the Communist world handles protest. More than 650,000 Soviet troops invaded Czechoslovakia to end the mild reforms instituted in that country during the Prague Spring. A general strike was called and twenty thousand brave Czechs marched in Prague under the guns of Soviet tanks. The strike lasted exactly one hour, and several hundred—some reporters said more than a thousand—Czechs were killed in scattered fighting.

Lyndon Johnson tried desperately to bribe the Communists into agreeing to peace in Vietnam. In June 1964 the President sent a message to Hanoi to assure Ho Chi Minh and his colleagues that the United States had no intention of trying to overthrow their regime. If Ho would lay off Laos as agreed in 1962 and abide by the "peace" signed with the French in 1954, Johnson promised to "assist all the countries of the area in their economic development."[12] He kept sending this offer to Hanoi for the nearly five more years he remained in office, dangling billions of dollars in aid in his quixotic attempt to lure the Communists into signing a "peace." Ho Chi Minh, reinforced in his resolve by Soviet arms pouring into Haiphong, replied by stepping up the war against the American and ARVN forces and murdering more innocent civilians.

To prove his good intentions, Johnson kept turning the war on and off, alternately ordering stepped-up bombing of North Vietnam or increased levels of land action, and then proclaiming bombing halts and virtual suspension of action on the ground. Johnson pursued this policy right down to the wire of the 1968 election. On October 31 he announced there would be a complete halt to all American air, naval, and artillery bombardment of North Vietnam as of eight o'clock the next morning, Friday, November 1. This was practically the eve of the November 4 election and it was perfectly obvious Johnson had declared the cease-fire to help the Democrat candidate, Hubert Humphrey, over the top in his nip-and-tuck race with Richard Nixon. But the announcement was badly timed. It had only the weekend and a bit more to sink into the public consciousness and that was not quite enough.

Nonetheless, the bombing halt did have an impact. Nixon barely squeezed by in one of the closest presidential contests in history and the false prospect of peace in Vietnam decided a number of close House and Senate races in favor of the Democrats. By then the American people were so weary of the interminable war that millions of them were willing to grasp any peace straw dangled before them.

Chapter 30.

Biting the Bullet

The clamor grew so great that Secretary of the Treasury John Connally, who disliked the idea of controls as much as I did, bluntly told me, "If we don't propose a responsible new program, Congress will have an irresponsible one on your desk within a month."

—Richard Nixon in *The Real War*[1]

The election of Richard M. Nixon did not end the era of trauma ushered in with the assassination of John F. Kennedy and suffered through excruciatingly with Lyndon Baines Johnson. Indeed, on a number of crucial fronts, including the Vietnam War and international trade and monetary affairs, the trauma deepened.

Nixon had pledged sweeping changes, particularly in the economy and in foreign policy. He kept part of the first promise but none of the second. During the campaign he had told Willard Edwards of the Chicago *Tribune* that he was going to shake up the foreign service and a few days later he repeated in a Dallas television interview that he would "clean house" at the State Department.[2]

However, the appointment of William P. Rogers as Secretary of State and Henry Kissinger as chief national security advisor demonstrated clearly that Nixon had no intention of keeping that promise. Both were members of the establishment that had been charting America's uncertain course. It was obvious they would help keep the country on that same tack, as events were to prove.

In trade and monetary matters, which had essentially become byproducts of foreign policy, the picture was much the same. Nixon's original Secretary of the Treasury, David Kennedy, was a Chicago banker with previous experience under

Democrat administrations. His undersecretary for monetary affairs was Paul C. Volcker, the hulking, cigar-chomping economist who had matriculated at all the right schools—Harvard, the London School of Economics, the New York Federal Reserve Bank, and Chase Manhattan. Volcker had also served the Kennedy-Johnson administration as head of the Office of Financial Affairs before returning to Chase in 1965. Now with Nixon he was to play a key role in the most important monetary decision since Bretton Woods.

Trade and balance of payments problems multiplied in the early Nixon years leading to a run-up in inflation, accompanied, to the surprise of the economists, by higher unemployment. The old Keynesian theory that bigger budget deficits and higher inflation inevitably produced more jobs was being disproven by the modern phenomena of unrestricted imports which not only did little to dampen inflation—and in the long run made it worse—but robbed Americans of their jobs. Even twenty years after Nixon's election to the presidency this equation is still not widely recognized, or at least publicly acknowledged.

Nixon reduced U.S. forces in Vietnam, warmed up to the Soviets, and prepared for his détente with Mao Tse-tung in China. None of this seemed to help the economy, which had slipped into recession soon after he took over and kept getting worse. The balance of payments ballooned to more than $30 billion and panic seized the Treasury. Fortunately for Nixon, and for the country, a man came on the scene early in 1971 to put a strong finger in the monetary dike threatening to burst upon us.

John B. Connally succeeded David Kennedy as Secretary of the Treasury in February 1971 and though he had little experience in international economics he proved a quick study. Connally had been governor of Texas and was wounded riding in the car with President Kennedy during the assassination in Dallas. He brought with him to Washington in 1971 an old-fashioned notion that America's interests ought to come first in dealing with other nations, all of whom were putting their own interests up front. Although Connally's approach was considered heresy by the people running U.S. foreign and trade policy, it succeeded in rounding up our cantankerous trading partners long enough for them to reluctantly cooperate in freeing the U.S. from Harry Dexter White's gold trap.

As Clyde Farnsworth wrote in his incisive economic history of postwar Europe, *Out of This Nettle*, "Western Europe was fat, prosperous, and not a little smug in the early 1970s."[3] Always inclined to look down their noses at what they regard as the naiveté of Americans, the Europeans had gone blithely on ignoring U.S. requests to shoulder a greater share of NATO's costs. Instead, they satisfied themselves with criticism of our policy in Vietnam, apparently believing we should simply raise the white flag and surrender to the Communists in the Orient while footing most of the bill for the defense of Europe. They had gotten away with criticizing Americans with complete impunity for so long that they were ill prepared for John Connally. He was the one American in a position of power who did not take kindly to outsiders carping about his country while they gorged themselves on profits from trade with the USA made possible by the aid we had given them and the investments we were still making in their industries.

High noon came in mid-August 1971 when the British ambassador, Lord Cromer, late of Barings and the Bank of England, asked the Treasury to take some of Britain's surplus dollars in exchange for $3 billion in gold. Since the U.S. monetary gold supply was already down to $10 billion—barely a third of its postwar level—the time had at last come for a shoot-out. Connally called the President and a meeting was arranged at Camp David the next day. On August 13 Connally and Nixon met there with Arthur Burns, chairman of the Federal Reserve Board, Paul McCracken, chairman of the President's Council of Economic Advisors, George Shultz, who was then director of the White House Budget Bureau, and Paul Volcker, still running monetary affairs at the Treasury. There were others, but these were the principal players. William Rogers and Henry Kissinger were conspicuous by their absence. For once major trade and monetary decisions were to be made without the foreign policy gang's guidance.

After sternly warning his financial advisors and other staff against leaking the proceedings to the press, Nixon, to use his own words, "turned the meeting over to Connally."[4] What Connally had come up with was an admixture of ideas supplied by Burns, Volcker, and Shultz, seasoned with a little patriotic pepper drawn from his own Texas upbringing.

The most important, and lasting, element of Connally's plan was to beat the British and others to the draw and simply slam the Treasury's gold window shut, letting the dollar float to seek its own level on the foreign exchange markets. John Connally was suggesting what no president had dared since Bretton Woods—slay the $35-an-ounce golden calf Harry Dexter White and his accomplices had sculpted for America to worship while its freedom was filched. Everyone at the Camp David meeting knew what this bold move implied.

Arthur Burns, as chairman of the Fed, strongly opposed the gold move, warning that it would play havoc with world trade, send the stock market into a dive, and likely bring on a worldwide depression of lasting dimensions. But for once Nixon "did not follow his recommendations" and years later he believed "this decision turned out to be the best thing that came out of the whole economic program" he was to announce two days later.[5]

The rest of the program Connally unveiled at Camp David contained additional strong medicine: a 10 percent surcharge on all imports, which Nixon said was designed as "mainly a bargaining chip to discourage foreign countries from depressing their currencies in order to promote their exports"[6] reinstatement of the investment tax credit to encourage business to build new plant and equipment in the United States instead of going offshore; a proposal for new income tax relief; repeal of an excise tax on automobiles to stimulate higher sales; and, lastly, a ninety-day freeze on wages and prices.

Connally and Nixon had both been against wage-price controls. But Arthur Burns, one of the long parade of ersatz conservatives who have marched through

Washington, was for the freeze. So were most other economists, led by John Kenneth Galbraith, the Great Guru of their dismal science. George Meany of the AFL-CIO had been pushing for controls and in those days, when Meany pushed, half the Congress fell to its knees. As Nixon recalled, "The clamor grew so great" that both he and Connally felt they had no alternative except to put the freeze in place. Nixon rued this decision, and later freely admitted it was wrong.

On Sunday night, August 15, 1971, President Nixon went on television to reveal his "New Economic Policy". (Perhaps he was not aware he was echoing exactly the same label Lenin had given *his* original Soviet economic policy.) The president's address was well received and next day the Dow-Jones average went up 32.93 points. But the struggle to reestablish a working international monetary exchange system in place of the Bretton Woods formula had just begun. Nearly two decades later it still is not completed.

Nixon took his authority for the sweeping moves made in the trade and monetary field from the Trading with the Enemy Act, though of course the countries affected were all supposed to be friends. His legal cover was later found to be invalid, but by that time most of the moves had been changed through negotiations with our trading partners.

The negotiations began almost immediately, some of them executed behind Connally's back by Arthur Burns and Henry Kissinger. Kissinger took the tack that Connally was destroying the NATO alliance while Burns tossed the ball to the European central bankers by asking Jelle Zijlstra, former prime minister of the Netherlands and then chairman of the Bank of International Settlements, to act as intermediary.[7]

Nonetheless, John Connally kept tight hold on the reins as he rode into Rome at the end of November for a meeting of the Group of ten finance ministers. Wasting no time, Connally started an auction with an offer to devalue the dollar against gold by 10 percent. The British chancellor of the exchequer, Anthony Barber, countered with 5 percent. But in the end Connally got his way and a little bit more.

After a meeting Nixon, Connally, and Rogers had with their French counterparts in the Azores on December 14, gold was pegged at just over $38 per ounce. French president Georges Pompidou was a banker who had come out of the Rothschild organization and his finance minister, Valéry Giscard d'Estaing, would succeed him. Nixon and Connally were dealing with men who could make decisions. The deal was cut.

There remained the formality of a conference to obtain the concurrence of the other members of the Group of Ten. This was held at the Smithsonian Institution in Washington later in December, where all the other currencies were revalued against the dollar to put the harness on the gold agreement. The Japanese, in their inevitable nitpicking way, kicked up a fuss about increasing the value of the yen by 17 percent. They finally settled at 16.9 percent.[8]

The combined revaluations were supposed to reduce the U.S. balance of payments by $9 billion. They fell far short of that target but what help they did provide came none too soon. For in 1971 the United States suffered its first trade deficit in modern times, a $2.3 billion shortfall, seemingly insignificant by the inflated standards of the late 1980s but a harbinger of bigger—and much worse—things to come. The following year the trade deficit jumped to $6.4 billion and with only two modest exceptions our trade balances have been in the red ever since.

At the Smithsonian meeting, in exchange for the monetary concessions extracted from the other nations, the United States not only dropped the 10 percent surcharge on imports but waived the investment tax credit it had planned to reinstate in order to promote capital investment in the United States. In spite of this unseemly collapse, Nixon called the Smithsonian pact ''the most significant monetary agreement in the history of the world.'' That was an obvious over-statement. It did not compare with Bretton Woods and what Harry Dexter White's plan had done to America in the intervening years. But Nixon's action on August 15, 1971, did at least save what was left of the nation's gold.

None of the other objectives were achieved, except in the very short term. The wage-price controls merely kept inflation steaming in the pressure cooker waiting for the chance to blow off the lid. The balance of payments problem was not solved and when the expected benefits of the Smithsonian Agreement failed to materialize the Federal Reserve increased the money supply by a record 9 percent in 1972 to provide the illusion that something good had happened.

Another attack on the dollar was sparked by an economic crisis in Britain during the spring of 1972. Harold Wilson's Labour government had passed the baton, and a crushing budget, to Edward Heath and his Conservatives earlier in 1969 after completing nationalization of the steel industry and touching off another inflationary spiral. However, Heath's halfway measures failed to get the beastly budget under control and inflation kept going strong. In March 1972 the Bank of England lost a third of its reserves within two weeks in a futile attempt to defend the pound at the $2.55 exchange rate set by the Smithsonian Agreement. In the end both the dollar and the pound were the worse for wear. The pound was devalued again and the U.S. balance of payments deficit hit $20 billion for 1972 forcing a second devaluation of the dollar against gold. This time the 10 percent cut in the dollar's international value upped the price of monetary gold to $42.22. It was a cosmetic price since U.S. monetary gold was not for sale then, though later our gold would be sold in repeated attempts to hold down the price of the precious metal.

This second devaluation came after John Connally had left the Treasury. It was executed under the aegis of Connally's successor, George Shultz, with Paul Volcker whispering in his ear. Volcker was a great one for promoting devaluations. He helped push two more, one under Carter, the other under Reagan, after the two engineered with Nixon. None of the four devaluations Volcker prescribed managed to staunch the flow of America's industrial lifeblood. More-over, they helped heat up inflation and one wonders how many times Paul Volcker had to be proven wrong. Still, our Presidents kept coming back to him for advice.

Having applied a few more patches to the monetary crazy quilt, Nixon went traipsing off with Henry Kissinger in search of a viable foreign policy. Soon after the Smithsonian Agreement was signed they departed for China, there to begin the process by which American workers are now forced to compete with the penny-ante wages that Communist state doles out to its long-suffering millions. (Now close to a billion!) In that same fateful year of 1972 our euphoric president gave the Soviet Union a credit to ''buy'' nearly fourteen million tons of wheat in the United States and encouraged our businessmen to increase the sale of their technology to the USSR. One result was the mammoth Kama River foundry designed and engineered by the Swindell-Dressler subsidiary of Pullman. Within five years this largest foundry in the world was turning out armored vehicles, some of which went into Afghanistan while others girded the Soviet frontier with Poland to threaten Solidarity later in the 1970s.

Basking in the warm glow of detente, Nixon went on to win reelection in 1972 by the biggest landslide in U.S. history, overwhelming the Leftist Democrat nominee, Sen. George McGovern of South Dakota. Only Massachusetts and the District of Columbia voted for McGovern, who gleaned a grand total of 17 electoral votes against Nixon's tally of 520. For one brief moment it appeared that the Left had been put in its proper place by the American people. But the moment quickly passed. Richard Milhous Nixon, under mounting pressure generated by the frenzy over Watergate, let the opportunity slip through his fingers.

Chapter 31.

The Petrodollar Bonanza

At the high watermark of the Nixon Presidency, as the White House and Mr. Agnew were hurling their rhetorical thunderbolts down upon the cohorts of the political left, Senate Minority Leader Hugh Scott (Republican, Pennsylvania) consoled his fretting liberal colleagues, "The conservatives get the rhetoric," he observed, and "we get the action."

Il n'y a que la vérité qui blesse. It is only the truth that hurts.
—Patrick J. Buchanan in
Conservative Votes, Liberal Victories[1]

As President, Richard Nixon ushered in the modern era of trade deficits and the superinflation that has accompanied them. After his stunning electoral victory of 1972, in which the Left was stripped of its claims to popular support by the American people, Nixon himself was soon deprived of the mandate he had won. From shortly after the inauguration until he was driven from office in August 1974, his was a crippled presidency.

One wonders why his opponents waited until after he was reelected before clubbing him with Watergate. After all, the break-in at the Watergate offices of the Democratic campaign committee had taken place in June 1972. The conventions and campaign came after that but the media gave Richard Nixon a virtually free ride on the Watergate issue all the way to the November election.

The two devaluations of the dollar, the first in 1971 and the second in the summer of 1972, had added fuel to the already burning fires of inflation. Commodities, traded primarily in dollars, soared nearly two-thirds in 1972. Inflation in the United States that year was reported (or misreported) at 7 percent, modest by comparison with Britain's 10 percent and Italy's 12 percent. But by mid-1973 the cost of living was in orbit. Food prices in the United States soared 14.5 percent for the year, much of that rise attributable to the loss of confidence in the government over the Watergate scandals.

Nixon had begun reducing the number of American troops in Vietnam in 1969. Essentially, he played the same vacillating game with the war as Lyndon Johnson had played before him and he followed Johnson's shameful example of rewarding the Soviets who were arming the Communist forces to kill our men in Vietnam. Nixon recalls that in March 1972 the North Vietnamese army launched "a full scale invasion" across the DMZ, the buffer zone theoretically protected by treaty.[2] Yet while the invasion was going on Nixon sent his Secretary of Agriculture, Earl Butz, to Moscow to "discuss trade agreements" with Brezhnev, and Nixon boasts that "during this period we signed several joint agreements dealing with education and cultural exchanges."[3]

Nixon dispatched Kissinger on a secret mission to Moscow that spring of 1972 to discuss Vietnam and disarmament. Toward the end of May the president flew to the Soviet Union to sign the SALT (Strategic Arms Limitation Treaty). This was the first of three summit meetings Nixon had with Brezhnev. At each one he gave away more of our nation's strategic and technological resources via trade "initiatives."

In January 1973 Nixon swallowed the transparently false "peace" Kissinger had worked out with the Vietnamese Communists in Paris. It took Hanoi's forces two years to mop up South Vietnam under cover of Kissinger's accord, probably because Ho Chi Minh's Soviet sponsors had more important fish to fry in the Nixon-Kissinger disarmament pan.

This appeasement, obviously calculated to buy favor with the media, failed to keep the hounds at bay. Every day Nixon climbed farther out on the Watergate limb. And every day he dreamed up some new ploy to soothe the pack that was after him. In the very early stages of the controversy he pushed through an end to the military service draft and replaced it with the costly all-volunteer army. Fresh announcements on the Vietnam peace talks and disarmament negotiations and plans for new summits poured forth from the White House in an unending stream.

Free trade has long been a popular item on the media's menu of priorities. So Nixon fed it to them in large doses. He boasted in his memoirs that he "pushed legislation through the Congress authorizing negotiations for reduction of trade barriers,"[4] thus launching the Tokyo Round of GATT negotiations that opened in September 1973. Nixon was also proud that he had "abolished numerous controls on international capital movements that had been imposed in the 1960s."[5] But he neglected to mention, that the reason these controls had been imposed in the first place was to slow the flight of American capital abroad where it was used to build industries that were destroying our own.

In June 1973 Nixon met again with Brezhnev, first in Washington and then in the more cozy setting of San Clemente, the presidential home on the California coast. More trade deals were made and plans formulated for funneling additional technology and industrial plants to the Soviet Union.

Still the hounds bayed at the President's heels. Nothing would shut them up while Richard Nixon remained in office. Actually, the press so relished its role of howling at the President it became a habit. Nixon's successors have all been treated much the same way, though the intensity of the attacks has never quite reached the same hysterical levels as Watergate.

Prior to the fall of 1973 oil had been regarded as one of the great boons to mankind, certainly not a problem to be worried about. World oil prices were low, as little as $1.80 a barrel in 1970, and oil was only a minor factor in the early U.S. trade deficits of that decade. Cheap oil gave the country inexpensive electric power, a wide range of petrochemical products, and affordable gasoline for the increasing number of cars and trucks on the roads.

In 1967 a luncheon meeting took place at the Duquesne Club in Pittsburgh, hosted by Gen. Arthur G. Trudeau, the brilliant former chief of research and development for the U.S. Army, who had become president of the Gulf Research and Development Corporation, a subsidiary of Gulf Oil. The General, who had once headed Army Intelligence, had invited several representatives of T. Mellon & Sons* to sit in, with some directors of Gulf Oil and executives of U.S. Steel and other Pittsburgh corporations, at a briefing on the Mideast conducted by several of his friends from the intelligence community.

An illuminated chart showed how the oil pumped out of Saudi Arabia, Iraq, Iran, and other countries of the region flowed to the West, providing much of the fuel for our energy industries. One of the men conducting the briefing identified Soviet agents active in the region and said there was evidence they were plotting a sudden massive cutoff of Mideast oil to the West, probably in conjunction with an attack by Egypt and Syria against Israel. Rather dramatically, the briefer flicked a switch that put out all the lights on the chart, visually showing what such a cutoff would do to the world.

When the oil stopped flowing on the chart, a director of one of Gulf Oil's British subsidiaries shifted heavily in his chair.

"Hrummph," he snorted. "That will never happen. *Never happen.*"

In October 1973 it did happen, and in precisely the way that General Trudeau's intelligence team had predicted a half-dozen years earlier. Spurred on by the Soviet Union, Egypt and Syria attacked Israel on October 6, the Yom Kippur holy day of atonement, and soon an oil embargo cut off the flow of oil to the West and to Japan. The conflict was by far the bloodiest of all the Arab-Israeli wars and initially Israel's forces were driven back. Spearheaded by Soviet tanks

---

*Gulf Oil had been founded by Andrew W. Mellon, who sent the McGuffey brothers from the Pennsylvania oil fields to Texas in 1900 to drill into a hill where Patricio Higgins had found oil. The National Geological Survey, a U.S. government agency, had previously informed Higgins there was no possibility that there was any oil in Texas or in the entire Southwest. Nonetheless, the McGuffeys brought in "Spindletop," the greatest gusher of all time. The Mellon family remained the major shareholder in Gulf Oil until shortly before its merger with Chevron in the 1980s.

and armored vehicles, the Egyptians hammered out a salient in the Sinai and poured in sixty thousand heavily armed troops.

The World Almanac records that "The Egyptian army's advance was greatly aided by the use of new Russian SAM–6 missiles which stymied the Israeli air offensive against the bridgehead."[6] Simultaneously, the Syrians gained two footholds in the Golan Heights.

For nearly a week the Israelis were on the defensive, but massive air and sea lifts of American arms and equipment made up for their losses of matériel in the Sinai and enabled them to counterattack. Within days the Israelis had regained all the lost ground, driven across the Suez to isolate an Egyptian army in the Sinai, and were nearing Damascus on their northern front.

On October 19 the Arab oil countries shut off petroleum shipments to the West. Three days later the UN Security Council unanimously passed a resolution jointly sponsored by the United States and the Soviet Union calling for a cease-fire. On October 25 Nixon placed American forces worldwide on a "precautionary alert." Two days after that the fighting stopped when the United States and the USSR agreed not to participate in sending a UN peacekeeping force to the region.

The truce in the Mideast did not bring an immediate end to the oil embargo. In fact, it lasted five more months, until March 18, 1974. By then the West was tied up in tight little knots. Long lines of automobiles stretched for blocks around gasoline stations in the United States. Western Europe, more dependent upon imported oil and gas than America, suffered through a winter of power dimouts and industrial shutdowns.

The price of oil quadrupled within a few months after the embargo was declared and kept rising even after it was called off. A new kind of dollar was introduced on world exchanges—the petrodollar. These were the enormous amounts of dollars paid to the Arab and other oil-producing nations for their petroleum products. The Arab members of the OPEC oil cartel were reveling in the ransom they were able to extract from the United States, Europe and Japan.

In a brilliant analysis for *Policy Review* of the impact of the 1973–74 oil cutoff and its aftermath, Paige Bryan, Scott Sullivan, and Steve Pastore added up the toll in the Fall 1982 issue of the Heritage Foundation quarterly. "By late 1974," they wrote, "the oil producing countries of the Middle East had accumulated an enormous dollar surplus as a result of the price rise ($65 billion), and the consuming nations had amassed the concomitant deficits ($33 billion for the industrialized West, and $21 billion for the developing countries). This was to be the largest peacetime transfer of wealth in world history."[7]

As the authors pointed out, the rise in oil prices (they went from under $2 a barrel to $35) "produced an historic restructuring of the global economy and a serious weakening of Western geopolitical security."[8] Europe was shoved into the arms of the Soviet Union and agreed to the natural gas pipeline which ties Germany, France, and the others to the USSR like an umbilical cord, making them dependent upon the Soviets for a large part of their energy requirements.

Western banks, finding themselves with a surfeit of petrodollars deposited by the Arabs, recycled a substantial portion of them—nearly $100 billion over the next decade—to the Soviet bloc as well as huge additional loans to the Third World. There can be no doubt that a very substantial portion of the Western loans to the East bloc served to greatly strengthen the Soviet Union's military power, directly and indirectly.

The petrodollars hyped up the worldwide hyperinflation already generated by the Eurodollars created by the United States's giveaway aid-and-trade policy and by the Vietnam War. The U.S. Cost-Price Index soared no less than 40 points in five years, from 121 in 1971 to over 161 in 1975. (In World War II it had risen less than 12 points between 1940 and 1945.) Although oil and other energy costs were obviously to blame for much of the astronomic inflation of the 1970s, our wide-open trade door, which robbed American companies of the benefits of economies of scale, and the hell-for-leather lending of the big banks, contributed mightily to soaring prices, not only in the United States but around the globe. Indeed, the more sensitive and less self-sufficient economies of undeveloped countries and LDCs suffered far more from hyperinflation than the U.S. They simply could not absorb in any orderly way the billions of dollars showered upon them by our reckless bankers.

That the bankers were themselves lighting the fuse of the debt bomb they were building in the Third World was obvious even at the time. But they had the bit of greed in their teeth and they were obsessed with lending dollars to all comers, including Communist states where there is no possible way of recovering loans in default. Thus, every working day American commercial banks figuratively tossed hundreds of millions of dollars out their windows.

The Bryan-Sullivan-Pastore team tell us that "the top twelve U.S. banks . . . which account for nearly two-thirds of the overseas activities of all U.S. banks, derived nearly 50 percent of their earnings from overseas business in 1977. By 1976 the Chase Manhattan Bank, which in 1972 earned only 34 percent of its income overseas, had more than doubled that share to 78 percent."[9] They cited a Senate Foreign Relations Committee study that showed international earnings for the thirteen largest banks rose from $177 million in 1970 to $836 million in 1975, while domestic earnings leveled off.

The effect of this tremendous shift was that our big banks, always international, now became *supranational*. Indeed, many believe the world economy is now supranational. As Howard Wachtel notes, "For every dollar in a bank or savings and loan association inside the United States, there is another 50 cents held in banks outside of the country that are beyond the regulatory reach of the banking safeguards we take for granted."[10]

Today, when a sheik in Kuwait or Saudi Arabia sneezes, bankers in New York and London reach for their aspirin. And the psychological and financial virus those bankers may contract from their foreign customers are transmitted to people in all walks of life in America, England, Europe, and the scores of countries dependent upon the West.

There are those, Wachtel among them, who believe the jump in oil prices gave the dollar a reprieve.[11] However, as he and others recognize, the temporary lift the dollar got in the early 1970s has since generated very serious problems. Wachtel is correct in stating that "the monetary upheavals of the 1970s have left the world with an international financial baggage that weighs down economies with a rigid monetary austerity. . . . "[12]

One result of the billions of dollars in loans the U.S. banks showered upon Brazil, Argentina, Poland, Romania, and a host of others, is that the banks now exert their considerable influence upon our government to keep American ports open to imports from these countries so they can service their debts to the banks. In short, American industries and workers and farmers are being auctioned off to the thoroughly irrational lending practices of bankers in Wall Street and our other financial centers.

Moreover, every time one of these less developed countries defaults on a debt to an American bank, or extracts another loan from the IMF or the World Bank to service that debt, the value of the dollar is shaved some more. The American consumer, who is supposed to benefit from free trade, actually gets taken both coming and going. His dollars are worth less as U.S. banks dish them out in unsecurable loans to the whole wide world, and he gets taken by the imports coming in which deprive domestic industries of their ability to keep costs and prices down. On top of that, there are those millions of Americans who no longer have jobs because of imports and search in vain for those allegedly created by exports. (Some jobs obviously are created by exports. But the Secretary of Commerce has yet to prove those fictional statistics his department keeps feeding the public.)

By 1974, the year Nixon resigned over Watergate, foreign products were flooding the country. Imports of goods and services topped $141 billion that year, nearly double the 1972 figure. This included $16 billion paid out in interest, dividends and other income on foreign investments in the United States and nearly $14 billion more spent by Americans overseas. But it did not include the money Americans paid for imported illegal narcotics or the growing trade in counterfeit goods passing through our overworked and understaffed Customs Service.

The federal budget was reflecting the pressures of the additional inflation imposed by the oil embargo and the lending sprees that followed. Government expenditures had shot up from $208 billion in 1970 to $340 billion in 1975. State and local government spending was rising at an even faster rate, going from a total of $150 billion to over $261 billion in the same five-year period.[13]

Our federal debt hit $544 billion in 1975, an increase of nearly 50 percent in five short years. The state and local indebtedness added another $221 billion, bringing our total government debt to well over $765 billion. Under free trade America was becoming the greatest debtor nation on earth. It was difficult for the average citizen to comprehend what the debt figures meant. But one man did try.

Willard F. Rockwell, Jr., chairman of the Tax Foundation, stated in his foreword to the foundation's annual report: "government expenditures for 1977 are projected at $9,607 per U.S. household. What that astonishing figure means is that Federal, state and local governments are spending money at an annual rate equal to almost half of the average household income."[14]

Chapter 32.

Another Yalta

About 50 percent of the hardware [trade items] sold to the USSR
is used to enhance the technical performance of Soviet weapons
systems. As the U.S. government has said, the assimilation of
Western technology is so broad that the U.S. and other Western
nations are subsidizing the Soviet military buildup.
—Anthony Harrigan, president,
United States Business and
Industrial Council[1]

Richard Nixon was nearing the end of his aborted presidency in June 1974 when
he journeyed with his alter ego, Henry Kissinger, to the Soviet Union for his
third and final summit with Leonid Brezhnev, the beetle-browed Russian leader
who was later cast into the Communist limbo by Mikhail Gorbachev. After initial
meetings in Moscow, Nixon and Brezhnev flew to the Crimea, where they
continued their talks at a villa on the outskirts of Yalta.

It was appropriate that Nixon went to Yalta, since he nearly rivaled the great
giveaway his predecessor, Franklin Roosevelt, had made in that same Crimean
resort when he turned over Poland and the rest of Eastern Europe to Stalin.
Nixon was sensitive to how the public back home might react if they had known
the summit was in Yalta. So he did what he had always done: he dissembled.
In his memoirs, however, he is quite frank about this particular evasion. "Since
the name Yalta still carried unfavorable connotations," he wrote, "we called
this the Oreanda Summit, after the area in which the [Brezhnev] dacha is situ-
ated."[2]

What this Yalta II meeting, and the Moscow sessions that bracketed it, produced, to use Nixon's own summation, was "the threshold test ban, further restrictions on ABMs, agreements to seek controls on environmental warfare and for cooperation in energy, the opening of additional consulates in both countries, and, most important, the oral agreement I made with Brezhnev for a mini-summit before the end of 1974 for the purpose of reaching agreement on limitations of offensive nuclear weapons."[3]

Actually, it is clear from Nixon's memoirs that it was Henry Kissinger who usurped and dominated the discussions with Brezhnev all during this summit while the President passed Kissinger notes with mild suggestions on SALT and other matters.[4]

Except to mention that "Brezhnev was very tough" on Vietnam,[5] Nixon does not even allude to the ominous fact that as he dallied at Yalta the Soviets were preparing their North Vietnamese surrogates for the invasion of South Vietnam and Cambodia in violation of the "peace" agreements Henry Kissinger had concocted in Paris eighteen months earlier. Though Nixon was gone from the White House when the Communist invasion came the following spring, this humiliating defeat must be laid at his administration's doorstep, with, of course, a cowardly Congress sharing the blame for refusing to help our Saigon allies as they went down to defeat.

Thus, at this disguised Yalta in 1974 Nixon tacitly reinforced the agreements already in place that would deliver many more millions of people into the hopeless hell on earth that communism creates for those it conquers. Moreover, it was not just Vietnam, Cambodia, and Laos that were handed over to communism by the Nixon-Kissinger treaties and the accompanying withdrawal of U.S. forces from Southeast Asia. Sixteen more countries fell to the Communists after the collapse of Vietnam, from Angola and other African states to Nicaragua in our Central American backyard.

There was one other agreement Nixon and Brezhnev entered into that may ultimately do more damage to the United States and the Free World than even the loss of Vietnam. This was creation of the U.S.-USSR Trade and Economic Council (USTEC), an organization brought into being by a protocol signed on June 22, 1973 by Nikolai S. Patolichev, the Soviet minister of foreign trade, and George P. Shultz, then Secretary of the Treasury. The short and innocuous-sounding document pledged increased cooperation between the USSR and the USA to develop "mutually beneficial trade between the two countries." The protocol envisioned a private-sector U.S.-USSR chamber of commerce which would eventually evolve from USTEC.

Anthony Harrigan, president of the U.S. Business and Industrial Council, the only major business organization consistently opposed to trading with avowed enemies of the United States, summed up some of the results of the USTEC and similar trade-promotion efforts in a speech at the University of Colorado in September 1987. Harrigan cited U.S. government statistics enumerating "over five thousand Soviet military research projects [that] benefit from U.S. information and hardware each year."[6]

Ironically, the U.S. government—which implicity condemns American and other Western subsidization of the Russian military moloch—sponsors and supports the U.S.-USSR Trade and Economic Council and other groups promoting increased trade with the Communist world. Indeed, it was the personal involvement of Richard Nixon when he was President that put USTEC into its high-powered orbit, and this at a time when the Communists were pressing the war in Vietnam with Soviet weapons.

There are an equal number of Soviets and Americans on the USTEC board of directors. The twenty-six U.S. members read like the *Who's Who* of American industry and finance, and there are two additional directorships reserved for representatives of the National Association of Manufacturers and the U.S. Chamber of Commerce. The original, or early, U.S. directors included David Rockefeller, chairman of the Chase Manhattan Bank; A. W. Clausen, president of Bank of America and later head of the World Bank; Armand Hammer, the ubiquitous chairman of Occidental Petroleum; Richard C. Gerstenberg, chairman of General Motors; Irving S. Shapiro, chairman of Du Pont, and the chairmen of 3M, Caterpillar Tractor, Union Carbide, International Harvester, Deere & Co., and Pan American Airways.

Most disturbing was the presence on the board of the then chairman of Rockwell International, the company that built the U.S. space shuttle and has been deeply involved in other space and defense projects. Another company with heavy defense-related activities represented on the board was Hewlett-Packard. Indeed, it was then represe·,ed by its chairman, David Packard, who has served as Undersecretary of Defense in the Pentagon. Still another early USTEC director from a corporation with sensitive national defense contracts was Reginald H. Jones of General Electric.

Nobody, except possibly a few people in the CIA or the Defense Intelligence Agency, had the faintest idea who most of the Soviet directors of USTEC were and are. However, the Heritage Foundation verified in a 1988 report by Ira Carnahan that the Soviet half of USTEC is under "KGB domination."[7]

There was, however, one Russian on the original USTEC board whom we were to hear more about in later years. He was Vladimir Alkhimov, then deputy minister of foreign trade for the USSR and co-chairman of USTEC with Donald Kendall, the chairman of Pepsico. Alkhimov met with a group of correspondents at the Duquesne Club in Pittsburgh in early 1974 when the Arab oil embargo was still in force and an hour's wait in line for gasoline was considered fortunate.

Alkhimov's ex officio hosts at the Duquesne Club were Samuel B. Casey, Jr., president of Pullman Inc. and a USTEC director, and Donald Stingel, president of Pullman's Swindell-Dressler subsidiary, which was designing the huge Kama River industrial complex for the Soviets. Casey had been an early supporter of Sen. Barry Goldwater for President a decade earlier but in Richard Nixon's administration much had obviously changed.

Stingel was later to become a governor of the Export-Import Bank in Washington during the Carter administration. (Trade cuts across all party lines—

Democrat, Republican, and Communist. Indeed, it frequently makes the lines dividing all three indistinguishable.)

Alkhimov made quite an impression on the assembled correspondents at the press conference that followed breakfast. He exhibited a mind that worked like a computer-driven steel trap and most of the newsmen appeared embarrassingly naive as he answered their questions in his brisk, businesslike way. Two exceptions were William Wylie, financial editor of the *Pittsburgh Press*, and Jack Markowitz, his counterpart from the *Post-Gazette*. They refused to let him off the hook on the relationship between trade and human rights, a question Alkhimov sought to dismiss as irrelevant.

Vladimir Alkhimov played a key role in the structuring and operation of the U.S.-USSR Trade and Economic Council during its formative years. However, in 1986 he suddenly dropped out of sight when his daughter defected to the West. His last known assignment was the chairmanship of the Soviet Union's central bank, their counterpart of the Federal Reserve. Ushering in USTEC was probably his most important achievement.

USTEC was, like so many of our foreign policy innovations of the 1970s, the creation of Henry Kissinger. Indeed, one of the early issues of the USTEC *Journal* displays a photograph of Secretary of State Kissinger beaming on a group of directors of the Council from his seat at the head of the table.

If Nixon thought he could save his presidency with trade promotion ploys like USTEC or the Kissinger disarmament schemes, he was badly mistaken. He had offered up John Mitchell, Chuck Colson, John Erlichman, Bob Haldeman, John Dean, and even his Vice President, Spiro Agnew, who had turned out to be, as our politicians so quaintly put it, on the take. Now, in the sweltering summer of 1974, he returned from Yalta and Moscow to find the pack, in and out of Congress, still in full cry for impeachment.

Within a month of Nixon's return from the summit the House judiciary committee voted to recommend impeachment on three counts, one involving a criminal conspiracy connected with the Watergate coverup, and another for abuse of power in failing to carry out his oath to defend the Constitution.

Early in August a number of his old supporters in the House and Senate said they would vote for impeachment. On August 9, 1974, Richard Milhous Nixon became the first President in the history of the United States to resign from office. He was replaced by Gerald Ford, a congressman from Michigan and former Republican leader of the House of Representatives, whom Nixon had named Vice President to replace Agnew.

Ford's very first public announcement after being sworn in was that he had asked Henry Kissinger to stay on as Secretary of State. It was an appropriate appointment. Next to Lyndon Johnson's McNamara-Rusk-Rostow triumvirate, Kissinger was the principal architect of the first loss of a war ever suffered by the United States of America. Vietnam was headed down the drain with Watergate.

Chapter 33.

Roulette at Rambouillet

We achieved the ultimate monetary reform that we all came to accomplish.
                                    —Secretary of the Treasury William E. Simon[1]

We have unanimously agreed that gold should be phased out of the IMF system.
                                    —Chancellor of the Exchequer Denis Healey[2]

Gerald R. Ford assumed the presidency of the United States at a moment when the very fabric of the republic appeared to be unraveling. If it were coming apart, as the media daily proclaimed during the Watergate scandals, it certainly was due to much more than the administration of the government during Richard Nixon's inept tenure. Forces set in motion long before were gnawing away at the foundations of American society and not the least among them was Washington's fanatic worship of free trade and the irrational monetary policies that sprang from that fraudulent theology.

Ford moved into the White House while the country and the world were still reeling from the impact of the Arab oil embargo. The U.S. trade deficit for 1974 was $5.3 billion, with petroleum products accounting for a large share of the imbalance. Moreover, the deficit would have been much worse but for the recycling of Arabian petrodollars into the American economy. Indeed, in 1975 this pulled the trade balance into the black by a healthy $9.1 billion. Alas, 1975 was to see the very last U.S. trade surplus for at least the next decade and a half. In the very next year, 1976, the trade deficit soared to $9.3 billion and hit $30.9 billion for 1977 as it rocketed toward the $200 billion range of the Reagan years.

The Ford administration was beset by more than trade and monetary problems. Gerald Ford had only been in office a few months when the electorate, driven to extremism by the furor over Watergate, sent to Washington the most radical Congress in our history. The House and Senate tied up the executive branch in impotent little knots and prevented Ford from taking action to save Vietnam, Cambodia, and several African countries that also fell to the Communists.

Moreover, the worst recession since the 1930s sent unemployment to its highest levels in a quarter-century while, contrary to accepted economic theory, inflation rose sharply. In the early 1970s the inflation had been partially spurred by a world steel shortage, and our trading partners took full advantage of this to raise their prices. Having knocked American steel producers out of some product lines entirely, the Japanese and others upped prices of their exports to the United States by as much as 300 percent. It was estimated that the theoretical savings American consumers had allegedly realized from steel imports in the preceding two decades were erased in a single year.

The flagrant gouging of the Japanese and others, coupled with a rising flood of all imports that reached $140 billion in 1974, prompted the outgoing and more conservative Congress to pass a new trade bill before the radicals took over. This Congress also restored the right of our citizens to own gold, a right they had been deprived of for more than forty years. At the same time, however, the U.S. Treasury, then headed by William E. Simon, began an all-out campaign to convince the public that gold wasn't really worth owning after all. One way Simon attempted this was in ordering a series of auctions of the nation's monetary gold in order to keep gold prices down.

In just two big Treasury auctions, the first in January 1975, the second in June of the same year, Simon sold off 1,253,500 ounces, or more than 46 tons of our monetary gold. The halls of Fort Knox were beginning to echo in their emptiness and the radar screens of the central banks in London, Paris, Bonn, and Zurich were bouncing with contradictory blips of both fear for the dollar and avid anticipation of more profits on the gold they were buying from those crazy Americans.

Gerald Ford and William Simon also made another major assault on the use of gold in international monetary transactions during a series of conferences that culminated in, or at least reached another anticlimax at, the economic summit held in Rambouillet, France, in the autumn of 1975. On the road to Rambouillet, the President had to weather a number of crises and suffer through interminable meetings with other heads of state. The first important one of these was with Leonid Brezhnev at Vladivostok toward the end of November 1974.

Henry Kissinger, the formulator of our foreign policy during the Nixon-Ford years, took the president along to Vladivostok to introduce him to the dazzling art of summitry. En route, the presidential party stopped off in Tokyo and Korea to visit with our principal Pacific trading partners, doubtless to reassure them that the new trade bill about to go into effect would not seriously impinge upon our trade relations with them.

When he arrived at the Soviet Union's easternmost colony Ford was taken for a ride by Brezhnev in a luxurious private railroad car to the resort ninety minutes away where the meetings took place. The principal topic during the several days of negotiations between the President and the Soviet leader was, as always, arms control. With Kissinger urging him on, Ford gave Brezhnev much of what the Soviets asked for. This included a provision to let the USSR catch up with the United States in MIRVs, the multiple warheads which had increased our strategic power in spite of all the efforts of the disarmament lobby to reduce our nuclear forces.

Ford and Kissinger also agreed to open the door wider to trade with the Soviet bloc. More credits to buy American grain at bargain prices were arranged and pledges to strengthen the U.S.-USSR Trade and Economic Council (USTEC).

THE FALL OF VIETNAM

While the Vladivostok talks were in progress, the Soviet's client state, North Vietnam, was preparing for its next and greatest invasion of South Vietnam in violation of the Paris peace accords which had earned Kissinger a Nobel Prize. As Ford and Brezhnev met, the USSR was shipping thousands of tons of armaments to mount the offensive. Our intelligence was well aware of this. The Communists could not hide whole shiploads of tanks as they were offloaded onto the docks at Haiphong. But the public was not adequately informed of the buildup until the invasion was unleashed.

The Communist offensive began soon after Vladivostok and heavy fighting raged in Vietnam through December 1974 into the new year. As if to add a little more "moral" support to the heavy arms shipments it had sent to make the invasion possible, the USSR announced early in January that it was nullifying the trade agreement Brezhnev had reached with Nixon in 1972. The pretext was the Jackson-Vanik amendment that tied U.S. trade with Russia to the emigration of Soviet Jews.

On January 9 the key Vietnamese stronghold of Phuoc Binh fell before the Soviet-sponsored onslaught. In some places the American-trained Army of the Republic of Vietnam (ARVN) fought courageously. But in others it cut and ran as the Communist offensive intensified. Ford did try to get congressional permission to lend U.S. air and naval support to the besieged ARVN forces. President Thieu sent an urgent message from Saigon reminding the United States of the firm commitments Nixon had made to persuade him to sign Kissinger's ersatz peace accords. But the Congress, dominated now by the new breed of surrenderists, refused to honor those commitments. Even the additional aid to the ARVN Ford asked for was rejected.

Toward the end of March Gen. Fredrick C. Weyand of the Joint Chiefs flew to Palm Springs, where Ford was vacationing, to warn that Vietnam would fall unless U.S. help was forthcoming at once. Ron Nessen, Ford's press aide, records in his book: "After the meeting, Kissinger drove to the press center to give a briefing. 'Why don't these people [the Vietnamese] die fast?' he moaned in the car. 'The worst thing that could happen would be for them to linger on.' "[3]

In Vietnam, the Communist forces drove southward as the few thousand remaining Americans in the country were evacuated. Ambassador Graham Martin resisted evacuation until the last possible moment. An hour before midnight on April 28, 1975, Martin, a few remaining members of his staff, some Marine guards, and a number of Vietnamese refugees, were lifted out of the embassy compound in helicopters.[4]

It had been fourteen years since President Kennedy ordered the first large-scale U.S. military unit into Vietnam. America's longest, most divisive war had ended, "not with a bang but a whimper."

On May 12, 1975, President Ford and the U.S. armed forces managed to salvage a little of America's tattered national honor in the *Mayaguez* incident. A Communist patrol seized the U.S. merchant ship and its thirty nine-man crew in the Gulf of Siam and took the American captives to an island off the Cambodian coast.

At the White House the President was bitterly criticized by Democrat Senate leaders Mike Mansfield and Robert Byrd when he informed them he was ordering air strikes to protect the Marines who had landed on the island to recapture the ship and rescue its crew.[5] But the action succeeded in forcing the Cambodians to free the crew of the *Mayaguez*, although American casualties in the operation were high—thirty-six dead and missing; fifty wounded. Nonetheless, it probably prevented other American vessels from being taken by Communists puffed up with their victory in Vietnam. Moreover, it sent a message to the Kremlin that the United States had not yet run up the white flag.

Ironically, as Vietnam was suffering the agony of defeat and preparing for the greater agonies to come under Communism, the United States sent a mission to Moscow to strengthen the trade ties between the two countries. The mission was headed by Secretary of the Treasury William E. Simon and Acting Secretary of Commerce John K. Tabor, who met with Brezhnev and his trade team in the Kremlin.

According to the communique issued after the meeting. "Both delegations expressed satisfaction that . . . bilateral trade continues at a high level."[6] It added that the United State and USSR had increased their trade to $1 billion in 1974— "four times what it was in 1970." This, despite a drop in U.S. farm exports to the Soviet Union, which obviously meant we were sending them much more machinery and technology.

Although the United States was then in the throes of its final defeat in Vietnam, William Simon and the others, according to the communique, "expressed sincere gratitude for the warm hospitality extended by the Soviet side during our stay in the USSR." Thus do U.S. officials bow to the commissars in the Kremlin, while their fellow Americans die on the battlefronts.

We need to be reminded that 58,021 Americans died in the Vietnam War and 153,303 more were wounded, many of them blinded or maimed for life. Most of the Americans were killed or wounded by weapons supplied by the Soviet Union at a time when our Presidents, Democrat and Republican, were currying favor with the USSR by increasing credits and trade and "cultural exchanges" with that country.

SPINNING THE WHEEL AT RAMBOUILLET

In the fall of 1975 one of the most severe recessions in the nation's history was deepening as the United States continued to lose confidence in itself and in the government. This erosion had been growing for several years, triggered by Watergate, accelerated by the loss of Vietnam, worsened by the internal decay as evidenced so tragically in America's growing consumption of narcotics.

The balance of payments problem had temporarily receded as wholesale Arab purchases of American products and services more than offset the outflow of dollars for oil. But everyone knew, or guessed, that this was but a temporary reprieve. The dollar was not yet dead (like the country, it proved amazingly resilient) but it was under constant siege. It was in the shadow of these less than happy circumstances that the industrial world's finance ministers and central bankers, augmented on one occasion by their heads of state, met in a series of conferences that are remembered, not entirely correctly, as the last gasp of the Bretton Woods monetary system.

The best known of these meetings was held at the luxurious Chateau Rambouillet in France, the country that more than any other respects and understands the value of gold. However, most of the decisions ratified at Rambouillet were actually made earlier at the International Monetary Fund's thirtieth annual meeting in Washington. Indeed, just *before* the IMF conference officially opened the finance ministers and central bankers of the leading industrial nations assembled in late August to forge the real agreements.

William Simon was determined to get the Europeans and Japanese to agree to wash out of the IMF system what remained of its original adherence to gold as an integral part of international payments. Simon reportedly took his foreign colleagues out on the presidential yacht *Sequoia* for a sail down the Potomac and kept them sweltering there until they professed to see things his way.[7] What came out of this uncomfortable cruise was more bad news for the dollar.

The centerpiece of the agreement reached on the Potomac was a commitment to exchange gold among central banks at the free market price, then hovering around $140 per ounce, as opposed to the $42.22 at which it had been pegged in the wake of John Connally's 1971 shoot-out. However, a codicil to the 1975 agreement forbade the banks from buying new gold, thus pumping up the private market for the next two years.

The effect of the *Sequoia* agreement and subsequent accords was the development of a new world monetary arrangement which might be called Rambouillet roulette, a high-stakes gambler's game in which national currencies were put on the line every day. Simon had assigned Edwin H. Yeo, a Pittsburgh banker who

had become Udersecretary for Monetary Affairs at the Treasury, to work out
the details of the new game with the Europeans' French emissary, Jacques de
Laroisiere, later managing director of the International Monetary Fund. The deal
Yeo and de Laroisiere cut allowed each country to pick its own exchange rate
system—free floating, managed floating, pegged to SDRs, pegged to foreign
currencies, pegged to a basket of currencies, "*pegged to anything but gold.*"[8]
As the game played itself out, however, the Europeans very wisely contrived
their own side-game with gold, though at the outset, in 1975, they followed the
bad example of the United States and actually gave some gold away.

Under the Washington agreements, a third of the IMF's gold supply—or 50
million ounces—was disposed of to satisfy Simon's campaign to demonetize
gold. A healthy share of the IMF gold was auctioned off and donated to Third
World countries. Even Communist Romania and Yugoslavia shared in this largesse. It is not clear by what authority Simon gave away America's large share
of the IMF gold. This, however, was merely the first of several similar donations
of American and European gold to less developed countries via IMF auctions.

Simon wanted to erase all vestige of gold in the IMF's payments transaction
and replace it with fiat paper. In this he largely succeeded, but the effect was
to transfer much of the IMF's payments authority to the central banks, which
still clung to gold as the true measure of their nations' wealth. The Bank of
International Settlements in Basle assumed new importance after the autumn of
1975. The central bankers who regularly assemble there call most of the shots
on payments transfers in international exchange though they often defer to their
own governments.

The agreement reached on Simon's *Sequoia* outing in August 1975 was ratified
after Labor Day by the IMF annual meeting and the C-20 group, the committee
comprised of representatives of twenty nations evenly divided between the
"rich" industrial countries and the "poor" LDCs. (The Group of ten industrial
nations had been augmented by a like number of LDCs to give the latter a greater
voice in world trade and monetary affairs.)

President Ford and the other "Big Five" heads of state put their seal of
approval on the IMF and C-20 arrangements at Rambouillet later in the fall of
1975. (The "Big Five" was comprised of the United States, Britain, France,
Germany, and Japan. Italy and Canada joined later to make it the "Big Seven.")
Ford had come to Rambouillet some weeks after two assassination attempts had
been made on him in California and he may have welcomed the chance to relax
for a few days in the security of the lovely chateau.

There were still some untidy odds and ends to clean up after Rambouillet and
these were tackled by the "experts" at Kingston, Jamaica, in January 1976. It
was here that a second third of the IMF's gold was disposed of with the same
formula Simon steamed out of his colleagues on the Potomac the previous August.
The Third World countries were again the big beneficiaries. The Jamaica meeting,
said the South African minister of finance, O. P. F. Horwood, "reaffirms and
entrenches the monetary role of gold."[9] This, of course, sent the South Africans

home happy since they produce more than half of the world's newly mined gold, but it was the direct opposite of what the Treasury's Simon had intended.

It is interesting to note that the United States played the leading role in concocting a large international giveaway for the Third World at a time when our own country was mired in recession, with unemployment at the highest levels in thirty-five years, interest rates at an all-time record, inflation soaring out of reach, and the federal government facing unprecedented peacetime deficits.

Thibaut deSaint Phalle in *The Federal Reserve: An Intentional Mystery* shows how the Fed encouraged the commercial banks to make more loans offshore. Then he adds: "Surely, this is not to the country's advantage—particularly in a period of recession. Nor can it be of any advantage to the [American] depositors who are risking their savings in Zaire, Mexico, and Brazil rather than in the development of business (and, consequently, of employment) in our own country."[10]

Unfortunately, in seeking a cure for the recession neither Gerald Ford nor any of his advisors gave serious consideration to the one policy that could have pulled the country out of the doldrums—a return to a sound trade policy. By the mid-1970s all memory of America's historic economic experience had been erased.

Chapter 34.

The No-Escape Clause

If I were ever again to suggest another escape clause case to my board of directors, they would shoot me.[1]
—Fawn Evenson, President,
Footwear Industries of America
in 1989

The Trade Act of 1974, signed into law by President Ford on January 3, 1975, held out a measure of hope for industries and workers being driven to the wall by the massive invasion of imports that multiplied exponentially in the troubled decade of the 1970s. Tragically, the new law failed to fulfill the hope it promised.

Thanks largely to the efforts of Sen. Russell B. Long of Louisiana, then chairman of the Senate Finance Committee, the act sought to tighten enforcement of the anti-dumping and countervailing duty statutes already on the books. But the greatest expectations centered on Section 201, the so-called "escape clause" designed in the new legislation to give companies and their employees an easier route to protection when they were injured by imports. No longer did they have to prove that imports were the *major* cause of injury; it was now deemed sufficient that they show imports had been "*a substantial cause of serious injury, or the threat therof.*"[2]

Under the escape clause procedure industries and labor organizations were supposed to be able to obtain relief within eight months after a complaint was lodged. The name of the federal agency handling such cases was changed from the Tariff Commission to the United States International Trade Commission (ITC), obviously in deference to the vastly changed conditions now prevailing in the nation's trade with the rest of the world. After all, the United States was just one player in the big international trade game and foreign players had equal standing before the law with our own companies and workers. In practice, alas, the foreigners turned out to have *more* standing.

Although the 1974 act appeared to promise a faster track for 201 cases, the procedures were still laborious. First of all, in spite of the specific wording of the new law it was futile for an industry to file a case unless it had been severely injured for some time. Secondly, even if it did get a finding of injury and a favorable recommendation for a remedy from the ITC, the President could reject it. The law provided that the Congress could override the presidential decision and institute the ITC recommendation. But in practice this was not feasible, and if attempted could stretch out the case interminably while more companies and jobs fell by the wayside.

It quickly became apparent, moreover, that most cases could not get beyond the injury barrier, let alone have a remedy approved by the President. Of the first three dozen cases filed under the new law, only five managed to achieve some degree of relief from imports for the injured industries. Of those five successful cases, those involving the Specialty Steel Industry of the United States, the Footwear Industries of America, and the Committee to Preserve American Color Television (COMPACT) * were the three most visible escape clause cases fought between 1975 and 1979. A review of the fate of each of these industries will show that in the long run the Trade Act of 1974, and the 1979 Trade Agreements Act that succeeded it, provided no escape for American companies and workers.

KEEPING SPECIALTY STEEL ALIVE

The specialty steel industry in the United States is acknowledged by its foreign competitors to be the most technologically advanced industry of its kind in the world. Indeed, in the 1975–76 escape clause case, and in subsequent trade actions, the foreign producers argued that the U.S. specialty steel industry did not need relief from imports because it was so up-to-date and efficient, unlike much of the larger carbon steel industry.

Actually, specialty steel is on the cutting edge of modern technology. The high-alloy metals produced in America's specialty steel mills keep many of the country's other industries going. Electric power generation, oil and gas production, the aerospace and transportation industries, food processing, mining, communications, computers—these and many more depend upon reliable sources of specialty steel products. Surgical instruments and the latest medical diagnostic equipment are made from stainless steel and other alloys. Moreover, specialty steels are absolutely essential for the nation's defense effort, as a Senate Armed Services subcommittee found after hearings and a lengthy investigation.[3]

Yet in spite of the obviously crucial role it plays in the nation's economy,

___

*The author was a consultant to all three of these industries on these and other trade cases.

health, and defense, specialty steel production was on the ropes in 1975. The industry had won several anti-dumping cases earlier in the decade. But the government had refused to enforce its own rulings against illegal imports with the result that most mills were operating well below capacity and unemployment in the industry was over 40 percent. The United States Steel Corporation had closed down a stainless wire rod plant in Cleveland when import penetration topped 70 percent in that product line. Other mills had also ceased production and for some the stoppages would be permanent.

The industry and the United Steelworkers of America jointly filed the escape clause case in mid-1975 and hearings were held in October. The cavernous hearing room in the old Tariff Building in Washington was overcrowded with participants and spectators and the press tables were filled. The atmosphere was charged with expectation, since this was the first major test of the most important provision of the new Trade Act.

Battle lines were clearly drawn. Representatives and witnesses for the domestic industry were seated on one side of the huge room; the lawyers and economists of the foreign producers filled the other, with the ITC commissioners perched on their high judicial bench in between. The American industry was represented by a then relatively small and unknown law firm—Collier, Shannon, Rill & Scott. Donald de Kieffer was the senior partner supervising the case and Stanley Nehmer, a distinguished economist and former Commerce Department official, had prepared the statistical testimony that told the sad tale of a vital industry decimated by imports.

Arrayed against the Americans were attorneys for some of the most high-powered law firms in Washington and New York. They were there to do battle for the various Japanese and European steel companies. It was no coincidence that most of these same law firms also represented the governments of the countries producing the imported steels.

Why? Because their client foreign governments were the actual owners of most of the foreign companies involved. Indeed, nothing demonstrated more dramatically than this ITC hearing room face-off what privately owned American corporations are up against: i.e., the *governments* of Japan, Britain, France, Germany, Sweden, Austria, et al.

But government ownership and subsidization was not at issue in a 201 case. Proof of injury was the decisive question, and several obviously injured industries, including the hard-pressed industrial fastener manufacturers, had already been turned down by the ITC under the supposedly broader criteria of the new law.

Miraculously, the Specialty Steel Industry of the United States (then called the Tool and Stainless Steel Industry Committee) and United Steelworkers of America prevailed in this landmark case. The ITC found imports had done serious injury to the companies and their workers and the commissioners voted, four to one, to recommend the president grant import quotas for five years. Another bitter fight followed, this time against the State Department, which sees itself as the protector of the trade interests of all foreign nations in stark contrast to the aggressive commercial role played by the foreign ministries of other countries in behalf of their own industries.

Fortunately, by this time it was election year. And all trade cases, particularly escape clause cases, are highly political. President Ford granted part of the remedy recommended by the ITC, but he cut the import restrictions from five to three years and he cloaked the import quotas in a thin disguise by negotiating an Orderly Marketing Agreement (OMA) with Japan. Surprisingly, the Europeans refused to accept this more diplomatic arrangement and the President was forced to impose quotas on specialty steel imports into the United States from most nations of Europe.

In the years since, the specialty steel industry and the steelworkers have waged constant warfare against unfair imports. President Carter tried to lift the import quotas after barely a year and, though he was dissuaded, Carter ultimately refused to grant the full five-year respite recommended by the ITC. His special trade representative, Robert Strauss, led the industry to believe it would get the complete term the ITC had voted. But Strauss had already secretly promised the Europeans that the quotas would be phased out in the last two of those years, and warehouses in U.S. ports were bulging with imported stainless and other alloy steels waiting for the U.S. markets to open again. When they did, an avalanche of subsidized specialty steels hit the market, and the American companies, like a ton of steel bricks.

Ronald Reagan did somewhat better by the specialty steel industry than Jimmy Carter. In spite of his impassioned advocacy of free trade, President Reagan came to see that this crucial industry had made a very heavy investment to maintain its technological leadership and had held down its prices. He also came to understand that foreign governments were unfairly subsidizing the competition. In 1982 Reagan took the unusual step of instituting a second escape clause case in behalf of the industry and its workers. In July 1983 he granted another import program, a combination of quotas and higher tariffs for four years. Tool steels and a few other products covered by quotas fared well. But the industry's bread-and-butter stainless sheet and strip, accounting for some 70 percent of the total volume, was hard hit by record imports in the following years because higher tariffs did not work. The governments of the foreign producers simply increased their subsidies to overcome the tariffs Reagan had imposed.

Although the specialty steel industry is still alive, and a few of the companies have thrived under the restraint programs, the attrition has been severe. Of the two dozen companies that belonged to the industry coalition in 1975, only half are still in the business of producing specialty steels. U.S. Steel got out of high-alloys almost entirely; Bethlehem Steel abandoned tool steel production when import penetration went over 50 percent; Colt Industries Crucible Steel mill in Midland, Pennsylvania, which once employed nearly five thousand people, was closed, a remnant of one section of the big plant operated by another company. Nearly a half-dozen specialty steel companies have been forced into bankruptcy, though a few were coming back in 1987–89 under Chapter 11. Of the sixty-five thousand jobs that depended upon specialty steel production in 1975, less than thirty thousand were left in 1990.

For more than half the highly skilled workers, research metallurgists, executives and marketing personnel in the specialty steel industry, the escape clause in the Trade Act of 1974 provided no escape.

THE FOOTWEAR FIASCO

Disappointing as the failure to enforce U.S. trade laws has been to the specialty steel industry, it does not begin to compare with the disenchantment of many other industries, including the volume steel producers, automobile industry, textiles, computers, communication equipment, television manufacturing, and literally scores of others. Indeed, specialty steel is counted as a success story in the annals of recent trade wars. It is still alive, whereas many other industries that have sought relief from imports under our trade laws are either dead or dying. The footwear industry is a good example of how the United States government has permitted a once thriving industry to decline, in this instance to be sacrificed to the interests of the Third World whose industrial base our taxpayers financed and our technology developed.

By the end of the Johnson administration, nonrubber shoe imports had already climbed to more than 20 percent of the U.S. market. Within the next six years the penetration nearly doubled. More than three hundred footwear factories had closed, scores of companies had gone out of business, thousands of workers had lost their jobs.

Many shoe plants were family-owned enterprises located in small towns scattered over nearly forty states. Often, the shoe factory was the only large employer in the community. When it shut down, the economic base of the whole town died with it.

In August 1975 the Footwear Industries of America (then the American Footwear Industries Association) and two shoe-worker unions jointly filed an escape clause case with the ITC. The injury could not be denied and the commission recommended import restraints. President Ford, perhaps because he had so recently been blistered as a "protectionist" for his specialty steel decision, turned down the footwear industry and instead implemented a program of adjustment assistance—what George Fecteau and John Mara, the presidents of the shoe unions, had called "burial insurance" for the jobs of their members.

Angered at the President's flaunting of the new trade law in an industry obviously savaged by unfair imports, the Senate Finance Committee took the unusual step of petitioning the ITC to reopen the footwear case. The ITC again recommended import relief but the new president, Jimmy Carter, appeared to hesitate under the barrage of criticism accusing him of considering violation of the holy policy of free trade.

Jacob Clayman, the able lawyer who had succeeded the Steelworkers' I. W.

Abel as president of the AFL-CIO's Industrial Union Department, rallied the unions to lodge strong protests with the President they had just helped elect. Lane Kirkland, who was soon to succeed George Meany as head of the AFL-CIO, delivered a withering attack on the bureaucrats in the federal government wearing Gucci shoes and driving to work in Honda and Mercedes luxury autos, while they frivolously decided the fate of whole industries and thousands of workers.

Jimmy Carter got the message, but not all of it. Instead of imposing a real import restraint program, he directed his trade representative, Robert Strauss, to negotiate Orderly Marketing Agreements with Taiwan and Korea, the two countries accounting for the largest shares of footwear exports to the United States. By this time shoe import penetration was over 50 percent and that is the level Strauss substantially settled for, although other countries immediately increased their exports and Taiwan and Korea never fully observed their agreements.

In June 1981 President Reagan permitted the OMA with Taiwan and Korea to expire and shoe imports shot up to over 60 percent, accounting that year for $2.5 billion of the overall trade deficit. Within months the situation in the shoe industry was desperate. Employment, which had been nearly 240,000 in 1968, was cut in half to 120,000 by mid–1982, and another 80,000 jobs in support industries had disappeared. Plant closings had climbed by more than four hundred during the same period for a total of some seven hundred in less than twenty years.

A bipartisan group of senators and congressman called upon the President to invoke Section 301 of the Trade Act, which provided for retaliation against countries which subsidized exports or barred their own markets to American products.

At a press conference in the Capitol on September 29, 1982, Sen. John Heinz of Pennsylvania emphasized that "American shoe manufacturers are not losing sales because they are not competitive. Rather, unfair trade restrictions on the part of other producers have closed foreign markets to American products and made the U.S. market the dumping grounds for the world's exports."[4]

Sen. John C. Danforth of Missouri charged that the United States was practicing "unilateral free trade in footwear" so that while we kept "our market wide open to all . . . our major competitors maintain severe barriers to imports."[5] Sen. George J. Mitchell of Maine reported that two thousand of his state's remaining seventeen thousand shoeworkers had "already lost their jobs as a result of the President's pursuit of free trade in the year since import restraints were jettisoned."[6]

George Q. Langstaff, president of Footwear Industries of America, warned that his industry and the jobs that still depended upon it faced "potential extinction" unless U.S. trade laws were enforced.[7] The executive branch and other exponents of free trade tend to treat statements like this as "alarmist." But Langstaff's warning proved all too accurate. By 1989 footwear imports were an astronomical 82 percent, 316 more plants had closed, and thousands of additional jobs had disappeared.[8]

The footwear industry filed several more trade cases in the late 1980s and eventually tied its effort to the textile and apparel industry's campaign for import relief. The ITC consistently found serious injury had been done to all these industries, but the President refused to defend them against the unfair tactics indulged in by their subsidized competitors abroad. Ronald Reagan, like so many of his predecessors in the White House, continued to ignore the trade laws of the United States as he bowed to foreign policy considerations and the tinsel god of free trade.

Fawn Evenson, who succeeded George Langstaff as president of Footwear Industries of America, said in 1989: "Our only hope for keeping the remaining plants and jobs is the Congress."[9] Unfortunately, the Congress had long since surrendered its Constitutional authority over trade to the President.

Chapter 35.

The TV Sell-Out

The Treasury Department has thrown up one administrative roadblock after another to thwart the levying of duties against Japanese television manufacturers who have flagrantly flouted the law for more than a decade.
—Jacob Clayman and Allen W. Dawson
in joint statement for COMPACT, 1978[1]

American television manufacturing, once the great cornucopia of capital for the entire electronics industry, is *the* classic case of an industry that died because the United States government adamantly refused to enforce its own trade laws. In anything other than a trade matter it would be judged a case of criminal negligence and those guilty of sacrificing more than twenty-five companies and tens of thousands of jobs to the conspirators in Japan, Taiwan, and Korea would have been sentenced to federal penitentiaries to reflect upon their betrayal of their fellow citizens.

Television was, of course, invented in America and TV sets were produced here experimentally before World War II and on a commercial basis from the mid-1940s onward. For better or worse, TV revolutionized our society. It also brought about a revolution in the electronics industry, which has continued into the present age of video recorders and personal computers. It would be difficult indeed to imagine the world without those millions of screens that give us instant information on everything from the latest events in the Persian Gulf or Panama to up-to-the-minute stock prices and available airline seats.

There were twenty-eight U.S. companies making TV sets by the 1960s when the Japanese Ministry of Trade (MITI) approved the plan of its electronics companies to target this high-technology American industry. By the end of that decade they were selling both black-and-white and color TV sets in our market at the rate of several million per year. The dumping was so redolent our Customs Service could smell it all the way from Tokyo. The 19-inch color TV set that sold at Sears, Roebuck stores for less than $295 cost Japanese consumers $750 on the Ginza. Dumping margins were even wider for the bigger 25-inch sets: $700 here, up to $2,100 in Japan.[2]

In 1968 the domestic manufacturers and key suppliers like Corning Glass, which once had five plants turning out glass parts for TV sets, filed an anti-dumping case through a committee of the Electronics Industries Association of America. Three years later, after an exhaustive investigation by the Tariff Commission, the Secretary of the Treasury got around to issuing a finding of dumping. The Treasury then administered a light slap on the wrist, fining the Japanese and their U.S. importers a piddling $1 million when everyone knew the actual dumping duties should have been well over $100 million.

For the next half-dozen years the Treasury gave the Japanese a free ride as they increased their penetration of our TV market. By 1976 imports had grabbed 75 percent of the black-and-white TV market and soared over 50 percent in color TV sales. At this point a brilliant young lawyer named Paul Cullen, who was then associated with Corning Glass, contacted Thomas F. Shannon's law firm and they organized a coalition of companies and labor organizations under the banner of COMPACT—the Committee to Preserve American Color Television. Monochrome (black-and-white) TV production was judged too far gone to defend, but color television was still a profitable domestic industry with annual sales of $2.5 billion.

Amory Houghton Jr., then chairman of Corning Glass and later congressman from his upstate New York district, saw quite clearly that his company and its customers—RCA, Westinghouse, and Zenith among them—were engaged in what he called "all-out war." He assigned one of Corning's top executives, Allen W. Dawson,* a pioneer of the television manufacturing industry, as co-chairman of COMPACT. Jacob Clayman, president of the AFL-CIO's Industrial Union Department, became the labor cochairman, and there were no less than ten major unions lined up to fight side-by-side with the few companies that dared join the coalition. Some of the largest TV manufacturers, like RCA and General Electric, had such extensive interests in Japan that they did not want to jeopardize them by signing up with COMPACT, though they were to reap the biggest benefits if it won the case.

The COMPACT coalition filed its Section 201 escape clause petition in the fall of 1976 and it immediately became the great trade cause célèbre of the year. When the prime minister of Japan, Takeo Fukuda, came to Washington on a

---

*Allen W. Dawson became chairman of Siecor, the Siemens-Corning joint venture which is re-wiring the world with the fiber-optics cables Corning Glass developed. Dawson later was named chairman of Siemens U.S.A.

state visit in March 1977 the color TV case was at the very top of the agenda in his White House meeting with President Carter.[3]

Jimmy Carter had not been very well briefed and he blurted out that the United States would accept an annual import level of color TVs from Japan in the range of 2.5 million sets. One of Fukuda's aides interrupted and, speaking rapid Japanese, advised the prime minister not to accept the President's offer because Mr. Carter was sure to lose face when he found that the import level acceptable to the U.S. industry and its workers was half that figure. Diplomatically, Fukuda smiled and remained silent.

Nonetheless, Carter's gaffe encouraged the Japanese to hold out for a higher number of color TV exports to the United States than they probably had planned. Soon after the White House meeting, Robert Strauss, the high-flying Texas lawyer-politician, jetted to Tokyo within forty-eight hours of his Senate confirmation as the president's special trade representative to negotiate the TV import controversy. There the MITI negotiators confronted him with a very high import demand for color TVs on the order of the figure President Carter had mistakenly offered Prime Minister Fukuda. Strauss and his own negotiators had a difficult time getting the Japanese down to a more realistic number.

In the end, Bob Strauss made a secret side agreement with the Japanese to junk the still existent anti-dumping finding against them. Of course, Strauss had no legal authority to make such a promise and leading members of his own party in the Congress were shocked when they found out about it in House trade committee hearings a year later.[4] However, that did not prevent Bob Strauss from becoming Jimmy Carter's campaign chairman in 1980.

In 1977 Strauss bounced from Tokyo to London where President Carter had hoped to announce a settlement of the TV case at the April economic summit being held there. But a few loose ends remained and the announcement had to wait. When it was made, the Orderly Marketing Agreement with Japan permitted some one million color TV imports from that country but did not cover other nations.[5]

The agreement did revive the American industry for a while, or at least until the Japanese could rev up their joint-venture TV plants in Taiwan and Korea and expand their production in the United States. Then the end runs around the Carter-Strauss OMAs began and within two years color television imports were back to their pre–escape clause levels of nearly two million sets a year. Monochrome production, not involved in the 201 case but still covered by the Treasury's earlier dumping finding, had almost vanished from the American scene and General Electric closed its last monochrome plant in North Carolina a few years later.

Color television manufacturing hung on for another decade. But instead of the twenty-eight U.S. companies once involved in producing TV sets, by 1990 there were but a few left and only Zenith was still a major producer, though most of its components were made abroad. After the RCA-GE merger of 1987, both of those companies all but gave up the TV ghost.

Once-prosperous American television manufacturers like Magnavox, Motorola, Emerson, Philco, Admiral, Sylvania, and Westinghouse had all been either knocked out of TV set production or had fallen under foreign ownership. The Japanese, Koreans, Taiwanese, and even the Dutch have either taken over the formerly American TV plants or built their own in the United States, mostly to assemble parts made in their own countries to get around our anti-dumping laws.

"Free Trade Zones," now dot America's landscape like so many privileged sanctuary DMZs through which foreign products invade the country with total impunity.[6] One of these trade zones was established in Forrest City, Arkansas, so Japan's Sanyo could bring in color TV picture tubes which were under import limitations.[7] The result was that another Corning Glass plant in Indiana bit the dust. Corning, which invented the glass parts that made television receivers possible, has gone from five TV glass plants to one. Other suppliers of the almost extinct U.S. TV industry have also been forced to shut down: furniture factories that made TV set cabinets, plants that produced television picture tubes, electronics laboratories that turned out the latest circuitry components. All are now gone, and with them, plus the assembly plants they supplied, have gone more than one hundred thousand American jobs.

Television manufacturing was not an antiquated "smokestack" industry. It was one of the most modern industries in the country and its plants were among the nation's most efficient and cost-productive. Until the import invasions of the 1960s, the U.S. companies had taken advantage of the economics of scale provided by our growing home market to hold prices down. Indeed, color television sets that sold for $1,000 or more in the 1950s were selling for half that and less a decade later—*before* the Japanese targeted our market with their hidden export subsidies, dumping and other illegal trade practices, all a matter of record in the forgotten files of a government which chose to ignore the evidence in the name of "free" trade.

There is, however, much more to the demise of television manufacturing in America than appears on the record of the International Trade Commission or in the annals of the Treasury and Commerce Departments, or even in the secret deals made by White House wheeler-dealers.

In June 1977 *Time* broke a story, "Kickbacks in Living Color,"[8] which revealed that, with the exception of Sony, Japanese TV manufacturers had been involved for years in making illegal rebates to some of America's biggest retail chains in order to get around the TV dumping duties, which the Customs Service found now totaled $400 million, a whopping run-up from the $1 million fine the Treasury had imposed in 1971. All kinds of deals had been worked out with the U.S. retailers. Double invoicing was the key to most of them.

As *Time* reported, "the Japanese manufacturer quotes the U.S. importer an official price equal to the Japanese (market) price, then makes under-the-table payments—in effect, illegal rebates—that allow the U.S. company to offer the set at prices that undercut U.S.-made TVs by $100 or more. Sometimes the payments are disguised as rebates or 'credits' for advertising or shipping."[9] In one case, the rebates were made in cash to five executives in a big retail chain in the upper Midwest. The chairman of the company, who was not in on the deal, fired all five on the spot when he was confronted with the evidence.

Several other retail chains were indicted, including Sears, Roebuck and Company, which a Los Angeles grand jury found had been working the kickback scheme with the Japanese for more than a decade.[10] A friendly judge subsequently quashed the indictment, ignoring the false statements Sears executives had repeatedly made on Customs declarations. There was said to be a total of more than eighty retail companies indulging in the schemes that helped put the American TV manufacturing companies out of business.[11] But charges were only brought against two—Sears, Roebuck and Alexander's Inc. of New York. The latter got off with a small fine and Sears escaped punishment entirely.

In 1978 the Customs Service sent out notices to all ports of entry to begin collection of the $400 to $600 million then due the Treasury in dumping fines against the importers and Japanese television manufacturers. All hell broke loose at the Treasury and the White House. John J. Nevin, then chairman of Zenith, the leading American TV manufacturer, revealed during a stockholders' meeting that ''On Wednesday, March 29, officials of the Japanese embassy and counsel representing Japanese television manufacturers met with high-level Treasury personnel. As a result of that meeting, a cable was sent to Customs field locations instructing those locations to block out of the notices prepared earlier any items relating to dumping duties for the period subsequent to June 30, 1977.''[12] A few days later the Treasury announced it was settling $400 million in TV dumping fines for $46 million, a little more than ten cents on the dollar.

The Treasury's handling of the TV dumping case was so odorous the Congress deprived it of jurisdiction over future cases and transferred the responsibility for all anti-dumping cases to the Commerce Department in the Trade Agreements Act of 1979. Incredibly, Commerce proceeded to give the Japanese an even better deal on the TV duties then the Treasury. They were permitted to settle the balance of the now estimated $800 million for $68 million, much less than the 10 percent previously assessed.

Many Commerce Department, Treasury and other government officials dealing with trade matters wind up gliding through the ''revolving door'' into high-paying jobs for the Japanese and other foreign interests, a practice so common in Washington that Sen. Strom Thurmond of South Carolina introduced legislation to bar the door in 1988. Unfortunately, Senator Thurmond's ethics bill was vetoed by President Reagan in the waning days of his administration.

Far more than the American television manufacturing industry and its suppliers were victims of the government's refusal to enforce our trade laws. The whole consumer electronics field was sold out. Video tape recorders, invented in America, were never made here because the big multinational corporations, seeing how the U.S. government surrendered their TV production, sent their VCR technology to Japan on the theory that it was better to have a piece of the action than none at all. Eventually, of course, the Japanese grabbed everything and they still had virtually none at all. But at the time the instant profits from licensing and joint ventures with Japan looked very attractive for the next balance sheet and that is as far as most of our corporate managers are permitted to see.

It was an enlightening coincidence that the same issue of *Time* that revealed the Japanese television kickback conspiracy also carried a story about the debt buildup in the Third World. The article cited estimates by Yale economist Robert Triffin that "foreign loans made by the world's private banks surged from $100 billion in 1969 to $548 billion last year [1976]." The Swiss, French, and Germans were all fairly big players in the rapidly expanding international lending game. "But," *Time* reported, "U.S. banks and their overseas branches were by far the most aggressive lenders."[13]

Gerald R. Ford had played the same role as all his predecessors since Franklin Roosevelt in the showering of dollars on the world and in encouraging U.S. banks to follow the federal government's bad example in financing competition for American industry and workers. But the pace was picking up and, as the loan money poured out, the value of the dollar shrank dramatically. Double-digit inflation was just around the corner when Gerry Ford turned over the keys to the White House to Georgia's Jimmy Carter.

Chapter 36.

The Trilateralist

The tragedy of the Carter administration was that the President failed to live up to the ideals that he preached on the campaign trial in 1976. . . . He permitted personal cronyism and pressure group politics to dictate essentially all of his appointments. . . . His eagerness to accommodate all sides on all issues resulted in his pleasing no one and being regarded as a weak and wishy-washy president.

—Clark R. Mollenhoff in
The President Who Failed[1]

Jimmy Carter came out of nowhere in 1976 to snatch the Democratic nomination from old professionals like Hubert Humphrey and Henry (Scoop) Jackson and go on to defeat President Gerald R. Ford, who first came to Washington when Carter was still in school. No one knew much about Carter, except that he had been governor of Georgia and he wanted to be President. He had been adopted by the Trilateralists, an esoteric society organized under the aegis of David Rockefeller to tie more closely together the three sides of the developed world's trade triangle—the United States, Europe, and Japan.

How did Rockefeller come to pick Carter for the Trilateral Commission? Zbigniew Brzezinski, the first director of the group and later President Carter's national security advisor, told *London Sunday Times* correspondent Peter Pringle the Trilateralists had been looking for somebody from the South and "we were impressed that Carter had opened up trade offices for the state of Georgia in Brussels and Tokyo. That seemed to fit perfectly into the concept of the Trilateral."[2]

Carter flew from Atlanta to New York in November 1971 for an audience with David Rockefeller, and a little lunch, in the Chase Manhattan Bank's board of directors dining room.[3] He obviously passed the Trilateralist test. Soon Rockefeller and the rest were quietly talking up Jimmy Carter for President and arranging for him to acquire some foreign affairs background by sending him off to confer with prime ministers and commissars.

The Ford-Carter campaign of 1976 was the dullest presidential contest since Thomas E. Dewey departed from the political scene. *Business Week* commented in an editorial that October: "Neither candidate has talked hard specifics that would solve the problem of stubborn structural unemployment in an economy with a violent inflationary bias. . . . *Neither has shown any understanding of the peculiar problems that arise in world trade when a market-oriented economy competes with socialized or semi-socialized systems.*"[4](Emphasis added.)

The election was not decided on economic issues, however. If it had been, Ford should have been elected since the economy was bouncing back from recession at the time, though a bit erratically. What Ford did was to prove, that after more than two years as President and a quarter-century in the Congress, he knew *less* about world affairs than Jimmy Carter, who knew almost nothing. This startling disclosure came in one of their television debates when Max Frankel of the *New York Times* asked Ford how the Helsinki agreement was working. In defending that "human rights" *soufflé*, Ford unbelievably declared, *"There is no Soviet domination of Eastern Europe and there never will be under the Ford administration."*[5] (Emphasis added.)

Carter may not have known much, but he was clever enough to seize the big chance. When asked to comment in rebuttal he said: "I would like to see Mr. Ford convince the Polish-Americans and the Czech-Americans and Hungarian-Americans in this country that those countries don't live under the domination and supervision of the Soviet Union behind the Iron Curtain."[6]

The American public, obviously not as susceptible to Henry Kissinger's brainwashing as Gerald R. Ford, decided right then and there that the President should be sent to the showers. Better an unknown like Jimmy Carter, than a chief executive who hadn't heard the countries of Eastern Europe were under Soviet suzerainty. Carter won the election comfortably, gleaning 41.8 million votes to 39.1 million for Ford and taking the Electoral College, 297 to 240.

But Jimmy Carter had barely been elected when observers were already having reservations. Just four days after his victory the *Wall Street Journal*, hardly a protectionist gazette, sounded a bit worried about the President-elect's "attitude on . . . international economic issues."

"For example," the *Journal* reported, "he is a strong free-trader and favors additional aid to the developing countries through such international lending agencies as the World Bank. He also accepts as a fixture the floating exchange rate system. . . ."[7]

The same article noted that only the week before "top economists" had gathered in Washington under the auspices of the Trilateralists' favorite front organizations—the Brookings Institution, Germany's Kiel Institute for World Economics, and the Japan Economic Research Center. The assembled sages, blandly displaying their antiquated Keynesian bias, had concluded that "domestic economic policies geared to stimulate economic activity should now be adopted by Germany, Japan, and the U.S."[8]

These recommendations were taken to heart by Jimmy Carter, who hyped up the economy with bigger budget deficits just as soon as he took office. The German and the Japanese governments were more prudent. In fact, they did not choose to follow Carter down the Trilateralist path, which helps explain why a decade later they had replaced the United States as the dominant trade and finance centers of the globe.

The line-up of Carter's cabinet read like Lyndon Johnson's second and third team, with a few holdovers from Nixon-Ford's more undistinguished bench-warmers. At least sixteen of the more visible Carter nominees were members of David Rockefeller's Trilateral Commission. These included Harold Brown, Robert McNamara's protégé, as Secretary of Defense; W. Michael Blumenthal as Secretary of the Treasury; Paul C. Warnke, director of the U.S. Arms Control and Disarmament Agency; Elliot Richardson as ambassador-at-large for the UN Law of the Sea Conference; and Andrew Young, who was named ambassador to the UN.

Others, not necessarily Trilateralists, but definitely of the same ilk, were Cyrus Vance, who was appointed Secretary of State; Joseph A. Califano, a former aide to Johnson, named to head the multibillion-dollar Health, Education and Welfare Department and, as the new energy commissar, James R. Schlesinger, whom Ford had fired as Secretary of Defense.

Backstopping Blumenthal at the Treasury was Anthony Solomon, who became Undersecretary for Monetary Affairs. A New York businessman and economist, Solomon fancied himself as a sculptor and he did his best to reshape U.S. trade and monetary policy in a yet more global mould. He was later rewarded with the presidency of the New York Federal Reserve Bank and held that post well into the Reagan years. The Assistant Secretary of the Treasury for International Monetary Affairs was another wunderkind cut out of the same cloth, C. Fred Bergsten, one of the "geniuses" who matriculated at the Brookings Institution. Bergsten had testified virulently against import restraints in the specialty steel escape clause case, predicting they would cause higher inflation. The fact that the specialty steel import quotas imposed by President Ford proved *anti-inflationary* was, like most other economic realities, lost upon the Bergstens of this world.

In the trade cockpit at the White House was Robert Strauss, who as chairman of the Democratic National Committee had helped Jimmy Carter's presidential aspirations by naming him chairman of the Democratic Campaign Committee in 1974. The other key player in the Carter trade game was Juanita Kreps, a soft-spoken economist from North Carolina who became Secretary of Commerce.

More remotely concerned with trade, but ultimately involved in the new president's overall economic policy plans, was his Georgia crony, Bert Lance, who had a traumatic time of it in Washington after it was revealed that he was using the Calhoun National Bank, of which he was still chairman back in Georgia, for questionable practices. This and other embarrassing disclosures cut short Bert Lance's term as director of the Office of Management and Budget and President Carter accepted Lance's resignation only nine months into his term.

Jimmy Carter's first act as President was to pardon the draft evaders who had sat out the Vietnam war in Sweden, Canada, and other sanctuaries. Three days later, on January 24, 1977, he called for a nuclear test halt and three days after that he unveiled his economic plan while his Vice President, Walter Mondale, journeyed around the world urging the Europeans and Japanese to adopt the Trilateralist formula and stimulate their economies so their own consumers could buy more of the goods they were funneling into the United States.

Increasingly, America's trade deficits were being blamed on the prudent fiscal behavior of Europe and the inexplicable unwillingness of the Japanese to slow down their exports to the U.S. Oil was the other great alibi for our growing trade imbalances, and in this case it was, at least partially, a genuine excuse. In 1977 alone the United States spent $45 billion on imported petroleum products, about a third of it paid over to the Mideast.

With all the inflationary forces so obviously closing in on the country, Carter and his incompetents picked this moment to boost the federal budget some more. They shoveled an extra $30 billion onto the already burning fires, increasing the budget deficit to $70 billion. No one, except the President, was surprised when inflation rose by nearly 30 percent in 1977 to nearly 7 percent from the already worrisome 4.8 percent of the year before.

Energy was the chief concern, particularly when a bone-chilling stream of Arctic air put much of the country in the deep freeze through January 1977 and into February. Some cities imposed brown-outs to save electric power and many factories shut down so that home power needs could be supplied. It was a bitter winter, made all the more so by the slowly dawning realization that the nation's government was in the hands of people who did not seem to know what they were doing.

Blumenthal, the Secretary of the Treasury, indulged in the dangerous game of benign neglect of the dollar, a policy which Solomon and Bergsten had apparently told him would solve our trade problems by boosting exports. (This had become the eternal solution that never worked, though new excuses for its failure were ingeniously invented each year.)

As the dollar sank in value in international exchange, it fed the already raging fires of domestic inflation, robbing retirees of their pension security, millions of people of their savings, and everyone of much of their purchasing power. The federal budget deficits were providing more than enough fuel for inflation, and Blumenthal's de facto devaluation made matters worse.

The Federal Reserve, which could have slowed inflation somewhat, instead poured more gasoline on the flames. Arthur Burns's term as chairman of the Federal Reserve Board was due to expire in January 1978 and he obviously wanted to stay on. To ingratiate himself with Jimmy Carter, who thought his first priority was to stimulate the economy, Chairman Burns loosened up on the money supply and the presses at the U.S. Mint worked overtime printing still more Federal Reserve notes, alias dollars.

In his 1987 book, *Secrets of the Temple: How the Federal Reserve Runs the Country*, William Greider calls Burns "a domineering egoist who bullied and manipulated fellow governors of the Fed."[9] Greider also says "Burns discreetly courted key members of the Carter Administration, hoping to win their friendship and approval" for his reappointment as Fed chairman.[10]

For all his pains, Arthur Burns failed to win a second term. Instead, the President appointed G. William Miller, chairman of Textron, Inc., as the new chairman of the Federal Reserve Board. Miller's qualifications for this position were not immediately apparent, but he was looked upon with favor by David Rockefeller, and apparently that was sufficient to place him at the helm of the mighty Federal Reserve System.

RUMBLES AT THE RIVER CLUB

G. William Miller attended a private dinner hosted by David Rockefeller at the River Club on March 21, 1977, in honor of Sen. Russell Long, the chairman of the Senate Finance Committee. Senator Long had been widely acknowledged as the savior of American business when he had thwarted a radical tax bill only a year earlier. Some two dozen businessmen were present, including the chairmen of such corporations as General Motors, United States Steel, IBM, Exxon, Bethlehem Steel, and Pfizer, in addition to the presidents of Mobil, TRW, TWA, Goodyear, Union Carbide, and the vice-chairman of General Electric. And then there was G. William Miller, the chairman of Textron, a company that was hardly in the same league with the others represented at Rockefeller's party.[11]

The dinner was to be the unveiling of a project Senator Long had envisioned for some time. Deeply concerned about the rapid decline of American industry before the ever-rising flood of illegal imports, he proposed an "umbrella organization" to coordinate the scattered, and for the most part ineffectual, efforts to combat the trade invasion. It was obvious that the U.S. Chamber of Commerce and the National Association of Manufacturers were not defending the interests of their members, and they certainly were not getting the real and present dangers of free trade across to the press and public.

Russell Long carried the case for a more sane trade policy right into the lion's den. David Rockefeller, who headed the Chase Bank had come to the Senator when he got wind of the plan. There was no more devoted and consistent advocate of free trade in America than Mr. Rockefeller and he was ever on guard against the faintest whiff of protectionism. He had invited Senator Long to outline the project to a group of leading corporate executives assembled for the occasion.

Senator Long laid the case right on the line. "It is my firm conviction," he said, "that the free economic system, which has sustained America and served our people so well, is nearing the end of its long and successful run. Already, vast areas of the world are laboring under state-controlled economic systems of one form or another. The number of nations that still enjoy relatively free economies has dwindled to a bare handful. . . . ''

"What this means is that many of you, in operating your businesses, are no longer competing against your private sector counterparts abroad. Instead, you are increasingly forced to compete against governments overseas that own or subsidize industries in order to artificially stimulate their economies and export their unemployment to the United States.''

Russell Long pointed out that "misnamed" reformers were working in Washington to "pursue international trade policies that allow foreign producers to enjoy full protectionism and subsidies while they capture our markets both at home and abroad.''

He outlined why present business organizations were not getting their message across and he called for "an umbrella organization dedicated to the preservation and improvement of our free economic system but not dominated by any one industry or other group.''

Senator Long said the organization he proposed "must have labor membership from those parts of the labor movement that agree that our free economic system is worth preserving.''

In conclusion, Senator Long spelled out how he personally felt about industry's failure to defend itself in the public arena.

"I don't relish the role of forever standing in the breach trying to defend our free economic system while the business community goes off helter-skelter pursuing its narrow interests and failing to even try to develop sufficient support for the moderate position which offers the only chance to win. Gentlemen, with the proposed Committee for a Free Economy I present you with an opportunity to prove to me and the other members of Congress that you wish to preserve our free democratic society,and that you believe it can be done.''[12]

When the Senator had finished, David Rockefeller rose and invited questions, rather pointedly calling upon G. William Miller to ask the first one. Miller made some suitable noises, but he did not really respond to Russell Long's challenge. Neither did any of the leaders of American industry present at the dinner. Not one of them addressed himself to the trade problem Long had so precisely identified, though that was certainly the No. 1 problem faced by many of them, especially by Edgar B. Speer, the chairman of U.S. Steel, Lewis W. Foy of Bethlehem Steel, and Frank T. Cary, the IBM chairman, all of whom were present.

The last comment came from Thomas A. Murphy, the chairman of General Motors, who obviously knew the reason for the lack of response around the table. "Senator," he said, "you've been talking tonight about the economic illiteracy of much of our society, but perhaps what we should really be talking about is the political ignorance of the business community.'' No one laughed, and David Rockefeller ended the discussion right there.

The prologue to this dinner at the River Club was a well calculated and expensive effort to lead the chairman of the Senate Finance Committee into believing this project was being activated when it wasn't. The Business Round Table, comprised of the top people in U.S. finance and industry, retained a consulting firm to conduct interminable surveys in California and elsewhere to determine whether there was a "market" for the Senator's proposal. The surveys and studies went on for several years with, of course, no conclusive results.

Senator Long had more than enough to do on the Finance Committee fighting off the Carter administration's inflationary schemes. The opportunity to change the nation's trade policy passed. David Rockefeller had cleverly deflected it; it was simply unrealistic to think that the chairman of the Chase Bank, with hundreds of millions of dollars in loans to foreign industries, would want to pull in those loans to rebuild American industry.

As the years go by and the Chase, Citibank, and all the others, are forced to write off more and more of those foreign loans, we can hardly take any satisfaction from their losses. After all, it is our dollars, as well as theirs, that are being shredded in the process. And it is our country that is the victim of their free trade folly.

Rockefeller apparently considers America merely a space station en route to the One World heaven. His Trilateralist recruit, Jimmy Carter, shared that notion. In August 1977 when the *Voyager 20* spacecraft was launched it carried the following message from the president of the United States:

"This Voyager spacecraft was constructed by the United States of America. We are a community of 240 million human beings among the more than 4 billion who inhabit the planet earth. We human beings are still divided into nation states but these states are rapidly becoming a single global civilization. We hope someday, having solved the problems we face, to join a community of galactic civilizations."[13]

Chapter 37.

Through the Looking Glass

With the triumph of monetarism the supranational economic order was now able to impose conditions not only on private citizens and foreign governments, but on the U.S. government as well.

—Howard M. Wachtel
in *The Money Mandarins*[1]

It was during the dismal Carter years that all the vagrant vultures set loose over decades by the government's free trade policy finally came home to roost. They had been dropping out of the sky for years to pick the bones of American industry. Now they came zooming in en masse from all points of the global compass to gobble up the dollar.

The trade deficits the United States had been running since 1971 provided the developed nations of the world, and increasingly the LDCs, with a surfeit of dollars to use at their own discretion. The Arabs bought airports and supermarkets for their cities, security systems for their palaces, and oil field equipment complete with technicians from Texas; and they stuffed their bank accounts in Zurich and London with vast hordes of dollars. The Japanese bought our coal and ores and oil and other raw materials to help them manufacture the steel, automobiles, and television sets they dumped on us in fulfillment of MITI's mercantilist policy. The Europeans bought as little as possible from the U.S.A, prudently preferring to make their own products and live off the profits of their exports. The Soviets and some of their colonies absorbed huge quantities of American grain, most of it on credit at interest rates that should have made our own farmers, or even manufacturers enjoying the U.S. prime rate, very envious indeed.

Still, there were so many dollars left over after all these various needs and wants were satisfied that the foreigners found it profitable to buy pieces of America with their mounting surpluses of Federal Reserve notes. The Arabs bought Treasury bills, and so did the Japanese, though more and more the latter were also acquiring our industrial plants or building their own in our country. The Europeans liked U.S. government securities too, but with the dollar losing value under the Carter regime they felt cheated and their central banks are said to have quietly given the nod to their "private" banks—many of them government-owned—to start buying shares of U.S. companies on the New York Stock Exchange[2] while the dollar remained depressed under Blumenthal's "benign neglect."

The Dow soared in the spring of 1978 as the European money came flowing into the stock market. But the boom was short lived and by the time President Carter journeyed to Bonn in July for another economic summit the bloom was already off the Wall Street rose. This made the Europeans angry, almost arrogant, for now they felt doubly cheated, first on the decline of the dollar, and then in the stock market. Even the Japanese were upset, though they had been slyly selling the dollar short for months, a revealing display of their peculiar double-think, for their trade policy dictated that they keep the yen rigged high against the dollar, as they had successfully done for years, while it also appeared to be in their own self-interest to prop up their large accumulations of Treasury paper. Still, it was hard for the Japanese to resist the temptation of a short-term gain against the dollar, especially when they knew the United States government would protect their long-term trade interests, no matter what they did.

At the Bonn economic summit the President of the United States was sternly advised to get his house in order. In particular the other heads of state thought America should cut back on its energy consumption. The Europeans had always been envious of our ability to keep energy costs low; now that they were high they were miffed because it cut into the value of their dollar holdings and made their exports to the U.S. less of a bargain to our consumers. There just was no satisfying the Europeans, especially now that they were prosperous.

Actually, if the British, French, Germans, et al. had looked a little closer at the U.S. market, as the Japanese were doing, they would have seen that higher prices of imports did not deter many Americans from buying them. Price might keep our people from purchasing some domestic products like automobiles, but certainly not imports. Jaguars and Mercedeses and Hondas were all the rage. Fashion dictated that every up-and-coming yuppie have at least one, and, preferably, several.

Toyota boosted its prices in the U.S. twice within eight weeks in 1978, the second time by 5.4 percent. But the *Wall Street Journal* reported "soaring foreign car prices failed to dampen demand."[3] In fact, the higher prices on imports were pushing the prices on American cars up. Foreign cars were grabbing nearly 20 percent of the U.S. market, robbing General Motors, Ford, Chrysler, and American Motors of their traditional economies of scale so their costs naturally rose.

However, the U.S. auto makers were afraid to raise their prices on their own with the federal government ready to pounce on them, as Carter had on the steel industry for an attempted price rise even before his inauguration. But with foreign car prices zooming, more modest price increases by GM and the other domestic auto manufacturers were now much more easily accomplished. The age of the inexpensive American family car was nearing an end, shot down by our government's free trade policy.

At Bonn, there was something ironic, even tragic, about Jimmy Carter being bawled out by his foreign counterparts for failures of American trade and monetary policy. Two of the countries these heads of state represented, Germany and Japan, had been defeated by the United States three decades earlier and then had been lifted by American aid from the ruins of the war they had started. Two others, England and France, had been rescued from defeat by the U.S., and largely rebuilt by our taxpayers via the Marshall Plan.

Moreover, America was bearing more than its share of NATO's costs for the defense of Europe and giving Japan a completely free ride on defense expenditures by serving as its strategic shield. Nonetheless, Jimmy Carter ate humble pie in Bonn. He was, Martin Mayer wrote, "compelled by the pressure of his colleagues to promise not only a reduction in American energy consumption but also a lid on American inflation."[4]

The international currency markets ignored President Carter's promises. The dollar kept falling after the Bonn summit and gold began gearing up for its flight to the moon. Anthony Solomon, the Treasury's monetary commissar, pronounced the market "irrational."[5] Obviously the market felt the same way about Mr. Solomon.

The annual meeting of the International Monetary Fund in September 1978 resembled a wake. The finance ministers and the central bankers and their numerous attendants kept up appearances during the lavish parties laid out for them in Washington. They still rode two blocks from the Carlton or Hay-Adams hotels to the Treasury or IMF buildings in their chauffered stretch limousines and they still consumed caviar and quail at the groaning banquet tables. But behind the scenes the mood was one of foreboding.

The dollar was in the process of falling 38 percent against the Swiss franc, which was widely believed to be the next best thing to gold. The U.S. trade deficit, allegedly $31 billion the year before (it was actually much more) was heading even higher in 1978. Inflation in America was officially 8 percent that year, but everyone knew the real figure was well above that. A sampling of real estate prices in the Washington metropolitan area would have shown a rise of 20 percent in a matter of months. It all made our foreign guests very nervous about the Eurodollars and Treasury bills they still possessed. And a month later they had a lot more to be nervous about.

As if it thought the dollar could defy the law of gravity, Congress passed a tax cut calculated to send inflation skyrocketing; and just for good measure it approved the Humphrey-Hawkins full-employment bill, which was guaranteed to add substantially to the already backbreaking budget deficits. (In all, the Congress was to enact a total of no less than 261 social programs during Carter's four years in the White House, most of them at his administration's behest.)[6]

At the Federal Reserve, a befuddled G. William Miller was still trying to learn the ABCs of monetary manipulation, which apparently seemed to him to consist primarily of daily telling the printers at the Mint to "Let 'em rip!" The dollars came flying off the presses in ever-increasing quantities, dramatically adding to the inflationary spiral.

During the last week of October 1978 the stock market took another sharp dive and by October 27 the world exchange markets discovered there were virtually no buyers for the dollar. The once almighty dollar had passed through Purgatory and appeared headed for Hell in defiance of all doctrine, theological or terrestrial. (Theology holds that if a soul suffers long enough in Purgatory it will eventually gain admittance to Heaven. But the dollar, which obviously has no soul, was going in the other direction.)

Carter, Blumenthal, and Miller moved to concoct a belated defense of the dying dollar. The Treasury scared up every asset it could think of, even tapping into Harry Dexter White's old Bretton Woods loan window, the IMF's General Arrangement to Borrow, which had been used only by the most down-and-out less-developed countries for years. Then they found $10 billion in Treasury paper denominated in foreign currencies and $5 billion in SDRs tucked away in various vaults, including the aforementioned IMF loan. Our trading partners were urgently called upon to help by accepting healthy increases in the exchange swap lines: $6 billion with the Germans, $5 billion with the Japanese, $4 billion with the Swiss.[7]

The heaviest part of the burden of bailing out the sinking dollar was to be borne by that old standby, gold. Only a short time before, at the IMF meeting in September, the Treasury had been issuing dire warnings against the "remonetization" of gold. The Treasury pledged to sell 1.5 million ounces a month at free market prices for as long as it took to get the dollar back to something approaching normal. The question, which nobody wanted to ask, let alone answer, was just how long could the U.S. gold supply last with both the trade and budget deficits orbiting in outer space?

Over Halloween the Treasury played "Trick or Treat" with the world's central bankers, who knew that they had to supply the swap-line billions or go bust with that free-spending old reprobate, Uncle Sam. Then, on All Saints Day, November 1, the President appeared at a press conference with his secretary of the Treasury and the chairman of the Federal Reserve Board. The reporters, with a few exceptions, had little idea of the fires Carter, Blumenthal, and Miller had been walking through, and that was probably just as well. If they had grasped the full dimensions of the problem, they would only have added to the panic already in full flight on the international exchanges.

The President announced that the United States intended to defend the dollar at last; and such is the power of the presidential pulpit that even a very weak incumbent can reassure a populace willing to believe almost anything just as long as it doesn't interfere with their watching their favorite television show. The New York Stock Exchange went up on Carter's pledge. Fortunately, most of the European money markets were closed for All Saints' Day, a holy day of obligation in much of Europe. This gave the New York market's rise a chance to buoy up the currency exchanges in London, Paris, and Zurich. Miraculously, the dollar rose.

Against gold, however, the rise of the dollar soon proved illusory. And once again this raised the unanswerable question: how much gold did the United States still have?

THE ALCHEMISTS

The U.S. gold reserve was 265 million ounces in 1978, according to Martin Mayer, who presumably got this figure from official Treasury sources.[8] However, a full five years earlier, on November 30, 1973, the Bureau of the Mint had issued an "Inventory of Gold Bars" which placed the monetary gold supply at 255,460,150 ounces.[9] How could the U.S. gold stock have grown by some 10 million ounces in those intervening years when we had horrendous trade deficits adding to the already mountainous balance of payments? Moreover, the Treasury had conducted a number of auctions in its war against gold. In just two of these, in January and June 1975, 1,253,500 ounces, or over forty-six tons of gold, had been sold off on the orders of Treasury Secretary William Simon. And more gold sales followed these before the monthly Treasury auctions were instituted in November 1978.

Had the United States discovered some secret source of gold to replenish its constantly auctioned monetary supply? Total domestic mining operations in 1975 had produced less than thirty-five metric tons, far less than the forty-six tons the Treasury had sold in only two auctions in the first half of that year. Were we buying gold from South Africa? The Soviet Union? Canada? All of those countries had far more gold production than we did. Indeed we were down to 2.4 percent of the world's total mined gold in 1975, as compared with 52.2 percent for South Africa, 28.9 percent for the Soviet Union, and 3.6 percent for Canada. Even little Ghana was mining 21.4 metric tons of gold, or 1.5 percent of the 1975 world supply.[10]

But if the U.S. was buying foreign gold, where were we getting the money to buy it with? We owed practically every other country in the world for the chronic trade imbalances against us. And why would the Treasury be selling gold, most of which it had acquired at $35 an ounce, in order to buy more at free market prices already over $300 an ounce in 1978? Apparently the Treasury and the Federal Reserve, like the fabled alchemists of old, had come up with a magic formula. Only this modern alchemy far outdid the Medieval magicians, who at least used metals, however base, in cooking their fairy-tale gold. The

U.S. Treasury and the Fed must have been making their gold by burning paper dollars.

This legerdemain was so mysterious that no one could decipher the magic formula, least of all the Secretary of the Treasury or the chairman of the Federal Reserve. The media was naturally mystified and didn't bother to prominently, or even intelligibly, report what was fast becoming the second most dangerous strategic imbalance of our time, next to our rising deficit with the Soviet Union in nuclear weapons.

From 64 percent of the world's monetary gold supply in the 1950s, the U.S. stock had skidded all the way down to —*what*? No one seemed to know, but the percentage drop was deep indeed. What was known is that the European central banks and monetary authorities admitted to owning 1, 187 billion ounces of gold in mid–1979.[11] This made the U.S. monetary stock of 265 million ounces look puny and pathetic by comparison. We had less than one-fourth of the gold the central banks controlled, and in all probability much less than that. The Europeans had obviously broken their promise not to buy gold, but with the dollar going to hell in a hand basket who could blame them?

In the spring of 1979 the Treasury gold auctions were abruptly cut in half from 1,500,000 ounces to 750,000. Obviously someone had at last posed the question: *How long could our monetary gold supply hold out?*

Chapter 38.

Never-Never Land

The threat is nearly invisible in ordinary ways. It is a crisis of
confidence. It is a crisis that strikes at the very heart and soul
and spirit of our national will. We can see this crisis in the
growing doubt about the meaning of our own lives and in the
loss of a unity of purpose for our Nation.[1]

—President Jimmy Carter
in a television address
to the Nation, July 15, 1979

The year 1979 was one of deepening disenchantment for the American people.
Nothing the Carter administration did seemed to come out right and the electorate
began to lose confidence in the government again. The trade deficit had soared
to nearly $40 billion the year before and the public finally perceived the trade
wars being waged against the United States as a major crisis.

Fueled by the constant rise in imports, inflation went into double digits. The
consumer price index increased 13.3 percent for the year and kept climbing.
Gold, a more accurate barometer of inflation, went past the $500-per-ounce
mark, despite all the Treasury's frantic efforts to hold it in check. The Federal
Reserve discount rate zoomed to 13 percent in February, the highest in the Fed's
six decades of abject failure. The commercial banks' prime rate, spurred on by
the Fed, was on its way to an incredible 20 percent as the year ended.[2]

Bad as the economic scene was, international events were worse. The year
started off with the departure from Iran of its Shah, Mohammad Reza Pahlavi,
who was advised to leave by a U.S. General dispatched to Teheran by President
Carter. The Shah had paid a state visit to Washington in 1977 and as he stood

on the South Lawn of the White House with the President a mob of exiled Iranians, augmented by cadres from our native-born Left, stormed the high iron fence guarding the grounds. Tear gas had to be used to disperse the demonstrators and an ill wind blew it back into the faces of the dignitaries. The Shah and the President wept.

Instead of rounding up the more violent Iranians and deporting them, the American authorities permitted them to continue their crazed demonstrations in our nation's capital. The rioting proved contagious, and soon thousands of Iranians were screaming for the Shah's scalp in Teheran and other Iranian cities. The Shah had been accused of sanctioning police torture of dissidents, but after the Shah left, much of the populace was whipped to a frenzy by religious fanaticism, and Iran was transformed into a vast torture chamber rivaling its northern neighbor, the Soviet Union, in crimes committed against humanity.

The crisis in Iran that followed the Shah's journey into exile slowly began to strangle the oil supply from the Persian Gulf, creating another energy crisis with long lines at gasoline stations by the summer.

The world had oil on the brain during much of Carter's tenure in the White House. OPEC kept upping the price of crude, in spite of the generally moderating influence of Saudi Arabia, Kuwait, and the Gulf emirates. Muammar Qaddafi was one of the firebrands urging price increases and Americans were shocked when the President's brother, Billy Carter, registered as a foreign agent for the government of Libya.

Oil was seen as the primary cause of the trade imbalance and inflation. It certainly was a major factor, but oil was not the only force propelling the trade deficit and inflation. In fact, the thing that saved the dollar from utter incineration during this period was that the world oil trade was done in dollars. Whenever the price of crude went up there was a worldwide rush to buy the dollar, and its value increased on international money exchanges, thereby slowing inflation in the U.S.

Although no economist would confess, the explosion of world trade was the primary propellant driving global inflation into the nuosphere. In just six years, 1972 to 1978, world exports had tripled from $400 billion to $1,286 billion, according to the President's 1978 annual report on the Trade Agreements Program.[3]

It was, however, the import side of the trade ledger that revealed where the real damage was being done to America's economic infrastructure. The President's 1978 trade report disclosed, "automotive imports advanced by 30 percent, nearly twice the rate recorded in 1977."[4] Moreover, truck imports were up over 40 percent in 1978; steel imports 26 percent; food 10 percent, and consumer goods as a whole 29 percent.

The trade deficit with Japan alone was $11.6 billion, with Canada $5.2 billion, and with the developing countries, including oil producers, the deficit was a staggering $18.4 billion. It must be added that all of these statistics are suspect, and the real value of imports was undoubtedly much higher, as were the dollar amounts of the deficits. A chart in the 1978 presidential report would have us believe that exports totaled $143.1 billion and imports $172.0 billion for a deficit of $28.3 billion. But elsewhere, buried in the text, one finds the confession that the trade deficit "expanded by $3.2 billion to $39.6 billion" in 1978.[5] (It was actually much more than that.)

Even if you accept the government figures, keep in mind that they do not include the billions of dollars in drugs, other contraband, counterfeits, and kickbacks. But why the discrepancy in the government's reporting of its own trade statistics? The explanation given is the differing methods of measuring: f.a.s. (free alongside ship) versus c.i.f. (including charges for freight and insurance). The f.a.s. value when used for both exports and imports gives the $28.3 billion trade deficit the President was trying to palm off on us for 1978. But when the f.a.s. value of exports is measured against the c.i.f. value of imports, which is the traditional and more accepted method, the trade deficit rises to $39.6 billion. In short, more than a fourth, or $10.3 billion of our trade deficit was airily dismissed by a wave of the statistical wand.

To finance our reckless binge of buying up the world's surplus goods, Americans borrowed from the Europeans and, to a lesser extent in the 1970s, from the Japanese. The more sophisticated Europeans didn't mind lending to us to buy their goods. But when we used their money to buy Japanese imports and then let the value of the dollar fall, Europe got upset.

The Europeans were not as avid as the Japanese in their approach to trade with the United States. Indeed, the President's 1978 trade report claimed the United States had a trade *surplus* with Western Europe of $7.1 billion in 1977 and $3.4 billion in 1978. Presumably, much of this surplus was in military hardware the U.S. sold to NATO. But America was no longer sending nonmilitary aid to Europe and the Europeans were even beginning to privatize some of their nationalized industries. With some exceptions like Greece and Spain, they were behaving in a more adult manner in trade and monetary matters than the United States. One example of this was their attitude toward gold.

Not long before the Bonn economic summit in the summer of 1978 representatives of the nine member countries of the European Economic Community assembled in the German port city of Bremen to set up the European Monetary System. The world monetary system established at Bretton Woods in 1945 had been scuttled by Richard Nixon in 1971 and the chaos that had prevailed since was intolerable. The members of the new European group agreed by treaty to contribute 20 percent of their monetary system's reserves in gold. One sensed the Europeans were acting to defend themselves against the erratic actions of the antigold Americans.

At Bremen, the ECC created the European Currency Unit, or Ecu. The name harked back to the old French *ecu*, various gold and silver coins bearing the figure of a shield, issued from the reign of Louis IX until 1794, well into the French Revolution. (Revolutions, whether violent as in France and Russia, or secret overthrows blessed by compliant legislators, as in the United States, always give high priority to attacking gold and silver and replacing them with ersatz currencies of baser metals or plain paper.)

The Europeans, in 1978, were edging their way back to gold. In fact, they had been doing this for a quarter-century, as they acquired more and more of America's monetary gold and augmented it with newly mined gold from South Africa, Russia, Canada, and Ghana. France had led the way up the golden stairs in the 1960s, with its central bank increasing gold holdings by over 115 percent. Although France let up somewhat in its monetary gold buys between 1970 and 1975, Germany, Switzerland, Italy, Portugal, Denmark, and the Benelux countries all sustained or increased the rate of their gold purchases. Moreover, the Japanese had early joined the gold parade, keeping pace with France (though it was starting from a smaller gold base) in increasing its central bank holdings in the decade ending 1970. But from 1970 to 1975 Japan far outdid all the nations of Europe, boosting its monetary gold stock by more than 123 percent.[6]

In short, while the U.S. Treasury and Federal Reserve System were warring against gold, the Europeans and Japanese were making gold their monetary ally. The Ecu was only to be used in exchange transactions between European countries, but each country knew approximately how much gold was behind the currencies of all the others. Thus, when the Swiss suddenly went off the steep end in 1978 and began printing francs by the carload, their currency began to look, and smell, more like Swiss cheese than the solid gold-backed notes of the past. Inflation climbed, and for a time it appeared the Swiss franc preferred the thin air at the peak of the Matterhorn to the more sensible climate around Zurich or Lake Geneva.

Actually, gold was back by the late 1970s but no one was talking about it in monetary circles, except in fearful whispers in the United States and Britain, and very quietly in Europe and Japan. There was a tacit understanding that the rest of the world would simply let the United States float euphorically on its paper dollars while all the other developed countries used our market to dump their products and bought gold with their surplus dollars to stuff the coffers of their central banks.

A number of countries were minting gold coins by 1975, and not just for numismatic collectors. South Africa was successfully selling its Krugerrand as an investment and they were exporting them everywhere, including to America. Even the Soviet Union was busy stamping out new gold coins for the expanding world market.

It was not, however, only gold coins that were feeding the gold rush. It was bullion. Americans had just regained the right to own gold that Franklin Roosevelt had deprived them of in 1933 and they were entering the gold market by the thousands. At first they bought gold as a hedge against inflation. But as inflation soared beyond everyone's worst expectations, a speculative boom in gold and silver began.

By the time he got to Tokyo for the 1979 economic summit Jimmy Carter must have known his presidency was on the ropes. A strong movement was afoot among Democrats to draft Sen. Edward Kennedy for their party's 1980 nomination. The slogan being laughed around that summer was ''ABC—Anybody But Carter.'' But in Tokyo the Japanese politely pretended they had not heard and treated the President with correct courtesy.

Masayoshi Ohira, Japan's prime minister, played host to Carter and the other heads of state attending the summit. Oil was much on their minds. That, and the continued decline of the dollar, prompted more lectures aimed at the American president about cutting U.S. energy consumption and propping up the dollar.

En route home the President apparently decided a cabinet shake-up would be just the thing to reassure our disgruntled trading partners. After communing with the shade of Franklin Roosevelt at Camp David (FDR had called it Shangri-La), Carter let the axe fall in midsummer. Out went his attorney general, Griffin Bell, Transportation Secretary Brock Adams, and HEW Secretary Joseph Califano. But these were not all.

Michael Blumenthal was dismissed from the Treasury and James Schlesinger from the new Department of Energy. William Miller was shifted from the Federal Reserve to become Secretary of the Treasury and ten days later the old monetary hand, Paul Volcker, was brought down from the New York Federal Reserve Bank to become chairman of the Fed board. The appointment of Volcker reassured the markets. He was known to be an advocate of higher interest rates, which normally might have scared off investors but which now, with inflation scaring everybody more than anything else, had the opposite effect.

The lift Volcker's appointment gave the markets was however, short-lived; the new Federal Reserve chairman did not reduce the money supply, as expected, but actually increased it. This, of course, fed more inflation into the already bloated economy. Talk in Congress of another tax cut that would send inflation yet higher, scared off the expected infusion of capital from abroad and by September the dollar was taking another dive with gold doing another somersault upward.

In the middle of that month the Big Five finance ministers held a secret meeting in Paris to hammer out the script for the upcoming IMF meeting being held that year in Belgrade. The Europeans and Japanese found themselves at loggerheads with the obstinate American position on gold and other monetary concerns. When word of the meeting—and its failure—leaked out, the dollar absorbed another severe beating. The Arabs, and everyone, else, wanted out. They exchanged their dollars for gold, silver, Deutsche marks, Swiss francs, even British pounds. ABC had become ABD: ''Anybody But Carter'' translated abroad, and even on domestic exchanges, into ''Anything But the Dollar.'' Eurodollar accounts were up to nearly $1 trillion and the dollar had declined almost 29 percent since 1977.[7]

A pall hung over the IMF meeting at Belgrade. The site had been selected as an obvious attempt to build a better economic bridge from the West into the Communist world. But there were more pressing concerns than East-West trade on everyone's mind. The American delegation, headed by Paul Volcker of the Fed and the Treasury's Bill Miller, was greeted with more dire warnings from the central bankers and their cohorts. Volcker must have taken the warnings seriously because he cut his stay in Belgrade short and headed back to Washington to develop a ''monetarist strategy designed to prevent the dreaded free-fall of the dollar.''[8]

Early in October, Volcker, with the full support of a chastened President, unveiled a new policy of monetarism. The Federal Reserve Board pledged to reduce the growth rate of the money supply, raise interest rates still further, and hope that this would prop up the dollar. It is to Carter's credit that he agreed to accept the new regimen of tighter money with an election looming. However, apparently neither Carter nor Volcker ever seriously considered biting the gold bullet, as the Europeans and Japanese had done without breaking *their* teeth.

By 1979 the relentless trade wars had so weakened the dollar and the U.S. industrial base it once represented that America was forced to do the bidding of foreign governments on the economic stage, as Paul Volcker's hasty retreat from Belgrade revealed.

A demonstration of weakness in one sphere of a nation's life often transfers into others. It is doubtful that there was any direct link between America's knuckling under to foreign demands at Belgrade and what was to follow in Teheran soon after Volcker's monetary announcement. However, there is no doubt whatever that the widening world perception that the United States lacked the will to defend itself on any front—be it trade, the strategic arms race, crime, narcotics, or dealings with other countries—certainly invited the seizure of our embassy in Iran on November 3, 1979.

Night after night for the next fourteen months the nation was subjected to the painful and humiliating spectacle of savage Iranian mobs burning the American flag, shaking their clenched fists in defiance of our country on the TV evening news. Concern for the lives of the sixty-five Americans and a score of other hostages wrenched our hearts, but the ordeal our country was subjected to by the Iranians numbed our souls.

The Ayatollah Khomeini had spurred on the ''students'' who seized the embassy in an attempt to force the United States to turn over the exiled Shah, who was being treated for cancer in a New York hospital. To mollify the Ayatollah, the Shah was shunted off to Panama, and then to Egypt, where Anwar Sadat gave him a place to die.

Nearly six months after the hostages were taken, Carter ordered a rescue attempt. The mission was aborted when one of the six helicopters sprung a leak in its hydraulic system. During the pullout, another helicopter collided with a C-130 transport. Eight men were killed, and their bodies were left behind with the abandoned helicopters as the rest of the task force escaped in the five remaining transports.

Over Christmas 1979, as the hostage crisis in Iran neared the end of its second month, six Soviet army divisions invaded Afghanistan, spearheaded by mechanized armor made in the Kama River plant designed by Pullman-Swindell in Pittsburgh, USA. A KGB Spesnatz team assassinated the Afghan ruler, Hafizullah Amin, in the presidential palace and Babrak Karmal, the indigenous Communist chief, was proclaimed the new despot.

President Carter expressed shock at the Soviet invasion and said the explanation Brezhnev had sent him was "obviously false." He recalled the U.S. ambassador from Kabul, announced he would ask the Senate to delay consideration of the SALT arms limitation treaty with the USSR, cut back on cultural exchanges, and declared an American grain embargo against the USSR. Soon Soviet forces were on the Afghan-Iranian border and it was feared they might invade Iran and strike through to the Persian Gulf.

On January 23, 1980 the President went before Congress and in his State of the Union address he declared that the United States must be prepared to go to war if necessary to protect the oil trade routes in and out of the Gulf. Whatever Jimmy Carter's past mistakes, he redeemed himself in the Afghan crisis. His strong stand may well have prevented a Soviet strike into Iran and perhaps into Pakistan. The Kremlin was obviously not yet ready for an all-out war with the United States.

Chapter 39.

The Gold Rush Trade Act

The Trade Agreements Act of 1979 will implement multilateral
trade negotiations which were anticipated internationally with
the signing of the Tokyo Declaration in September 1973....[to]
"achieve the expansion and ever-greater liberalization of world
trade...through the progressive dismantling of obstacles to
trade and the improvement of the international framework for
the conduct of world trade."
                          —Report of the House Committee on Ways
                     and Means on the Trade Agreements Act of 1979[1]

The Trade Agreements Act of 1979, which evolved from the Tokyo Round of
the GATT's never-ending marathon, was a monument to the persuasiveness of
Robert Strauss, the fast-talking Texas lawyer Jimmy Carter installed as his special
trade representative. Seldom has the Congress been mesmerized by as many
empty promises as Ambassador Strauss fired at it in the spring of that eerie year.
Pious pronouncements issued forth daily from Strauss's office reassuring the
senators and representatives that the bill sponsored by the Carter administration
to implement the Tokyo Round of Multinational Trade Negotiations (MTN)
would ultimately improve America's competitiveness in world trade and, at least
in relative terms, reduce the frightening trade deficits that were helping fuel
inflation.

A decade later it is possible to look back on the carnage wrought by the 1979
Trade Act and wonder how the Congress could have been so gullible. The trade
deficits that were then running in the $30 to $40 billion range doubled and tripled
in the early 1980's and were five times as high by 1986 and six times as high

in 1987 as they were when Bob Strauss staged his talkathon at the expense of
the American people. Yet the Congress was so taken by Strauss's performance
that it passed the Trade Act of 1979 almost unanimously. There were only three
votes against it in the Senate and just seven in the House.

Only a few voices were raised against the Tokyo Round and none of them
were really heard over the din of Ambassador Strauss's barrage. I delivered
several speeches that year against the trade bill, including one in Washington.
In another address before the United States Business and Industrial Council I
warned that the treaty signed in Geneva, which the trade bill was to implement
and mesh into U.S. law, ultimately "threatens to transform us into a nation of
warehouses where we will all be ungainfully occupied in distributing and selling
other countries' products."

The treaty would, I said, eventually "affect not only our present trade laws,
but a host of other federal, state and local laws enacted over a long period of
time" to protect American industries and workers.[2] These laws were not concerned exclusively with trade but reached into realms affecting the health and
safety of whole communities and regions of our country. Laws which had taken
generations to develop in order to uphold standards of production and quality
of products were about to be written off by adoption of a treaty a few bureaucrats
had signed in Geneva with Jimmy Carter's blessing.

"Buy American" laws which required the Department of Defense and other
agencies of the government to purchase U.S.-made products were about to be
jettisoned to satisfy the "deals" our negotiators had struck with the Japanese,
Europeans, and others participating in the negotiations.

Worst of all, the Congress had to accept or reject the treaty drawn up in
Geneva on a straight "up or down" vote. Take it *all* or leave it. This arrangement
generated excruciating pressure on members of Congress for their approval of
the whole GATT concoction, as the final vote tallies in both houses attest.

President Carter had wanted to take the package to the Tokyo economic summit
in late June 1979 but, because of the inefficiency of his own trade negotiators,
the recommended enabling legislation was not ready in time. The GATT agreements under Section 102 were not submitted to the Congress until June 19. The
senators and congressmen did not want their constituents to think they had acted
on such an important and intricate bill without "due consideration and reflec-
tion." The House Ways and Means Committee report on H.R. 4537, alias the
Trade Agreements Act of 1979, was itself 453 pages long.[3] Carter took off for
Tokyo toward the end of the month empty-handed.

After the Fourth of July recess the Congress came back and within a few days
the House had passed H.R. 4537. There had been no real debate. A few perfunctory questions were asked, and quickly answered with the usual obfuscations
reserved for issues dealing with trade. The bill was bipartisan. The Republican
members of the Congress had copped out of their Constitutional responsibilities
along with the Democrats. It was essentially a One Party–One World vote and
the homogenized Congress voted up the Strauss-Carter delivery of more Amer-

ican industries, millions of jobs, and another large slice of U.S. sovereignty to the New World Order and the GATT.

The Trade Act of 1979 was, like all its predecessors since the Roosevelt-sponsored law of 1934, a fraud. It was sold to the public, and to both business and labor, as a great opportunity for American industry to gain access to foreign markets previously barred to our products. Title III of the legislation, dealing with government procurement, promised that the treaty "will open more than $20 billion in foreign government purchases to U.S. bidders, according to the House committee's report."[4]

This promise proved as illusory as all the others made or implied by the new law. But in return for this particular $20 billion mirage, the report said "the President is authorized to waive application of discriminatory government procurement law, such as the Buy American Act, with respect to approximately 15 percent of U.S. Government purchases."[5] Since 15 percent of our government's purchases in one year far exceed the $20 billion U.S. industries were supposed to get over the next *eight* years, the treaty and implementing legislation were loaded against our companies and workers before even the first bid could be made abroad.

The Trade Act of 1979 flung open the door to imports into the United States still wider. We could no longer "discriminate" against foreign products that did not meet our statutory standards. Tariffs on civil aircraft were eliminated entirely to make it still easier for the government-owned-and-subsidized aero industries abroad to penetrate our market. It reduced duties on imported wines to make it more difficult for our growers in California and other states to compete. It implemented a number of bilateral agreements affecting imports of cheese and other dairy products that wiped out thousands of American farmers. It amended the Meat Import Act to provide a *minimum* "access or floor for imports of 1.2 Billion pounds annually." It made it easier for foreign countries to appeal anti-dumping and countervailing duty judgments against them, further discouraging American companies from seeking redress from illegal imports under these cumbersome statutes.

In short, what little remained of America's historic trade policy was now gone with the wind of the Tokyo Round. But if, by some accident, there was anything left with which to defend U.S. industries and workers from unfair imports, the President was authorized to scuttle it at will. Title XI gave him "authority to enter into trade agreements on nontariff measures [for] an additional eight years" and it authorized the auction of "import licenses" by the executive branch to give foreigners more ready access to the U.S. market.[6] Moreover it cleared the way for completely free trade treaties with North American countries. (Canada cashed in on this during the Reagan administration but Mexico and the Central American states have not, as of this writing.)

After stripping our industries and wage-earners and farmers of any chance to compete on an even basis with their foreign counterparts, the Trade Agreements Act of 1979 added one last ironic note: it required a "Presidential review of export trade functions and a study of U.S. competitiveness."[7] Not a review to determine the extent of the damage to America's jobs and industrial base. But merely of "export trade functions" and "competitiveness."

Jimmy Carter in his naiveté and Bob Strauss in his eagerness flimflammed the Congress without difficulty in 1979. But they could not fool the markets. The dollar kept descending as gold, silver, collectibles, and almost anything that had some liquidity, lifted off. Bankers love trade, and it has become the great growth industry for American lawyers representing foreign governments and their socialized industries. But markets deal with real capital and investment money, and they tend to take a different view, as the events of 1979 so dramatically disclosed.

Gold prices on the commodities futures exchanges started to soar right after Carter-Strauss put over the Trade Agreements Act in mid-1979. The market apparently perceived what the Congress and Carter were blind to, i.e., that the new trade law had to spell more trouble for American industry and for the dollar. Gold had been slipping in the Ford administration and touched $100 an ounce shortly before the 1976 election. Thereafter it began to climb, slowly at first, but steadily, and it did not dip until the latter part of 1978 when it hit what everyone thought was an unsustainable high approaching $250 per ounce. After a brief drop to just below $200, gold futures began to go up again.

Gold passed $300 an ounce while the Congress was taking its cursory glance at the trade bill and it did not look back after that until near the end of the year. The rise was not initially due to any earth-shaking international event, as most experts now claim, attributing gold's rise to the crises in Iran and Afghanistan, both of which came months after the rise began. Gold's great climb had begun at the very end of 1978 and went up $100, or more than a third, in six months.

Gold rose and the dollar burned while Jimmy Carter fiddled at the Tokyo economic summit, pushed the Congress to pass the trade bill, and guillotined his cabinet just after Bastille Day. Gold passed the $400 mark when our embassy was seized in Iran and the Treasury auctioned more gold in a vain effort to depress the price. Although Paul Volcker's appointment as chairman of the Federal Reserve Board helped boost the Dow for a while, it had virtually no effect on gold, which just kept rising. The world wanted to get rid of its Federal Reserve notes as fast as it could and gold appeared to be at the very least a temporary haven.

Silver had an even more meteoric rise than gold. From a little above $4 an ounce when Carter was elected it went to $8 in mid-summer 1979 as the Trade Act zipped through Congress. From there it zoomed to $20 in early December, reaching almost $30 by the end of that month and hitting $48.80 on January 17, 1980. In terms of its multiple, silver outdistanced gold. It had gone up twelve times while gold was multiplying by eight since 1976.

But it is an old market truism: what goes up must come down. And silver came down with a resounding crash. Bunker Hunt and his brothers can tell you all about silver. They not only rode the silver rocket to $48.80, the Hunts rode it all the way back down to $10.80 when it hit its 1980 low on March 27. At its high, the silver held by the Hunts was estimated to be worth a profit of $7.3 billion.[8] But in less than three months they lost $7.7 billion, not only on silver but on other holdings and properties the family had to sell off to cover their open positions in the futures market. By 1988 the Hunts, once one of America's wealthiest families, went into bankruptcy.

Did the Hunts fall into a trap? The crash came on the Monday after the silver market reached its $48.80 high on January 17. The COMEX (Commodities Market Exchange) board actually did ''what no one thought an exchange could do,'' wrote Peter Cavelti, ''they prohibited the buying of silver by anybody.''[9] The COMEX board had simply pulled the plug on the Hunt silver fortune.

According to Cavelti, ''the Hunt brothers lost more money in the silver market than even the U.S. Government had lost in dumping the Treasury's silver to hold down the market.''[10] Trapped, hornswoggled, or just plain victims of their own greed, the Hunts had taken the greatest roller coaster ride in the history of financial markets. Their paper profits at the peak of the silver boom were as high as the trade deficit of the United States in the last quarter of 1979. And their loss equaled the nation's trade imbalance for the entire first quarter of the following year.

Gold, meanwhile, was experiencing its own rise and fall. Having passed $400 in the early stages of the Iran hostage crisis, it went all the way up to $852 after the Soviet invasion of Afghanistan. Gold began to fall with silver (the metals markets often interact) and tumbled to under $450 in the early spring. Although it had not multiplied in value like silver on its way up, neither did it fall proportionately as far. Gold lost nearly half its value in early 1980, but silver plummeted by a factor of almost five.

Aside from the arbitrary shutdown of the COMEX market on January 21, there were other factors affecting the drop in precious metals. The boom in gold and silver was originally touched off by the public's general loss of confidence in the Carter government many months before the Iranian and Afghan crises. But those two events, coming as they did one right after the other, caused the whole world to sit up and take fearful notice. For a time it appeared the balance of power was about to shift dramatically in favor of the Soviets and against the United States. If there had been a futures market for the ruble it may have rivaled gold and silver in December 1979 and early January 1980.

However, when James Earl Carter took a firm stand and leveled at least some trade actions against the Soviet Union after the invasion of Afghanistan, the tide turned. His State of the Union message to the Congress on January 23, 1980 made it plain the United States was not yet ready to roll over and play dead. The President promised that America would protect the oil trade routes in and out of the Persian Gulf even if it meant war. When the markets next opened the dollar went up as gold and silver plummeted.

The intricate relationship between a nation's currency and its will, plus its military capabilities, was never more apparent than during this crisis. If Carter had not reacted forcefully, gold and silver would have resumed their rise and the dollar would have gone to hell, taking the country, and the world, with it.

Gold did resume its rise in the spring. But it lost steam and the dollar began to recover strength as it became apparent that Jimmy Carter would likely be replaced in the White House by Ronald Reagan.

Chapter 40.

Enter Reagan

I'm not frightened by what lies ahead and I don't believe the American people are frightened. Together, we are going to do what has to be done.

—President-elect Ronald Reagan,
Victory statement in Los Angeles,
November 4, 1980

Ronald Reagan, twice governor of California, was elected President of the United States on his third try. He had failed to get the nomination of the Republican Party in 1968 and again in 1976 but in 1980 he decisively defeated the incumbent President, Jimmy Carter, capturing 489 electoral votes to only 49 for Carter. The American people had given Reagan a mandate for change and elected a Republican Senate to help him achieve the goals he had set for the nation.

Trade never became an issue in the 1980 campaign. In the only debate between the two major candidates, in Cleveland on October 28, the emphasis had been on nuclear weapons. Carter said his daughter Amy thought that was the most important issue and he warned it would be ''dangerous'' to place nuclear weapons under the control of Ronald Reagan.

Just that morning, a *Washington Post* headline had proclaimed, ''Carter Goes Into Debate With Lead in New Poll.'' But to more objective observers it was perfectly obvious long before the debate that Reagan would win. Frank van der Linden, Washington correspondent for the *Sacramento Union* and author of *The Real Reagan*, had predicted a landslide for Reagan right after the Republican convention in Detroit in July.

The transition period between the election and inauguration of a new President is the critical time during which an incoming administration takes shape. Although conservatives were claiming a great victory, and the Heritage Foundation even published its own agenda for the "Reagan Revolution," political veterans watching the key appointments made by Reagan that winter of 1980–81 could tell the new government would be something much less than expected.

On his very first visit to the capital after the election, Ronald Reagan went out of his way to pay his respects to the High Priestess of Washington, Katherine Meyer Graham, board chairman of the *Washington Post*. Mrs. Graham, whose father, Eugene Meyer, had parlayed a seat on the Federal Reserve Board into ownership of one of the two most powerful newspapers in America, graciously received the incoming President at a dinner party in her Georgetown home. The *Post* shares the honors with the *New York Times* in arranging the national agenda every day for the rest of the mass media and, thus for the Congress, the executive branch, and even the Supreme Court.

In his revealing 1988 book Donald T. Regan candidly admits, "I was shocked by the extent to which the press determined the everyday activities, and even the philosophical tenor, of the Presidency."[1] Regan might not have been so shocked by this if he had not been so insulated from the political scene in Wall Street all those years before he joined the Reagan cabinet as Secretary of the Treasury and then switched jobs with James Baker to become chief of staff to the President in 1985.

Donald Regan wrote in *For The Record* that the "fascination" of the Reagan administration's inner circle with "image" meant everything had to be done towards "stimulating a positive effect in the media, with the result that the press, not the people, became the President's primary constituency."[2] Although Don Regan doesn't say so, this state of affairs is actually subtle sabotage of the whole idea of majority rule by turning over the governance of the country to the media minority. Thus, the press very largely decides how, and in what light, the people will see their President and other public officials.

Indeed, there are many thoughtful journalists who are as concerned as the public about the hostile aggressiveness of the media toward the men and women in government. Fred Barnes, the White House correspondent of *The New Republic*, wrote in a *Reader's Digest* article in 1988 that "For the past two decades, the American media have been growing more combative, arrogant, outspoken, critical, negative and opinionated. . . . Reporters often allow their political views to shape what they cover and how they cover it. They treat America's political, business and social leaders as targets. Presidents are fair game."[3]

And what part of the political spectrum are most of these mediacrats coming from? An extensive survey by two university professors, S. Robert Lichter and Stanley Rothman, was taken in 1980 and thus did not record how what they called the "media elite" voted in the Reagan-Carter election. But a clue was provided by their past performance. "In 1972," the professors said, "when 62 percent of the electorate chose Nixon, 81 percent of the media elite voted for George McGovern." Four years later in 1976 they picked Jimmy Carter over

Gerald Ford by "exactly the same margin." And in 1964 they went overboard for Lyndon Johnson against Senator Barry Goldwater "by the staggering margin of 16 to 1, or 94 to 6 percent."[4]

The media elite were out of step with the majority of the American people on every issue or attitude included in the Lichter-Rothman survey. Yet these are the same people who day after day are interpreting the news for the nation and every President, not just Ronald Reagan or George Bush, knows he must stay within the bounds they set.

Free trade is one of the issues no President has yet dared oppose. On the whole, correspondents covering the trade beat in Washington are a capable, hard-working group. I have known many of them personally over the years and, with a few exceptions, I admire their professionalism. But I have never known one who would fit the description of a "protectionist" and virtually all of them believe free trade is the only way to go, although I have detected a major modification of that attitude in recent years as the terrible damage caused by unrestricted imports has become more apparent.

Permitting the media elite to delineate the boundaries of his administration, Ronald Reagan was naturally cautious in his appointments. For the most part he selected faceless men, and women, who had little or no political exposure prior to the 1980 campaign and, in many instances, precious little in the campaign itself. One exception was Alexander Haig, an Army general well known as a protégé of Henry Kissinger, who was named as Secretary of State. This was seen as the tipoff that nothing substantive was to be changed in America's approach to foreign policy and that the State Department would continue to be left to its own devices.

In trade matters, what this meant was that every foreign country had one of the most powerful departments of the U.S. government as its advocate in import disputes arising between America's privately owned industries and the government-subsidized industries of the rest of the world. This had been the formula set by the antiquarian free-trader Cordell Hull when he was Secretary of State under Franklin Roosevelt. It would be the same formula embraced by Alexander Haig and, later, by George Shultz, under Ronald Reagan.

At the Commerce Department's helm Reagan placed the unknown Malcolm Baldridge, who was to occasionally defend domestic industries against the more flagrantly illegal foreign incursions but who on the whole docilely followed the primrose path of free trade. The Secretary of Labor, Raymond Donovan, may have weighed in on the side of American workers against unfair imports but Mr. Donovan was besieged, unfairly as it turned out, by a court case involving his past business dealings. He never had a chance to make his policy, if any, known or felt.

William Brock was first named as President Reagan's trade representative and later succeeded Donovan as Secretary of Labor. Like Baldridge, Brock infrequently rose to the defense of American industries and workers when sufficient political pressure was applied. But for the most part he helped keep the doors wide open as the greatest flood of imports in history inundated the U.S. market, wiped out hundreds of industrial plants and thousands of farms, and piled up nearly a trillion dollars in trade deficits during the Reagan years. Brock did have one distinction, however. He was not as politically faceless as most of his colleagues in the cabinet. He had been a congressman and senator from Tennessee and chairman of the Republican National Committee. If the others could plead innocence, Brock could not.

Other officials with responsibility for trade matters included the Secretary of the Treasury, Donald T. Regan, who was succeeded by James Baker. Both of them were thoroughgoing free traders with little or no knowledge of international monetary affairs, as Baker was to demonstrate most dramatically with his 1985 devaluation of the dollar. (Regan, as White House chief of staff then, probably at least acquiesced in Baker's damaging action.)

The Treasury had been stripped of its jurisdiction over antidumping in the Trade Act of 1979 because of its failure to enforce the law in the television dumping case against Japan. Nonetheless, it retained important consultative powers in trade cases and the Customs Service remained under Treasury's broken wing.

Caspar Weinberger, at the helm of the Defense Department, appeared to believe there was no real necessity for maintaining the nation's industry for national security purposes. The appraisal of the outgoing Army chief of staff, Gen. John A. Wickham Jr., in mid-1987—that there was no national production base to support even a limited conventional war—tells the whole sad story of Weinberger's attitude toward trade. It seemed more important for him to mollify our allies and open up bidding on defense contracts to the Japanese than to preserve American industries.

As a result, the department of the government charged with protecting the nation against attack refused to protect the industrial base on which the United States has to rely for its defense. One example, among many, serves to illustrate this point.

Lawrence J. Brady, a former Commerce Department official who had blown the whistle on the Carter administration's transfer of technology to the Soviet Union, was appointed Assistant Secretary of Commerce for International Trade Administration early in Reagan's first term. Among the many cases that came before Brady at Commerce was one concerned with nonferrous metals imports, which had all but eliminated domestic capacity to produce these materials so vital to national defense. The case had been brought under a provision of the trade laws designed to protect those industries considered absolutely essential to America's security.

Lawrence Brady issued a ruling to save what was left of America's nonferrous metals production and was promptly overruled by the Department of Defense. Incredulous, Brady called his counterpart at the Pentagon and asked the key question, "Where would we get these metals if there was a war?" The answer from the Pentagon was "from Japan."

The Defense Department respondent obviously had never heard of the diffi-
culties the U.S. and British navies encountered during both world wars in keeping
supply lines open across the world's oceans. Hundreds of ships and thousands
of brave men went to the bottom in the Atlantic, Pacific, the North Sea, the
Mediterranean, and the Indian Ocean trying to transport critical materials at a
time when the industrial base of both Britain and the United States were much,
much less dependent upon imports than they are today.

Another Reagan appointee concerned with the national security aspects of
trade was William J. Casey, director of the Central Intelligence Agency. Like
Reagan, Casey's heart was in the right place but his head was often in the clouds.
Moreover, his practical knowledge of intelligence was shaped during his World
War II service with the Office of Strategic Services (OSS) under Gen. William
J. Donovan and he knew precious little about the game—or its players—since
that time.

The CIA plays an important role in strategic international trade. It is charged
with surveillance of the economies of other nations, including the Soviet Union.
There is a long list of the agency's failures to detect major developments in
defense production inside the Soviet bloc and this list was unfortunately lengthened considerably under Casey.

Most important trade cases are reviewed by an interagency group comprised
of the Secretaries of State, Commerce, Labor, the Treasury and Defense Departments, with a key role reserved for the president's trade representative. The
International Trade Commission also has an important role, especially in Section
201 escape clause cases, but in dumping and countervailing duty cases as well.
From time to time there were knowledgeable and, more rarely, experienced
people on the commission. But for the most part the ITC has been manned by
political appointees with little or no experience in industry. This became even
more apparent in the Reagan years than previously, and some of the decisions
handed down by the ITC defied logic. Literally hundreds of industrial facilities
and an enormous number of jobs were destroyed by the erratic actions of this
commission between 1981 and 1989.

One of the more far-reaching cases decided by the U.S. International Trade
Commission was a 201 escape clause case brought by the Ford Motor Company
near the end of the Carter administration. In 1980 the American automobile
industry was suffering through its worst year since the fierce depression of 1921.
Chrysler reported a loss of $1.71 billion for the year and was forced to seek
loan guarantees from the government to stay in business. Ford also registered
an unhealthy deficit and General Motors, although it then sold 45 percent of all
cars purchased in the United States, experienced its first full-year loss in nearly
sixty years. The combined red ink spilling over the ledgers of the Big Three
automakers was a staggering $4 billion for 1980. Yet the U.S. International
Trade Commission, ruling on the escape clause case brought by Ford, refused
to recommend import relief as provided by law.

The Reagan White House worked out a loose agreement with the Japanese to voluntarily limit their auto exports to the United States for four years. But shipments obviously increased and the Customs Service, completely snowed under by imports of all kinds, may not have been able to accurately count the many thousands of foreign autos coming into the country.

David A. Stockman, the self-proclaimed "campus Marxist" whom Ronald Reagan placed in charge of the Office of Management and Budget (OMB), almost went up in smoke when the prime minister of Japan, Nakasone, announced the limitations on auto exports. In his tell-all book, Stockman complained that "This cover-up protectionism really frosted me." But then, almost everything "frosted" Stockman, especially actions that conflicted with his free trade theology. "Free markets don't stop at the border," he sermonizes in his book.[5]

While Stockman was advising the President on budget and trade matters, he was pouring out the innermost secrets of the White House to William Greider, then of the *Washington Post*. When Greider published Stockman's confessions, which portrayed Ronald Reagan as Washington's village idiot, in a cover story in the December 1981 issue of *Atlantic Monthly*, there was another one of those temporary tempests that so tantalizes the capital. No one thought Stockman would be kept on, but he was. The President dressed down his budget director—and then let him stay for another four years. Ronald Reagan's tolerance apparently knew no bounds.

Although serious concerns were raised about the level of the President's understanding, and about the integrity of many people around him, there is no question that Ronald Reagan turned in a magnificent performance during his first term in the White House. Indeed, this writer, in common I'm sure with many other citizens, repeatedly thought that if William Shakespeare was right, and all the world really is a stage, then Ronald Wilson Reagan most certainly was *the* greatest actor who ever trod the boards of this Old Globe.

The day Reagan was inaugurated, the Ayatollah Khomeini, apparently believing the new President might be a throwback to the breed of U.S. chief executives who believed their fellow citizens ought to be defended, quickly released the hostages he had been holding in Teheran since the seizure of the U.S. embassy more than a year before. This action itself gave the morale of the American people, and of the whole Western world, a marvelous lift.

Reagan then appeared to move decisively to restore the nation's defenses, so badly neglected under Carter. He recommended increased expenditures for the armed services and at the same time asked for substantial budget cuts for domestic programs. The budget he submitted to the Congress for fiscal year 1982 was $695 billion, with an anticipated deficit of $45 billion. Although that was painfully high, it represented a $41 billion reduction in overall spending from the budget Reagan had inherited from Carter.

The President also called for a tax cut stretched over the next three years in an effort to give his vaunted "supply side" economics a fair trial. Throughout our history increased defense spending called for higher taxes, which the people almost always willingly paid. Now, however, Reagan reversed this long-established tradition.

Initially, Reagan's fiscal policy, which in another era would have been judged dangerously reckless, appeared to work. There was an almost immediate improvement in the economy, although unemployment remained high and neither inflation nor interest rates fell as fast as the President had hoped. The Federal Reserve Board, under the chairmanship of Paul Volcker, appeared reluctant to cooperate, and in retrospect that was probably just as well, though the Fed's policies undoubtedly helped deepen the recession that fell on the land the following year.

Nonetheless, the prime rate began a slow descent from the 21.5 percent usury that had helped propel mortgage rates beyond reasonable reach and had crippled the real estate and home building industries. Inflation, which peaked at 12.4 percent for 1980, began to come down and fell more rapidly after the recession struck.

Even before hard times hit, the trade picture had darkened. The United States absorbed no less than $241 billion in imports from other countries in 1980 and although the merchandise trade deficit was announced at $20 billion, many suspected it was in reality much higher. Fortunately, the balance of payments was partially covered by a rush of foreign capital in quest of the astronomic interest rates prevailing in America.

STANDING TALL

Emerging from the side entrance of the Washington Hilton hotel off Connecticut Avenue on March 20, 1981, President Reagan was shot in the chest by a would-be assassin. Three other members of his party were wounded: his press secretary, James S. Brady, who suffered a serious head wound; a Secret Service agent, Timothy J. McCarthy, shot in the abdomen, and a Washington police officer, Thomas K. Delahanty. A Washington wag at Billy Martin's tavern in Georgetown, apparently not realizing the seriousness of the incident, blurted out at the bar: "My God! It's open season on the Irish. Bar the door!"

Ronald Reagan, badly wounded as he was, joked himself as he was being sped to the George Washington University Hospital on Washington Circle. The quick and skillful action of the doctors saved Reagan's life and, miraculously, within a month he appeared before a joint session of the Congress to ask approval of his plans for cutting the budget.

Only a mean-spirited Scrooge would turn the President down after a performance like that. Unfortunately, we had one in the person of the Speaker of the House, Thomas P. (Tip) O'Neill. Donald Regan notes in *For The Record* that O'Neill's personal "antipathy to Reagan . . . affected nearly every issue."[6] At times, O'Neill was downright insulting to the President, even banging his fist on the table and cussing during a meeting of congressional leaders with Reagan at the White House.[7]

The President went far out of his way to mollify the speaker, but there was no making peace with the man. O'Neill's deep-seated dislike of Reagan probably made Tip dig in his heels and refuse to cut spending even when it was apparent that's what the country wanted. If O'Neill had been as obstinate on trade matters as he was on almost everything else the Reagan administration proposed, some progress might have been made on this beleaguered front. Unfortunately, the speaker showed little understanding for the fundamental problems faced every day by American industries and workers forced to compete with foreign governments.

Even Ronald Reagan, avowed champion of free trade, occasionally demonstrated more insight into this aspect of the trade problem than Tip O'Neill and his associates on Capitol Hill. Indeed, for just a little while in 1982 it appeared the President had learned an important lesson about foreign government subsidization of exports to the United States.

Chapter 41.

The Battle Against Subsidies

Our manufacturing economy will continue to go down the drain.
After thirteen years fighting against [subsidized imports from]
Europe and then Japan and now Korea, Spain, Sweden, Finland,
Brazil, Mexico and Italy . . . I know how Custer felt when he said,
"Where did all those bleeping Indians come from?"[1]
— Richard P. Simmons,
chairman of the
Specialty Steel Industry
of the United States,
in April 1985

In the winter of 1981–82, the Specialty Steel Industry of the United States—always on the cutting edge of the trade issue as it was in 1975–76 when it won the first major escape clause case under the 1974 Trade Act—filed a Section 301 action charging the domestic industry was being injured by imports illegally subsidized by the European Community and by the governments of a half-dozen countries. Four of the countries were members of the European Community: Britain, France, Italy, and Belgium. The other two were Austria and Sweden.

This was another landmark case, perhaps the most important ever filed under U.S. trade law, for it clearly joined the most crucial issue faced by the nation's industry and its workers in the escalating trade wars waged against America: the subsidization by foreign governments of exports to the United States.

If the Reagan administration recognized this central problem, and acted accordingly to protect the country's industries, a new day would dawn in international trade. American companies and their workers would be given new hope for the future. Investment in research, new plant and new equipment would stop flowing abroad and be centered once again in the U.S.A. No longer would the nation have to depend so heavily upon foreign capital for the token industrial facilities the Japanese, Koreans, and others buy or build in our country to assemble the profitable components they make at home. Hundreds of depressed communities in the rust belt and all across the land could look forward to a brighter tomorrow.

It was a case seemingly made for President Reagan to put the chaotic trade puzzle in sharp focus and to affirm his oft-expressed dedication to our free economic system as opposed to government intervention. And for just a little while—for a few eloquent sentences—Ronald Reagan appeared to respond to the trade subsidy challenge. Alas, the opportunity flickered by. But it is worth recording what transpired.

On the morning the Specialty Steel Industry and the United Steelworkers of America jointly filed the Section 301 antisubsidy case against the European countries and Brazil, a press conference was called to brief the media. The late Lloyd McBride, president of the Steelworkers, pointed out that there was well over 20 percent unemployment in the nation's specialty steel mills. Eugene March of Colt Industries, then chairman of the industry coalition, stated the case for the domestic companies.

"Our industry is acknowledged by other countries to be *the* technological leader of the world," March pointed out. "But no matter how efficient we are, foreign companies can always undercut us on price. Why? Because almost all of them are either owned outright or are heavily subsidized by their governments. In the United Kingdom, the steel industry is 79 percent owned by the government. In Brazil it is 68 percent; Italy 57 percent; Sweden 59 percent."[2]

"Moreover," March added, "in France the National Assembly just recently approved the state takeover of two of the major steelmakers. And on top of everything the European Community has for many years granted generous low-interest loans to specialty steel industries of its member countries."

McBride made the point that "this is not competition. . . . It is the penalization of our people for being the most productive, the most efficient, the hardest working. Foreign countries are shipping their unemployment to America."[3]

Richard P. Simmons, president of Allegheny Ludlum Steel Corporation of Pittsburgh, and chairman of the specialty steel industry both before and after this case was filed, warned that if protection against the subsidized imports was not forthcoming soon the industry in the United States would have to be drastically restructured within the next year or two.[4]

Unfortunately, Simmons's prediction came to pass. At the time there were seventeen U.S. member companies producing specialty steels, down from the twenty-five in the original coalition that filed the escape clause case in 1975. Before the legal procedure initiated in December 1981 was decided by President Reagan more than a year and a half later, five more companies had bit the dust. Three of them had filed for bankruptcy; Colt Industries closed its big Crucible stainless steel mill in Midland, Pennsylvania, and another company simply gave up the ghost and vanished from America's industrial scene. These were all members of the most crucial industry in the country, one whose products virtually no other modern industry can do without.

What President Reagan did in stretching out the procedure was typical of his administration's handling of trade actions. Halfway measures were almost always employed in efforts to mollify our trading partners while American industries and jobs fell by the wayside.

On November 17, 1982, nearly a year after the 301 antisubsidy case was originally filed, the president issued a memorandum to the U.S. trade representative, William Brock. This presidential memo must stand as one of the best examples of the double-think, double-speak, double-do indulged in by our government officials on the trade issue.

While acknowledging that foreign governments had been subsidizing their specialty steel exports to America in violation of our laws and the GATT code, Reagan said, in effect, that attacking subsidies is *not* the way to go in solving the trade problem.

"The United States believes that subsidies have been provided . . . ," the president said, even enumerating the various ways the European Community and its members had provided them: "preferential loans, loan guarantees, capital grants, 'recapitalization' of financial losses, interest rebate programs, exemptions from taxation and other practices."[5] Reagan also owned up that "the injury to the domestic industry is clear" and he gave the specialty steel companies and their skilled workers a nice pat on the back. They are, he said, "efficient, technologically up-to-date and export oriented." Moreover, he allowed they were members of "an advanced, innovative and competitive industry." He also admitted that the industry's "output is used in a wide range of demanding applications critical to an industrial economy."[6]

The President even went so far as to concede that, because of the subsidized imports, "the industry is facing an unprecedented challenge . . . and a number of its member firms are fighting for survival." In addition, he pointed out that "imports were at historically high levels, with import penetration ratios ranging . . . [up to] more than 50 percent. . . . "[7]

What was Ronald Reagan's answer to specialty steel's problems, which he had freely acknowledged were primarily caused by foreign subsidies? It was, believe it or not, to sweep the subsidy issue under the rug and, instead of ruling on the Section 301 case, he instituted a Section 201 escape clause case with the ITC on behalf of the industry. This had the effect of stretching out the whole procedure for nearly eight more months, during which time more companies drowned in red ink and thousands more workers lost their jobs.

It is not difficult to fathom the sophistry involved in Ronald Reagan's convoluted specialty steel decision. The last thing he wanted that day was a controversy with the Europeans over the subsidy issue. There were simply too many other balls bouncing on the international scene to toss in yet one more. NATO had to be preserved at all costs (which it should be) and the President could not afford to offend its members. However, if he had bit the subsidy bullet on specialty steel, a made-to-order case of a technologically advanced industry savaged by illegal imports, the President may have been able to eventually persuade our European and other trading partners to face up to reality. As it was, the outcome of the compromise escape clause case he initiated satisfied no one.

On July 5, 1983 the President granted, as Clyde Farnsworth put it in his Page 1 story for *the New York Times*, "four years of trade protection to American producers of specialty steel in a move that angered nations that export steel to the United States and only partly appeased the domestic industry."[8] The exporting nations, of course, would have been angry with *any* American action that denied them what they had come to regard as their "right" to total access in the U.S. market.

The domestic specialty steel companies were "only partly appeased" because instead of placing import quotas on all product lines, as they had requested, the president applied these restrictions to tool steels and some other products, and merely imposed higher tariffs on stainless steel sheet and strip, the industry's "bread-and-butter" output. Reagan had been warned that higher tariffs would not deter imports because the exporting countries would simply increase their subsidies to overcome the increased Customs duties. However, the warning went unheeded and within months the industry and its workers were faced with an increased invasion of imports.

One year after the President's attempt to play Solomon with steel imports, he received a letter from Lynn R. Williams, the new president of the Steelworkers union, and Paul R. Roedel, CEO of Carpenter Technology Corporation and chairman of the Specialty Steel Industry of the United States. They reported that the higher tariffs "have failed to slow the inexorable increase in subsidized imports. In the first five months of 1984, imports of stainless sheet and strip products increased no less than 62 percent over the same period last year, *before* your import restraint program was initiated."[9] Roedel and Williams asked Reagan to replace the tariffs with import quotas but no action was ever taken. Reagan had opened one eye for the specialty steel industry. He kept the other tightly closed.

At the time President Reagan was deciding the specialty steel case, the U.S. trade deficit was beginning its exponential leap toward outer space. In August 1983, the merchandise trade imbalance set another new record and the Associated Press reported "the widening of the deficit brought the shortfall for the first half to $47.2 billion . . . compared with $36.4 billion for all of last year." Imports were now coming in at the annual rate of almost $500 billion, but Secretary of Commerce Baldridge said imports merely reflected the country's "strong economic growth."[10]

By 1984 the annual trade deficit hit $123.3 billion and the following year it went up another 20 percent to nearly $150 billion. The federal budget deficits were making their big jump at the same time: from $60 billion in 1981 to $128 billion in '82, to $195 billion in '83, over $200 billion for '85, and an astronomical $220.7 billion by 1986. Oddly, no one in the Reagan administration—certainly not Stockman, let alone Regan or Baker—appears to have made the connection between the rise in trade deficits and the rocketing upward of the federal budget deficits.

By blinding themselves to this obvious reality, the people in Reagan's Treasury Department, and in the Office of Management and Budget, had permitted the nation to plunge into the abyss of deeper debt and created an industrial terrain splattered with closed plants and steel mills. The root of their error was more philosophical than fiscal, although it was plainly both.

Reagan and most of his financial advisors were married to the free market philosophy of Milton Friedman, the Nobel Prize–winning economist who had created a new school of thought at the University of Chicago. Friedman's advocacy of freeing the economy from governmental restraint was correct—up to a point. Where it went wrong—terribly wrong—was in confusing the international market with the American market. Unfortunately, there is very little resemblance between the two.

The world outside the United States is mostly ruled by socialist, quasi-socialist, Shinto socialist, and communist governments. Their economies differ from ours to varying degrees but they all work on the common principle that government ownership or subsidization of major industries, and often smaller ones as well, is the central sun around which their economic lives revolve. The United States, with its privately owned industries, simply cannot compete against even the smallest of these essentially socialist states, as Hong Kong, Korea, Singapore, and Taiwan have demonstrated to our sorrow. When the more powerful units of Japan and the European Community are weighed in this same scale, the tilt against America becomes dangerous indeed.

Milton Friedman's thinking was shaped in the 1930s, forged in the caldron of the World War II upheaval, and frozen in the immediate postwar period. Tragically, the thinking of Ronald Reagan and his advisors was similarly frozen. The world has changed dramatically, but they have refused to recognize the change. They occasionally appear to detect the change in other areas of endeavor, but not in international trade.

Milton Friedman's influence over Ronald Reagan was all-pervasive in fiscal, monetary, and trade matters. This can be verified from numerous sources, including Donald Regan, the Treasury secretary cum White House chief of staff. Regan noted that "Friedman is a strong believer in monetarism, which holds that the level of economic activity is most directly affected by the money supply, or, in institutional terms, by the Federal Reserve."[11]

Ronald Reagan's "Reaganomics"—or supply-side theorism—derived from "many sources," according to Don Regan, not the least of which was that old

Scot curmudgeon, Adam Smith. In short, "Reaganomics" had its origins in the eighteenth-century theory as filtered through Friedman, whose own thinking was frozen in the postwar era of American ascendancy and had not thawed sufficiently to awaken to the new conditions that prevailed in international trade and monetary affairs.

Chapter 42.

Down with the Dollar

We have lost control of our economy because we now depend upon foreigners to finance us.
—Peter Peterson, former secretary of commerce, on CBS "Evening News," October 24, 1987[1]

Ronald Reagan won reelection to his second term as President by the largest landslide in history, drawing more than 54 million votes to 37 million for Walter Mondale. The margin of Reagan's electoral college victory was even more impressive. He captured 525 electoral votes, more than any candidate before him, to only 13 for Mondale, who took only one state, Minnesota, plus the District of Columbia.

In spite of this, the Republicans lost several seats in the Senate and gave ground in the House. It was a personal victory for Reagan but a comedown for his party, which the President had done little to build during his first four years. He was to do even less in the next four.

Almost immediately after his second inauguration things started to go wrong for Reagan. The economy had recovered from the worst recession of the postwar era but unemployment was still quite high and the trade and budget deficits were soaring out of control.

The President was roundly criticized over the Bitburg incident in the spring of 1985. His trip to Germany to participate with Chancellor Helmut Kohl in the laying of wreaths at a soldier's grave in the cemetery at Bitburg coincided with the Bonn economic summit. This was yet another of those largely ceremonial annual events that theoretically draws the nations of the world closer together. Reagan's first summit in this series was at Montebello, Franklin Roosevelt's old hideaway in Canada. There Reagan had charmed his counterparts from Britain, France, Germany, Italy, and Japan by putting the discussions on a first-name basis.

The earlier economic summits of the Reagan years were strongly influenced, though not dominated, by the European socialists, particularly Helmut Schmidt of Germany and François Mitterand of France, and by Pierre Trudeau of Canada, whose country came to be included in what evolved into the Big 7. Schmidt, particularly, seemed to delight in lecturing President Reagan on what was wrong with the American economy and Reagan's own fiscal and monetary policies. Fortunately, Margaret Thatcher supported Reagan on most issues that arose and helped him to gain confidence in himself, a condition that was vital to Reagan's performance on every stage.

The Bonn summit of 1985 was more congenial in some respects than the earlier meetings Reagan had attended. Helmut Schmidt had been replaced by Chancellor Kohl, a Christian Democrat conservative much closer to Reagan's economic position. Moreover, the acerbic Trudeau had been supplanted by Brian Mulroney, a handsome Canadian-Irishman who found he had much in common with Ronald Reagan, particularly a tendency to avoid controversy at all costs and "keep it light."

The main concern at Bonn was the strength of the dollar. This was now being blamed for the horrendous trade deficits America was piling up, replacing all the previous myths that had been offered for the same problem when the dollar was weak in international exchange. Reagan had been hearing this same argument from the Treasury and his other economic advisors back home and although he at first couldn't see anything wrong with the dollar being strong, the dialectics began to wear him down.

Free trade must be defended at all costs, the other heads of state hammered at Reagan. The strong dollar was the real reason for those trade deficits, they said. Let the dollar fall and U.S. exports will rise and that will take care of your problem. There he was Ronald Reagan, surrounded by his friends and allies, all telling him the same thing—and he was the odd man out. It was a hard argument to resist. Maybe all those earnest people were right. Those darn trade deficits. It might just be the dollar *was* too high.

Sometime between May and September of 1985 Ronald Reagan abandoned his instinctive belief that a strong dollar was a good thing. There was a cabinet meeting at the White House on September 3. Many things were discussed: tax reform; the budget deficits (the U.S. debt ceiling had almost doubled in five years under Reagan and was approaching the magic $2 trillion mark); the farm problem, also getting much worse; the controversy in Congress over aid to the Nicaraguan freedom fighters; South African sanctions,[2] which would cut off the source of vital metal ores to our steel and other industries but the pressure was growing intense and we might have to shoot ourselves in *that* foot, too.

The question of the dollar's strength came up, if at all, almost in passing, whispered *sotto voce* into the presidential ear by the Secretary of the Treasury,

James Baker. Did the President nod? Or was he just catching forty winks? Whichever, the thing was done. The dollar would be shot down as soon as possible and that would take care of those awful trade deficits.

On a Sunday later in September the finance ministers and central bankers assembled at the Plaza Hotel on New York's Central Park South off Fifth Avenue. James Baker, speaking for the U.S. Treasury, revealed after the closed-door meeting that the nations represented—Japan, and the larger European states, and Canada—had agreed to let the dollar fall. Details of the agreement were still secret but no one was hiding the reason for the decision to shoot down the dollar.

The real target was protectionism, which was mounting in the Congress as the ever-rising invasion of imports killed off more American factories, farms and jobs. Karl Otto Pohl, the president of West Germany's central bank, told reporters on Monday, the day after the Plaza Pact was agreed upon, that it was hoped the "change in the exchange rate will put up [i.e., generate] resistance to the protectionist threat" growing in America and in the Congress.[3]

On that same day, President Reagan revealed the other tong of the pincer attack against that old devil, protectionism. Stuart Auerbach of the *Washington Post*, whose story was carried on the front page of the *International Herald Tribune* (jointly owned by the *Post* and the *New York Times*), reported on the president's new "package of trade actions which, with a coordinated international attack on the high dollar, are aimed at blunting a surge of protectionist pressures in Congress."[4]

The presidential package included proposals that allegedly would, Auerbach wrote, "make it easier for American companies and the U.S. government to pursue unfair trade complaints against foreign countries and to fight piracy and counterfeiting of intellectual property protected by patents and trademarks." Reagan's proposals also called for a $300 million U.S. government fund to "counter subsidized financing by other countries that mix aid and liberal credit terms to win contracts away from American companies."[5]

"We will take all the action that is necessary to pursue our rights and interests in international commerce," Reagan promised. He added that the federal government intended "to see that other nations live up to their obligations and their trade agreements with us."[6]

"I will not stand by and watch American businesses fail because of unfair trading practices abroad," Reagan stated. "I will not stand by and watch American workers lose their jobs because other nations do not play by the rules."[7]

This was not only the most protectionist speech Ronald Reagan had ever made, it was the most protectionist address *any* American president had delivered since William McKinley was shot in 1901.

The dollar began to fall just as soon as the Plaza Pact, and Reagan's trade actions, were revealed. In London, it fell six cents against the pound on the first day, nearly fourteen pfennigs against the Deutschemark and forty centimes against the French franc. The Tokyo markets were closed that Monday, but when they opened the dollar went down sharply against the yen.

Four previous attempts to cure the trade and balance of payments problem by devaluation had failed—the first under Lyndon Johnson in 1968; Richard Nixon's two-step attempt in 1971 and 1972; and Jimmy Carter's "benign neglect" of the dollar in the later 1970s. All these efforts not only had failed to cure the trade-payments problem but had ended by spurring inflation.

Devaluations are doomed to failure because they focus on the wrong reason for America's trade maladies. Devaluations aim at increasing exports, a laudable goal, but not one that will enable the nation to score any real victories in the trade and monetary wars stacked so sharply against us by foreign subsidies. This is the economic equivalent of the kind of no-win war we fought in Vietnam.

The central problem is unrestricted imports financed by socialist or quasi-socialist governments abroad and our own fanatical adherence to free trade. At best, exports can only have a minimal effect upon the U.S. economy, and even if they rise sharply it does the country little good while our factories and mills continue to be put out of business by imports.

Depressing the value of the dollar abroad fuels inflation at home. Among other things, it increases the prices of the raw materials and other imports the nation needs to operate its industries. As world commodity prices rise, particularly in scarce metal ores and oil, domestic industries feel the additional squeeze of higher costs. While unfair and illegal imports keep right on depressing the market price for U.S. products, foreign governments find ways to offset the increase in dollar value of their exports to us caused by devaluation. Not the least of these are subsidies, often hidden, but more devious means are employed as well, including unlawful kickbacks to U.S. retailers, one of the dodges used by the Japanese to put America's television manufacturers out of business.

Devaluation is a desperation measure. It is a confession that the United States no longer has suzerainty over its own currency or its own economy. And we depend upon foreigners because we have surrendered our markets to them, permitting them to, in effect, pay for the imports we buy from their countries by borrowing from them, or worse, selling off our real estate and industrial plants, to reimburse them for the imports.

The Plaza Pact failed to correct America's chronic trade deficits. In the year it was promulgated, 1985, the U.S. trade shortfall hit a record $150 billion. The following year it soared to over $180 billion; came close to $200 billion in 1987 and allegedly subsided to under $140 billion in 1988. The total cumulative trade deficit for these four years was thus nearly $670 billion, approaching even the astronomic budget deficits which they helped fuel and sustain. Imports into the United States were still an unsustainable $460 billion in 1988, the last year of the Reagan presidency, and had totaled nearly $2 trillion in the four years 1985 through 1988.

The devalued dollar made it cheaper for foreign companies, backed by their governments, to buy American industries. At the end of 1988, while the Treasury congratulated itself on an increase in U.S. exports, foreign direct investment in the United States rocketed to over $1 trillion. Britain was by far the biggest buyer, committing $32.5 billion in 1988 alone to purchase control of no less than four hundred American companies, among them Pillsbury, Brooks Brothers, Koppers Corporation, and the Farmers Group insurance firms. Japan grabbed another $12 billion worth of U.S. industries and even little Holland was a major player in the international "Buy Up America" game. Thus, devaluation helped spur what John Burgess of the *Washington Post* called "one of history's greatest cross-border movements of capital. . . ."[8]

Gold is another measure of the failure of devaluation. When the Plaza Pact was unveiled in September 1985 gold was hovering around $300 an ounce and had been under that not long before. A year later gold was over $400 and the year after that it had cracked $500 when the stock market crash came and sent all markets downward.

Yet even through the panic days of the 1987 crash, while the Dow dived in October nearly 1,000 points below its August high, gold remained reasonably stable. It subsided, rather than crashing, like the other markets. When it began to rise again the following spring, as the dollar continued to fall, Secretary of the Treasury Baker let it be known that the same group that put together the disastrous Plaza Pact, the central bankers and foreign ministers, would again go on the offensive against gold. This meant the Treasury and the Federal Reserve could sell off more of our gold supply to keep the market price of gold down.

Once again, the old question arose: How much gold did the United States have left?

And once again, no one answered.

Chapter 43.

The Prologue Is Past

George Bush faces problems that no American president has faced before. He has lost sovereignty. If he wants to undertake some new policy, he has to clear it first with the bankers in Frankfurt or Tokyo or they will dink the dollar or cause a panic on Wall Street.

—Stephen S. Cohen, co-director,
Berkeley Roundtable on the
International Economy[1]

George Herbert Walker Bush became the forty-first President of history's longest-running and most successful republic on January 20, 1989. The previous November he had soundly defeated Governor Michael Dukakis of Massachusetts, the Democratic candidate who came off as a caricature in the bitterly fought campaign, which Dukakis and his party had tried to focus on the vice-presidential aspirants, Sen. J. Danforth Quayle of Indiana and Sen. Lloyd Bentsen of Texas.

The international trade and monetary crisis, which had figured fairly prominently in the early presidential primary campaigns of 1988, receded after Governor Dukakis won a majority of the "Super Tuesday" delegates in March. Congressman Richard Gephardt of Missouri had opened up the issue by attaching an allegedly protectionist amendment to the trade bill then wending its interminable way through the House and Senate. Gephardt did glean much more than a million votes on Super Tuesday but he finished behind Dukakis, Sen. Albert Gore of Tennessee and Jesse Jackson.

After that trade faded as an election issue. Although Dukakis made several halfhearted attempts to revive it late in his campaign against Bush, he obviously had no wish to push the issue as forcefully as Gephardt had done, which may explain why he lost several key states by narrow margins, among them Illinois, Missouri, and Pennsylvania. Capturing them would not have given him a victory over Bush, who won by 426 electoral votes to just 112 for Dukakis. But they would have made the Democrat's defeat less humiliating.

Perversely, the American people voted to increase the Democrat margins in both the House and Senate, thereby guaranteeing that the President they had elected by some seven million votes would have a difficult time governing with the Congress in the firm grip of the opposition.

International trade and monetary issues were high on the list of major problems President Bush inherited. However, Bush barely touched on them in his first message to the Congress, centering instead on the federal budget as tradition demanded. It is doubtful if any of the President's top advisors had caught up with the connection between the budget and trade deficits, a connection that was still only furtively whispered in Washington.

Fortunately, announcement of the 1988 trade deficit in mid-February 1989 showed a drop in that worrisome imbalance. But the shortfall was still well over $137 billion, hardly a figure to stand up and cheer. Moreover, imports were flooding into the American market at an alarming rate—nearly $460 billion in 1988 alone. An increase in exports to $322 billion helped narrow the trade gap so the Treasury could at long last claim the 1985 devaluation of the dollar was having some effect. But no one bothered to count devaluation's serious side effects, most especially its impetus to inflation, which was again becoming a serious concern.

Nearly 40 percent of the 1988 trade deficit was caused by Japan, which officially shipped almost $90 billion of its products to the United States while absorbing less than $38 billion of ours. Taiwan was second in piling up trade surpluses against America, accounting for nearly $13 billion of the total. Germany was third with $12 billion; Canada fourth with $10 billion, and Korea next with almost $9 billion, having unloaded more than $20 billion of their goods on our home market.

One of the very few trade surpluses registered by the U.S. was with Britain. It was a small one, but an improvement over the $3.2 billion deficit against us the year before. Indeed, the improvement in the overall U.S. trade imbalance was helped substantially by a drop in the surplus the twelve-nation European Community ran up against us, which was cut from well over $20 billion to $9 billion.

Quite obviously, Japan and other Oriental countries were taking the biggest toll in the unrelenting trade wars waged against America. Stuart Auerbach, trade correspondent of the *Washington Post*, pointed out that Japan increased its exports to the U.S. so much in the last quarter of 1988 that "If the deficit for those three months had lasted a year, the annual trade deficit with Japan would have been $64.4 billion—higher than it was in 1987."[2]

Yet less than a month before George Bush took office another trade war with

Europe claimed public attention. "U.S. retaliates in European trade dispute," proclaimed the *Miami Herald* banner headline across the top of its front page,[3] and other media gave this latest battle prominent coverage. The Europeans had used hormones injected in U.S. livestock as an excuse to ban $120 million in U.S. meat exports to the EC. The outgoing Reagan administration struck back by increasing tariffs 100 percent on Danish hams, Italian canned tomatoes, French wine coolers, and other products.

During the election campaign George Bush pledged to extend the "voluntary" limitations on steel imports which had finally given the American steel industry and its decimated workers a respite from the most serious trade invasion of all. The industry had chalked up its first two profitable years of the decade after losing an aggregate $9 billion through 1986 and the import restraints were slowly bringing steel back to life. The overall steel industry, following the example of the high-alloy specialty steel producers, was reinvesting a substantial share of its profits in new plant and equipment though its debt ratio remained high due to the earlier losses.

In September 1989 President Bush extended the import restraints on a reduced basis but added they would be eliminated entirely within two years if other steel producing countries phased out their export subsidies. It was a very big "if" and few in the U.S. industry expected foreign governments or the European Community to actually end subsidies.

The domestic semiconductor industry won an important federal court case against Japan in February 1989. The decision handed down in favor of Intel Corporation against Japan's NEC makes it possible for U.S. chipmakers to use copyright laws to protect their products.[4] Moreover, Intel announced the same month that it had scored a major breakthrough by developing technology to store one million pieces of information on a chip half the size of a postage stamp.[5] In spite of all the doom-and-gloom articles and books about "the loss of America's competitive edge" our industries were proving they could still lead in many areas of technology.

Against the few promising signs were arrayed a strong regiment of economic problems facing the new president, not the least, of course, the budget and trade deficits. The savings and loan crisis, festering for a decade, would require massive federal intervention and Bush candidly conceded the bailout could cost the taxpayers up to $40 billion over the next ten years. (Other estimates ranged as high as $200 billion.)

The corporate takeover craze, which gushed a record $311 billion in buyouts in 1988, was bringing warnings to Mr. Bush from many quarters that something had to be done to slow this dangerous trend. For one thing, it was running up corporate debt to potentially explosive levels as the takeover artists borrowed to buy up companies, and the companies borrowed to defend themselves. No matter which side won, domestic industries were almost inevitably weakened in their fierce battles against international competition.

Economic consultant Henry Kaufman warned that the price paid for the takeover mania was "decapitalization of U.S. business, through the substitution of new debt for outstanding equity."[6] He added that in just five years the debt of America's nonfinancial corporations had risen $840 billion and interest on the loans was siphoning off more than 25 percent of their internal cash flow.

Third World debt was another deep concern of the incoming Bush administration. Latin American countries were working toward a united front that threatened to pull the plug on the world economy. The Group of Seven finance ministers and central bankers met in February 1989 to search for a solution but the best they could come up with were recommendations to strengthen the roles of the International Monetary Fund and the World Bank, the two leading *causes* of the debt problem as well as the related trade wars they had helped ignite by financing Third World industries to compete with the United States and Europe.

Meanwhile, America's own foreign debt was rapidly increasing as our trade and balance of payments deficits mounted. It was estimated that by the early 1990s we would owe the rest of the world over $1 trillion, more than the present debt owed by the entire Third World.

It was perfectly plain, though seldom acknowledged, that our skyrocketing foreign debt, and the trade deficits that fueled it, combined with the damaging devaluation of the dollar, were major contributors to the new spurt in inflation. Differing views on how to deal with the debilitating increase in the cost of living were again causing tensions between the government and the Federal Reserve.

Alan Greenspan, chairman of the Federal Reserve Board, openly challenged the new President in testimony before several congressional committees. He seemed to go out of his way to stake out disputes with Bush, even questioning the economic forecasts issued by the administration.[7] But the most acrimonious debate centered on the Fed's methods of fighting inflation. Once again the privately owned Federal Reserve Bank was taking the self-serving route of upping interest rates to hold down wage and price increases. And once again our nation of borrowers was feeling the painful pinch as the prime rate rose toward the levels of the Carter years.

Less than a week after his inauguration George Bush sent a shot across the Fed's bow. In contrast to Ronald Reagan, who almost always backed the Federal Reserve no matter what it did, Bush pointedly disagreed with Greenspan's tactics.

"I haven't talked to Alan lately," the president said, "but I don't want to see us move so strongly against fear of inflation that we impede growth. We have to keep expanding opportunities for the working men and women of this country." He added that he was encouraged that the markets "have been saying that things are reasonably stable. . . . There [are] no signals out there in the markets that this economy is in real trouble."[8]

A few days later the Dow-Jones average reached 2324, its highest point since the crash of October 1987.[9] Not long after that Ford and General Motors announced healthy increases in earnings for 1988. However, larger shares of the automakers' revenues were coming from operations abroad. In fact, Ford's U.S. earnings fell 9 percent from the year before despite a rise in its share of the domestic market.[10]

In the international political arena Uncle Sam was still standing tall, despite the epidemic of gloomy prophecies counting America out. Thirty years earlier Walter Cronkite of CBS News had consigned the USA to the status of a "second class power" following the Soviet launch of *Sputnik*. Fortunately his fellow citizens had ignored the Cronkites in their midst and gone right on doing their own thing each day. The accumulated result of their combined efforts is that America—despite its many problems—is still No. 1, while the Soviet Union has fallen farther and farther behind the United States and Europe in the economic realm.

The Soviet army pulled out of Afghanistan in February 1989, leaving a million people dead behind it and a population cut almost in half by flight to other countries. U.S. military aid to the Afghan rebels, who fought with amazing courage and tenacity, helped bring about the victory, though the eventual outcome was yet to be decided.

The year 1989 was to become one of the most momentous in recent history. The Communist system was ostensibly overthrown in Poland, though the Party kept control of key ministries while permitting Lech Walesa and Solidarity to select a prime minister and other cabinet members and begin the transition to a less state-controlled economy. The bloodless revolution in Poland quickly spread throughout Eastern Europe, though in Romania it became violent and hundreds died before a new regime replaced the executed despot Nicolae Ceausescu.

Mikhail Gorbachev stood passively by in Moscow and took no immediate action to slow down the upheavals in Poland, Romania, Hungary, Bulgaria, Czechoslovakia or East Germany. He appeared to draw the line at secession of the Baltic states incorporated into the USSR in 1940 with the approval of Nazi Germany, but as this is written in the early spring of 1990 it is still uncertain what the Soviet would do about Eastonia, Latvia and Lithuania.

The biggest surprise came in East Germany. Mass demonstrations in the autumn of 1989 toppled Erich Honneker and many of the other Communists who had ruled the five eastern provinces of Germany with an iron hand. In March 1990 the Christian Democrat coalition backed by West German Chancellor Helmut Kohl won a resounding victory over both the Communists and the Socialists in the first free election in East Germany since 1932. Unification of the two Germanies appeared inevitable but most observers believed it would take time, perhaps several years—and then only if the Russian bear kept its claws sheathed.

Central America also underwent a revolutionary transformation. After years of trying to oust the Panamanian dictator Manuel Noriega, by more subtle methods, President Bush ordered U.S. combat troops into that country in December 1989 when Noriega's men began shooting American soldiers stationed in the Canal Zone. Within hours, the Americans established control and placed in power the previously elected government, which Noriega had suppressed.

In February 1990 the Nicaraugan people voted out Daniel Ortega and his Communist Sandinistas after a decade of disastrous rule. The Communists were replaced by a coalition headed by Violeta Chamorro, a courageous newspaper editor, and Nicaragua appeared on the road to freedom. In nearby El Salvador, however, the Communist revolution continued and Fidel Castro remained in apparently complacent control of Cuba.

Colombia became the focus of attention when the arrogant drug lords stepped up their terrorism in 1989. But President Virgilio Barco and his armed forces fought back and by early 1990 the Colombians seemed to be slowly restoring a semblance of order in their country. Nonetheless, narcotics imports into the United States from Colombia and other countries were still at very high levels and continued to pose a pervasive threat to the societies of both the exporting and importing nations.

There was a growing recognition in the world that free trade had spawned some disastrous situations. One of them was the poison gas plant the Germans, Japanese, and others had built for the Libyan terrorist government of Muammar Qaddafi. Another was the two thousand people killed and thousands more injured in the disaster at a Union Carbide pesticide plant in Bhopal, India. Although there was evidence that the escape of the fatal gas fumes from the plant had been caused by the negligence, and perhaps sabotage, of native Indian employees, the U.S. company was held responsible. In early 1989 Union Carbide settled with the government of India for $470 million, a sum that could not bring back the dead but might help comfort the survivors. It was a costly and tragic lesson for both the American corporation and the Indian victims that free trade, which had promoted construction of the Bhopal plant, was a mixed blessing.

One traumatic byproduct of free trade was the flood of drug imports into the United States. If the chief of the new Office of National Drug Control, former Secretary of Education William Bennett, hoped to get a handle on the drug problem he would have to come to grips with the trade issue. If he did not, Bennett would spend his time in office whistling into the narcotic-laced winds blowing at the United States from every point of the compass.

Other Bush appointees concerned with trade included the Secretary of Commerce, Robert A. Mosbacher. A Texas oil millionaire, he promised tough enforcement of U.S. trade laws during his confirmation hearing before the Senate Commerce Committee. If the pledge was kept, it would go a long way toward reversing the multiple defeats the nation had suffered in the trade wars.

The secretary of the treasury, Nicholas F. Brady, had served in that post at the end of the Reagan administration and before that was chairman of the White House commission that investigated the causes of the 1987 market crash. If, as reported, Brady found that large Japanese sales of Treasury bonds brought on the crash, he may have received an invaluable education to prepare him for his role in the trade wars that lay ahead. At a minimum, it was hoped he would find a way to reduce dependence upon Japanese investment in U.S. government securities.

Secretary of State James Baker III must also have earned a number of useful lessons during the Reagan years for his inevitably prominent part in future trade combat. For one thing, by 1989 he must have known that devaluation of the dollar would not solve the trade problem, as Paul Volcker and others led him to believe before he engineered the damaging Plaza Pact of 1985 in the early stages of his tenure as Secretary of the Treasury.

The most worrisome of the Bush appointments to key posts dealing with trade was the naming of Carla Hills as U.S. trade representative, an important cabinet post. Anthony Harrigan, president of the United States Business and Industrial Council, revealed that Mrs. Hills, her husband, and their daughter had all worked for Japanese and other foreign clients in the international trade field. In fact, Mr. Hills had lobbied Congress in an effort to soften the sanctions against Toshiba, which had delivered the most sensitive American technology to the Soviet Union, enabling the USSR to equip its nuclear-armed submarines with quiet propellers our Navy could not detect for critical tracking purposes. Not only did the Toshiba actions, in tandem with a Norwegian government-owned firm, cause a grave national security problem for the United States, but it would cost U.S. taxpayers billions of dollars in the effort to restore adequate detection of Soviet submarine movements. Still, Carla Hills promised during her confirmation hearings that she would not hesitate to recommend that the President take retaliatory action against foreign governments that violate our trade laws.

Another cause for concern was the Deputy Secretary of State—Lawrence S. Eagleburger, a protégé of Henry Kissinger and president of Kissinger Associates for four years. Clients of this consulting firm included some of the largest multinational and foreign corporations. The chairman of American Express, James Robinson, justifying huge fees to AmEx director Kissinger, credited the former Secretary of State with helping him get the Japanese government and business leadership " . . . to bring Nippon Life [an insurance firm] into . . . Shearson Lehman," an American Express subsidiary.[11] Eagleburger's own clients numbered firms like Sweden's Volvo, South Korea's Daewoo Group, Italy's Fiat, and the Midland Bank, Britain's fourth largest commercial bank.

Toward the end of February 1989, as his appointment of former Sen. John Tower of Texas was in deep trouble, President Bush flew to Tokyo to attend the funeral of Emperor Hirohito, who had given his personal blessing to the Japanese bombing of Pearl Harbor. Upon his arrival the President of the United States found he had been relegated to a back row among the heads of state at the funeral on the ludicrous ground that he did not have enough seniority to sit up front with the really big boys. It was a rather too obvious gesture that the Japanese wanted to humble the American leader in the eyes of the world. Last-minute protests were lodged and some correction was made in the seating arrangement. Nonetheless, the message the Japanese delivered with this rude gaffe was not lost on those with even a modicum of knowledge of the Orient. Japan, in its newfound prosperity, was prepared to continue waging all-out trade war against America.

The only question was how would George Bush, the World War II Navy pilot and hero, respond? Obviously, it would be out of character for him, and for his country, to seek revenge for such a petty slight. However, if it helped the

President understand more clearly the nature of America's chief adversary in the destructive trade wars being waged against the United States, the incident in Tokyo could ultimately prove useful.

Even more useful, however, would be full recognition of the most damaging weaponry used by all our adversaries in the global economic struggle—subsidization of exports. For far too long foreign governments have targeted American industries and workers in this fierce ongoing war. They have shut down thousands of U.S. factories, killed off millions of jobs, turned hundreds of communities into economic ghost towns, and transformed whole regions of the nation into not one but many rust belts.

If the United States is to survive the current trade wars, it must adopt an adequate defense. For a start it must strictly enforce the trade laws already on the books and stop winking at the wholesale violations of our dumping and countervailing duty statutes by our adversaries.

The next step must be an American call for desocialization of the world economy. The world has been experimenting with Marxism and its various mutants since 1917, and in Germany, France, and a few other countries since the end of the nineteenth century. It is widely acknowledged today that socialism is a failure. Yet governments continue to pursue this mirage, less internally in recent years, but more and more in their external trade and monetary relations with other countries.

America must make it clear that we will no longer accept imports when they are subsidized to knock out our own industries and workers. The President and his trade officials must draw the line: the United States will not take the products of countries that export their unemployment and other social problems to our shores.

Desocialization of the world economy cannot be accomplished overnight. The barring of subsidized imports into the American market cannot be done all at once. But they can be reduced over time on an equitable schedule that gives other countries sufficient chance to reconsider and reconstruct their own systems.

If the United States refuses to adopt a realistic approach to trade and monetary policy, it will continue to decline as the doomsayers project. However, if the American Plan suggested here is adopted, the industries and communities that have been crippled or killed by the trade wars can be revived, and the standard of living of those countries which accept our free economic system will also be improved.

The hour is late and time is running out. But for two centuries America has defied the prophets of despair. We can continue to confound them through at least the twenty-first century if we act in the 1990s to restore our traditional trade and monetary policies, while pointing the way for the rest of the world to follow.

Notes

INTRODUCTION

1. American Iron and Steel Institute, "Current Statistics, American Steel Industry" (Washington, September 10, 1988).

2. U.S. Bureau of Labor Statistics, "Study of Displaced Workers" (Washington: GPO, 1988).

3. "Brady Blames Japan," *Washington Post*, April 23, 1988.

4. Ibid.

5. *Harvard Business Review*, March-April 1979. Chart accompanying article, "State-owned business abroad: new competitive threat," by Kenneth D. Walters and R. Joseph Monsen.

CHAPTER 1.

1. John Berry, "Nation's Need for Foreign Capital Reached New High in 4th Quarter," *Washington Post*, February 12, 1988.

2. "Tokyo Tops New York as Bank Center," *Washington Post*, February 10, 1988.

3. United Press International dispatch from Tokyo, July 8, 1987.

4. Lindley H. Clark Jr., "Why Are Our Banks Disappearing So Fast?" *Wall Street Journal*, November 25, 1986.

5. Ibid.

6. J. Peter Grace, "The Problem of Big Government," *Imprimis* (January 1988).

7. Cornelius F. Foote Jr., "Area House Prices Up 25 Percent in a Year, Survey Finds," *Washington Post*, May 25, 1988.

8. "U.S. to Change Way it Reports Trade Deficit," *Washington Post*, January 23, 1988.

9. American Iron and Steel Institute, *Steel News* (Washington, June 11, 1986).

10. American Iron and Steel Institute, News Release, February 12, 1988.

11. American Iron and Steel Institute, *Steel News* (Washington June 2, 1987).

12. Peter Samuel, "INF Now Even Worse, Say Former Reagan Aides," *Washington Inquirer*, May 27, 1988, p. 1.

13. Ibid.

14. George C. Wilson, "General Sees Army Short of Supplies," *Washington Post*, June 17, 1987.

CHAPTER 2.

1. Ernest Ludlow Bogart, *Economic History of the American People* (New York: Longmans, Green and Co., 1935), 78.

2. Ibid., 123–4.

3. Ibid., 127.

4. Ibid.

5. Ibid.

6. John A. Logan, *The Great Conspiracy* (New York: A. R. Hart & Co., 1886), 13–14.

7. Alexander Hamilton, *Report on the Subject of Manufactures*, Delivered to the House of Representatives, December 5, 1791.

8. Charles Parkin, *The Moral Basis of Burke's Political Thought* (London: Cambridge University Press, 1956), 22.

9. Hamilton, op. cit.

10. Davis Rich Dewey, *Financial History of the United States* (New York: Longmans, Green and Co., 1931), 112–23.

11. Ibid., 115.

12. Ibid., 101.

13. Ibid., 121

14. Ibid.

CHAPTER 3.

1. Dewey, op. cit., 178.

2. Logan, op. cit., 15–16.

3. Dewey, op. cit., 164.

4. Logan, op. cit. 15.

5. Dewey, op. cit., 152 ff.

6. Marquis James, *The Life of Andrew Jackson* (New York: Bobbs-Merrill, 1938), 394.

7. Dewey, op. cit., 178–80.

8. Ibid., 181.

CHAPTER 4.

1. James, op. cit., 590.

2. Ibid., 604.

3. Ibid.

4. Ibid., 613.

5. Ibid., 621.

6. Ibid.

7. Paul Studenski and Herman E. Krooss, *Financial History of the United States* (New York: McGraw-Hill, 1963), 88.

8. James, op. cit., 590.

9. Ibid., 601.

10. William D. Kelley, M. C., *Speeches, Addresses and Letters on Industrial and Financial Questions* (Philadelphia: Henry Carey Baird, 1872), v.

11. Ibid., ix–x.

CHAPTER 5.

1. Dewey, op. cit., 300.

2. F. W. Taussig, *The Tariff History of the United States* (New York: G. P. Putnam's Sons, 1931), 164.

3. Ibid.

4. Ibid., 165.

5. Dewey, op. cit., 299.

6. Ibid., 315.

7. Ibid., 355.

8. Ibid., 321.

9. Ibid.

10. Ibid., 322.

11. Charles L. Prather, *Money and Banking* (Chicago: Richard D. Irwin, Inc., 1951), 220–22.

12. Dewey, op. cit., 369.

13. John Kenneth Galbraith, *Money: Whence It Came, Where It Went* (Boston: Houghton Mifflin, 1975), 105.

14. Studenski and Krooss, op. cit., 169.

15. Ibid., 181.

16. Ibid., 183.

CHAPTER 6.

1. Diana Knox, *The Industrial Revolution* (London: George G. Harrup & Co., Ltd., 1974), 5.

2. Bogart, op. cit., 612.

3. Ibid., 648.

4. Ibid., 554.

5. Ibid.

6. Ibid., 559.

7. Ibid., 511–13.

8. Ibid., 500.

9. U.S. Census Bureau.

10. Arthur S. Link and William B. Catton, *American Epoch*, 3d ed. (New York: Alfred A. Knopf, 1967), 58.

11. Bogart, op. cit., 595.

12. Dewey, op. cit., 410

13. Bogart, op. cit., 665–66.

14. Dewey, op. cit., 431–33.
15. Ibid., 436.
16. Ibid., 437.
17. Bogart, op. cit., 667.

CHAPTER 7.

1. Otis L. Graham Jr., *The Great Campaigns* (Englewood Cliffs, N.J.: Prentice-Hall, 1979), 79.
2. Dewey, op. cit., 465–66.
3. Ibid., 474, 94.
4. Bogart, op. cit., 667.
5. Taussig, op. cit. 363.

CHAPTER 8.

1. Edward Mandell House, *The Intimate Papers of Colonel House*, ed. Charles Seymour, vol. 1 of 4 (Boston: Houghton Mifflin, 1926), 44.
2. Ibid., 114.
3. Albert C. Ganley, *The Progressive Movement* (New York: Macmillan, 1964), 69–70.
4. House, *Papers*, vol. 1, 34.
5. [E. M. House], *Philip Dru, Administrator* (New York: B. W. Huebsch, 1912).
6. Ganley, op. cit., 72.
7. House, *Papers*, vol. 1, 45.
8. House, *Papers*, vol. 3, 224.
9. House, *Papers*, vol. 1, 265.
10. Ibid., 47.
11. Taussig, op. cit., 410.
12. Dewey, op. cit., 489.
13. Taussig, op. cit., 441.
14. Dewey, op. cit., 490.

CHAPTER 9.

1. Thibaut de Saint Phalle, *The Federal Reserve: An Intentional Mystery* (New York: Praeger, 1985), xiv, from preface by Charles E. Lord.
2. Lincoln Steffens, quoted by Peter Collier and David Horowitz in *The Rockefellers: An American Dynasty* (New York: Holt, Rinehart and Winston, 1976), 93.
3. Eustace Mullins, *Secrets of the Federal Reserve* (Staunton, Va.: Bankers Research Institute, 1983), 1.
4. Bertie Charles Forbes, in *Current Opinion* (December 1916): 382.
5. Ibid.
6. Mullins, op. cit.
7. Frank Vanderlip, *From Farm Boy to Financier*, quoted in Mullins, op. cit. 9.
8. House, *Papers*, vol. 1, 50.
9. Ibid., 91–96; 102; 161–65.

10. Lindley H. Clark Jr., "The Federal Reserve Policy: Steady as She Goes," *The Wall Street Journal*, November 24, 1986, p. 1.

CHAPTER 10.

1. House, *Papers*, vol. 3, 114–15.
2. Graham, op. cit., 93.
3. Ibid.
4. Ibid.
5. House, *Papers*, vol. 1, 272–74.
6. Robert K. Massie, *Nicholas and Alexandra* (New York: Atheneum, 1967), 264.
7. Ibid., 271
8. House, *Papers*, vol. 3, 98–99.
9. Graham, op. cit., 64.
10. Dewey, op. cit., 512.
11. Graham, op. cit., 64.
12. Ibid., 93.
13. Ibid.
14. Ibid., 61, 65.
15. Ibid., 74.
16. Ibid.
17. House, *Papers*, vol. 2, 451–454.
18. Ibid., 457–58.
19. Ibid., 465.

CHAPTER 11.

1. Woodrow Wilson, "Message to the Congress," April 2, 1917.
2. House, *Papers*, vol. 3, 1.
3. Massie, op. cit., 397.
4. House, *Papers*, vol. 3, 42–46.
5. Ibid., 112.
6. Ibid., 114.
7. Ibid., 15–16.
8. Mullins, op. cit., 84–88.
9. Letters and Friendships of Sir Cecil Spring-Rice, quoted in Mullins, op. cit., 89.
10. House, *Papers*, vol. 3, 149–168.
11. Ibid., 322.
12. Ibid.
13. Woodrow Wilson, Point VI of Fourteen Points, "Message to the Congress," January 8, 1918.
14. Ibid., Point III.
15. House, *Papers*, vol. 4, 37.
16. B. H. Liddell Hart, *Strategy* (New York: Frederick A. Praeger, 1967), 216, 218.
17. House, *Papers*, vol. 4, 75–76.
18. Ibid., 87.
19. Ibid., 143.

CHAPTER 12.

1. Paul Warburg, speech of October 22, 1915, quoted in Mullins, op. cit., 44.
2. Dewey, op. cit., 494.
3. Ibid., 509.
4. House, *Papers*, vol. 4, 243.
5. Ibid., 126.
6. Wilhelm Roepke, *What's Wrong With the World?* (Philadelphia: Dorrance & Co., 1932), 65.
7. House, *Papers*, vol. 4, 127–28.
8. Ibid., 418.
9. Ibid., 176.
10. Ibid., 304.
11. Gene Smith, *When the Cheering Stopped* (New York: William Morrow & Co., 1964), 47.
12. House, *Papers*, vol. 4, 467.
13. Ibid., 487.
14. Ibid., 518.

CHAPTER 13.

1. John Pollock, *The Bolshevik Adventure* (New York: E. P. Dutton & Co., 1919), xiv.
2. Gene Smith, op. cit., 82.
3. Ibid., 89, 106.
4. Ibid., 125.
5. House, *Papers*, vol. 1, 47.
6. Gene Smith, op. cit., 141.
7. Studenski and Krooss, op. cit., 342.
8. Graham, op. cit., 111–12.
9. Ibid., 112.
10. Pollock, op. cit., xv–xvi.
11. House, *Papers*, vol. 3, 36.
12. William Hard, *Raymond Robins' Own Story* (New York: Harper & Brothers, 1920), 10–11.
13. Mullins, op. cit., 86.
14. Christopher Lasch, *The American Liberals and the Russian Revolution* (New York: McGraw-Hill, 1972), 72.
15. Ibid., 184.
16. R. H. Bruce Lockhart, *Memoirs of a British Agent* (London: Macmillan, 1974), 309.
17. Ibid., 311.
18. Maj. Gen. William S. Graves, *America's Siberian Adventure 1918–1920* (New York: Jonathan Cape & Harrison Smith, 1931), 7–9 (quotations from Aide Memoir to Graves from Department of State).
19. *World Almanac & Book of Facts*.
20. Eugene Lyons, *Herbert Hoover* (Garden City, N.Y.: Doubleday, 1964), 146.
21. Pollock, op. cit., xviii.

CHAPTER 14.

1. Studenski and Krooss, op. cit., 329.
2. Graham, op. cit., 111.
3. Ibid.
4. Taussig, op. cit., 453.
5. Martin A. Larson, *The Federal Reserve and Our Manipulated Dollar* (Old Greenwich, Conn.: Devin-Adair Co., 1978), 85.
6. Ibid.
7. Ibid.
8. John Kenneth Galbraith, *The Great Crash: 1929* (New York: Time Inc., Book Division, 1962), 15–16.
9. Studenski and Krooss, op. cit., 341.
10. Ibid.
11. Ibid., 341–42.
12. Benjamin H. Williams, *Economic Foreign Policy of the United States*, (New York: McGraw-Hill, 1929), 226.
13. Edmund A. Walsh, *The Last Stand* (Boston: Little, Brown, 1931).
14. Ibid., 134.
15. Ibid., 145–48.

CHAPTER 15.

1. Thibaut de Saint Phalle, op. cit., 64.
2. George W. Malone, *Mainline* (New Canaan, Conn.: Long House, Inc., 1958), 14.
3. Donald W. Bedell, "Tariffs Miscast as Villain in Bearing Blame for Great Depression: Smoot-Hawley Exonerated," *Congressional Record*, May 9, 1983, entered by Sen. John Heinz of Pennsylvania.
4. Ibid.
5. Sen. John Heinz, *Congressional Record*, May 9, 1983.
6. Broadus Mitchell, *Depression Decade* (New York: Holt, Rinehart and Winston, 1961), 26.
7. Thibaut de Saint Phalle, op. cit., 61.
8. Ibid.
9. Galbraith, *The Great Crash*, 33.
10. Ibid., 156.
11. Ibid., 152.
12. Richard J. Whalen, *The Founding Father: The Story of Joseph P. Kennedy* (New York: New American Library, 1964), 136.
13. Galbraith, *The Great Crash*, 165.
14. David E. Koskoff, *The Mellons: The Chronicles of America's Richest Family* (New York: Thomas Y. Crowell Company, 1978), 313.
15. Ibid., 330.

CHAPTER 16.

1. Broadus Mitchell, op. cit., 15.
2. James McGregor Burns, *Roosevelt: The Lion and the Fox 1882–1940*, (New York and London: Harcourt Brace Jovanovich, 1956), p. 130.
3. Ibid.
4. Ibid., 143.
5. William E. Leuchtenberg, *Franklin D. Roosevelt and the New Deal 1932–1940* (New York: Harper & Row, 1963), 10–11.
6. Studenski and Krooss, op. cit, 354.
7. Ibid., 355.
8. Mitchell, op. cit., 11.
9. Ibid., 16.
10. Jesse Jones, *Fifty Billion Dollars: My Thirteen Years with the RFC (1932–1945)* (New York: Macmillan, 1951), 6.
11. Ibid., 19.
12. Studenski and Krooss, op. cit., 388.
13. Ibid., 387.
14. Franklin D. Roosevelt, first presidential "Fireside Chat," March 12, 1933.

CHAPTER 17.

1. Norman and Jeanne MacKenzie, *The Fabians* (New York: Simon & Schuster, 1977), 43.
2. Studenski and Krooss, op. cit., 387.
3. The *New York Times*, July 4, 1933.
4. Studenski and Krooss, op. cit., 388.
5. James McGregor Burns, op. cit.
6. Studenski and Krooss, op. cit., 402.
7. Malone, op. cit.
8. Leuchtenberg, op. cit., 206–7.
9. Ibid., 207.
10. Robert Lekachman, *The Age of Keynes* (New York: Random House, 1966), 73.
11. Ibid., 123.
12. Ibid., 124.
13. Ibid., 125.
14. Studenski and Krooss, op. cit., 392.
15. Ibid., 392–93.
16. Ibid., 393.
17. Ibid.
18. Mitchell, op. cit., 367.
19. Ibid., 40.
20. Ibid., 445.
21. Ibid., 444.
22. Ibid.

CHAPTER 18.

1. Arthur S. Link, *American Epoch* (New York: Alfred A. Knopf, 1961), 481.
2. U.S. Office of Price Administration, *First Quarterly Report*, Period Ended April 30, 1942 (Washington: GPO 1942), 2–4.
3. Ibid.
4. Link, op. cit., 470.
5. Franklin D. Roosevelt, speech in Boston, October 30, 1940.
6. Link, op. cit., 487.
7. Ibid.
8. Armand Van Dormael, *Bretton Woods: Birth of a Monetary System*, (New York: Holmes & Meier, 1978), 40.
9. Lekachman, op. cit., 179–80.
10. William Adams Brown, *The United States and the Restoration of World Trade* (Washington: Brookings Institution, 1950), 49.
11. Howard M. Wachtel, *The Money Mandarins: The Making of a New Supranational Economic Order* (New York: Pantheon Books, 1986), 48.

CHAPTER 19.

1. John Kenneth Galbraith, *Money: Whence it Came*, 257.
2. John Maynard Keynes, speech before the House of Lords, May 1944, quoted in Robert Lekachman's *The Age of Keynes*, 184.
3. Ibid., 184–85.
4. William Adams Brown, op. cit., 53.
5. Martin Mayer, *The Fate of the Dollar* (New York: Truman Talley Books, Time Books, 1980), 45.
6. Ibid., 45–46.
7. Lekachman, op. cit., 187.
8. Van Dormael, op. cit., 219.
9. Wachtel, op. cit., 47.
10. William A. Rusher, *Special Counsel* (New Rochelle, N.Y.: Arlington House, 1968), 95–98.
11. Ibid., 10.
12. Anthony Kubek, *The Red China Papers* (New Rochelle, N.Y.: Arlington House, 1975), 97.
13. Anthony Kubek, *How the Far East Was Lost* (Chicago: Henry Regnery Company, 1963), 178.
14. *World Almanac & Book of Facts*.
15. Edgar Ansel Mowrer, *Triumph and Turmoil* (New York: Weybright and Talley, 1968), 366.
16. Link, op. cit., 506.
17. Carroll Quigley, *Tragedy and Hope* (New York: Macmillan, 1966), 900.
18. Hugh Scott, *Come to the Party: An Incisive Argument for Moderate Republicanism* (Englewood Cliffs, N.J.: Prentice-Hall, 1968), 29–30.
19. Ibid., 30.

CHAPTER 20.

1. Arthur M. Schlesinger, "The Future of Socialism," *Partisan Review* (September 1947).

2. Studenski and Krooss, op. cit., 443.

3. Ibid., 436.

4. Ibid., 441–42.

5. Ibid., 451.

6. *World Almanac and Book of Facts*.

7. C. Hartley Grattan, "What the War Cost," *Harper's Magazine* (April 1949).

8. William Henry Chamberlin, "The Bankruptcy of a Policy," in *Perpetual War for Perpetual Peace*, ed. Harry E. Barnes (Caldwell, Idaho: Caxton Printers, Inc., 1953), 524.

9. Ibid., 519.

10. Eugene W. Castle, *The Great Giveaway* (Chicago: Henry Regnery Company, 1957), 13.

11. Ibid.

12. Ibid.

13. Malone, op. cit., 27.

14. Ibid.

CHAPTER 21.

1. William Adams Brown, Jr., op. cit., 15.

2. Allen Drury, *A Senate Journal 1943–1945* (New York: McGraw-Hill, 1963), 446.

3. Ibid.

4. Erich Roll, *The World After Keynes* (New York: Praeger, 1964), 99.

5. Malone, op. cit., 34.

6. Ibid., 36.

7. John M. Dobson, *Two Centuries of Tariffs*, U.S. International Trade Commission, (Washington: GPO, 1976), 116–17.

8. Ibid., 117.

9. Ibid., 118.

CHAPTER 22.

1. R. H. S. Crossman, ed., *New Fabian Essays*, preface by Clement R. Attlee (London: Turnstile Press, 1952).

2. William Henry Chamberlin, op. cit., 526.

3. Gen. Albert C. Wedemeyer, *Wedemeyer Reports!* (New York: Henry Holt & Co., 1958), 394–5.

4. Ibid.

5. Interview with Lt. Gen. Arthur G. Trudeau, Washington, D.C., January 29, 1988.

6. Robert Murphy, *Diplomat Among Warriors* (Garden City, N.Y.: Doubleday, 1964), 317.

7. Harry S. Truman, *Memoirs*, vol. 2, (Garden City, N.Y. Doubleday, 1955), 456.

8. General of the Army Douglas MacArthur, *Reminiscences* (New York: McGraw-Hill, 1964), 368.

9. Ibid., 369.

10. *Look*, September 6, 1966.

11. Lewis E. Lloyd, *Tariffs: The Case for Protection* (New York: Devin-Adair Co. 1955), 54.

12. Ibid.

13. "Inflation and Unemployment," *Congressional Quarterly* (Washington: 1975), 74.

14. Studenski and Krooss, op. cit., 494–95.

15. Ibid., 497.

16. Ibid., 507.

17. Ibid., 510.

CHAPTER 23.

1. Willard F. Rockwell, *The Rebellious Colonel Speaks*, ed. Alfred Lief (New York: McGraw-Hill, 1964), 35.

2. Edward S. Flash Jr., *Economic Advice and Presidential Leadership* (New York: Columbia University Press, 1965), 115.

3. Ibid., 163.

4. Link, op. cit., 593–94.

5. Ibid., 592.

6. Ibid., 593.

7. Ibid., 595.

8. Ibid., 596.

9. American Iron and Steel Institute, News Release, February 18, 1988.

10. Lloyd, op. cit., 181.

11. *Report of the Tax Foundation, Inc. for 1977*, 33.

12. Richard Bolling and John Bowles, *America's Competitive Edge* (New York: McGraw-Hill, 1982), 5.

13. Dobson, op. cit., 118.

14. Martin Mayer, op. cit., 83.

CHAPTER 24.

1. Wachtel, op. cit., 64.

2. Studenski and Krooss, op. cit., 529.

3. Ibid., 528.

4. *The Federal Reserve System*, 2d ed., Board of Governors of the Federal Reserve System (Washington: GPO, 1947).

5. Malone, op. cit., 47.

6. Ibid., 50.

7. Ibid.

8. Ibid., 51.

9. Ibid.

10. Ibid., 48.

11. Ibid., 51

12. Ibid., 48.

13. Statistics on U.S. Flag Vessels provided to author in 1988 by Maritime Administration, Department of Transportation, Division of Trade Statistics.

14. *World Almanac and Book of Facts*.

15. Ibid.

16. Rockwell, op. cit., 171.

17. U.S. Treasury Department, *Maintaining the Strength of the United States Dollar in a Strong Free World Economy* (Washington: GPO, January 1968), 94.

18. Martin Mayer, op. cit., 81.

CHAPTER 25.

1. Theodore White, *The Making of the President 1964* (New York: Atheneum, 1965), 20.

2. Testimony of William J. Crockett, Deputy Under Secretary of State for Administration, Senate Judiciary Committee, Subcommittee on Internal Security, May 1965.

3. Martin Mayer, op. cit., 86.

4. Ibid., 87.

5. Ibid.

6. Ibid.

7. Wachtel, op. cit., 59.

8. Arthur M. Schlesinger, Jr., *A Thousand Days: John F. Kennedy in the White House* (Boston: Houghton Mifflin, 1965), 652.

9. Sen. Strom Thurmond, *Congressional Record*, April 15, 1969.

10. Walt W. Rostow, *The United States in the World Arena* (New York and Evanston: Harper & Row, 1960), 537.

11. William J. Gill, "The Most Dangerous Period of the Cold War," *Washington Report* (Washington: American Security Council, June 29, 1964).

12. "Scholar Who's No. 2 at the White House," *Business Week* (March 25, 1967).

13. Senate Preparedness Subcommittee of the Armed Services Committee, *Report on Missiles in Cuba* (Washington: GPO, April 1964).

CHAPTER 26.

1. Rostow, op. cit., 537.

2. Wachtel, op. cit., 69–70

3. Ernest H. Preeg, *Traders and Diplomats: An Analysis of the Kennedy Round of Negotiations Under the General Agreement on Tariffs and Trade* (Washington: Brookings Institution, 1970), 47–48.

4. Ibid., 46.

5. Ibid., 46–47.

6. Ibid., 49–50.

7. Ibid., 50.

8. Lloyd, op. cit., 188–89.

9. *Congressional Quarterly*, op. cit., 103.

10. Schlesinger, *A Thousand Days*, 895.

11. *The Times*, London, May 1, 1963.

12. Preeg, op. cit., 6.

13. Ibid., 7.

14. Ibid., 11.
15. Lyndon Baines Johnson, *The Vantage Point* (New York: Holt, Rinehart and Winston, 1971), 6.
16. Ibid., 1.

CHAPTER 27.

1. Johnson, op. cit., 42.
2. Ibid., 26.
3. Ibid.
4. Ibid., 40.
5. Ibid., 43.
6. Martin Mayer, op. cit., 131.
7. Wachtel, op. cit., 74.
8. Johnson, op. cit., 314.
9. Dobson, op. cit., 122.
10. Johnson, op. cit., 311.
11. Preeg, op. cit., 197.
12. Ibid., 238.
13. Johnson, op. cit., 314.
14. Ibid., 314.
15. Wachtel, op. cit., 78.
16. Martin Mayer, op. cit., 151.

CHAPTER 28.

1. Martin Mayer, op. cit., 141.
2. Johnson, op. cit., End Papers.
3. *World Almanac and Book of Facts*
4. Johnson, op. cit., 93.
5. Graham Wallas, *The Great Society* (London: Macmillan, 1914).
6. Ibid.
7. Sen. Barry Goldwater, *Congressional Record*, March 6, 1985.
8. Johnson, op. cit., 44.
9. Ibid., 46.
10. Interview with Rep. Mendell Rivers, September 15, 1966.
11. "Prospectus for Un-Intelligence," *Washington Report* (Washington: American Security Council, January 18, 1965).
12. Ibid.
13. Martin Mayer, op. cit., 140.
14. Ibid., 141.
15. Ibid., 143.

CHAPTER 29.

1. Ludwig von Mises, "Inflation" *The Freeman*, Foundation for Economic Education, Irvington-on-Hudson, N.Y. March 1967.

2. Johnson, op. cit., 287.

3. Ibid., 294.

4. Ibid., 300–1.

5. James M. Ennes Jr., *Assault on the Liberty* (New York: Random House, 1979), quote from caption under photo between pp. 146 and 147.

6. Ibid., 78.

7. Ibid., 137.

8. Martin Mayer, op. cit., 162.

9. Wachtel, op. cit., 77.

10. Martin Mayer, op. cit., 162.

11. *World Almanac and Book of Facts*.

12. Johnson, op. cit., 67.

CHAPTER 30.

1. Richard Nixon, *The Real War* (New York: Warner Books, 1980), 219.

2. The *Washington Post*, October 14, 1968, report on Nixon television interview of October 13 on WFAA-TV, Dallas.

3. Clyde Farnsworth, *Out of This Nettle* (New York: John Day Co., 1973), 5.

4. Richard Nixon, *The Memoirs* (New York: Grosset & Dunlap, 1978), 519.

5. Ibid., 520.

6. Ibid., 519.

7. Martin Mayer, op. cit., 196.

8. Ibid., 201.

CHAPTER 31.

1. Patrick J. Buchanan, *Conservative Votes, Liberal Victories* (New York: Quadrangle, 1975), 3.

2. Nixon, *Memoirs*, 586.

3. Ibid., 587.

4. Ibid., 521.

5. Ibid.

6. *World Almanac & Book of Facts*, 1976, 738.

7. Paige Bryan, Scott Sullivan, and Steve Pastore, " Capitalists and Commissars," *Policy Review* (Fall 1982): 19.

8. Ibid.

9. Ibid., 20.

10. Wachtel, op. cit., 92.

11. Ibid., 86.

12. Ibid., 87.

13. Tax Foundation, Inc., *Facts and Figures on Government Finance*, 1977, 15.

14. Ibid., 5.

CHAPTER 32.

1. Anthony Harrigan, "East-West Trade and National Security," address at University of Colorado at Boulder, September 24, 1987.

2. Nixon, *Memoirs*, 1029.

3. Ibid., 1036.

4. Ibid., 1032.

5. Ibid., 1028.

6. Harrigan, op. cit.

7. Ira Carnahan, "USTEC: Determined to Sell Moscow the Rope that Could Hang America," *Institution Analysis* (Washington: Heritage Foundation, February 5, 1988), 8.

CHAPTER 33.

1. William E. Simon, quoted in *The War on Gold* by Antony Sutton (Seal Beach, Calif.: '76 Press, 1977), 158.

2. Denis Healey, quoted in ibid.

3. Ron Nessen, *It Sure Looks Different from the Inside* (Chicago: Playboy Press, 1978), 98.

4. Ibid., 111–12.

5. Ibid., 123–24.

6. William E. Simon, *A Time for Truth* (New York: McGraw-Hill, 1978), 16.

7. Martin Mayer, op. cit., 238.

8. Ibid., 240.

9. Sutton, op. cit., 156.

10. deSaint Phalle, op. cit., 9.

CHAPTER 34.

1. Fawn Evenson, president, Footwear Industries of America, interview with author, March 8, 1989.

2. Trade Act of 1974, *Summary of the Provisions of H. R. 10710* (Washington: GPO, December 30, 1974).

3. "Essentiality of Specialty Steels to National Security," Senate Committee on Armed Services, Subcommittee on General Legislation, April 7, 1972.

4. Sen. John Heinz, press conference in the Capitol, Washington, September 29, 1982.

5. Sen. John C. Danforth, ibid.

6. Sen. George J. Mitchell, ibid.

7. George Q. Langstaff, ibid.

8. Statistics provided author by Footwear Industries of America, 1989.

9. Evenson, op. cit.

CHAPTER 35.

1. Jacob Clayman and Allen W. Dawson, COMPACT news release, March 14, 1978.

2. U.S. Customs Services statistics.

3. White House agenda for meeting of President Carter and Prime Minister Fukuda of Japan, March 21, 1977.

4. Ways and Means Committee, Subcommittee on Trade, House of Representatives, *Hearings*, 1977–1978 (Washington: GPO, 1979).

5. Office of the President's Special Trade Representative, June 1977.

6. A. Kent MacDougall, "U.S. Foreign Trade Zones: Boon or Bane for Production, Jobs," *Los Angeles Times*, April 18, 1982.

7. "Free Trade Zone Decision Will Not Come Before June," *Economic World* (New York, April 1982).

8. "Kickbacks in Living Color," *Time* (June 13, 1977): 63.

9. Ibid.

10. John Holusha, "Import Penalties on Japanese TVs Eased After Parley," *Washington Star*, April 28, 1978, p. D-6.

11. Seymour M. Hersh, "Testimony on Fraud in Importing TV Sets From Japan Is Studied," *New York Times*, January 24, 1979, p. 1.

12. John Holusha, op. cit.

13. "Shaky Mountain of Debt," *Time* (June 13, 1977): 63.

CHAPTER 36.

1. Clark R. Mollenhoff, *The President Who Failed* (New York: Macmillan, 1980), 254.

2. Peter Pringle, *London Sunday Times*, quoted by Victor Lasky in *Jimmy Carter: The Man and the Myth* (New York: Richard Marek Publishers, 1979), 160.

3. Lasky, Ibid.

4. "Ducking the Real Issues," *Business Week* (October 11, 1976).

5. Gerald R. Ford, quoted by Ron Nessen, op. cit., 268.

6. Jimmy Carter, quoted by Ron Nessen, ibid., 269.

7. Richard J. Levine, "Carter Faces World Economic Ills," *The Wall Street Journal*, November 8, 1976.

8. Ibid.

9. William Greider, *Secrets of the Temple: How the Federal Reserve Runs the Country* (New York: Simon & Schuster, 1987), 66.

10. Ibid.

11. Dinner hosted by David Rockefeller at the River Club, Program & List of Guests, New York, March 21, 1977.

12. Sen. Russell Long, address at the River Club, New York, March 21, 1977.

13. President Jimmy Carter, quoted in the *Washington Post*, August 1, 1977.

CHAPTER 37.

1. Wachtel, op. cit., 135.

2. Martin Mayer, op. cit., 261.

3. "Toyota Increases Its U.S. Prices by 5.4%," *Wall Street Journal*, April 17, 1978, p. 4.

4. Martin Mayer, op. cit., 283.

5. Ibid., 289.

6. Lasky, op. cit.

7. Martin Mayer, op. cit., 294.

8. Ibid., 305.

9. Bureau of the Mint, "Inventory of Gold Bars," in Sutton, op. cit., 114–115.

10. "Gold 1975," Consolidated Gold Fields Ltd., London, 1975.

11. Martin Mayer, op. cit., 306.

CHAPTER 38.

1. President Jimmy Carter, television address, July 15, 1979.

2. *World Almanac and Book of Facts (1981).*

3. *The 23rd Annual Report of the President of the United States on the Trade Agreements Program:* Washington: GPO, 1978, p. 4.

4. Ibid., 7.

5. Ibid., 5.

6. Sutton, op. cit., 118.

7. Wachtel, op. cit., 133.

8. Ibid., 134.

CHAPTER 39.

1. *Trade Agreements Act of 1979*, Report of the Committee on Ways and Means, House of Representatives (Washington: GPO, 1979).

2. William J. Gill "American Industry and Foreign Competition, A Projection: 1980–2000," address before United States Business and Industrial Council Forum, November 1, 1979.

3. Trade Agreements Act of 1979, op. cit.

4. Ibid., 2.

5. Ibid.

6. Ibid., 4

7. Ibid.

8. Peter C. Cavelti, *New Profits in Gold, Silver and Strategic Metals* (New York: McGraw-Hill, 1985), 56.

9. Ibid.

10. Ibid.

CHAPTER 40.

1. Donald T. Regan, *For the Record* (New York: Harcourt Brace Jovanovich, 1988), 246.

2. Ibid.

3. Fred Barnes, "Can We Trust the News," *Reader's Digest* (January 1988): 33.

4. S. Robert Lichter and Stanley Rothman, "The Media Elite," *Washington Post*, April 23, 1980.

5. David A. Stockman, *The Triumph of Politics* (New York: Harper & Row, 1986), caption under photographs between pp. 118 and 119.

6. Regan, op. cit., 278.

7. Ibid.

CHAPTER 41.

1. Richard P. Simmons, comments to the Association of Iron and Steel Engineers, April 8, 1985.
2. Eugene March, specialty steel press conference, Washington, December 8, 1981.
3. Lloyd McBride, ibid.
4. Richard P. Simmons, ibid.
5. President Ronald Reagan, memorandum to U.S. Trade Representative William Brock, November 17, 1982.
6. Ibid.
7. Ibid.
8. Clyde Farnsworth, "U.S. Curbs Imports of Specialty Steel," *New York Times*, July 6, 1983, p. 1.
9. Paul R. Roedel and Lynn R. Williams, letter to President Regan, July 3, 1984.
10. Associated Press dispatch, August 5, 1983.
11. Regan, op. cit., 157–58.

CHAPTER 42.

1. Peter Peterson on *CBS Evening News*, October 24, 1987.
2. Regan, op. cit., 269.
3. Axel Krause, "Traders React as U.S. Vows to Intervene," *International Herald Tribune*, September 24, 1985.
4. Stuart Auerbach, "Reagan Acts to Reduce Unfair Trade," *International Herald Tribune*, September 24, 1985.
5. Ibid.
6. Ibid.
7. Ibid.
8. John Burgess, "British Investments in U.S. Outpace Japan's, Study Finds," *Washington Post*, January 27, 1989.

CHAPTER 43.

1. Stephen S. Cohen, quoted by Stuart Auerbach in "Bush Faces a Complex Trading Environment," *Washington Post*, January 15, 1989.
2. Stuart Auerbach, "Trade Deficit for Year Falls for First Time Since 1980," *Washington Post*, February 18, 1989.
3. Tom Webb, "U.S. retaliates in European trade dispute," *Miami Herald*, December 28, 1988.
4. Evelyn Richards, "U.S. Chipmakers Backed in Copyright Suit," *Washington Post*, February 9, 1989.
5. *New York Times*, February 12, 1989.
6. Henry Kaufman, "Bush's First Priority: Stopping the Buyout Mania," *Washington Post*, January 1, 1989.
7. John M. Berry, "Fed's Greenspan Disagrees With Bush Economic Forecast," *Washington Post*, February 1, 1989.
8. John M. Berry, "Bush Signals Disagreement With the Fed," *Washington Post*, January 26, 1989.

9. Dow-Jones Average of 30 Industrials for January 30, 1989.

10. Associated Press dispatch, February 16, 1989.

11. Walter Pincus, "Eagleburger to Limit Role in Dozen Countries," *Washington Post*, February 16, 1989.

Bibliography

Adams, Arthur E. *The Russian Revolution and Bolshevik Victory: Why and How*? Boston:
    D. C. Heath & Co., 1960.
Aliber, Robert Z. *The International Money Game*. New York: Basic Books, 1979.
Alperovitz, Gar, and Jeff Faux. *Rebuilding America*. New York: Pantheon Books, 1984.
American Iron and Steel Institute, "1988 Annual Statistical Report," Washington, 1989.
Armbruster, Frank. *The Forgotten Americans: A Study of Values, Beliefs, and Concerns
    of the Majority*. New Rochelle, N.Y.: Arlington House, 1972.
Ball, George W. *The Discipline of Power: Essentials of a Modern World Structure*.
    Boston: Little, Brown, 1968.
Barnes, Harry Elmer, Ed. *Perpetual War for Perpetual Peace: A Critical Examination
    of the Foreign Policy of Franklin Delano Roosevelt and its Aftermath*. Caldwell,
    Idaho: Caxton Printers Ltd., 1953.
Barnes, Fred. "Can We Trust the News," *Reader's Digest*, January 1988.
Baruch, Bernard M. *Baruch: The Public Years*. New York: Holt, Rinehart and Winston,
    1960.
Bass, Herbert J., Ed. *America's Entry into World War I*. New York: Holt, Rinehart and
    Winston, 1964.
Bedell, Donald W. "Tariffs Miscast as Villain in Bearing Blame for Great Depression:
    Smoot-Hawley Exonerated." *Congressional Record*, May 9, 1983. Entered by
    Sen. John Heinz of Pennsylvania.
Belgion, Montgomery. *The Worship of Quantity: A Study of Megapolitics*. London:
    Johnson Publications, 1969.
Bogart, Ernest Ludlow. *Economic History of the American People*. New York: Longmans,
    Green and Co., 1935.
Bolling, Richard, and John Bowles. *America's Competitive Edge: How to Get Our
    Country Moving Again*. New York: McGraw-Hill, 1982.
Bowers, Claude G. *Beveridge and the Progressive Era*. New York: The Literary Guild,
    1932.

Bradford, Frederick A. *Money and Banking*. New York: Longmans, Green and Company, 1946.

Braudel, Fernand. *The Wheels of Commerce: Civilization and Capitalism, 15th–18th Century*. Vol.2. New York: Harper & Row, 1982.

Brown, Anthony Cave, and Charles B. MacDonald, *On a Field of Red: The Communist International and the Coming of World War II*. New York: G. P. Putnam's Sons, 1981.

Brown, Constantine. *The Coming Whirlwind: 1914–1952*. Chicago: Henry Regnery Company, 1964.

Brown, William Adams, Jr. *The United States and the Restoration of World Trade: An Analysis and Appraisal of the ITO Charter and the General Agreement on Tariffs and Trade*. Washington: Brookings Institution, 1950.

Bruce-Briggs, B. *The Twilight of Free Trade*. Alexandria, Va.: American Policy Institute, 1983.

Bryan, Paige with Scott Sullivan and Steve Pastore, "Capitalists and Commissars," *Policy Review*, Fall 1982.

Bryce, James, *The American Commonwealth*. New York: Macmillan, 1910.

Buchanan, Patrick J. *Conservative Votes, Liberal Victories*. New York: Quadrangle, 1975.

Bullock, Alan, and Maurice Shock. *The Liberal Tradition: From Fox to Keynes*. New York: New York University Press, 1957.

Burke, Edmund. *Reflections on the Revolution in France*. New Rochelle, N.Y.: Arlington House, 1965.

Burnham, James. *The Managerial Revolution*. New York: John Day Co., Inc., 1941.
———. *Suicide of the West*. New York: John Day Co., 1964.

Burns, Arthur F. *Frontiers of Economic Knowledge*. Princeton, N.J.: Princeton University Press, 1954.

Burns, James McGregor. *Roosevelt: The Lion and the Fox 1882–1940*. New York and London: Harcourt Brace Jovanovich, 1956.

Carabini, Louise, Ed. *Everything You Need to Know Now about Gold and Silver*. New Rochelle, N.Y.: Arlington House, 1974.

Carnahan, Ira. "USTEC: Determined to Sell Moscow the Rope that Could Hang America." *Institution Analysis*, Heritage Foundation, February 5, 1988.

Cary, James. *Japan Today: Reluctant Ally*. New York: Praeger, 1962.

Castle, Eugene W. *The Great Giveaway: The Realities of Foreign Aid*. Chicago: Henry Regnery Company, 1957.

Caute, David. *The Great Fear: The Anti-Communist Purge Under Truman and Eisenhower*. New York: Simon & Schuster, 1978.

Cavelti, Peter C. *New Profits in Gold, Silver and Strategic Metals*. New York: McGraw-Hill, 1985.

Chamberlain, Joseph. Preface to *The Case Against Free Trade*, by W. Cunningham. London: John Murray, 1911.

Chamberlain, John. *The Enterprising Americans*. New York: Harper & Row, 1963.
———. *The Roots of Capitalism*. Princeton, N.J.: D. Van Nostrand, 1965.

Chamberlin, William Henry. "The Bankruptcy of a Policy" in *Perpetual War for Perpetual Peace*. Edited by Harry E. Barnes. Caldwell, Idaho: Caxton Printers, Ltd., 1953.

Churchill, Winston S. *Triumph and Tragedy*. Boston: Houghton Mifflin, 1953.

Clemens, Diane Shaver. *Yalta*. New York: Oxford University Press, 1970.

Cluster, Dick, and Nancy Rutter. *Shrinking Dollars, Vanishing Jobs: Why the Economy Isn't Working for You*. Boston: Beacon Press, 1980.

Collier, Peter, and David Horowitz. *The Rockefellers: An American Dynasty*. New York: Holt, Rinehart and Winston, 1976.

Congressional Quarterly, "Inflation and Unemployment," Washington, 1975.

Considine, Bob. *The Remarkable Life of Dr. Armand Hammer*. New York: Harper & Row, 1975.

Cook, Fred J. *Walter Reuther: Building the House of Labor*. New York: Encyclopaedia Britannica Press, 1963.

Cotton, Sen. Norris. *In The Senate: Amidst the Conflict and the Turmoil*. New York: Dodd, Mead, 1978.

Crocker, George N. *Roosevelt's Road to Russia*. Chicago: Henry Regnery Company, 1959.

Crossman, R. H. S., ed. *New Fabian Essays*. Preface by Clement R. Attlee. London: Turnstile Press, 1952.

Culbertson, John M. *International Trade and the Future of The West*. Madison, Wis.: 21st Century Press, 1984.

Cunningham, W. *The Case Against Free Trade*. London: John Murray, 1911.

Davenport, John. *The U.S. Economy*. Chicago: Henry Regnery Company, 1965.

de Kieffer, Donald. *Doing Business with Romania*. New Canaan, Conn.: Business Books International, 1985.

de Kieffer, Donald, and Les DeVilliers. *Doing Business with the U.S.A.* New Canaan, Conn.: Business Books International, 1984.

DeLamaide, Darrell. *Debt Shock: The Full Story of the World Crisis*. Garden City, N.Y.: Doubleday, 1984.

Dell, Sidney. *Trade Blocs and Common Markets*. New York: Alfred A. Knopf, 1963.

de Saint Phalle, Thibaut. *The Federal Reserve: An Intentional Mystery*. New York: Praeger, 1985.

de Saint Phalle, Thibaut. *Trade, Inflation, and the Dollar*. New York and Oxford: Oxford University Press, 1981.

de Tocqueville, Alexis. *Democracy in America*. New Rochelle, N.Y.: Arlington House, 1965.

de Toledano, Ralph. *The Greatest Plot in History*. New York: Duell, Sloan & Pearce, 1963.

Dewey, Davis Rich. *Financial History of the United States*. New York: Longmans, Green and Co., 1931.

Dickson, Douglas N., ed. *Managing Effectively in the World Marketplace*. New York: John Wiley & Sons, 1983.

Dobson, John M. *Two Centuries of Tariffs*. U.S. International Trade Commission. Washington: GPO, 1976.

Drury, Allen. *A Senate Journal: 1943–1945*. New York: McGraw-Hill, 1963.

Dulles, Foster Rhea. *Labor in America: A History*. New York: Thomas Y. Crowell Company, 1966.

Eibling, Harold H., Carlton L. Jackson, and Vito Perrone. *Two Centuries of Progress: United States History*. River Forest, Ill.: Laidlaw Brothers, 1974.

Elias, Christopher. *Fleecing the Lambs*. Chicago: Henry Regnery Company, 1971.

Ennes, James M., Jr. *Assault on the Liberty*. New York: Random House, 1979.

Facts and Figures on Government Finance. 19th Biennial Edition. New York: Tax Foundation, Inc., 1977.

Fairchild, Henry Platt. *This Way Out.* New York: Harper & Brothers, 1936.

Faith, Nicholas. *Safety in Numbers: The Mysterious World of Swiss Banking.* New York: Viking Press, 1982.

Farnsworth, Clyde H. *Out of This Nettle: A History of Postwar Europe.* New York: John Day Co., 1973.

The Federalist Papers. By James Madison, Alexander Hamilton, and John Jay. New Rochelle, N.Y.: Arlington House, 1965.

The Federal Reserve System: Purposes and Functions. Board of Governors of the Federal Reserve System, Washington: GPO, September 1974.

Fellner, William, Project Dir. *Essays in Contemporary Economic Problems: Demand, Productivity and Population.* Washington: American Enterprise Institute, 1981.

Ferguson, C. E., and Juanita M. Kreps. *Principles of Economics.* New York: Holt, Rinehart and Winston, 1965.

Flash, Edward S., Jr. *Economic Advice and Presidential Leadership: The Council of Economic Advisers.* New York: Columbia University Press, 1965.

Forbes, Bertie Charles. In *Current Opinion*, December 1916.

Freemantle, Anne. *This Little Band of Prophets: The Story of the Gentle Fabians.* New York: Macmillan, 1960.

Galbraith, John Kenneth. *The Affluent Society.* Boston: Houghton Mifflin, 1958.

————. *The Great Crash: 1929.* New York: Time Inc., Book Division, 1962.

————. *Economics and the Public Purpose.* Boston: Houghton Mifflin, 1973.

————. *Money: Whence it Came, Where it Went.* Boston: Houghton Mifflin, 1975.

————. *The Age of Uncertainty: A History of Economic Ideas and their Consequences.* Boston: Houghton Mifflin, 1977.

————. *A Life in Our Times: Memoirs.* Boston: Houghton Mifflin, 1981.

Gale, W. K. V. *The Iron and Steel Industry: A Dictionary of Terms.* New York: Drake Publishers, Ltd., 1971.

Ganley, Albert C. *The Progressive Movement: Traditional Reform.* New York: Macmillan, 1964.

Gannon, Robert, *The Cardinal Spellman Story.* New York: Doubleday 1962.

Gilder, George. *Wealth and Poverty.* New York: Basic Books, 1981.

Gill, William J. "American Industry and Foreign Competition, A Projection: 1980–2000," Address before United States Business and Industrial Council Forum, November 1, 1979.

Gill, William J. "Prospectus for Un-Intelligence." *Washington Report*, American Security Council. Washington, January 18, 1965.

Gill, William J. "The Most Dangerous Period of the Cold War." *Washington Report*, American Security Council. Washington, June 29, 1964.

Goldwater, Barry. *The Conscience of a Majority.* Englewood Cliffs, N.J.: Prentice-Hall, 1971.

Goldwater, Barry. *Congressional Record* (Senate). Washington, March 6, 1985.

Grace, J. Peter. "The Problem of Big Government." *Imprimis*, January 1988.

Graham, Otis L., Jr. *The Great Campaigns.* Englewood Cliffs, N.J.: Prentice-Hall, 1979.

Grattan, C. Hartley. "What the War Cost." *Harper's Magazine* (April 1949).

Graves, William S. *America's Siberian Adventure 1918–1920.* New York: Jonathan Cape & Harrison Smith, 1931.

Greider, William. *Secrets of the Temple: How the Federal Reserve Runs the Country.* New York: Simon & Schuster, 1987.

Grunwald, Joseph, and Kenneth Flamm. *The Global Factory: Foreign Assembly in International Trade.* Washington: Brookings Institution, 1985.

Gurley, John G. *Challengers to Capitalism: Marx, Lenin and Mao.* Stanford, Calif.: Stanford Alumni Association, 1975.

Hacker, Andrew. *The End of the American Era.* New York: Atheneum, 1971.

Hansen, Roger D. et al. *The U.S. and World Development: Agenda for Action 1976.* New York: Praeger, 1976.

Hard, William. *Raymond Robins' Own Story.* New York: Harper & Brothers, 1920.

Harrigan, Anthony. *The National Interest.* Brentwood, Tenn. USIC Educational Foundation, 1986.

————. "East-West Trade and National Security." Address at University of Colorado at Boulder, September 24, 1987.

Hawkins, William R. *The National Interest: The Private Enterprise Perspective.* Washington: USIC Educational Foundation, 1987.

Hayek, Frederick A. *The Road to Serfdom.* Chicago: University of Chicago Press, 1944.

Hazlitt, Henry. *Will Dollars Save the World?* Irvington-on-Hudson, N.Y.: The Foundation for Economic Education, Inc., 1947.

————. *What You Should Know about Inflation.* Princeton, N.J.: D. Van Nostrand Company, 1960.

————. *The Failure of the "New Economics": An Analysis of the Keynesian Fallacies.* New Rochelle, N.Y.: Arlington House, 1973.

Heilbroner, Robert, and Aaron Singer. *The Economic Transformation of America: 1600 to the Present.* New York: Harcourt Brace Jovanovich 1984.

Heller, Walter W. *New Dimensions of Political Economy.* Cambridge: Harvard University Press, 1966.

Henderson, W. O., *The Industrial Revolution in Europe.* Chicago: Quadrangle, 1961.

Hitch, Charles J., and Roland N. McKean. *The Economics of Defense in the Nuclear Age.* New York: Atheneum, 1965.

Hoffman, William. *David: Report on a Rockefeller.* New York: Lyle Stuart, Inc., 1971.

House, E. M. *Philip Dru, Administrator,* New York: B. W. Huebsch, 1912.

————. *The Intimate Papers of Colonel House.* Edited by Charles Seymour. 4 vols. Boston: Houghton Mifflin, 1926, 1928.

Howland, Charles P. *Survey of American Foreign Relations: (1929).* Published for the Council on Foreign Relations. New Haven, Conn.: Yale University Press, 1929.

Hufbauer, Gary Clyde, and Joanna Shelton Erb. *Subsidies in International Trade.* Washington: Institute for International Economics, 1984.

Humphrey, Sen. Hubert H. *War on Poverty.* New York: McGraw-Hill, 1964.

International Monetary Fund, *Staff Papers.* Volume XXXII. Washington: IMF, 1985.

Interstate Commerce Commission. *43rd Annual Report, Nov. 30, 1929.* Washington: GPO, 1929.

Ireland, Thomas R. *Monetarism.* New Rochelle, N.Y.: Arlington House, 1973.

Jacobs, Jane. *Cities and the Wealth of Nations: Principles of Economic Life.* New York: Random House, 1984.

James, Clifford L. *Principles of Economics.* New York: Barnes & Noble, 1960.

James, Marquis. *The Life of Andrew Jackson.* New York: Bobbs-Merrill, 1938.

Johnson, Lyndon Baines. *The Vantage Point: Perspectives of the Presidency 1963–1969.* New York: Holt, Rinehart and Winston, 1971.

Jones, Jesse H., and Edward Angly. *Fifty Billion Dollars: My Thirteen Years with the RFC (1932–1945.)* New York: Macmillan, 1951.

Jordan, George Racey. *Gold Swindle: The Story of our Dwindling Gold.* New York: The Bookmailer Inc., 1959. Revised edition 1961.

Kamin, Alfred, ed. *Western European Labor and the American Corporation.* Washington: The Bureau of National Affairs, 1970.

Kelley, William D., M.C. *Speeches, Addresses and Letters on Industrial and Financial Questions.* Philadelphia: Henry Carey Baird, 1872.

Kirk, Russell. *Edmund Burke: A Genius Reconsidered.* New Rochelle, N.Y.: Arlington House, 1967.

Kirk, Russell, and James McClellan. *The Political Principles of Robert A. Taft.* New York: Fleet Press Corp., 1967.

Kirkland, Edward C. *Industry Comes of Age: Business, Labor, and Public Policy 1860–1897.* Vol. 6. New York: Holt, Rinehart and Winston, 1962.

Kirkpatrick, Jeane J. *The Strategy of Deception: A Study in World-wide Communist Tactics.* New York: Farrar, Straus & Co., 1963.

Knox, Diana. *The Industrial Revolution.* London: George G. Harrup & Co., Ltd., 1974.

Koskoff, David E. *The Mellons: The Chronicle of America's Richest Family.* New York: Thomas Y. Crowell Company, 1978.

Kubek, Anthony. *How the Far East Was Lost: American Policy and the Creation of Communist China, 1941–1949.* Chicago: Henry Regnery Company, 1963.

———. *The Red China Papers.* New Rochelle, N.Y.: Arlington House, 1975.

Lacey, Robert. *Ford: The Men and the Machine.* Boston: Little, Brown, 1986.

Lambro, Donald. *The Federal Rathole.* New Rochelle, N.Y.: Arlington House, 1975.

Lamont, Douglas F. *Foreign State Enterprises: A Threat to American Business.* New York: Basic Books, 1979.

Landauer, Carl. *Germany: Illusions and Dilemmas.* New York: Harcourt, Brace, 1969.

Lapp, Ralph E. *The New Priesthood: The Scientific Elite and the Uses of Power.* New York: Harper & Row, 1965.

Larson, Martin A. *The Federal Reserve and our Manipulated Dollar.* Old Greenwich, Conn.: Devin-Adair Co., 1978.

Lasch, Christopher. *The American Liberals and the Russian Revolution.* New York: McGraw-Hill, 1972.

Lasky, Victor. *Jimmy Carter: the Man and the Myth.* New York: Richard Marek Publishers, 1979.

Lee, Dwight E., Ed. *The Outbreak of the First World War: Who was Responsible?* Lexington, Mass.: D. C. Heath & Co., 1963.

Lekachman, Robert. *The Age of Keynes.* New York: Random House, 1966.

———. *Economists at Bay: Why the Experts Will Never Solve Your Problems.* New York.: McGraw-Hill, 1977.

Leuchtenberg, William E. *Franklin D. Roosevelt and the New Deal 1932–1940.* New York: Harper & Row, 1963.

Lewis, John P. and Valeriana Kallab, Eds. *Development Strategies Reconsidered.* Washington: Overseas Development Council, 1986.

Liddell Hart, B. H. *Strategy.* New York: Praeger, 1967.

Lindbergh, Charles A., Sr. *Your Country at War*. Philadelphia: Dorrance & Co., 1934 edition of original 1917 book copyrighted by Charles A. Lindbergh Sr.

Link, Arthur S. *American Epoch*. New York: Alfred A. Knopf, 1961.

Link, Arthur S. and William B. Catton. *American Epoch*. 3d ed. New York: Alfred A. Knopf, 1967.

Lloyd, Lewis E. *Tariffs: The Case for Protection*. New York: Devin-Adair Co., 1955.

Lockhart, R. H. Bruce. *Memoirs of A British Agent*. London: Macmillan, 1974. (Original Edition 1932.)

Lodge, George C. *The New American Ideology*. New York: Alfred A. Knopf, 1975.

Logan, John A. *The Great Conspiracy: Its Origin and History*. New York: A. R. Hart & Co., 1886.

Lohbeck, Don. *Patrick J. Hurley*. Chicago: Henry Regnery Company, 1956.

Lyons, Eugene. *Herbert Hoover*. Garden City, N.Y.: Doubleday, 1964.

MacArthur, Douglas. *Reminiscences*. New York: McGraw-Hill, 1964.

MacKenzie, Norman and Jeanne MacKenzie. *The Fabians*. New York: Simon & Schuster, 1977.

Malone, George W. *Mainline*. New Canaan, Conn.: Long House, Inc., 1958.

Marcosson, Issac F. *Wherever Men Trade: The Romance of the Cash Register*. New York: Dodd, Mead, 1945.

Martin, Rose L. *Fabian Freeway: High Road to Socialism in the U.S.A. 1884–1906*. Chicago: Heritage Foundation, 1966.

Massie, Robert K. *Nicholas and Alexandra*. New York: Atheneum, 1967.

Mayer, Martin. *The Fate of the Dollar*. New York: Truman Talley Books, Time Books, 1980.

Mayer, Thomas. *Monetary Policy in the United States*. New York: Random House, 1968.

McCarran, Sister M. Margaret Patricia. *Fabianism in the Political Life of Britain 1919–1931*. Chicago: Heritage Foundation, 1954.

McClintick, David. *Stealing from the Rich: The Home-Stake Oil Swindle*. New York: M. Evans & Co., 1977.

McCloy, John J. *The Challenge to American Foreign Policy*. Cambridge: Harvard University Press, 1953.

Meier, Gerald M. and Robert E. Baldwin. *Economic Development: Theory, History, Policy*. New York: John Wiley & Sons, 1963.

Mintz, Morton and Jerry S. Cohen. *America, Inc.: Who Owns and Operates the United States*. New York.: Dial Press, 1971.

Mises, von, Ludwig. "Inflation." Irvington-on-Hudson, N.Y. *The Freeman*, Foundation for Economic Education, March 1967.

Mitchell, Broadus. *Depression Decade: From New Era through New Deal 1929–1941*. New York: Holt, Rinehart and Winston, 1961.

Mollenhoff, Clark R. *The President Who Failed*. New York: Macmillan, 1980.

Molnar, Thomas. *Utopia: The Perennial Heresy*. New York: Sheed and Ward, 1967.

Morris, James. *The Road to Huddersfield: A Journey to Five Continents*. New York: Pantheon Books, 1963.

Mowrer, Edgar Ansel. *Triumph and Turmoil: A Personal History of our Times*. New York: Weybright and Talley, 1968.

Mullins, Eustace. *Secrets of the Federal Reserve*. Staunton, Va.: Bankers Research Institute, 1983.

Murphy, Robert. *Diplomat Among Warriors*. Garden City, N.Y.: Doubleday, 1964.

Myrdal, Gunnar. *Beyond the Welfare State: Economic Planning and its International Implications*. New Haven, Conn.: Yale University Press, 1960.

————. *Challenge to Affluence*. New York.: Pantheon Books, 1963.

————. *The Challenge of World Poverty: A World Anti-Poverty Program in Outline*. New York: Pantheon Books, 1970.

Myrdal, Jan. *Confessions of a Disloyal European*. New York: Pantheon Books, 1968.

Nessen, Ron. *It Sure Looks Different from the Inside*. Chicago: Playboy Press, 1978.

Nettles, Curtis P. *The Emergence of a National Economy: 1775–1815*. New York: Holt, Rinehart and Winston, 1962.

Nixon, Richard. *The Memoirs*. New York: Grosset & Dunlap, 1978.

————. *The Real War*. New York: Warner Books, 1980.

North, Douglass C. *The Economic Growth of the United States 1790–1860*. Englewood Cliffs, N.J.: Prentice-Hall, 1961.

Nourse, Edwin G. and Associates. *America's Capacity to Produce*. Washington: Brookings Institution, 1934.

Nussbaum, Arthur. *A History of the Dollar*. New York: Columbia University Press, 1957.

Packard, Vance. *The Pyramid Climbers*. New York: McGraw-Hill, 1962.

Page, Walter H. *The Life and Letters of Walter H. Page*. 3 volumes. Edited by Burton J. Hendrick. Garden City, N.Y.: Doubleday, 1925.

Palyi, Melchior. *Managed Money at the Crossroads: The European Experience*. Notre Dame: University of Notre Dame Press, 1958.

Paris, Alexander P. *The Coming Credit Collapse*. New Rochelle, N.Y.: Arlington House, 1974.

Parkin, Charles. *The Moral Basis of Burke's Political Thought*. Cambridge: Cambridge University Press, 1956.

Parkinson, C. Northcote. *Parkinson's Law and Other Studies in Administration*. Boston: Houghton Mifflin, 1957.

————. *The Law and the Profits*. Boston: Houghton Mifflin, 1960.

Petro, Sylvester. *The Labor Policy of the Free Society*. New York: The Ronald Press Co., 1957.

Pickersgill, Gary M., and Joyce E. Pickersgill. *Contemporary Economic Systems: A Comparative View*. Englewood Cliffs, N.J.: Prentice-Hall, 1974.

Pines, Burton Yale, Ed. *A World Without A U.N.: What Would Happen if the U.N. Shut Down*. Washington: Heritage Foundation, 1984.

Pirenne, Henri. *Economic and Social History of Medieval Europe*. New York: Harcourt, Brace, 1937.

Pollock, John. *The Bolshevik Adventure*. New York: E. P. Dutton & Co., 1919.

Prather, Charles L. *Money and Banking*. Chicago: Richard D. Irwin, Inc., 1951.

Preeg, Ernest H. *Traders and Diplomats: An Analysis of the Kennedy Round of Negotiations Under the General Agreement on Tariffs and Trade*. Washington: Brookings Institution, 1970.

Quigley, Carroll. *Tragedy and Hope: A History of the World in Our Time*. New York: Macmillan, 1966.

Rabbeno, Hugo. *American Economical Policy*. New York: Garland Press, 1974.

Read, Leonard E. *Students of Liberty*. Irvington-on-Hudson, N.Y.: Foundation for Economic Education, Inc. 1950.

Reagan, Michael D. *The Managed Economy*. London: Oxford University Press, 1963.

Regan, Donald T. *For the Record*. New York: Harcourt Brace Jovanovich, 1988.

Rickenbacker, William F. *Death of the Dollar: Personal Investment Survival in Monetary Disaster*. New Rochelle, N.Y.: Arlington House 1968.

Ridgway, Matthew B. *The Korean War*. Garden City, N.Y.: Doubleday, 1967.

Rock, Vincent P. *A Strategy of Interdependence: A Program for the Control of Conflict between the United States and the Soviet Union*. New York: Charles Scribner's Sons, 1964.

Rockwell, Willard F. *The Rebellious Colonel Speaks: The Selected Papers of Willard F. Rockwell*. Edited by Alfred Lief. New York: McGraw-Hill, 1964.

Roepke, Wilhelm. *What's Wrong with the World?* Philadelphia: Dorrance & Co., 1932.

———. *A Humane Economy: The Social Framework of the Free Market*. Chicago: Henry Regnery Company, 1960.

Rogers, Donald I. *How to Beat Inflation by Using It*. New Rochelle, N.Y.: Arlington House, 1970.

Roll, Erich. *A History of Economic Thought*. New York: Prentice-Hall, 1939.

———. *The World After Keynes*. New York: Praeger, 1964.

Roosevelt, Franklin D. First Presidential "Fireside Chat," March 12, 1933.

Rostow, W. W. *The United States in the World Arena*. New York and Evanston: Harper & Row, 1960.

———. *The Stages of Economic Growth: A Non-Communist Manifesto*. Cambridge: Cambridge University Press, 1964.

Rusher, William A. *Special Counsel: An Inside Report on the Senate Investigations into Communism*. New Rochelle, N.Y.: Arlington House, 1968.

Ruttenberg, Harold J. *Self-Developing America*. New York: Harper & Brothers, 1960.

Scheibla, Shirley. *Poverty Is Where the Money Is*. New Rochelle, N.Y.: Arlington House, 1968.

Schiff, Irwin A. *The Biggest Con: How the Government is Fleecing You*. New Rochelle, N.Y.: Arlington House, 1976.

Schlesinger, Arthur M., Jr. "The Future of Socialism." *Partisan Review* (September 1947).

———. *A Thousand Days: John F. Kennedy in the White House*. Boston: Houghton Mifflin, 1965.

Scott, Hilda. *Does Socialism Liberate Women? Experiences from Eastern Europe*. Boston: Beacon Press, 1975.

Scott, Hugh. *Come to the Party: An Incisive Argument for Moderate Republicanism*. Englewood Cliffs, N.J.: Prentice-Hall, 1968.

Sennholz, Hans F. *Money and Freedom*. Cedar Falls, Iowa: Center for Futures Education, Inc., 1985.

Servan-Schreiber, Jean Jacques. *The American Challenge*. New York: Atheneum, 1968.

Silver Anniversary Forum. *The Future of Industrial Research*. New York: Standard Oil Development Company, 1945.

Simon, William E. *A Time for Truth*. New York: McGraw-Hill, 1978.

Sinclair, James E., and Harry D. Schultz. *How the Experts Buy and Sell Gold Bullion, Gold Stocks & Gold Coins*. New Rochelle, N.Y.: Arlington House, 1975.

Smith, Adam. *The Wealth of Nations*. New Rochelle, N.Y.: Arlington House, 1965.

Smith, Edward Garstin. *The Real Roosevelt*. Chicago: The States Publishing Company, 1910.

Smith, Gene. *When the Cheering Stopped.* New York: William Morrow & Co., 1964.

Snider, Delbert A. *Introduction to International Economics.* Homewood, Ill.: Richard D. Irwin, Inc, 1963.

Spencer, Daniel L., and Alexander Woroniak, eds. *The Transfer of Technology to Developing Countries.* New York: Praeger, 1967.

Steel, Ronald. *Walter Lippman and the American Century.* Boston: Little, Brown, 1980.

Stein, Herbert. *Washington Bedtime Stories: The Politics of Money and Jobs.* New York: Free Press, 1986.

Stern, Philip M. *The Great Treasury Raid.* New York: Random House, 1964.

Stockman, David A. *The Triumph of Politics.* New York: Harper & Row, 1986.

Studenski, Paul and Herman E. Krooss. *Financial History of the* United States. New York: McGraw-Hill, 1963.

Sutton, Anthony C. *Western Technology and Soviet Economic Development 1930 to 1945.* Stanford: Hoover Institution Press, 1971.

———. *The War on Gold.* Seal Beach, Calif.: '76 Press, 1977.

Taussig, F. W. *The Tariff History of the United States.* New York: G. P. Putman's Sons, 1931.

Teixeira, Bernardo. *The Fabric of Terror.* New York: Devin-Adair Co., 1965.

Truman, Harry S. *Memoirs,* vol. 2. Doubleday, 1955.

Tyrrell, R. Emmett Jr., ed. *The Future That Doesn't Work: Social Democracy's Failures in Britain.* Garden City, N.Y.: Doubleday, 1977.

U.S. Bureau of Labor Statistics, "Study of Displaced Workers," Washington: GPO, 1988.

U.S. Congress Office of Technology Assessment. Special Report. *Plant Closing: Advance Notice and Rapid Response.* Washington: GPO, 1986.

U.S. House of Representatives. Report of the Committee on Ways and Means. *Trade Agreements Act of 1979.* Washington: GPO, 1979.

U.S. House of Representatives. Report of the Subcommittee on Oversight and Investigations of the Committee on Energy and Commerce. *Unfair Foreign Trade Practices: Criminal Components of America's Trade Problem.* Washington: GPO, 1985.

U.S. International Trade Commission. *Two Centuries of Tariffs: The Background and Emergence of the United States International Trade Commission.* By John M. Dobson. Washington: GPO, 1976.

U.S. Office of Price Administration, First Quarterly Report. Washington; 1942.

U.S. Office of Technology Assessment, Congress of the United States. *Technology and Steel industry Competitiveness.* Washington: GPO, June 1980.

U.S. Senate. Hearings before a Subcommittee of the Committee on Manufactures. *A Bill to Establish a National Economic Council: Oct. 22 to Dec. 19, 1931.* Washington: GPO, 1932.

U.S. Senate. Report of the Committee on Finance. *Trade Reform Act of 1974.* Washington: GPO, 1974.

U.S. Treasury Department. *Maintaining the Strength of the United States Dollar in a Strong Free World Economy.* Washington: GPO, January 1968.

Van Allen, Edward J. *The Trouble with Social Security.* Mineola, N.Y.: Omnipress, 1969.

Vandenberg, Arthur Hendrick. *If Hamilton Were Here Today.* New York: G. P. Putnam's Sons, 1923.

Van Dormael, Armand. *Bretton Woods: Birth of a Monetary System*. New York: Holmes & Meier, 1978.

van der Linden, Frank. *The Real Reagan*. New York: William Morrow, 1981.

Vieira, Edwin, Jr. *Pieces of Eight: The Monetary Powers and Disabilities of the United States Constitution*. Old Greenwich, Conn.: Devin-Adair Co., 1983.

Von Mises, Ludwig. *Theory and History: An Interpretation of Social and Economic Evolution*. New Rochelle, N.Y.: Arlington House, 1977.

Voss, Earl. *Nuclear Ambush*. Chicago: Henry Regnery Company, 1963.

Wachtel, Howard M. *The Money Mandarins: The Making of a New Supranational Economic Order*. New York: Pantheon Books, 1986.

Wallas, Graham. *The Great Society: A Psychological Analysis*. London: Macmillan, 1914.

Walsh, Edmund A. *The Last Stand*. Boston: Little, Brown, 1931.

Walters, Kenneth D. and R. Joseph Monsen, "State-Owned Business Abroad: New Competitive Threat," *Harvard Business Review* (March–April 1979).

Ward, Benjamin. *The Conservative Economic World View*. New York: Basic Books, 1979.

Wedemeyer, Albert C. *Wedemeyer Reports!* New York: Henry Holt & Co., 1958.

Weil, Gordon L. *A Handbook on the European Economic Community*. New York: Praeger, 1965.

Wellborn, Fred W. *The Growth of American Nationality: 1492–1863*. New York: Macmillan, 1947.

Whalen, Richard J. *The Founding Father: The Story of Joseph P. Kennedy*. New York: New American Library, 1964.

White, Theodore. *The Making of the President 1964*. New York: Atheneum, 1965.

Wile, Frederich W. *Men Around the Kaiser*. Indianapolis: Bobbs-Merrill, 1914.

Williams, Benjamin H. *Economic Foreign Policy of the United States*. New York: McGraw-Hill, 1929.

Williamson, Thames Ross. *Introduction to Economics*. New York: D.C. Heath & Co., 1923.

Wooldridge, William C. *Uncle Sam, the Monopoly Man*. New Rochelle, N.Y.: Arlington House, 1970.

Index

ABOUT THE AUTHOR

William J. Gill, author and historian, has also served as a consultant on international trade to several major American industries. He has participated in more than a score of cases involving illegal imports into the United States, including subsidies by foreign governments that were found to be in violation of both U.S. trade law and the international GATT code. Currently, he is president of the American Coalition for Competitive Trade in Washington, DC.

This is Mr. Gill's fourth book on international affairs and domestic politics. An award-winning correspondent for UPI and *The Pittsburgh Press* earlier in his career, he has contributed to many publications, among them *Time, Life, Fortune*, the *National Geographic*, and *Nation's Business*. He was also associated with the Chase Manhattan Bank in New York and was chief executive officer of the Allegheny Foundation, T. Mellon & Sons, Pittsburgh, for six years. He is a graduate of the University of Missouri and is a member of the National Historical Society.